Developing and Evaluating Educational Research

Gary W. Moore
University of Colorado at Colorado Springs

Little, Brown and Company
Boston   Toronto

Library of Congress Cataloging in Publication Data

Moore, Gary W.
  Developing and evaluating educational research.

  1. Educational research—Handbooks, manuals, etc.
I. Title.
LB1028.M643 1983   370'.7'8   82–18675
ISBN 0-316-57959-9

Library of Congress Catalog Card No. 82–18675

ISBN 0-316-57959-9

9 8 7 6 5 4 3 2

MV

Published simultaneously in Canada
by Little, Brown & Company (Canada) Limited

Printed in the United States of America

Credits

Chapter 1, pages 10–11, 12–13, 15–17, 18–19, 20–21; *Chapter 11,* pages
331–332: From E. K. Morris, C. F. Surber, and S. W. Bijou, Self-pacing versus
instructor-pacing: achievement, evaluations, and retention, *Journal of
Educational Psychology,* 1978, 70 (2), 224–234. Copyright 1978 by the
American Psychological Association. Reprinted by permission of the publisher
and authors.

Chapter 1, pages 26–34: From H. J. Walberg, D. Schiller, and G. D. Haertel,
The quiet revolution in educational research, *Phi Delta Kappan,* November
1979, 179–183. Reprinted by permission. Facsimile courtesy of the Boston
Public Library.

Chapter 3, pages 73–74: From R. P. Travis and P. Y. Travis, Self actualization
in marital enrichment. Reprinted from Volume 2, Number 1 of *Journal of
Marriage and Family Counseling.* Copyright 1976 American Association for
Marriage and Family Therapy. Reprinted by permission.

Chapter 4, pages 97, 98, 99, 100; *Chapter 11,* pages 325–330: From M. S.
Ashby and B. C. Wittmaier, Attitude changes in children after exposure to
stories about women in traditional or nontraditional occupations, *Journal of
Educational Psychology,* 1978, 70 (6), 945–949. Copyright 1978 by the
American Psychological Association. Reprinted by permission of the publisher
and authors.

continued on page 424

Preface

Since the body of knowledge in education grows significantly every five to ten years, teachers, prospective teachers, and other professionals interested in education must develop skills to conduct and evaluate research. Most textbooks written primarily to train research methodologists, however, have not always met practitioners' needs for a clear, straightforward description of how to understand and evaluate research. *Developing and Evaluating Educational Research* is designed to fit that need. More specifically, it is intended as a first exposure to educational research for students who will become users or consumers of research literature. The content of this book has been used successfully in an introductory research and statistics course for undergraduates; also, it has been used with masters and doctoral level students.

Organization

One main strength of this text is its organization. The concepts and principles of educational research are presented within the overall context of the research-based journal article. The structure of the journal article offers a natural vehicle for organizing and communicating the needed information. The article format also allows students to integrate and apply the concepts of eduational research more quickly.

After an overview of the research process in Chapter 1, the text is organized into four main parts, which coincide with the major sections of a research article. In Part 1, Chapters 2, 3, and 4, the Introduction section of the article is analyzed. In each of the three chapters we consider a key component of the research process—the statement of purpose, formulation of hypotheses, and review of the literature. In addition, strategies for integrating these three components into a coherent Introduction section are discussed at the end of Chapter 4.

The second component of a research article, the Method section, is presented in Part 2. In Chapter 5 we describe the steps in constructing a sample. In Chapter 6 we analyze the types of variables and threats to validity and in Chapter 7 we discuss the types of research designs and present suggestions for developing the Procedure section. In Chapter 8 we look at the Instrumentation section and present the various types of tests and core interpretations. Pertinent technical information for administering standardized tests is included.

Part 3 is devoted to the Results section. Chapter 9 summarizes the basic descriptive statistics and Chapter 10 is focused on inferential statistics and we suggest a format for organizing and evaluating the Results section.

Finally, the Discussion section of the article and the task of writing the research report are examined in Part 4.

In the appendixes at the end of this book, you will find additional useful supplementary information. Appendix A is a discussion of specific tests used within education. Appendix B provides information on test publishers, and Appendix C reprints the American Personnel and Guidance Association's policy statement on responsibilities of users of standardized tests. Finally, in Appendix D we present various statistical tables.

Format

Imbedded in this text are several distinctive features to help facilitate comprehension and retention of content.

At the beginning of each chapter we present overview questions that preview major points. We have also developed a visual representation of the chapter's main concepts. Students have found these aids very useful in developing an overall image of each chapter's organization and content.

At the end of each chapter is a summary and a list of key terms. To promote application of the chief lessons in each chapter, performance type objectives are supplied. These follow the chapter summary.

The narrative of each chapter is augmented by several original illustrations based on key concepts of themes. Each illustration provides an opportunity to extend your skills of observing, integrating, and understanding. The illustrations are designed to stimulate the search for meaning and insight into the process of educational research.

Acknowledgments

Many people have supported me in writing this text and I would like to thank them for all their support and assistance. Mylan Jaixen, Senior Editor at Little, Brown, has supported me since the text was barely more than a thought in my mind. Sally Stickney and David W. Lynch also have been very helpful in preparing the manuscript for publication. David Bruce Porter, the illustrator, has shared with me many creative and useful ideas to improve the clarity of text as well as having developed highly original and creative drawings to support the text narrative.

The text could not have been written without the help of colleagues who teach courses for which the book is intended. I wish to express my gratitude to: Harvey Bleecher, Central Washington University; Dorothy Reeves, Western Kentucky University; Royce Ronning, University of Nebraska, Lincoln; and Carmine Yengo, Trenton State College. Although they caused many sleepless nights on my part, the comprehensiveness and usefulness of their critical comments were invaluable in my efforts to improve the clarity and precision of the material.

I am grateful to the Literary Executor of the late Sir Ronald A. Fisher, F.R.S., to Dr. Frank Yates, F.R.S., and to Longman Group Ltd., London for permission to reprint Tables III, IV, VII, and XXXII from their book *Statistical Tables for Biological, Agricultural and Medical Research* (6th Edition, 1974).

The organization, editing, and typing of the manuscript were enhanced significantly by the fine work of Ann Higgins and Missye Bonds. Evelyn Clossen and Connie Wroten also typed major portions of earlier drafts of the manuscript.

I would also like to thank my wife, Carol, for her support and encouragement. Finally, I would like to express my deep appreciaton to my two young sons, Matthew and Michael, who lovingly and patiently nudged me on with their happiness of life.

Brief Contents

Contents

Chapter **3**

Formulating Hypotheses   60

Chapter **4**

Reviewing the Literature   78

PART 2

Developing the Method Section of the Research Article   106

Chapter 5

Developing the Sample   108

Chapter 6

Constructing a Procedure: Types of Variables   134

Chapter 7

Constructing a Procedure: Types of Research Designs   160

Chapter 8

Evaluating the Instruments   194

PART 3

Analysis of the Results Section   234

Chapter 9

Descriptive Statistics   236

Chapter **10**

Inferential Statistics   266

PART **4**

Analysis of the Discussion Section and Writing the Research Report   318

Chapter **11**

Discussing the Results   320

Chapter **12**

Writing the Research Article   350

Developing and
Evaluating
Educational Research

Understanding the
Research Process

How do human beings acquire knowledge of the world?

How does the scientific method facilitate the acquisition of knowledge?

What are the four components of the research article, and how are the steps of the scientific method related to these components?

What is the purpose of each component of the research article and what does it include?

What are the two tangential components of the research article and what do they contribute?

What is the basic vocabulary of the research article?

How has the research literature furthered our understanding of educational principles and concepts?

Format of the Research Article

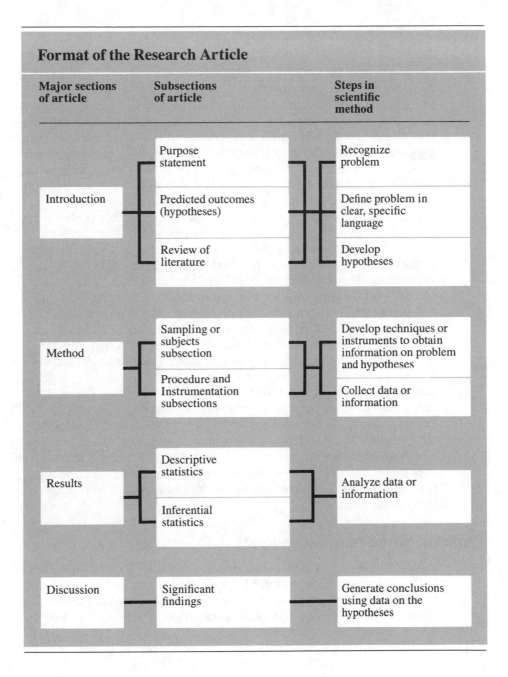

Major sections of article	Subsections of article	Steps in scientific method
Introduction	Purpose statement	Recognize problem
	Predicted outcomes (hypotheses)	Define problem in clear, specific language
	Review of literature	Develop hypotheses
Method	Sampling or subjects subsection	Develop techniques or instruments to obtain information on problem and hypotheses
	Procedure and Instrumentation subsections	Collect data or information
Results	Descriptive statistics	Analyze data or information
	Inferential statistics	
Discussion	Significant findings	Generate conclusions using data on the hypotheses

No two human beings have exactly the same experiences. Consider two people who see a movie together. Their experiences will not be exactly the same. If one believes that people are basically just and fair and the other believes that they are inherently cruel and unpredictable, the meaning assigned to their movie experience will differ according to their views of the world. Thus, one way in which we assign meaning to our experiences is to construct models or maps of the way we believe the world to be. The model or map then becomes one way of representing reality, and we use it to help make our way through the world. This representation will determine what our experience of the world will be, how we will perceive it, and what our choices will be.

Another example of a model of reality relates to parents' perception of the role and value of teachers. Some might perceive teachers as glorified babysitters; others might view them as dedicated, caring, skilled professionals who provide an invaluable service. Still others may have beliefs ranging between these two positions. The representation they have constructed will influence the personal experiences they encounter and affect the meaning they subsequently attach to those experiences.

Thus the model we create to guide us in the world is based upon our experiences. Each one of us, then, may construct a different model of our shared world. Because of these different models or maps of the world that we construct, the accurate communication of knowledge becomes difficult. As Korzybski states (1958): "A map is not the territory it represents, but if correct, it has a similar structure to the territory, which accounts for its usefulness . . ." (p. 58). Historically, there have been many ways of constructing maps of our world. As the accuracy of the map increases, the error in representing the terrain of our experiences decreases.

Popular Sources of Knowledge

In addition to personal experience, alternate ways of obtaining knowledge about the world exist. These other maps of the world that help provide meaning to our experiences have included authority, tradition, expert opinion, and church-state-ancient scholarship. For instance, an example of *authority* as a source of knowledge is the famous football quarterback who promotes popcorn poppers by saying: "I know which popcorn popper is best, and this is it!" An example of *tradition* as a source of knowledge would be the appeals of a mother recommending *Kool-Maid:* "I loved *Kool-Maid* as a child, and my mother trusted it for me, so I trust it as a mother, too." An example of *expert opinion* as a source of knowledge is the official-looking expert with lab coat and clipboard who tells us that: "Jimmie was in the *Crust* group which had 37 percent fewer cavities." He goes on to state: "Jimmie's group used

Crust with fluoride, while the other group used *Crust* but with a non-fluoride formula." Finally, an example of *church-state-ancient scholarship* as a source of knowledge is given by the federal economic spokesman reassuring us a few years ago that: "Interest rates for housing will not rise significantly above the 9 percent current rate. They will probably rise a point or two temporarily and then return."

All these maps of the world provide us with different sources of knowledge. However, knowledge claims derived from these models should be carefully examined to ensure that subjectivity, bias, vested interests, or important deletions and distortions of information have not occurred. Would the quarterback's perception be biased because he received $25,000 to recommend that product? Deletions of pertinent facts may also occur, such as the revelation that the mother who recommends *Kool-Maid* now wears false teeth because of excessive sugar in her diet as a child. Distortions in knowledge also can occur, as with the *Crust* tests. Since both groups received *Crust,* did it really produce the 37 percent fewer cavities? Or, since one group received it with fluoride and the other with no fluoride, wasn't the presence of fluoride the main factor that produced the 37 percent fewer cavities and not the use of *Crust?* Thus, any toothpaste with fluoride should obtain similar results! Vested interests, subjectivity, and bias may influence official state spokesmen to "adjust" their knowledge or predictions in a favorable direction.

Since different and frequently faulty models of the world are employed, securing accurate and useful knowledge is difficult. However, there is another way of constructing a map to obtain valid and useful knowledge.

The Scientific Method

The scientific method is an objective, systematic, testable process for obtaining knowledge about our world. It includes seven main steps that enable us to systematically test and analyze knowledge. These steps are:

1. Recognize a problem.
2. Define the problem in clear, specific language.
3. Develop hypotheses.
4. Develop techniques or instruments to obtain information related to the problem and hypotheses.
5. Collect data or information.
6. Analyze the data or information.
7. Generate conclusions based upon data related to the hypotheses.

As an explicit process by which anyone may confirm or replicate findings, the scientific method appears to be the most systematic, purpose-

The Scientific Method

ful, valid, and reliable way of obtaining knowledge. It is currently our best "map of the territory." But, as in any generalization, exceptions do occur. These exceptions frequently occur because of the nature of scientific investigation.

Limitations of the Scientific Method

Scientific investigation does not have a corner on absolute objectivity. Pure objectivity does not exist. However, scientific investigations can be very useful. Since the scientific method is used by researchers who may apply the procedures relative to their own differing realities, one main goal of the scientific method is to reduce or minimize error. We can decrease but never eliminate error because of the complexity and changeability of human beings as well as the complexity of stimuli they respond to. To claim that error can be eliminated would be to imply that we all have exactly the same model of the territory or the same meaning derived from exactly the same experiences. Obviously, we don't.

For instance, a type of error can be introduced into the scientific method just by the way a researcher asks a question. Two researchers are studying Piaget's theory of cognitive development; each has a young child determine that two clay balls have the same amount of clay. The child is then asked by each to roll one ball into a hot dog. Each researcher then asks: "Is there the same amount of clay in the hot dog as there is in the ball, or is there more in one than in the other?" Both children respond: "There's more in the hot dog." Now the first researcher asks: "Is that because the hot dog is longer?" But the second researcher asks: "How do you know that?" Because of the nature of the questions, the first researcher will be assessing his own level of development embedded within the child's responses, but the second researcher is increasing the probability that she will be assessing the child's reasoning level; and she is minimizing the likelihood of errors in her research. Thus, even so small a variable as the wording of the investigator's question can influence the research process.

Error is a very common phenomenon. It is reflected in all the preceding popular sources of knowledge as well as in the scientific method. However, it is often not apparent to the observer. Just as it is easy for an audience to forget that a puppeteer is pulling the strings of the figures they see frolicking on the stage, so it is easy for a consumer of knowledge to overlook the potential sources of error in the information he or she is receiving. This danger is particularly great when observers do perceive what they expect to see or hear.

One definition of *error* is that it is anything which causes predictions to vary from what actually occurs. There are several reasons why our predictions differ from what actually happens. One is that our past observations were not really accurate; that is, we really didn't see what we thought we saw. A second reason is that some conditions or circumstances have changed since we made the prediction. The error in our observations or measurements may be caused by changes in these un-

Sources of Knowledge

controlled situations or extraneous variables operating as well as by our selective perception or bias occurring.

The assumption that human beings are static and unchanging also frequently results in erroneous predictions. Even if our observations are accurate and complete and we have controlled all the possible confounding variables that were salient, our predictions still may be filled with error. Many researchers as well as philosophers would relate this left-over or residual error to the inherent variability in human behavior or human free will.

Historically, individuals have relied on these sources of knowledge: authority; tradition; expert opinion; church, state, and ancient scholars; as well as their own personal experience, because of the human need for certainty. Often we deal with uncertainty and the anxiety that accompanies it by creating or relying on social institutions or phenomena that offer absolute answers or universal truths. An equally strong rationale can, however, be developed for the reverse relationship. That is, the human need for certainty and reliance on institutions and phenomena which offer absolute and universal answers often generates error. Error is likely to flourish in a garden of dogma free from questions.

Thus, historically, as humans began to reason systematically, the scientific method evolved as a procedure to test numerous assumptions and so-called facts about the world. As mentioned earlier, the scientific method never eliminates error; rather it attempts to identify and minimize the effects of error to determine what is real or true knowledge from that which is not.

The scientific method is employed as a systematic, formal process in educational research. The purpose of educational research, like that of any area of inquiry which incorporates the scientific method, is to *understand, predict,* and *control* the phenomena it examines. To *understand* the observed phenomena is to account for relationships among variables in terms of the laws of logic and reasoning. To *predict* is to be able to determine the value of one variable by knowing the value of another. For instance, by knowing your pretest score on a research test, I can predict with greater than chance accuracy what your final grade will be. To *control* is to manipulate a variable so that it will produce effects in a second variable. For instance, the level of mathematical achievement is controlled by, or related to, the quantity of mathematical instruction received. Each of the three purposes is important for understanding an organized body of knowledge and to the further understanding, discovery, or refinement of that body of knowledge.

Knowing the scientific method and being able to use and apply it through the knowledge and skills of the research process is one powerful way of minimizing error so that the knowledge obtained can be maximally useful. Thus, one main goal in planning and conducting research is to reduce error in our process of acquiring knowledge. Perhaps in a hundred years a better map will be available, but humankind will have to wait for it, and when it comes, it will probably be tested using our old "map of the territory."

Relating the Scientific Method to the Journal Article

The seven steps of the scientific method comprise one useful map for obtaining knowledge about the world. These seven steps relate directly to the different procedures in the research process as seen in a research journal article. Any journal article that is based on research shares a common organization or flow. This relationship between the scientific method and a research-based journal article will now be expanded to emphasize the importance of each.

The Introduction section. A research article typically has four main components: *Introduction, Method, Results,* and *Discussion* sections. Each main component usually has several subsections. Typically, the *Introduction* part of the research article contains a *statement of the problem* or *purpose*, one or more *predicted outcomes* or *hypotheses*, and a *review of the literature.* These three subsections are usually integrated with the literature review serving as a rationale and background to the purpose and hypotheses. It is a conceptual description of what the researcher intends to study. Read the following Introduction and see if you can identify the three main subsections.

Self-Pacing Versus Instructor-Pacing: Achievement, Evaluations, and Retention

Edward K. Morris
Department of Human Development
and Family Life
University of Kansas

Colleen F. Surber
University of Illinois
at Urbana-Champaign

Sidney W. Bijou
University of Arizona

For educators and students alike, the self-pacing component of personalized systems of instruction (PSI) has traditionally been one of its most popular features (Carroll, 1963; Keller, 1968; Kulik, Kulik, & Carmichael, 1974; Sherman, 1974; Whitehurst & Whitehurst, 1975; Lloyd, Note 1). Self-pacing allows students to work at their own rates and plan for competing assignments from other courses. In the end, it serves to promote uniform subject mastery.

Recent research, however, indicates that self-pacing may not be one of the necessary conditions outlined by Keller (1968) that promotes effective learning (Bijou, Morris, & Parsons, 1976; Bitgood & Segrave, 1974; Burt, 1975; Lloyd, 1971; Lloyd & Knutzen, 1969; Mawhinney et al., 1971; Miller, Weaver, & Semb, 1974; Semb, Conyers, Spencer, & Sosa, 1974; Sutterer & Holloway, 1974). For example, within PSI courses, students who are permitted to self-pace are more likely to withdraw than those who are under instructor-paced contingencies (e.g., Semb et al., 1974). Moreover, in self-paced PSI courses (a) rates of test taking decline over a semester until students cram toward the end (Atkins & Lockhart, 1976; Burt, 1975; Lloyd & Knutzen, 1969; Lloyd, McMullin, & Fox, in press; Mawhinney et al., 1971; Robin & Graham, 1974); (b) undergraduate teaching assistants are inefficiently used; (c) study centers become overcrowded; and (d) mastery criteria sometimes deteri-

orate (Semb et al., 1974; Sutterer & Holloway, 1974).

To counteract these problems, some instructors have implemented required instructor-paced schedules for student progress (Lloyd, 1971; Malott & Svinicki, 1969; Miller et al., 1974; Stalling, 1971; Sutterer & Holloway, 1974), while others have introduced more flexible combinations of instructor- and student-paced point systems (Bijou et al., 1976; Bitgood & Segrave, 1974; Burt, 1975; Powers, Edwards, & Hoehle, 1973; Semb et al., 1974). Both types of pacing systems have been found effective in reducing student procrastination and withdrawal (Semb et al., 1974). However, we have few comparisons between self-pacing and instructor-pacing in terms of student achievement. The available data indicate that neither learning (Atkins & Lockhart, 1976; Bitgood & Segrave, 1974; Burt, 1975; Lloyd et al., in press; Robin & Graham, 1974; Semb et al., 1974) nor course satisfaction (Bitgood & Segrave, 1974; Robin & Graham, 1974; Semb et al., 1974) is affected by whether students self-pace or meet an instructor's pacing requirements. Given that no differences are found, the logistics of teaching assistant workloads and efficient, effective student management seem to favor the use of instructor-paced teaching systems.

Despite the equivalence of final examination scores and course evaluations, little is known about retention of material following course completion. A few studies have shown that students learning under a PSI system retain knowledge repertoires better than those learning under a lecture–discussion format (Cole, Martin, & Vincent, 1974; Cooper & Greiner, 1971; Corey & McMichael, 1974; Moore, Hauck, & Gagné, 1973), but these differences may reflect differential content acquisition more than they do differential retention per se (Lloyd, 1960).

Only one study (Robin & Graham, 1974) has been reported that compares the content retention by students whose pacing is evenly regulated by pacing contingencies with content retention by students who self-pace. In the Robin and Graham study, no retention differences were found; however, interpretation of the results was complicated by student self-selection, small comparison groups, differential withdrawal rates, and a retention interval of only 3 weeks. Thus, the present study was designed both to replicate research comparing self-paced to flexible instructor-paced approaches and to extend these findings to a more meaningful follow-up assessment of content retention.

Here the review of literature encompasses all six paragraphs. In the last sentence of the Introduction the statement of purpose or problem is presented explicitly. However, the various studies reviewed are used as a rationale for examining the main variables; for example, type of pacing: self versus instructor; academic achievement; retention of information; and course evaluations.

No hypotheses or predicted outcomes are presented. Thus we have an exception to our earlier generalization that the Introduction contains three subsections. With some types of research, a predicted outcome is not presented because of lack of support for doing so or because of a rationale weak in theory, past research, or personal experience. Thus, studies without a hypothesis frequently imply in their Introduction the research question: "What differences exist among groups?"

The Introduction relates directly to the first three steps of the scientific method: *(1) Recognize a problem; (2) Define the problem in clear, specific language; (3) Develop hypotheses.* The recognition or perception of a problem is usually developed from some aspect of theory, prior research, or personal experience. It requires intuition and sensitivity to discern a problem and clear reasoning to further specify and define it. For instance, the creative and bored children in the classroom, the resistant clients, or the bothersome truths of a favorite theory may be accepted by some people as realities that must be tolerated. Others may perceive a problem and want to test the effectiveness of different curricula for the creative child, various psychotherapeutic techniques in establishing rapport, or the advantages of one theoretical implication over another.

The ability to define the problem in clear, specific words is one key to minimizing the probability that error or chance will operate. If the researcher is clear about the purpose, that clarity will positively affect the other components of the research process. If researchers do not know where they are going, it becomes difficult to know how to get there. Losing clarity is analogous to losing the direction key to your map; you have your map, but the direction in which you are going becomes obscured.

The development and presentation of a hypothesis is simply a researcher's best professional prediction about the outcomes related to the problem or purpose. If a researcher wishes to include a prediction, it is presented along with an accompanying rationale derived from theory, research, or personal experience. If you do not have a prediction that can be supported, you take the conservative path and do not present a hypothesis. With or without a hypothesis, the Introduction should provide a clear foundation for the rest of the article.

The Method section. The second main component of the research article is the *Method* section. This part typically includes a *Sampling* or *Subjects* subsection and *Procedure* and *Instrumentation* subsections. The main purpose of the Method section is to explain clearly and specifically how the study was conducted or implemented. Read the following Method section and identify the various subsections.

Method

Subjects

One hundred forty-nine students were enrolled in a PSI section of an introductory child development course. Freshmen, sophomores, juniors, and seniors were randomly assigned to the self-paced and instructor-paced contingencies. Seventy-five students were placed in the former group and 74 in the latter.

General Procedures[1]

Course materials[2] were divided into 15 units of approximately equal size, 1 for each week of the semester.

---

[1] See Bijou et al. (1976) for a more detailed description of course management procedures, especially in regard to the pacing system.

[2] Course materials included *Child development: The basic stage of early childhood* (Bijou, 1976); *Child development I: A systematic and empirical theory* (Bijou & Baer, 1961); *Child development II: Universal stage of infancy* (Bijou & Baer, 1965); *Child development: Readings in experimental analysis* (Bijou & Baer, 1967); and *Course guide* (Bijou, Note 2).

At the completion of each unit's assignment, students came individually to a study center where they were required to pass a 10-item, short-answer essay quiz and an oral examination; both were graded by undergraduate teaching assistants. Ninety percent mastery was required. If one question was missed, it was included on the quiz for the next unit; if more than one question was missed, a make-up quiz was required.

Experimental Manipulations

The course syllabi given to the students in the self-paced and instructor-paced groups were identical except for the section describing grading procedures.

Self-paced condition. Students assigned to the self-paced group were permitted to complete the course at their own rate within the semester's time. A student's final grade was based solely on the number of units mastered: 15 units = A, 14 units = B, 13 units = C and 12 units or less = F.

Instructor-paced condition. Students assigned to the instructor-paced group worked within a flexible point system. As with students in the self-paced group, they could proceed as quickly as they desired; the number of units completed had the same relationship to their final grade. However, these students also had to meet a point criterion which generally required them to master at least one unit of material each week.

Failure to meet this criterion resulted in a one-letter drop in grade (i.e., from A to B, B to C, etc.). Completing each unit by the Thursday or Friday of its respective week earned the students enough points to meet the point criterion; however, the system was flexible in that more points could be earned for passing unit quizzes earlier in a week (see Table 1). Thus, the student who fell behind had some opportunity to make up points by mastering subsequent units on Mondays, Tuesdays, or Wednesdays of the following weeks. If a student failed to acquire the requisite number of points, the grade could still be maintained by completing a term paper of A quality with one opportunity for a revision.

Achievement Measures

The primary achievement measure was student performance on a 53-item multiple-choice test. Three or four items from all but the first unit were included and randomly ordered. Because the weekly unit quiz was of the short-answer, essay variety, none of the questions on the criterion test was the same, even though the material covered was identical.

The multiple-choice test was administered as a pretest during the students' first visit to the study center when they turned in their quiz for the first unit, a take home. A rerandomized posttest was administered

Table 1
Instructor-Pacing Point Schedule

Variable	Monday	Tuesday	Wednesday	Thursday	Friday
Points for quiz x in week x	10	10	9	8	8
Points for quiz x in week x + 1	5	—	—	—	—

immediately after each student's completion of the last unit of the course. The students were informed each time that their performance on the test would not affect their final grade.

A course evaluation questionnaire was also administered upon completion of the course. Questions were designed to cover the students' (a) satisfaction with specifics of course organization (i.e., the oral and written quizzes, grading procedures, teaching assistants, and optional weekly lectures) and (b) general reactions to the course.

Nine months following completion of the semester, all students were contacted by mail and offered $2 to take a follow-up test on which items from the original were again rerandomized. In addition to this monetary inducement, when the students arrived, they were informed that they could earn an extra 2¢ for each question answered correctly.

The *Subjects* subsection is clearly labeled as the first paragraph. Ideally, the Subjects subsection should answer three main questions: (1) Who participated in the study? (2) How were they selected? (3) How many were there? The first question includes a description of the characteristics of the subjects, namely, age, sex, and so forth.

The second subsection is labeled *General Procedures.* However, this and the entire *Experimental Manipulations* subsection comprise the *Procedure* part of the research article. Both of these describe the steps in conducting the study. The Procedure subsection should be described in sufficient detail to allow an outside investigator to replicate the study.

The *Achievement Measures* subsection comprises the *Instrumentation* subsection of the research article. This subsection should always present the operational definitions for the study; that is, the tests or instruments that will be used to measure the conceptual variables.

The *Procedure* subsection usually includes a summary of each step conducted in implementing the research. It includes instructions to subjects, the formation of groups, any special manipulations unique to the study, and any control features designed to minimize error.

The *Instrumentation* subsection usually includes a brief description of the apparatus or materials used and their function in the research. If tests are used, a statement presenting norms, reliability, and validity of the test for the researcher's purposes is presented. In addition, scoring procedures and sample questions are frequently provided.

Thus the Method section corresponds to the fourth and fifth steps of the scientific method: *(4) Develop techniques or instruments to obtain information related to the problem and hypotheses; (5) Collect data or information.* Using instruments that relate to the conceptual variables presented in the Introduction is not usually a difficult task. We have a tendency to make it difficult when we are not sure of what we plan to study. An exaggerated example of this difficulty would be trying to determine the effectiveness of our school's Introduction to Psychology class by administering a Russian history test; a less exaggerated example would be administering a statistics test or a developmental psychology test to the same class. It is a more subtle distinction when we choose from among five nationally standardized tests that purport to measure introductory psychology knowledge and skills. More levels of difficulty can surface unless we have a clear map of the territory.

It is rare in educational research for the data-collection phase of the scientific method to proceed exactly as planned. Frequently, a deviation from the most workable procedure occurs. For instance, we may have to do several phone interviews when we had planned to collect all our information with mailed questionnaires. Sometimes we lose subjects from one or more of the groups. Often subjects do exceptionally well because someone is watching them. Even more stable elements can betray us. One researcher who had planned to gather information from a one-way viewing screen ended up observing through a closet door that the subjects continually tried to open! The discrepancy between the intended procedures and the actual procedures needs to be examined in order to determine if the discrepancy produced significant artificial changes in the information collected. If so, the artificial changes should be reported. Thorough reporting in the Method section is essential to our credibility in the rest of the article.

The Results section.   The third main component of the research article is the *Results* section. It is frequently the one section of the article that produces a type of irrational anxiety or panic in someone just learning to conduct and evaluate research. Will I ever learn what all this stuff means, let alone do it myself? Yes, without a doubt you will, because it is the most logical and systematic section of the research article. In addition, most research articles use a similar organization for the Results section.

After all the information has been collected from the various subjects, the researcher frequently will have a multitude of scores of different kinds for each person. We then calculate statistics in order to summarize or describe all this information into a coherent, sensible whole. Every statistic has a special role and purpose, and the ones to be used usually depend upon the nature of the data and the purpose of the study. All statistics, however, seem to be grouped into two main functions that come under one of these two questions: (1) Which statistics best describe and summarize all the data or information? (2) Which statistics best determine if there are significant differences among the groups? Those answering the first question are called *descriptive statistics.* Numerical values labeled *mean* or *average, standard deviation, variance,* and *correlation* are descriptive statistics, and each has a logical and orderly function. No mystery or magic exists; it's just a process of knowing the meaning of the new jargon and how to use it.

Those statistics which fall under the second question are called *inferential statistics.* They are used to find out whether we can infer that there are real differences among the groups or whether error or chance is operating too strongly. Inferential statistics may be labeled *t-test, analysis of variance, discriminant analysis, multivariate analysis of variance,* and *Scheffé.* (This is some of the jargon I warned you about!) Read the following Results section twice—the first time reading the statistical values and the second time without reading the statistics, concentrating on the narrative.

Results

Of the 149 students originally enrolled in the course, 127 received final grades at the end of the semester, 63 in the self-paced group and 64 in the instructor-paced group. Three students had to be given incompletes for medical excuses (two from the self-paced group and one from the instructor-paced group) while 19 dropped the course. However, there was no difference in course withdrawal rate between the self-paced and instructor-paced groups, as they lost 9 (12.3%) and 10 (13.7%) students, respectively. Nor were there any differences in the final grade distributions: over 90% of the students in both groups received an A. At the end of the course, the average number of units completed by each group was virtually the same: self-paced group = 14.77 and instructor-paced = 14.95. Finally, the two

groups performed almost identically on the 53-item pretest. The mean number of correct items for the self-paced group was 20.5, while it was 20.3 for the instructor-paced group.

There was, however, a statistically significant difference between the two groups in terms of the number of quizzes repeated over the course of the semester. Students in the self-paced group had to repeat 4.1% of their quizzes, whereas those in the instructor-paced group had to repeat 7.2% of theirs, $\chi^2(1) = 8.75, p < .01$.

Pacing

To compare the rates of progress of the two groups, the semester was divided into 15-day periods. The average number of units completed during each time period are shown in Figure 1. Only the first 4 of the 5

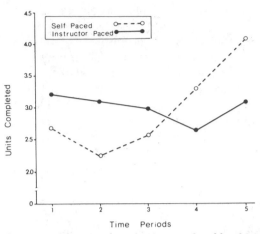

Figure 1. Mean number of units completed by the 5 15-day time periods of the course for the self-paced and instructor-paced groups.

time periods were used in a 2 × 4 (Pacing × Time) analysis of variance. The rationale for this was that since very few students failed to complete all 15 units, the information in the fifth time period is redundant with the first 4 (i.e., the score for Time Period 5 = 15 − sum of scores for Time Periods 1 through 4). This treatment of the data provides a conservative test of the pacing difference. The results showed a significant main effect for pacing group, $F(1, 125) = 7.86, p < .01$, and a significant Group × Time Period interaction, $F(3, 375) = 5.30, p < .01$. The significant interaction of pacing group and time period shows that the patterns of progress of the two groups through the course were not the same, as predicted by the contingencies.

Posttest Achievement Measure

The mean scores on the posttest were 32.6 for the self-paced group and 32.2 for the instructor-paced group. When compared with the pretest scores, an analysis of variance showed that the main effect of the pretest–

posttest was significant, $F(1, 124) = 412.9$, $p < .001$, while neither the main effect of the treatment (experimental conditions) nor the Treatment × Pretest–Posttest interaction approached significance. The performances of the two groups on the multiple-choice criterion tests increased significantly from the pretest to the posttest, but the two groups did not differ in their scores on either. In other words, it made no difference whether the students self-paced and procrastinated or whether they worked at an even rate under point incentives; they scored identically on the posttest achievement measure.

Course Evaluations

The course evaluation questionnaires completed at the end of the course yielded no differences in satisfaction on the dimensions evaluated. Both groups were equally positive about the course, as all ratings ranged from 2.90 and 3.45 on a 4-point scale.

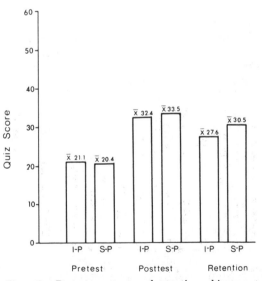

Figure 2. Pretest, posttest, and retention achievement scores for the follow-up samples from the self-paced (S-P) and instructor-paced (I-P) groups.

Retention Achievement Measures

Data were collected on 51 (40.2%) of the 127 students who received final grades in the course, 27 (42.2%) from the self-paced group and 24 (38.1%) from the instructor-paced group. Figure 2 shows the retention test scores for these samples along with their pretest and posttest scores. The latter scores for these follow-up students were similar to those of their groups as a whole. Moreover, the final grade distributions of the two follow-up groups also matched those of their respective groups.

Analysis of variance indicated a strong test (pre-, post-, retention) main effect, $F(2, 98)$ = 114.9, $p < .001$, but that the Group $\times$ Text interaction was not statistically significant, $F(2, 98) = 2.42$. However, the p value for the Group $\times$ Test interaction was .094 and suggested that the self-paced group performed somewhat better on the retention test than did the instructor-paced students. Finally, no relationships of any merit were found between the retention scores and posttest scores or the retention scores and procrastination.

Initially, it may be difficult to see any organization to this section. The first two paragraphs present the results of the descriptive statistics they calculated. For this study, percentages and average or mean scores were reported. Three of the following four sections present results obtained from the inferential statistics. Several comparisons were statistically significant, either $p < .05$, $p < .01$, or $p < .001$, while the last comparison for Group $\times$ Test interaction was not ($p = .094$, which is greater than $p < .05$). The course evaluations were analyzed insufficiently and seemed to be included only as a second thought. We don't know what dimensions were evaluated, nor do we know how the groups differed in rating each item or section of the questionnaire.

The Results section corresponds neatly with the sixth step of the scientific method: *(6) Analyze the data or information.* The goal of statistical analyses conducted on the original scores obtained from the subjects is to see whether the researcher can conclude that the differences obtained are real ones or due merely to error or chance. If they can be attributed to real differences among the groups, a *statistically significant difference* or *discrimination* is obtained. If the difference among groups cannot be considered a real one, it will be attributed to chance or error operating artificially. Thus, no statistically significant difference would be observed.

One main purpose of the Results section is to determine which differences are statistically significant and which are not. The questions the researcher must now answer are: "So what? What do these differences mean? What is the practical significance of this statistical difference?" Statistical significance is used as a baseline, so that we can assume that these differences are real and not due to error. Otherwise we would waste time trying to answer many more "So what?" questions about differences due to error or chance. Only after we have established statistical significance do we attempt to find out the practical significance.

The main function of the *Discussion* section is to present the implications of the results; that is, to attempt to answer "So what?" Thus, if the Results section is initially confusing, keep in mind that in the Discussion section we will usually try to focus on the main significant findings from the Results section. It will attach further practical meaning to them so as to increase our understanding of the research findings.

The Discussion section. The last main component of the research article is the *Discussion* section. In this we examine the main implications of the results by tying them into theory, past research, or personal experience. How are the results obtained in this study integrated into the existing body of knowledge? Is our knowledge base expanded, modified, or enriched by these findings? Read the following Discussion section.

Discussion

A comparison between a student self-paced instruction system and a flexible, instructor-paced point system revealed that students procrastinated when they self-paced, yet proceeded evenly through course material when given incentives to do so. As noted elsewhere, students do not *self*-pace; they pace according to the conditions that control the pacing behavior (Bijou et al., 1976). In most cases when we say a student self-paces, we are admitting that the conditions which produce pacing are unknown. These results are also in agreement with other research demonstrating that whether students self-pace or have their pacing regulated, they score similarly on criterion measures of course achievement (Atkins & Lockhart, 1976; Bitgood & Segrave, 1974; Burt, 1975; Lloyd et al., in press; Robin & Graham, 1974; Semb et al., 1974) and are highly and equally satisfied with the ways in which they were instructed (Bitgood & Segrave, 1974; Robin & Graham, 1974; Semb et al., 1974).

In addition to the similarity of course achievement and course satisfaction measures, the two groups showed no differences in (a) the number of units completed, (b) final grade distributions, or (c) course withdrawal rates. However, the self-paced group did have to repeat fewer quizzes, and this would seem to be an advantage. Why this difference occurred is not immediately apparent, but it could be that students took quizzes when they were prepared, rather than being forced to take them at the end of a week, prepared or not.

The data indicating that the self-pacing component had no differential effect on course withdrawal are particularly interesting. The PSI courses generally have higher withdrawal rates than lecture–discussion courses and the presumption is often that the self-pacing feature is the cause; however, there is only a small amount of empirical evidence for this latter claim (see Semb et al., 1974). Certainly the matter is not settled; the wide procedural variations from one PSI course to the next preclude a final answer. But the point can be made that self-pacing need not lead to greater student withdrawal. When it does, the other components of the PSI package should be scrutinized; indeed, they may be interacting with the self-pacing component, thereby inducing high withdrawal rates. This need not occur.

Although the results show striking similarities between the two groups on dependent measures relevant to educational achievement, many educators would still be troubled over student procrastination in the self-paced group. Course management logistics aside, cramming typically has been considered less desirable than regularly paced study; however, there are as yet no supportive data in the PSI literature for this conclusion (Burt, 1975). Therefore, the inclusion of a follow-up retention measure was a logical step for assessing possible differences. But no statistical retention differences were apparent. If anything, the data suggested that the benefit might go to the procrastinating self-paced group. Perhaps contingencies that allow self-pacing are important after all.

In addition to this retention trend, the difference between the two groups in quiz repeat rates was in favor of the self-paced group; they failed significantly fewer quizzes. But when all other achievement measures are the same, it is difficult to know how to interpret a high or low repeat rate. One conclusion is that more students in the instructor-paced group took quizzes before being adequately prepared. However, the supposedly aversive event of quiz failure did not seem to influence the course evaluation measures. On the other hand, it might be suggested that we did not measure the appropriate behaviors. Perhaps instructor-pacing and the quiz repeats are teaching students something else, something unrelated to achievement. Perhaps they are teaching pacing skills that will be more important to future learning than the content of any single course.

Future PSI research should attempt to determine whether pacing skills, once acquired in a course, will then be applied in subsequent courses. However, a caveat needs to be entered. Analogous to the difficulties of generalization from clinical and educational programs, pacing skills should not be expected to appear magically in other learning settings. They must be planned for and programmed. Perhaps instructor-paced systems would be part of the program, perhaps not. But we should begin to find out. If instructor-paced systems are not part of a learning-to-self-pace program, then we must examine the possible benefits of self-paced systems for content retention despite the course management problems they generate.

The Discussion section corresponds to the last step in the scientific method: *(7) Generate conclusions based upon data related to the hypotheses.* An organized format for discussing the conclusions or implications relates the findings back to the hypotheses stated in the Introduction. Thus, ideally, the major sections of the research article will be interwoven and logically integrated.

Two other tangential but important components of the research article are typically included: the *Reference Notes and References* and the *Abstract.* The Reference Notes and References usually contain the complete source of other articles cited in the research article. The Abstract is a short synopsis or summary of the entire article, usually presented at the beginning of the article prior to the Introduction. It is a useful procedure to read the Abstract first to determine if the entire article is of use, importance, or interest; if so, then the rest of the article is available.

Student procrastination is an important concern in personalized systems of instruction. This study compared progress made on course work by two groups of students—one self-paced (n = 75) and one instructor-paced (n = 74)—along with measures of course achievement and evaluations and a 9-month content retention test. Results showed that even though the self-paced group procrastinated, while the instructor-paced group did not, both scored similarly on pre-, post-, and retention tests and were equally satisfied with the course. Moreover, no differences were found in the number of units completed, final grade distributions, or course withdrawal rates. The withdrawal rate data and the tendency for the self-paced group to score better on the retention test are discussed in terms of educational objectives.

Reference Notes

1. Lloyd, K. E. *Behavior analysis and technology in higher education.* Unpublished manuscript, Drake University, 1975.

2. Bijou, S. W. *Course guide.* Unpublished manuscript, University of Illinois at Urbana-Champaign, 1973.

References

Atkins, J. A., & Lockhart, K. Flexible vs. instructor-paced college quizzing: A behavioral analysis of preference and performance. In L. E. Fraley & E. A. Vargas (Eds.), *Behavior research and technology in higher education.* Gainesville: Society for Behavioral Technology and Engineering, University of Florida, 1976.

Bijou, S. W. *Child development: The basic stage of early childhood.* Englewood Cliffs, N.J.: Prentice-Hall, 1976.

Bijou, S. W., & Baer, D. M. *Child development I: A systematic and empirical theory.* Englewood Cliffs, N.J.: Prentice-Hall, 1961.

Bijou, S. W., & Baer, D. M. *Child development II: The basic stage of infancy.* Englewood Cliffs, N.J.: Prentice-Hall, 1965.

Bijou, S. W., & Baer, D. M. *Child development: Readings in experimental analysis.* Englewood Cliffs, N.J.: Prentice-Hall, 1967.

Bijou, S. W., Morris, E. K., & Parsons, J. A. A PSI course in child development with a procedure for reducing student procrastination. *Journal of Personalized Instruction,* 1976, *1,* 36–40.

Bitgood, S. C., & Segrave, K. Comparison of graduated and fixed point systems of contingency managed instruction. In J. M. Johnston (Ed.), *Behavior research and technology in higher education.* Springfield, Ill.: Charles C Thomas, 1974.

Burt, D. W. Study and test performance of college students on concurrent assignment schedules. In J. M. Johnston (Ed.), *Behavior research and technology in higher education.* Springfield, Ill.: Charles C Thomas, 1975.

Carroll, J. A model of school learning. *Teachers College Record,* 1963, *64,* 723–733.

Cole, C., Martin, S., & Vincent, J. A comparison of two teaching formats at the college level. In J. M. Johnston (Ed.), *Behavior research and technology in higher education.* Springfield, Ill.: Charles C Thomas, 1974.

Cooper, J. L., & Greiner, J. M. Contingency management in an introductory psychology course produces better retention. *Psychological Record,* 1971, *21,* 391–401.

Corey, J. R., & McMichael, J. S. Retention in a PSI introductory psychology course. In J. G. Sherman (Ed.), *Personalized systems of instruction: 41 germinal papers.* Menlo Park, Calif.: Benjamin, 1974.

Keller, F. S. "Good-bye, teacher . . . ." *Journal of Applied Behavior Analysis,* 1968, *1,* 79–89.

Kulik, J. A., Kulik, C., & Carmichael, K. The Keller Plan in science teaching. *Science,* 1974, *183,* 379–383.

Lloyd, K. E. Retention of responses to stimulus classes and to specific stimuli. *Journal of Experimental Psychology,* 1960, *59,* 54–59.

Lloyd, K. E.   Contingency management in university courses.   *Educational Technology*, 1971, *11*, 18–23.

Lloyd, K., & Knutzen, N. J.   A self-paced programmed undergraduate course in the experimental analysis of behavior.   *Journal of Applied Behavior Analysis*, 1969, *2*, 125–133.

Lloyd, K. E., McMullin, W. E., & Fox, R. A.   Rate of completing unit tests as a function of student-pacing and instructor-pacing.   In T. Brigham, R. Hawkins, J. Scott, & T. F. McLaughlin (Eds.), *Behavior analysis research in education: Self-control and reading.*   Dubuque, Iowa: Wm. C. Brown, in press.

Malott, R. W., & Svinicki, J. G.   Contingency management in an introductory course for one thousand students.   *Psychological Record*, 1969, *19*, 545–556.

Mawhinney, V. T., et al.   A comparison of students studying behavior by daily, weekly, and three-week testing schedules.   *Journal of Applied Behavior Analysis*, 1971, *4*, 257–264.

Miller, L. K., Weaver, F. H., & Semb, G.   A procedure for maintaining student progress in a personalized university course.   *Journal of Applied Behavior Analysis*, 1974, *7*, 87–91.

Moore, J. W., Hauck, V. E., & Gagné, E. D.   Acquisition, retention and transfer in an individualized college physics course.   *Journal of Educational Psychology*, 1973, *64*, 335–340.

Powers, R. B., Edwards, K. A., & Hoehle, W. F.   Bonus points in a self-paced course facilitates exam taking.   *Psychological Record*, 1973, *23*, 533–538.

Robin, A. L., & Graham, M. Q.   Academic responses engendered by teacher pacing versus student pacing in a personalized instruction course.   In R. S. Ruskin & S. F. Bono (Eds.), *Personalized instruction in higher education: Proceedings of the First National Conference.*   Washington, D.C.: Center for Personalized Instruction, 1974.

Semb, G., Conyers, D., Spencer, R., & Sosa, J. J. S.   An experimental comparison of four pacing contingencies in a personalized instruction course.   In J. M. Johnston (Ed.), *Behavior research and technology in higher education.*   Springfield, Ill.: Charles C Thomas, 1974.

Sherman, J. G.   PSI: Some notable failures.   In J. G. Sherman (Ed.), *Personalized system of instruction: 41 germinal papers.*   Menlo Park, Calif.: Benjamin, 1974.

Definition of Basic Terms

Because the meanings we attach to words vary, we will define several terms and give examples. The definition of terms helps to clarify their meaning, thereby increasing communication and understanding.

Variable: a measurable characteristic that may assume different values. A variable is the opposite of a constant like *pi* (π), which always has the same value: 3.14. . . . Examples of variables include height, intelligence, birth order, and marital status.

Operational definition: specifying a variable by expressing the activities or operations required to measure it. To *operationalize a variable* is to convert it from a concept-level statement to a measurable, objective operation. For example, the concept of *intelligence* can be measured by the Stanford-Binet Intelligence Scale; the concept of *self-actualization* by the Personal Orientation Inventory; *creativity* by the Remote Associates Test; and *achievement* by the Iowa Test of Basic Skills.

An understanding of what an operational definition is and its relationship to a variable is vital in educational research. Both relate to what a *construct* or *concept* is. A *construct* or *concept* is an abstraction derived from some aspect of behavior in humans that varies among individuals. For instance, *creativity* is a concept and it is also a variable because human beings have different levels of creativity. We investigate numerous concepts in education. Other examples include *intelligence, self-actualization, anxiety, achievement,* and *motivation.* These concepts are also variables since people vary in each.

According to Kerlinger (1975, p. 31), two types of operational definitions of concepts are possible, a *measurement* type and an *experimental* type. A *measurement type of operational definition* describes how a concept will be assessed or measured. We could operationalize the concept of *intelligence* in any of the following ways: by using the Cognitive Abilities Test, the Wechsler Intelligence Scale for Children—Revised, or the teacher ratings of students' level of intelligence. Each researcher will select how to measure each variable; that is, each will determine what the operational definition of each concept will be.

An *experimental type of operational definition* specifies how a researcher will manipulate a variable. That is, this type of operational definition will delineate the various manipulations of a variable the researcher has chosen to study. For instance, we could operationalize the variable *type of instruction* as lecture, group discussion, peer tutoring, small group, independent study, computer-assisted, or any of a number of other ways. The experimenter will determine for each study how to manipulate or specify the variable; this includes not just how to manipulate the variable but also into how many different levels or types.

Thus, operational definitions are indispensable to educational research. If we study a particular concept, we develop a corresponding operational definition of that variable. We either delineate how we will measure it or how we will manipulate it. Operational definitions make replication and verification possible in all fields of research.

Data (singular *datum*):   values derived from the operational measurement of a variable. These include, for example, frequency of disruptive behaviors, leadership ratings, creativity scores, or seconds involved on a motivation task.

Population: an entire group of individuals or objects having some common observable characteristic. At times, people confuse *population* with an earlier understanding of the word. Actually, the only defining criterion for a population is that the group have some common, observable characteristic. Thus a population may be defined anywhere within a very broad range and can be as inclusive or as exclusive as the researcher deems necessary. Examples of populations include: (1) students currently enrolled in section 01 of Introduction to Research and Statistics; (2) students who completed Introduction to Research and Statistics between 1979 and 1982; (3) psychology students currently enrolled in section 01 of Introduction to Research and Statistics.

Sample: any subgroup of a population. The term *sample* does not place any restriction on how the sample was obtained, that is, what procedure was used. It is simply some smaller set of that population sharing a common observable characteristic. A sample may include: (1) the first ten students through the door who are currently enrolled in Introduction to Research and Statistics; (2) every third student on the class list; (3) all students who volunteer; (4) twenty students whose names were taken from a hat.

Parameter: a characteristic of a population that is measurable and can take on or be represented by different values. It is a definition similar to the one for *variable.* The difference is that the parameter relates to a population characteristic whereas the variable relates to a sample characteristic. For instance, intelligence for a sample group of third graders is called a variable; intelligence for a population of third graders in the United States is called a parameter.

One important concept that is related to a greater understanding of the relationship of the sample to the population is *sampling bias.* Sampling bias is the result of inadequately representing the salient characteristics or parameters of the population in the sample. Because of a nonrandom sampling of the target population, sampling bias may be introduced, for instance, into a study of college students by selecting subjects from the student union pub after a Monday night football game. These students will not be representative of college students in general. This concept relates to our general discussion of error presented earlier since the greater the bias the less the accuracy and representativeness of our results.

The following definitions distinguish among areas of research, the evaluation of programs, and the assessment of students.

Basic research: Also known as *pure* or *fundamental research,* basic research is conducted with the primary focus of generating new knowledge in order to refine or expand existing theories. It is usually conducted in controlled laboratory situations and often uses animals as subjects. There is no consideration of the practical application of the findings to actual problems.

Applied research: Applied research is conducted with the primary intention of testing theoretical concepts in actual situations in order to develop generalizable applications. Most educational research falls under this category of research, which is an attempt to develop generalizations, for instance, about the instructional, motivational, and learning process.

Action research: Action research is conducted with the primary intention of solving a specific, immediate, concrete problem in a local setting. The development of theory or generalizable applications is not of concern. Most school teachers probably will be involved in action-oriented research where the goal is to examine a specific classroom practice and to apply the research process skills to solve the problem systematically and scientifically. Problems with disruptive students or questions about which instructional method is most effective with my class are examples of action-oriented research questions.

Curriculum or program evaluation: Curriculum or program evaluation is concerned primarily with assessing the effectiveness of a product, process, or program in terms of specific goals and objectives. Typically, some judgment related to the continuance or termination or revision of a program is made. Criteria for evaluating a program's effectiveness may include its educational impact, cost, time, and resources needed. An evaluation project will generate a conclusion leading to recommendations which bring about changes or modifications in what was evaluated. An evaluation project provides answers to such questions as: Should we have year-round schools? What text should we use? Should we change our group standardized testing plan? Is this handwriting system effective?

Assessment: Whereas an evaluation project attempts to evaluate the effectiveness of a particular product, process, or program, in an assessment project we attempt to estimate, assess, or describe the achievement level of a large population of individuals—usually students, who have had varying educational (e.g., public, private, or parochial school) instructional, and environmental (e.g., geographical or urban-rural) influences. For instance, since 1969 a nationwide testing program of students in the fields of science, mathematics, literature, reading, and social studies has been conducted by the National Assessment of Educational Programs (NAEP).

These basic terms, plus the three earlier ones—error and descriptive and inferential statistics—will help establish an initial baseline for facilitating communication and understanding. Others will be defined as they are encountered within the context of the research process.

Importance of Educational Research

Historically, the integrated use of the scientific method in educational research has revised our understanding of matters that were assumed to be obvious or useful. The results of applied research produced a change in the models of reality shared by individuals; their maps of the territory had to be redrawn based on the new explorations.

For many years parents and grandparents believed that they should inhibit or discourage the learning and growth of their very bright or precocious children. They believed that precocious children would grow up to be dullards or inferior adults. "They'll use up all their 'smarts' too early and won't have any left as adults," it was thought. Not until research results came in from Lewis Terman's longitudinal study of gifted children, started in 1921 at Stanford, did this stereotype begin to fade. The results from this still-continuing research have produced a tremendous amount of knowledge about gifted and talented individuals as children and adults (Terman, 1925; Seagoe, 1975).

Herrnstein (1971) summarized the Terman evidence to support the conclusion that superior children do become superior adults. Of the original 1,000 gifted children with IQs of over 140, Herrnstein found from a sample of their productivity in their middle forties:

> ... about 2,000 scientific and technical articles, 60 books, 33 novels, 375 short stories or plays, 325 miscellaneous publications, 230 patents, not to mention the hundreds of radio and television

Ready to Begin the Journey

scripts, newspaper stories, pieces of art and music.... By the mid-1950's they had spawned (with spouses who were themselves significantly brighter than average) about 2,500 children whose average IQ appears to be above 130—not as brilliant as their exceptional parents, but still among the top 5 percent of the population (Herrnstein, 1971, p. 43).

Another belief accepted as common knowledge was that the more intelligent child is unpopular among his classmates. Other children resent them for their higher grades and greater acceptance by the teacher. Gronlund (1959), in his review of the research examining the relationship between intelligence or achievement and social acceptance or popularity, found that, as a group, gifted and high-achievement students were the ones most accepted by their peers rather than those least accepted.

Many other examples of the usefulness of the scientific method and educational research in producing a positive influence can be found. For instance, Walberg, Schiller, and Haertel (1979) summarized a systematic set of research reviews on instruction and related research during the 1969–1979 decade. The effect of the educational research process just over the last decade is extensive and significant. Positive findings regarding the effects of innovative curricula, behavioral instruction, mastery learning, programmed instruction, and motivation and learning are only a few of the educational research topics that have been further clarified. Their article from the *Phi Delta Kappan* is reprinted below.

The Quiet Revolution In Educational Research

by Herbert J. Walberg, Diane Schiller, and Geneva D. Haertel

Mr. Walberg and his associates marshal impressive evidence that, properly funded, the research community in education can produce (and has produced over the past decade) highly useful findings.

The past decade of educational research has shown us the means to attain our educational goals much more fully than ever before. We shall attempt in this article to verify that surprising statement. After all, we were told only a dozen years ago, by reputable observers, that results of most research on the teaching-learning process were not significant. In fact, John Stephens, after reviewing several decades of research, said that most educational techniques seem to hinder as often as they aid learning.[1] There was good reason for this conclusion a decade ago. As Gene Glass pointed out, the total of human effort on behalf of research in education, at least that part officially supported by public and private funds, was less than 2,000 person-years in 1968.[2] In the same year, 15,000 full-time researchers investigated agricultural productivity; 60,000 persons engaged in research and development in the health sciences. Since that time, however, the U.S. Office of Education, the National Institute of Education, the National Science Foundation, and other public and private agencies have increased the funding of educational research notably, with sound results, as we shall see.

The impressive accumulation of educational research findings in the last decade seems to have gone unnoticed by many educators and the general public. It might indeed be concluded from widely publicized reports that the schools are pathological institutions and that neither educators nor research workers know how to cure their problems and increase their productivity. Charles E. Silberman's popular book, *Crisis in the Classroom*, reached this conclusion.[3] Stephens, the reviewer cited above, argued that learning is spontaneous; that is, maturational forces within the student cause learning to proceed at a given rate notwithstanding wide variations in educational conditions.[4] Christopher Jencks and his colleagues concluded that luck is the most important determinant of educational and occupational attainment and that improvements in schooling do not increase the educational and social mobility of the poor.[5] The *Equality of Educational Opportunity* survey by James Coleman and his associates was also interpreted as showing a lack of relationship between educational conditions and student learning.[6] The Neville Bennett study in England appeared to show that progressive teaching methods hinder student learning.[7]

But most of these accounts failed to consider the hundreds of *other* learning studies, the results of which are tabulated below, along with many studies on other relations between educational means or conditions and learning outcomes.

Since the public and practicing educators seldom read the voluminous and scattered technical literature on education, we assembled a systematic collection of research reviews published from January 1969 to the present on instructional and related research conducted in elementary and secondary schools and institutions of higher education. We examined the *Current Index to Journals in Education* under the topics "Literature Reviews" and "State of the Art," the American Educational Research Association's *Review of Educational Research* and *Review of Research in Education*, and reviews cited in these sources. We also included forthcoming work, but we selected for analysis only critical, evaluative reviews of at least four studies. Nearly all the research we included was carried out in classrooms rather than in laboratories under artificial conditions. Since the reviews present results of multiple studies and multiple comparisons within studies in a variety of ways, we imposed, where possible, a consistent framework: The numbers of positive and negative, as opposed to mixed, results of studies are given; and the percentage of positive results — those that support the superiority of the means or condition in question — of all positive and negative results is calculated.[8]

Exposure and Opportunity

A recent review uncovered 25 conclusive investigations of the relationship of increased time allocated for instruction (or devoted to learning by the student) to cognitive and affective learning. Table 1 shows that 24 of the 25 (96%) showed a positive relationship between time and cognitive learning. In view of this consistent relationship, several investigators whose work is forthcoming are studying the distribution of time that students engage in learning during the school day. Wayne C. Frederick of the Chicago

Public Schools found that after subtracting time lost in absences, tardiness, interruptions, disruptions, and inattentiveness, as little as 25% of students' time in lower-achieving schools is actually spent on learning. David Berliner of the University of Arizona found in a sample of elementary classes in California that there was as little as 30 hours of effective instruction in mathematics during the school year. It is apparent even in the best schools that students often get stuck on a problem and need to wait for the teacher to get them started again. It seems clear that increasing the time students engage in the learning process, at least up to a point, might lead to large gains in learning.

Another recent review considered comparisons of innovative and traditional curricula on measures both favorable and unfavorable to the new curricula. The results (Table 1) show that innovative curricula have consistent impact on tests that reflect the intent of the curricula. Similarly, students in traditional courses do better (but not with significant consistency) on measures that reflect the intent of the traditional courses. Thus the new curriculum elements a school chooses for its students are another decisive determinant of what the students learn.

Table 1 shows the results from several reviews of class size. All four comparisons show significant learning benefits for small classes. Better-analyzed studies show more consistent favorable effects and lend credibility to the results. Gene Glass and Mary Smith's very extensive analyses, moreover, reveal that studies that randomly assign students to small and large classes in true experiments show stronger positive benefits for smaller classes. This finding enhances confidence that smaller classes lead to greater achievement rather than that both are caused by other variables such as community wealth. Stronger size/learning relationships found by Glass and Smith in studies carried out after 1960 than in those before 1940 indicate the increasing sophistication of educational research. Although the inverse size/learning relationship is not the strongest or most consistent among the results summarized here, several estimates from the Glass and Smith work are impressive: Children who gain 1.0 grade equivalents on average per year in a class of 40 would gain 1.3 equivalents in a class of 20 and 1.6 if taught individually. If average pupils were taught in a class of 20 pupils from kindergarten through grade 6, they would be over two years ahead of similar pupils taught for the same length of time in a class of 40.

Nature of Instruction

Table 1 shows a variety of effects for behavioral instruction on college as well as elementary and secondary school students. The prevalent form of behavioral instruction at the college level is referred to as "Personalized Systems of Instruction" (PSI), which has the following components: reliance on the written word in the form of small units of instruction; student self-pacing through these units; mastery (that is, usually perfect or near-perfect performance required on each unit before proceeding to the next); and assessment by repeated testing administered by student proctors, with maximum credit for success and no penalty for failure. Students continue working at their own pace through the units until they reach a satisfactory grade in the course. Three reviews of behavioral instruction show the superiority of PSI and modified PSI techniques over conventional lecture and discussion methods at the college level. The findings are consistent across 12 subjects for small, medium, and large samples on achievement, retention, and attitudes and interest in the subject.

Mastery learning, more often found in secondary and elementary schools, has the following components: clear goals and procedures for what is to be learned, specific instructional objectives, small units of learning, corrective feedback on progress, flexible learning time, alternative modes of instruction, and cooperative learning with peers. Mastery learning is similar to PSI in assuming that each student can learn if given appropriate instruction and sufficient time. Mastery learning also shows results consistently superior to conventional instruction on achievement, retention, and attitudes.

Programmed instruction uses written materials in which instructional elements are presented in units called "frames." Each frame requires an active response from the student, and the length of the frame, varying from short paragraphs to several pages, is designed to suit the abilities of the typical student. Programmed materials usually enable students to skip rapidly over material that is already known, to "branch" to needed correctives, and to proceed at a suitable individual pace. The reviews (Table 1) indicate that programmed instruction has consistently more favorable effects on achievement and interest in the subject than traditional classroom procedures.

Research on instructional radio and television and computer-assisted instruction is beyond our scope, since most of the reviews were published before 1969 and concern learning in special rather than classroom settings. However, conclusions of a review by Dean Jamison et al. should be mentioned.[9] Radio, television, and computer-assisted instruction are about as effective as conventional instruction. Computer-assisted instruction, as a replacement or supplement, often results in substantial savings of student time. The authors point out the need for exploring the productivity and cost-efficiency of substituting capital for labor in education, since the unit costs of media and technology decline with increasing usage.

The term "mathemagenic" was coined by psychologists in the early 1960s from the Greek roots *mathema* ("learning") and *genic* ("give birth to"). Thus mathemagenic techniques give birth to learning or encourage it in some way that may be exemplified in the materials of instruction, the structuring of the content, or specific teaching strategies (Table 1).

"Adjunct questions" are those inserted in textual material; for example, a 2,000-word passage concerning the life of

Charles Darwin was divided into 20 paragraphs of 10 lines each. Students answer one or more questions before or after each paragraph. Adjunct questions consistently benefit recall of information when given after passages but are less consistent in enhancing transfer of the information to new situations when given before the text.

"Advance organizers" are used as an introduction to relate new content to what the student already knows. An advance organizer, for example, was used to point out the differences and similarities between Buddhism and Christianity before a three-day instruction session, since the material on Buddhism was new and the material on Christianity was familiar to most students. Such organizers are usually presented at a higher level of abstraction than the instructional elements themselves. Research on advance organizers shows inconsistent effects on learning.

"Analytic revision of instruction" refers to lesson development that includes instructional objectives and trial-and-error revision of methods and materials until the objectives are reached. For example, a lesson on writing mathematical ratios is presented and student performance is evaluated; the lesson is then revised on the basis of difficulties encountered by the students and presented a second time. The process continues until the objectives are met. Four studies of this technique support the hypothesis that it is more efficacious than conventional methods.

"Direct instruction" pertains to those methods in which the teacher controls the timing and sequencing of instruction, chooses materials, and monitors student performance. Direct instruction generally focuses directly on the content of achievement tests. Four studies of this technique showed greater effectiveness than conventional methods in producing achievement gains. Since analytic and direct instruction may amount to teaching the test and only four studies are available on each, the results should be interpreted cautiously.

Research at the college level yields in-

Table 1. A Selective Summary of a Decade of Educational Research

Research Topics	No. of Results	Percent Positive
Time on learning	25	96.0
Innovative curricula on:		
Innovative learning	45	97.8
Traditional learning	14	35.7
Smaller classes on learning:		
Pre-1954 studies	53	66.0
Pre-1954 better studies	19	84.2
Post-1954 studies	11	72.7
All comparisons	691	60.0
Behavioral instruction on:		
Learning	52	98.1
"Personalized Systems of Instruction" on learning	103	93.2
Mastery learning	30	96.7
Programmed instruction on learning	57	80.7
Adjunct questions on learning:		
After text on recall	38	97.4
After text on transfer	35	74.3
Before text on recall	13	76.9
Before text on transfer	17	23.5
Advance organizers on learning	32	37.5
Analytic revision of instruction on achievement	4	100.0
Direct instruction on achievement	4	100.0
Lecture versus discussion on:		
Achievement	16	68.8
Retention	7	100.0
Attitudes	8	86.0
Student- versus instructor-centered discussion on:		
Achievement	7	57.1
Understanding	6	83.0
Attitude	22	100.0
Student- versus instructor-led discussion on:		
Achievement	10	100.0
Attitude	11	100.0
Factual versus conceptual questions on achievement	4	100.0
Specific teaching traits on achievement:		
Clarity	7	100.0
Flexibility	4	100.0
Enthusiasm	5	100.0
Task orientation	7	85.7
Use of student ideas	8	87.5
Indirectness	6	83.3
Structuring	3	100.0
Sparing criticism	17	70.6
Psychological incentives and engagement		
Teacher's cues to student	10	100.00
Teacher reinforcement of student	16	87.5
Teacher engagement of class in lesson	6	100.00
Individual student engagement in lesson	15	100.0
Open versus traditional education on:		
Achievement	26	54.8
Creativity	12	100.0
Self-concept	17	88.2
Attitude toward school	25	92.0
Curiosity	6	100.0
Self-determination	7	85.7
Independence	19	94.7
Freedom from anxiety	8	37.5
Cooperation	6	100.0
Social-psychological climate and learning:		
Cohesiveness	17	85.7
Satisfaction	17	100.0
Difficulty	16	86.7
Formality	17	64.7
Goal direction	15	73.3
Democracy	14	84.6
Environment	15	85.7
Speed	14	53.8
Diversity	14	30.8
Competition	9	66.7
Friction	17	0.0
Cliqueness	13	8.3
Apathy	15	14.3
Disorganization	17	6.3
Favoritism	13	10.0
Motivation and learning	232	97.8
Social class and learning	620	97.6
Home environment on:		
Verbal achievement	30	100.0
Math achievement	22	100.0
Intelligence	20	100.0
Reading gains	6	100.0
Ability	8	100.0

teresting results on teaching techniques and locus of instruction (Table 1). Discussion is about equal to lecturing on achievement but is consistently superior on retention. Student-centered discussion, moreover, is superior to instructor-centered discussion on attitude; and student-led discussion is superior to instructor-led discussion on both achievement and attitude.

It is informative to compare these results with the impact on achievement of factual in contrast to conceptual questions. Four studies indicate that factual teacher questions have greater impact on achievement, perhaps because many teacher-made and standardized tests sample the lower levels of cognitive processes such as memory rather than comprehension and analytic skills. This finding must be interpreted cautiously but suggests that educators should consider the trade-offs between lower and higher levels of cognitive attainment, that research workers should include multiple measures of outcomes in future work, and that reviewers should tabulate results across studies separately for each learning outcome.

Table 1 shows the results of teaching techniques observed in elementary (mostly primary) classrooms. The reviewers, Barak Rosenshine and Norma Furst, appear somewhat inconsistent in reviewing this evidence, since in some cases they counted studies as positive that yielded one positive significant correlation among several that were calculated. N. L. Gage's independent and explicit review of the evidence on teacher indirectness, praise, acceptance, and criticism, however, confirms certain Rosenshine-Furst results with a high degree of statistical probability.[10] These results indicate that achievement is enhanced under teachers who are clear about their expectations, goals, and methods for learning; who are flexible in their responses to students; who show enthusiasm for the lesson and for student learning; who are businesslike and task-oriented; who use student ideas in leading the lesson; who attempt to elicit answers to questions by students rather

than tell the answers; who use structuring comments that inform the student of the purpose and organization of the lesson content; and who avoid excessive criticism.

Table 1 shows the results of a review of psychological studies of teacher behaviors that stimulate students and reinforce their desirable responses. Both teacher behaviors are consistently related to achievement and achievement gains. Moreover, teacher engagement of the class in the lesson as well as the amount of individual student engagement in the lesson as percentages of total time also show consistently superior results.

Table 1 shows an analysis of a review of many studies contrasting "open" with traditional education. Open education is similar to progressive education of the 1920s in that students in humane, enriched classrooms are given a degree of autonomy to plan jointly with the teacher the goals, pace, method, and evaluation of learning.[11] Since it is often confused with permissiveness or with open space classrooms, it is sometimes termed "informal education." Despite the fact that many people in the open education movement feared conventional evaluations because they were intent on going beyond traditional achievement test outcomes, 76 of the 102 studies comparing open and traditional methods show no significant differences between the two and 54.8% of the 26 significant studies actually favored open education on achievement measures. Thus it does not appear that open education, on average, impairs conventional achievement test performance.

On the other hand, open education, when it has a significant effect — probably when it is authentically implemented — produces consistently positive results on goals it is intended to attain in creativity, self-concept, school attitudes, curiosity, and independence. Because replication is the essence of science, the results should be informative to those who have concluded from the widely publicized Bennett study that open education has failed.[12] In addition, the results suggest that researchers should measure learning outcomes that go beyond achievement. There is no present basis for knowing, for example, whether behavioral instruction and Personalized Systems of Instruction, even though they may promote achievement and retention, lead to greater creativity, curiosity, and independence.

Social-Psychological Environments

Twelve studies report on correlations between measures of social-psychological climate of classes and various types of learning in the United States, Canada, Australia, and India.[13] Table 1 shows a tabulation of correlations of student perceptions of the climate and measures of cognitive, attitudinal, and behavioral learning outcomes (in most cases adjusted for intelligence and corresponding pretests). The cognitive measures tap factual knowledge as well as higher-level conceptual understanding; the attitudinal measures tap interest in the subject matter and in subject-related careers; and the behavioral indices are counts of extramural voluntary activities associated with course content. Greater amounts of all three types of learning take place, on average, in classes that students perceive as cohesive, satisfying, difficult or challenging, democratic, and providing the physical setting and materials required for learning. Perceived climate characteristics that are negatively correlated on average with learning gains are: friction among the class members, emphasis on subgroups or cliques within the class, apathy toward the lesson, disorganized content and procedures, and favoritism toward some class members. Results from other research indicate that characteristics of the students, the teacher, the subject matter, and instruction determine the nature of the social-psychological climate of the class. These effects appear to be mediated by student perceptions of the climate, which in turn predict various types of learning.

Many psychologists today have strong cognitive or behavioral persuasions. Social psychologists more often emphasize feelings and motivation as determinants of learning. Nearly all studies summarized in recent reviews (see Table 1) show that the degree of student motivation is consistently reflected in the amount of learning that takes place.

Student motivation and classroom climate are not completely under the control of teachers and other educators. Although educators may to some extent enhance these determinants of learning, the abilities, attitudes, and behaviors the child brings to school are influenced by home environment. Table 1 shows the consistency of correlations of social class and of parental stimulation in the home with achievement and ability. The results indicate that social-class measures are consistently but weakly correlated with student achievement in school and that measures of parental stimulation and encouragement of the child (obtained by interviews with the parent in the home) are much more valid predictors of achievement and abilities. Parental stimulation is strongly correlated with verbal achievement, moderately correlated with mathematics achievement and intelligence, and relatively weakly correlated with spatial and reasoning ability. Only one longitudinal study of home environments and achievements has been conducted. This British study of three age groups of boys and girls indicates that measures of home environment predict the amount of reading gains over a four-year period. Contrary to some speculations, the study showed that the correlations of parental stimulation and student achievement are about equal in samples of primary and middle school children and older adolescents. Two field evaluations of intervention programs that strongly concentrate school and parent resources on reading achievement in socially depressed areas of Chicago's inner city and of Flint, Michigan, revealed reading test gains comparable to those in middle-class neighborhoods.[14] These field evaluations require further replication to test the generalizability of such joint school-family programs to increase learning.

Conclusions

The tabulations of results of recent reviews on the relation of instructional and other educational conditions to learning outcomes yield a number of consistent, positive results with definite policy and practical implications. Greater funding of educational research in the last decade has brought a greater number of disciplined investigators to the field and allowed them to improve measurements of educational goals and means; to increase the statistical and experimental control of effects; and, while drawing on the theoretical insights from psychology and the social sciences, to relate research to practical issues of educational productivity.

We conclude that certain conditions and methods consistently produce certain outcomes but that no single method or set of conditions is superior on all outcomes. The greatest confidence can be placed in the effects of opportunity, exposure, and instruction on achievement, retention, and attitudes, because many experiments with random assignments of students to alternative conditions are available for analysis. Less confidence can be placed in the effects of social-psychological conditions, although many are plausible, because they have been less frequently investigated and are more often uncontrolled or statistically, rather than experimentally, controlled.

Much research remains to be done on certain conditions of learning and particularly on their effects on outcomes such as voluntary learning during and after instruction and on such traits as creativity, self-concept, independence, and ethical maturity. We also need to know more about applications in extramural settings. It is possible, although our survey yielded no creditable evidence, that some instructional methods are consistently more effective for some children; this is an area of needed research.

In summary, a large and growing body of research evidence that was unavailable a decade ago constitutes one useful basis not only of future research but of educational policy and decision making. Together with the values and wisdom of school board members, educators, parents, and students, continued scientific inquiry should contribute much to educational productivity in the future.

HERBERT J. WALBERG (University of Chicago—DePaul University Chapter) is research professor of urban education, University of Illinois at Chicago Circle. DIANE SCHILLER is research assistant and GENEVA D. HAERTEL is research associate in the Office of Evaluation Research at the same institution. The authors thank Maurice J. Eash and Harriet Talmage for collegial support in this research, which was funded by the National Institute of Education (HEW-NIE G-78-0090) and the National Science Foundation (NSF-78-17374). The points of view and opinions stated do not necessarily represent the official position or policy of either agency.

A three-page appendix listing the reviews that are the basis of this report may be obtained by writing Walberg at the College of Education, University of Illinois at Chicago Circle, Box 4348, Chicago, IL 60680, or by writing Diane Kliewer, Editorial Secretary, Phi Delta Kappan, Box 789, Bloomington, IN 47402.

1. John M. Stephens, *The Process of Schooling: A Psychological Examination* (New York: Holt, Rinehart and Winston, 1967).

2. Gene V Glass, "The Wisdom of Scientific Inquiry," *Journal of Research in Science Teaching*, vol. 9, no. 1, 1972, pp. 3-18.

3. Charles E. Silberman, *Crisis in the Classroom* (New York: Random House, 1970).

4. Stephens, op. cit.

5. Christopher Jencks et al., *Inequality: A Reassessment of the Effect of Family and Schooling in America* (New York: Basic Books, 1972).

6. James S. Coleman et al., *Equality of Educational Opportunity* (Washington, D.C.: U.S. Office of Education, 1966).

7. Neville Bennett, *Teaching Styles and Pupil Progress* (Cambridge, Mass.: Harvard University Press, 1976).

8. With obvious justification, many reviews tabulate not the overall results of each study but the results specific to several conditions, outcomes, and subgroups such as boys and girls in the same classes. Although such tabulations are valuable in ascertaining differential effects of conditions on outcomes and subgroups, they cannot be considered independent sources of evidence since, for example, what improves reading vocabulary may also improve comprehension and benefit both boys and girls. So as not to exclude such valuable reviews from our survey, they are summarized in their original detail. Because their results are not independent, they should be interpreted cautiously. In most cases, however, nonindependence is beside the point, because of the uniformity and extensiveness of the findings. University groups at Colorado, Harvard, Illinois at Chicago, Michigan, Stanford, Wisconsin, and Yale are analyzing not only the consistency of the results as reported here but their magnitude and combined probabilities. Such intensive analyses, we believe, will be even more impressive than our initial assessments of consistency.

9. Dean Jamison, Patrick Suppes, and Stuart Wells, "The Effectiveness of Alternative Media: A Survey," *Review of Educational Research*, vol. 44, no. 1, 1974, pp. 1-68.

10. N. L. Gage, *The Scientific Basis of the Art of Teaching* (New York: Teachers College Press, 1978).

11. Herbert J. Walberg and Susan C. Thomas, "Open Education: An Operational Definition and Validation in Great Britain and the United States," *American Educational Research Journal*, vol. 9, no. 3, 1972, pp. 197-202.

12. Bennett, op. cit.

13. Herbert J. Walberg, "The Psychology of Learning Environments," in Lee S. Shulman, ed., *Review of Research in Education*, vol. 4 (Itasca, Ill.: F. E. Peacock, 1976), pp. 142-78.

14. Mary B. Smith, "School and Home," in A. Harry Passow, ed., *Developing Programs for the Educationally Disadvantaged* (New York: Teachers College Press, 1968); Herbert J. Walberg, Robert E. Bole, and Herschel Waxman, *School-Based Family Socialization and Reading Achievement in the Inner City* (Chicago: University of Illinois at Chicago Circle, Office of Evaluation Research, 1976). ☐

SUMMARY

We have compared the advantages in minimizing error of the scientific method with other sources of knowledge. These include personal experience, authority, tradition, expert opinion, and church-state-ancient scholars. The goals of science to understand, predict, and control phenomena introduced the seven steps of the scientific method. We then examined the relationship of the steps in the scientific method to the main components of the research article. Several basic terms were introduced, followed by a statement of the importance of research to our educational system.

OBJECTIVES

Confirm your understanding of the material in Chapter 1 using the following objectives:

Compare the advantages of the scientific method with other sources of knowledge.

Describe the steps of the scientific method and their relationship to the sections of a research-based journal article.

Name and explain the purpose of each section of the journal article.

Define the basic terms used in educational research.

Discuss the importance of educational research over the last decade.

TERMS

action research
applied research
assessment
basic research
concept
construct
curriculum or program
  evaluation
data
descriptive statistics
error
experimental type of
  operational definition

inferential statistics
measurement type of
  operational definition
operationalize
parameter
population
sample
sampling bias
scientific method
variable

PART

Analyzing the Introduction Section of the Research Article

As Chapter 1 indicates, the research article begins with the Introduction. The Introduction is an attempt to answer three main questions:

1. What is the main focus of the present research process?
2. What is the prediction about the outcome of the research process?
3. What is the rationale for analyzing the problem and predicting the outcome?

The statement of purpose, one or more hypotheses, and the literature review are integrated into a coherent and logical framework that provides the foundation for the subsequent implementation component—the Method section of the research article. In Chapter 2 we will discuss the statement of purpose for conducting research, in which you attempt to answer the first question: What is the main focus of the present research process? In Chapter 3 we shall look at ways to formulate the hypotheses for the research process. Hypotheses attempt to answer the second question: What is the prediction about the outcome of the research process? Last, Chapter 4 contains information relating to the review of literature and how it is interwoven with the purpose and hypotheses to provide a rationale. The rationale in turn becomes the Introduction section of the research-based journal article.

Stating the Purpose

What is the main function of the statement of purpose?

What are the four criteria for developing and evaluating purpose statements?

How does each criterion facilitate understanding and communication within the journal article?

How can the variables and the population in the research be specified to enhance the reader's understanding of the journal article?

What are the main pitfalls in writing and evaluating the purpose statement and how can they be avoided?

What are the types of purpose statements found within educational research and what are the implications inherent in the use of each?

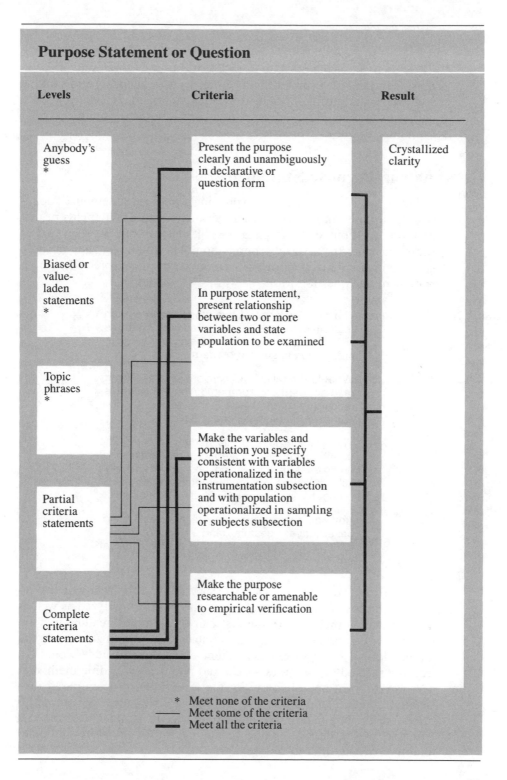

Purpose Statement or Question

Levels	Criteria	Result
Anybody's guess *	Present the purpose clearly and unambiguously in declarative or question form	Crystallized clarity
Biased or value-laden statements *	In purpose statement, present relationship between two or more variables and state population to be examined	
Topic phrases *		
Partial criteria statements	Make the variables and population you specify consistent with variables operationalized in the instrumentation subsection and with population operationalized in sampling or subjects subsection	
Complete criteria statements	Make the purpose researchable or amenable to empirical verification	

*   Meet none of the criteria
—— Meet some of the criteria
▬▬ Meet all the criteria

The statement of the purpose or problem is usually the result of an intensive inquiry into some general problem. It frequently means taking some thoughts, intuitions, or hazy ideas based upon personal experience and transforming those ideas into explicit, manifest statements that crystallize the inquiry process.

Creating the Purpose Statement

There are two main ways of expressing a purpose statement. The research purpose can be written as either one or more statements or one or more questions that express a possible relationship between two or more variables for a specific population. The following four purpose statements are derived from prior research and are expressed in both statement and question form:

> The main purpose of this study is to compare the effectiveness of two reading methods, sight and phonics, in increasing verbal comprehension in second graders.

> What is the relative effectiveness of the sight-reading method compared to the phonics-reading method in increasing verbal comprehension in second graders?

> The main purpose of this study is to determine if differences exist among three counseling techniques in decreasing test anxiety in high school juniors. Rational-emotive, gestalt, and no-counseling are the techniques examined.

> How do three counseling techniques—rational-emotive, gestalt, and no-counseling—differ in their effectiveness in decreasing test anxiety in high school juniors?

These four purpose statements clearly convey the focus of the research process. We are aware of the variables to be analyzed as well as the population included. In the first pair of examples, reading method and verbal comprehension are the variables, and second graders are the population. A more specific statement of the first variable would be: reading method of two *types*—sight and phonics; or reading method at two *levels*—sight and phonics. For the second pair of examples, counseling techniques and test anxiety are the variables, and high school juniors are the population. Again, a more specific statement of the first variable would be: counseling techniques at three *levels*—rational-emotive, gestalt, and no-counseling.

Based on just these examples, you can begin to see what the statement of purpose attempts to convey in the Introduction of the research article. It is the crystallization of an investigator's search into a particular territory of knowledge. Frequently, we start with many perplexing, confusing, and unanswered questions. But a clear statement of purpose will facilitate the subsequent research process.

Differences or Relationships

In addition to expressing a purpose statement as either a statement or a question, the researcher can specify that he or she will either test *differences* among variables or test the *relationship* among variables. For instance, the four previous examples of purpose statements would be testing *differences* among variables. Following are two examples of purpose statements that specify a *relationship* among variables:

> This study relates three measures of intelligence, two measures of creativity, and three learning styles in gifted and talented elementary students.

> What is the relationship among leadership skills, intelligence, and achievement motivation of high school seniors?

A main difference in these two types of purpose statements is in the use of two key words: *differ* or *differences* and *related* or *relationship*. These words have important implications for the type of research design and for subsequent statistical analyses. Using the words *relate* or *relationship* implies a type of study known as a *correlational* research study. We will elaborate on this type of research in a subsequent chapter. For now, you should realize that even a variation in one or two key words within a purpose statement can change the meaning communicated to the reader.

Thus, care and precision in selecting the right words to formulate the purpose statement are necessary because they affect the meaning conveyed as well as communicate to readers an indication of the quality of the research process. If the statement of purpose has not been clearly articulated it may be ambiguous, inconsistent, implied, biased, or irrelevant to the rest of the research process. Consider the following purpose statements:

> Creativity in selected children will be studied.

> Psychologists should examine the construct of consciousness.

> The effect of incentives in our school will be analyzed.
>
> Should the schools return to basics?

If the statement of purpose is clearly expressed, it will facilitate the research process. If it is not, as seen in the previous four statements, it will usually lead away from the problem for which answers are to be sought. It will also leave the reader confused, befuddled, and frustrated —unclear as to the goal or focus of the current research process.

Consider three ways in which the first purpose statement on creativity could be clarified:

> The purpose of this study is to compare differences between high and low achievers in the ninth grade on measures of originality and divergent thinking.
>
> The purpose of this study is to compare differences between high and low anxiety for second graders on a measure of elaboration.
>
> The purpose of this study is to determine the relative effectiveness of creativity training compared to no training in increasing flexibility of thought in college freshmen.

All these revised purpose statements are now sufficiently clear to enable us to understand the purpose. In the first statement about creativity, the variables and population are not clearly stated. The sentence is too vague and general. Thus we probably would experience difficulty operationalizing the subsequent research process. The three reworded purpose statements are only examples of many that could have been derived from the first general statement.

Developing and Evaluating Purpose Statements

The four criteria used for developing or evaluating a statement of purpose all relate to clarity. They include both editorial and substantive criteria. We will examine each separately and then integrate and interrelate them with a variety of purpose statements.

1. The purpose should be presented clearly and unambiguously in declarative or question form.
2. The purpose should present the relationship between two or more variables and state the population to be examined.

3. The variables and population specified in the purpose should be consistent with the variables operationalized in the Instrumentation subsection and with the population operationalized in the Sampling or Subjects subsection.

4. The purpose should be researchable or amenable to empirical verification.

Other educational researchers such as Kerlinger (1973, pp. 16–18) list three criteria that generally relate to criteria 1, 2, and 4. However, there

Components of the Purpose Statement

are some differences among these criteria. In the first criterion, Kerlinger recommends that a problem be stated always as a question. However, well-stated purposes or problems are commonly expressed either way in the research literature. Also, many beginning researchers confuse purpose statements or problem questions with hypotheses. Purpose statements and hypotheses are distinct and separate components of the research process; both should be clearly stated to increase the understanding of the novice researcher and reader. Comparing the second criterion with Kerlinger's, we see that he omits a statement that the population should be specified. The fourth criterion is comparable to Kerlinger's. If the four criteria above are applied in evaluating or writing a purpose statement, maximum clarity is achieved and the research article will flow in an integrated fashion from one component to the next. We shall elaborate on each of these criteria in the next four sections.

Using Declarative or Interrogative Statements

The first criterion for developing and evaluating the statement of purpose requires us to state it with maximum clarity and without ambiguity or inconsistency. As we have mentioned, this criterion serves as an overall organizer for integrating the others. Let us briefly expand this idea of clarity in the purpose statement to further our understanding.

One obvious implication of the preceding paragraph is that the experimenter should state the problem fully and precisely. The statement of purpose will have to be a grammatical sentence; topic phrases and clichés do not meet the criterion of clarity. Consider these purpose statements:

> Cognitive reasoning in students.

> Counseling will improve self-concept.

> The 3 R's are best for our children.

These purpose statements lack clarity and are ambiguous. The first is not a complete sentence; the other two exhibit bias in their wording. In the second example, "will improve" is a biased phrase implying that counseling will have a positive effect upon self-concept. In addition to the biased wording of the third statement ("best"), it is also a cliché.

Compare each of these three purpose statements with the following, reworded to increase clarity:

> How do male and female ninth graders differ
> on a measure of abstract reasoning?

> The main purpose of this study is to determine the effectiveness of group counseling compared to no counseling in increasing the level of self-esteem of first-grade children.

> What is the relative effectiveness of a traditional drill approach compared to a modern mathematics approach in increasing the retention of basic mathematics concepts in elementary school children?

In order to achieve a clear and explicit purpose statement, we must be able to see the general problem with utmost clarity. Many researchers argue that the one who investigates a research process should know, better than anyone else, what the main problem is. One reason we have difficulty stating it clearly is that we frequently do not spend the necessary time and effort in formulating the problem. Eager to plunge into the project, we neglect to specify clearly what we intend to investigate.

Specifying Variables and Population

The three criteria yet to be discussed for developing and evaluating a purpose statement will further elaborate on this criterion of clarity. The second criterion states that the purpose should present the relationship between two or more variables and state the populaton to be examined.

Basic considerations.   All the variables to be examined in our research process should be clearly specified in the purpose statement of the Introduction. The population should also be clearly specified. What do we mean when we say clearly specified? What level of clarity should the statement of purpose attain? On the one hand, a purpose statement should not be too general or incomplete so that it lacks meaning. For example:

> Reading and its effect on certain children.

On the other hand, it should not be so specific that the subsequent Instrumentation and Subjects subsections are a restatement of the purpose. For example:

> Standard score differences between 50 male and 50 female suburban middle-class fifth graders on the Iowa Test of Basic Skills (ITBS) Reading Comprehension subtest will be examined.

A good purpose statement will fall somewhere between these two extremes—not too general, yet not so specific that it becomes redundant. It will be presented at a general conceptual level. For example:

> The main purpose of this study is to determine differences between male and female fifth graders on a measure of reading comprehension.

This statement is clear and unambiguous; it specifies the variables, sex, and reading comprehension, and gives the population as being fifth graders.

The task of stating the variables and population with the proper specificity is not easy. Table 2.1 presents several variables and populations frequently encountered in educational research. Consider the different specification of variables for a given purpose statement.

Notice that many interpretations of the variable "intelligence" are possible. In a purpose statement, the term alone is frequently too general. On the other hand, "Wechsler Adult Intelligence Scale (WAIS) verbal IQ score" is too specific. Since the Instrumentation subsection will present an operational definition of the variable specified in the purpose, it is not necessary to include it in the statement of purpose. We need to settle on a point between the two extremes to avoid ambiguity and redundancy. Thus we arrive at the general conceptual level statement of the variable as "verbal intelligence."

The same framework for comparison applies to stating the population. For instance, giving the population as "counselors" is too general and subject to multiple interpretation. On the other hand, "first-year graduate level counseling majors" is too specific and duplicates the function of the Subjects subsection. It also lengthens the purpose statement unnecessarily and reduces clarity. Thus we state the general concept level population as "counseling majors," which falls between the two extremes.

A useful strategy for stating variables at the general conceptual level is found in the form or syntax of the variable. A variable stated as an unmodified noun is probably too general. A variable stated as a noun with multiple adjectives is probably too specific. However, a variable stated as a noun with one or two modifying adjectives is likely to fall within the general conceptual level category of maximum clarity with minimum ambiguity and redundancy.

Consider the two examples of the population specified as "children" in Table 2.1. Depending on how we choose to develop a research process, either of the general conceptual level statements given should be appropriate.

Table 2.1 Presentation of Variables at Different Levels of Specificity for the Statement of the Purpose

General conceptual level	Too general	Too specific
Verbal intelligence	Intelligence	WAIS verbal IQ score
Combinatorial logic	Reasoning ability	Performance on a colorless chemicals task
Reading comprehension	Reading level	ITBS reading comprehension subtest score
Originality	Creativity	Performance on Torrance Test of Creative Thinking scored for originality
Conservation of number	Conservation	Conservation of number at three levels: conserver, transitional, and nonconserver
Test anxiety	Anxiety	Self-report inventory of anxious situations while taking a test
Elementary school children	Children	Students in the first, third, and fifth grade at Bates Elementary School
Fifth graders	Children	Fifth-grade students at Roosevelt Elementary School
Counseling majors	Counselors	First-year graduate level counseling students

Complex research problems. If our research process is particularly complex and if many variables and their relationships are to be examined, the purpose statement may include several sentences in order to express these relationships. If such an extension is necessary, usually the main variables to be analyzed are given in the first sentence(s) and additional variables and groups are given in subsequent sentences. The statement then appears as a priority statement of variables based on their perceived importance to the research process.

Obviously, the fewer the variables and groups studied, the more simply the purpose can be stated. As we study more variables and groups, the statement of purpose becomes more elaborate and complex. The simplest research purpose has only one variable. Usually, we are interested in the performance of some population or group on that measure.

Questions that deal with comparisons or relative effectiveness are not usually of concern. Consider the following two purpose statements that reflect this one variable assessment:

> The main purpose of this study is to determine the level of reading comprehension in tenth graders who receive remedial reading instruction.

> What level of nonverbal acuity is obtained by first-year graduate counseling majors?

In the first statement, the variable is reading comprehension, and the population is tenth graders who receive remedial instruction. In the second, the variable is nonverbal acuity, and the population is first-year graduate counseling majors.

The statement of purpose can easily become more complex as two or three variables are introduced into the research process:

> What is the relative effectiveness of remedial reading instruction compared to traditional instruction in increasing reading comprehension in tenth graders?

> The main purpose of this study is to determine differences between counseling and engineering majors on a measure of nonverbal acuity.

For the first purpose statement, the two variables are reading comprehension and type of instruction—remedial and traditional; the population is tenth graders. For the second, the variables are nonverbal acuity and type of major—counseling and engineering; the population is graduate students. As we examine a problem, additional implications and unknowns usually arise that result in more variables to be examined. These, in turn, require a more complex statement of purpose. Consider these purpose statements expressing the relationship among three variables:

> The main purpose of this study is to determine differences among seventh-grade high, average, and low achievers on measures of verbal and performance intelligence.

> How do high- and low-anxiety groups of male and female college freshmen differ on a measure of academic achievement?

The three variables for the first purpose statement are: level of achievement, high, average, and low; verbal intelligence; and performance intelligence. The three variables for the second purpose are: anxiety level, high and low; sex; and academic achievement.

As mentioned before, complex purpose statements may require several sentences in which the primary focus is first delineated and the secondary focus follows. Consider the rewording of the second of the two preceding purpose statements:

> How do high- and low-anxiety groups of college freshmen differ on a measure of academic achievement? What sex differences exist?

Purpose statements become most complex when four or more variables are included. In such cases we may need a paragraph in order to express succinctly and clearly the statement of purpose. Consider these two examples:

> The present research investigates the effects of three test conditions—playlike, verbal-feedback, and nonverbal-feedback—on three measures of preschool children's creative abilities. The three measures of creativity are fluency, flexibility, and originality. Sex and ethnic-group differences are also examined.

> The main purpose of this research is to evaluate differences in language comprehension at two elementary grade levels with three ethnic groups. An additional purpose is to evaluate differences in vocabulary, word usage, and reading speed among the children. Socioeconomic status and sex differences are also assessed.

The variables for the first purpose are: type of test condition at three levels—playlike, verbal-feedback, and nonverbal-feedback; ethnic group at two levels—black and white; sex—male and female; fluency; flexibility; and originality. The population is preschoolers. The variables for the second purpose are: grade at two levels—first and third; ethnic group at three levels—black, Chicano, and white; socioeconomic status at two levels—lower and middle; sex—female and male; language comprehension; vocabulary; word usage; and reading speed. The population is elementary school children. Obviously, the greater the complexity of the research process, the greater the clarity required in stating the relationships among variables. If this clarity is cultivated, we are less likely to lose our way in the research process.

Ensuring Consistency Throughout Sections

The third criterion for developing and evaluating a purpose statement recommends that the variables and population specified in the purpose should be consistent with the variables operationalized in the Instrumentation subsection and with the population operationalized in the Sampling or Subjects subsection. This criterion is a further refinement and specification of the second one. All the variables examined in the research process should be given in the purpose statement of the Introduction. When the variables are operationalized in the Instrumentation subsection, the variables specified in both subsections should correspond exactly.

It is important to have a correspondence among variables. If there is a consistency among variables stated at a general conceptual level and variables that have been operationalized, the research article will flow more clearly from one component to the next. It will be more coherent and integrated. We will be able to follow the development of the research process from formulation to implementation to resolution of the problem. If there is no consistency among the sets of variables in each section, confusion will result. (For instance, the purpose may express two variables and the Instrumentation subsection three variables or variables that do not seem to relate to the earlier purpose statement.) This confusion generally causes us or those reading our research to ask such questions as: What are we attempting to study? How do we know if the original questions will be validly answered? Do we really know what we are trying to study?

As previously discussed, the research article is one manifestation of the research process. If the article lacks clarity and consistency, then the implementation of the research process usually does also. The consistency between the variables in the purpose and in the Instrumentation subsection is one instance of the need for clarity throughout all research components. As we continue to examine the research article, other interrelationships will be analyzed. Taken as a whole, the consistency of these relationships will usually reveal a clear picture of the quality of the research process we undertake.

The population specified in the purpose statement of the Introduction also should be consistent with the population operationalized in the Sampling or Subjects subsection. If there is no consistency between groups in the two sections (if, for instance, the purpose gives one population and the Subjects subsection a different or unrelated population), then confusion results over who is being studied. The relationship between the population stated in the purpose statement and in the Subjects subsection is another example of the need for clarity and consistency among research components.

Clarity and Consistency of the Purpose Statement

For instance, we might say in the purpose statement of our Introduction that we intend:

> To determine differences between seventh-grade high and low achievers on a measure of verbal comprehension.

Two variables, achievement at two levels—high and low—and verbal comprehension, are listed. The population is given as seventh graders.

In the Instrumentation subsection, however, in addition to the verbal comprehension measure that was operationalized by using a verbal comprehension subtest of a standardized achievement test, we find that a vocabulary, spelling, and language skills subtest was also administered to the seventh graders. Thus there is obviously a lack of consistency between the sets of variables stated in the purpose statement and those operationalized in the Instrumentation subsection. We could reword the purpose statement to include all the variables as follows:

> The main purpose of this study is to determine differences between seventh-grade high and low achievers on measures of language skills, reading comprehension, spelling, and vocabulary.

Consider another example to reinforce the need for consistency among research components. We may state in the Introduction that we shall attempt:

> To determine differences between counselors and noncounselors on a measure of self-disclosure.

The population to be assessed is counselors and noncounselors. But in the Subjects subsection of the research article, we may further elaborate the groups as "first-year graduate students in counseling and business administration." Clearly, the populations specified in the purpose statement and later operationalized in the Subjects subsection are not consistent and hence are misleading. One rewording of the purpose statement that would more accurately represent the population under study is:

> The main purpose of this study is to determine differences between counseling and business graduate students on a measure of self-disclosure.

In the preceding purpose statement a measure of self-disclosure is specified as one of the variables. Without a further knowledge of the variables operationalized in the Instrumentation subsection, several discrepant interpretations of this variable are possible. If the components of the research article are consistent with each other, then the first interpretation that follows would be most plausible. The most obvious interpretation would assume that one global measure of self-disclosure would be obtained. This interpretation would be most consistent given the wording of the purpose statement. A second interpretation might assume that self-disclosure would be the variable to be assessed but that several dimensions of the self-disclosing individual might be considered; for example, genuineness, empathy, and warmth. A third interpretation might assume that the statement of purpose did not include all the variables that were to be studied. For instance, a measure of verbal intelligence and ego strength are variables that may also have been examined. Thus accuracy and consistency are essential to the purpose statement and to the integrity of the research process and report.

Whatever we might intend in a study, consistency between the population and variables presented in the Introduction or purpose and later operationalized in the Subjects and Instrumentation subsections will reduce ambiguity and increase the clarity of the research process. Consider the change in the intended study as we alter the purpose statement to make it consistent with the different Instrumentation subsections.

> The main purpose of this study is to determine differences between counseling and business graduate students
>
> > on a global measure of self-disclosure.
> >
> > on three measures of self-disclosure—genuineness, empathy, and warmth.
> >
> > on measures of self-disclosure, ego strength, and verbal intelligence.

Frequently, our research is more complex than these examples in the sense of having more than one group and of examining many variables and their interrelationships. Regardless of the complexity of the research process, we must be consistent throughout all research sections. What will probably vary according to the complexity of the research is the *general conceptual level* at which the statement of purpose is to be presented. Usually the more complex the study, the more general the statement of purpose will be. This relationship will maintain the clarity of the statement of purpose and the consistency among research sections. The less complex the study, the more specific we can be in presenting the statement of purpose, as we explained with the preceding criterion.

Making Sure the Problem Is Researchable

Let us complete our examination of the criteria for evaluating a statement of purpose by considering the final criterion: The purpose should be researchable or amenable to empirical investigation.

A good statement of purpose presents a problem that is researchable. A researchable problem is one we can study by collecting and analyzing data. Problems which deal with philosophical or ethical issues, or which require value or judgmental statements, are not researchable questions that can be answered by scientific investigation. The research process could assess our attitudes about such issues, but research cannot resolve the specific problem. In the field of education, many issues have engendered a lot of debate but are not researchable problems—at least not as far as they have been currently presented. For instance:

Should the schools return to the basics?
Should the Lord's Prayer be allowed in the schools?
Minimum competency tests should be required.
Creationism should be taught with other theories of evolution.
Secular humanism should be taken out of the schools.

The statement of purpose should be phrased in a way that ensures that research into the question is possible; that is, it ensures that we can apply the steps of the scientific method. Consider the restatement and elaboration of the first issue, returning to the basics, into a statement of purpose that meets the four criteria:

> What is the relative effectiveness of the traditional drill approach compared to a modern mathematics approach in increasing the retention of basic mathematical concepts in elementary school children?

Here the variables are presented at a general conceptual level: retention of basic mathematical concepts, and type of instruction at two levels—traditional and modern. The population—elementary school children—also is stated. Value-laden words like "the basics" are eliminated. We could easily spend an entire professional lifetime attempting to determine whether "schools should return to the basics" and in doing so obtain relatively little reliable or valid information. But through a series of multiple studies, each with a carefully refined and specified purpose that results in a researchable problem, we can obtain reliable and valid results. These results may raise even more questions, but they should provide a few conditional answers to the original problem. A few philosophical or ethical issues may be amenable to scientific investigation, but most will not. We should be aware that if a purpose statement is biased or philosophical, then we will find it difficult to implement the research process.

In addition to stating the problem in a way that ensures that research is possible, we should be examining a problem that really is a problem. We should avoid the trivial and focus on problems that have theoretical or practical significance. If the reader's reaction to our statement of purpose is "So what?" or "Who cares?" then we have not made explicit the significance of the proposed research. Also, if after completing our statement of purpose we find that the problem can be answered by a

Significance of the Problem

simple yes or no, we know that it has not been suitably refined and specified. Deeper questions often surface when the statement of purpose moves from a simple yes-or-no distinction to one that requires answers to such questions as: "Why does this phenomenon occur?" or: "What is the significance of the relationship between these variables?"

In summarizing the basic criteria to be used when evaluating the statement of the problem, we have emphasized clarity. The statement of purpose presents in a clearly specified format the variables and their relationship to each other as well as to the population to be examined. The purpose statement also must be consistent with the variables and population later operationalized in the Instrumentation and Subjects subsections of the research article. Finally, the statement of purpose should be a researchable one rather than one which entails a philosophical or ethical issue, or which implies value or judgmental questions.

Levels of Purpose Statements

In developing our research following the scientific method, the first two steps require that we: (1) recognize a problem, and (2) define it in clear, specific language. In the preceding discussion on criteria for developing and evaluating purpose statements we have tried to facilitate these two steps by sharing concrete ideas on how they can be implemented. Now we shall explore the different levels of purpose statements found within educational research so that we can generate a new model to assist us further in evaluating our own purpose statements as well as others we encounter in the research literature. Keep in mind that we shall consider various criteria for evaluating or writing purpose statements that arise after the research process is completed.

Five main levels of purpose statements are suggested:

anybody's guess
biased or value-laden statements
topic phrases
partial statements of criteria
complete statements of criteria

In analyzing our own research writing as well as that of others, our first task is to identify the statement of purpose in the Introduction. Frequently, we will find purpose statements restated in a Discussion section or as the first or second sentence in the Abstract. Sometimes we have a tendency to write these statements more clearly because they are usually written later. Since we usually write the Introduction section first, we must remember to revise it so that it is consistent with the later sections.

Anybody's Guess

Something we might label *anybody's guess* is a sentence in the Introduction that is the closest to a purpose statement we can find. The purpose is not explicitly stated but rather implied from the tone and flow of the Introduction. It is the closest sentence approximating the implied focus of the research. Consider these examples of *anybody's guess:*

> One of the purposes of research in programmed instruction is to determine the effectiveness of individualized instruction.

> Can professors over thirty be trusted?

> Should foreign languages be taught to children in the primary grades?

These statements were the best presentation of the problem being investigated. Because they fail to present a crystallized purpose, the Introduction and subsequent sections also will lack clarity. To attempt to improve or make sense of such research, or to make practical decisions based on the research, is difficult. The haziness and cloudiness of the research process seems insurmountable.

Biased or Value-Laden Statements

Biased or value-laden statements are frequently given as the main focus of a research endeavor. One implication is that if we present a biased or judgmental statement in analyzing the problem we may have influenced the steps of the research process by that bias. We may represent our bias either very obviously or very subtly. Consider these obvious examples of biased or value-laden statements:

> The core curriculum is an enriching experience.
>
> Democratic education enhances social learning and citizenship.
>
> Authoritarian teaching methods should not be allowed in the public schools.

Each of these statements expresses an obvious bias of the researcher as well as unclear specification of the variables and population. Someone reading such statements could probably predict the results without reading beyond the Introduction. Surprisingly, we learn that the core curriculum, never operationalized, was far superior to other curricula! Democratic education did indeed enhance social learning and citizenship; and the authoritarian teaching method was inferior to other methods!

As mentioned in Chapter 1, a main goal of the scientific method is to reduce or minimize error in the inquiry. We need to minimize the influence of any experimenter bias we may have because it will affect the entire research process—both how the research is implemented and how the results are interpreted.

The previous examples were fairly obvious in their experimenter bias. Frequently, we express value judgments even more subtly in our purpose statements by the verbs we choose. Consider the differences between these verbs:

to show	to determine
to prove	to compare
to demonstrate	to investigate
to confirm	to differentiate

Verb phrases in column one reflect subtle bias and those in column two are more neutral. Purpose statements should be neutral expressions of the research focus. If we have a professional prediction—but not a bias—which can be supported by theory, research, or personal experience, then it should be presented as a hypothesis. Hypotheses are the only appropriate media for professional predictions.

Topic Phrases

In addition to purpose statements in research being anybody's guess or biased statements, we may write or read purpose statements that are only topic phrases. Topic phrases usually are the result of insufficient planning and inquiry into a problem area. It could easily be a heading or item in an outline rather than the statement of purpose which clearly conveys the focus of the research. Consider these topic phrases:

Creativity in the schools
Learning disabilities instruction for children
Dyslexia and remediation

We do not have a clear understanding of the research focus based on these topics. Understanding the research purpose would be delayed until we delineated or analyzed how the variables and population were operationalized. Only then could we return to the topic and accurately rephrase it into a statement of purpose meeting our four criteria. The presence of topics in our research usually implies incomplete and unorganized planning for the research. In addition, it is usually the foreshadowing of additional difficulties that will appear in the Method and Results sections. In a sense we can begin to apply our four criteria to topic phrases. Usually the topic phrase does not meet any of our four criteria for developing or evaluating statements of purpose.

Partial or Complete Statements of Criteria

The last two types of purpose statements will usually meet some or all of our criteria. Consider this example:

This study will investigate the use of incentives in schools.

In applying our four criteria, we observe that the purpose is unclear and not specific; the variable is generally stated; the population is omitted; the variables will not be consistent with the operationalized variables and population; and the purpose is not researchable as presented. Consider the following rewording:

What are the effects on pupil performance of different types of incentives?

Again, applying our criteria, it is still too general; variables, performance, and types of incentives need to be specified at that general conceptual level. The population of pupils also needs to be further specified. We still do not know if it will be consistent with operationalized terms, but it appears researchable as presented. Consider another rewording:

> This research investigates the relative effectiveness of two types of incentives, token and praise, on math achievement in high school sophomores. Sex differences are also analyzed.

This statement of purpose is clearly specified. The variables are presented at a general conceptual level: type of incentive at two levels—token and praise; mathematical reasoning; and sex. High school sophomores also are a clear specification of the population. Finally, the variables and populations are specified in such a way that we can determine if they are consistent with the variables and population operationalized in the Instrumentation and Subjects subsections.

SUMMARY

We have discussed the importance of a clear statement of purpose to the overall research process. Then we examined four criteria used in developing a purpose statement including numerous examples which varied in complexity. Finally, we have presented the five different levels of purpose statements encountered in educational research together with suggestions for writing our own purpose statements.

OBJECTIVES

In Chapter 2 we have considered the first component of the research article, the *statement of purpose*. Confirm your understanding of the material in Chapter 2 using the following objectives:

Identify the purpose statement in any journal article in your field.
Evaluate the purpose statement using the four criteria.
Write or rewrite any purpose statement so that it reflects an acceptable degree of clarity and specificity.

TERMS

purpose statements
research problem

Formulating Hypotheses

What are hypotheses and what is their purpose in the research process?

What are the three main types of hypotheses, and how are they represented symbolically?

What are the forms of hypotheses, and how are they used in the research article?

What is the notion of indirect proof, and how does it affect the planning of the research project?

What are the four criteria for developing and evaluating hypotheses?

What are the levels of hypotheses found within educational research, and what are the implications inherent in the use of each?

Hypotheses

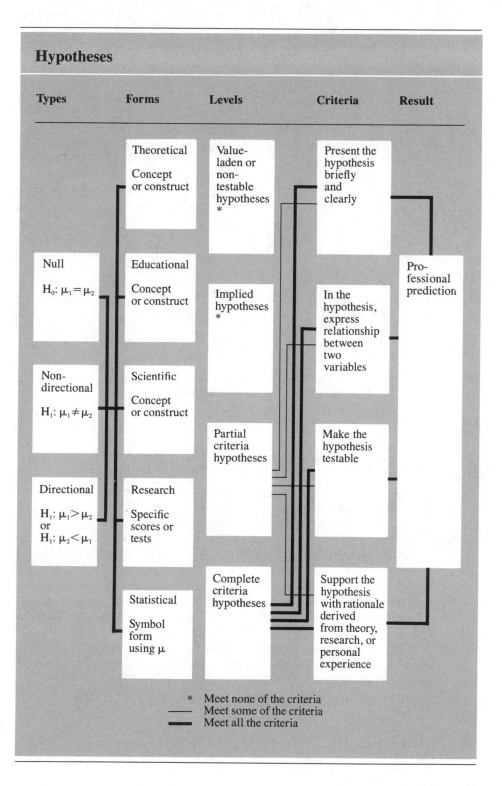

Types	Forms	Levels	Criteria	Result
	Theoretical Concept or construct	Value-laden or non-testable hypotheses *	Present the hypothesis briefly and clearly	
Null $H_0: \mu_1 = \mu_2$	Educational Concept or construct	Implied hypotheses *	In the hypothesis, express relationship between two variables	Pro-fessional prediction
Non-directional $H_1: \mu_1 \neq \mu_2$	Scientific Concept or construct	Partial criteria hypotheses	Make the hypothesis testable	
Directional $H_1: \mu_1 > \mu_2$ or $H_1: \mu_2 < \mu_1$	Research Specific scores or tests			
	Statistical Symbol form using μ	Complete criteria hypotheses	Support the hypothesis with rationale derived from theory, research, or personal experience	

*   Meet none of the criteria
——   Meet some of the criteria
━━   Meet all the criteria

The hypothesis is a researcher's tentative explanation or professional opinion predicting the main results of the research process. Supported by theory, research, or personal experience, it states the predicted results from the variables presented in the purpose statement. Unlike the statement of purpose, where all variables and their interrelationships are clearly presented as one statement, the hypothesis usually presents a predicted outcome between two measures. Since a number of measures may be involved, it is not unusual to include multiple hypotheses, each predicting an expected outcome. If there is no support for a proposed prediction, the statement of a hypothesis is frequently omitted. This chapter will consider the variety of hypotheses available to the researcher as well as the criteria for developing and evaluating them.

Types of Hypotheses

Writing Hypotheses

Consider these three hypotheses:

> No significant differences will be obtained between the sight reading method and the phonics reading method in increasing verbal comprehension scores.

> Significant differences will be found between the sight and phonics reading methods in increasing verbal comprehension scores.

> The sight reading method will obtain significant increases in verbal comprehension scores as compared to the phonics reading method.

These examples represent the three main types of hypotheses: the *null* hypothesis, the *alternative nondirectional* hypothesis, and the *alternative directional* hypothesis. The null hypothesis simply states that no real relationship exists among the variables. Unless statistically significant, differences in the perceived relationship will be attributed to chance or error.

The remaining two examples represent the two kinds of alternative hypothesis. Generally, any alternative hypothesis indicates a difference between the variables. The difference lies in the two kinds of alternative hypotheses—nondirectional and directional. In the second example, an alternative nondirectional hypothesis states that there is a real difference among the variables or groups, but the researcher is unsure of how the groups or variables differ. Which group will score better, poorer, higher, or lower than the other is not clear, based on theory, research, or personal experience. For instance, if there are conflicting or vague results in a problem area, the researcher may not have a strong rationale to predict a specific direction of outcome, and so a nondirectional hypothesis is stated. Thus, though we may be able to give a rationale for differences occurring, there is a stronger rationale for predicting that there is no direction of outcome. The nondirectional hypothesis is a conservative approach, while the directional hypothesis predicts a specific direction of outcome.

The third example, the alternative directional hypothesis, does state a specific relationship between the variables or groups; for example, increase, decrease, higher, lower, more or less adjusted, and so forth. A directional hypothesis includes one of two general outcomes, either greater than or less than, but the outcomes may be expressed by a variety of descriptors. Rewording the last example by replacing *increase* with *decrease* will not change the meaning as long as the expected relationship between the variables is maintained:

> Significant decreases in verbal comprehension scores will result from the phonics reading method as compared to the sight reading method.

Types of Hypotheses

With all three types, there is usually no statement of the population in the hypotheses because it has already been given in the purpose statement. Its inclusion would also diminish the clarity desired in stating the hypothetical relationships.

Educational researchers frequently use the following symbols to represent each kind of hypothesis:

1. H_0: $\mu_1 = \mu_2$ Null
2. H_1: $\mu_1 \neq \mu_2$ Nondirectional
3. H_1: $\mu_1 > \mu_2$
       or $\Big\}$ Directional
      H_1: $\mu_2 < \mu_1$

For this hypothesis, example 1 says that method 1 (sight) is equal to method 2 (phonics), a null hypothesis. Example 2 says that method 1 is *not* equal to method 2, an alternative nondirectional hypothesis. Example 3 says that method 1 is greater than method 2, an alternative directional hypothesis. Instead of using a capital letter to represent one method, variable, or approach, a general symbol is substituted to standardize the comparisons. The symbol used is the Greek letter mu (μ). It is always a representation for the *population* mean or average:

$$H_0: \mu_1 = \mu_2$$

Thus this null hypothesis states that the population mean of one group is equal to the population mean of the second group.

Forms of Hypotheses

Once we determine the type of hypothesis suitable for our research, we can determine the form of hypothesis to use. There are five main forms:

theoretical
educational
scientific
research
statistical

The first three forms usually refer to a hypothesis stated at a concept or construct level, similar to the first three hypotheses discussed above. For example:

> No significant differences are to be found between the sight reading method and the phonics reading method in increasing verbal comprehension scores.

The fourth form, a research hypothesis, is usually stated in terms of the specific scores and tests to be used; that is, the research hypothesis specifies the outcome using the operational definition of the conceptual level variable. You may want to reread the discussion of concepts and operational definitions in the basic terms section of Chapter 1.

> Statistically significant standard score increases will be obtained on the reading comprehension subtest of the Iowa Test of Basic Skills (ITBS) with the sight method compared to the phonics reading method.

The last form, a statistical hypothesis, is stated in symbol form using the Greek μ already indicated:

1. $H_0: \mu_1 = \mu_2$
2. $H_1: \mu_1 \neq \mu_2$
3. $H_1: \mu_1 > \mu_2$

We frequently encounter all five forms in educational research. However, in the Introduction section we usually find one of the first three forms stated at a conceptual level. Some researchers also prefer to state a research hypothesis in the Introduction or operationalize the variables in the Introduction. Both approaches tend to duplicate the function of the Instrumentation section. Thus, one recommendation is to place any research hypothesis, as well as operational definitions of the variables, in the Instrumentation subsection in order to avoid redundancy and to increase the flow and integration of various sections. Further conceptual level descriptions of the variables, if needed to increase the clarity of the Introduction section, should be appropriately stated there. The statistical hypothesis, when used, is stated in the Results section to provide a framework for the subsequent statistical analysis.

Notion of Indirect Proof

A concept that integrates the type of hypothesis with the results of the research process is the *notion of indirect proof.* The notion of indirect proof is an additional concept in the research process that integrates the various sections of the research article.

In developing a hypothesis for scientific investigation, we initially assume a null hypothesis that indicates no difference between our groups. As inquiry into the problem area proceeds, the researcher may find support for using either a nondirectional or directional hypothesis. Then, based on the results obtained from the research process, an investigator may support or not support the nondirectional or directional hypothesis presented earlier. In order to support or not support one of the alternative hypotheses, the researcher must proceed indirectly. It is indirect because the researcher must first reject the null hypothesis which assumed that no real differences existed between the groups. Then the alternative hypothesis that differences do exist can be supported indirectly.

We can never prove either a null or an alternative hypothesis. Since we usually sample only a subset of a population, other samplings may produce different or conflicting results; so, for a particular research investigation, *proof* does not exist for the hypotheses. Instead, we can *support* our alternative hypothesis by first rejecting the null of no differences. The distinction between proof and support is analogous to that between certainty and usefulness. We can never prove anything with certainty based on the findings of a single research study. As mentioned in Chapter 1, this is because of the nature of scientific investigation, which attempts to minimize error but which can never eliminate it entirely. One type of error discussed was *sampling bias;* if we do not accurately represent the characteristics of a population in our sample, we will err in generalizing our results back to the population as a whole. Because of this possibility of error, we can prove nothing with absolute certainty.

Although we cannot prove anything with absolute certainty, we can find support or usefulness for the findings derived from a single scientific investigation. If real differences do exist between groups, we can reject the null hypothesis and support the alternative hypothesis. Such support is indirect; the null hypothesis must first be rejected. If no real differences exist, we fail to reject the null hypothesis. We cannot prove the null either; we just fail to reject it for that study, since error may be operating as well.

One implication in conducting or evaluating the research process is that the null hypothesis is implied even though it is not stated explicitly. Commonly, researchers do not develop problems in order to determine that there are no differences among groups. Rather, they define a research problem in order to determine what differences, if any, there are among groups. Since a sample is a subset of a population and because the possibility of error exists, subsequent samples may reveal significant differences. Therefore, the null hypothesis of no differences may be the initial assumption and, only as a rationale is provided, is either a nondirectional or directional hypothesis proposed. In order to avoid redundancy, a null hypothesis is not usually stated but rather implied, and only alternative hypotheses are stated and supported in the research article.

Another implication of the notion of indirect proof relates to the Results and Discussion sections. As alternative hypotheses are presented,

Notion of Indirect Proof

they provide a framework for comparing the results. Results can be discussed in terms of whether they do or do not support alternative hypotheses. Presented in the Introduction, the alternative hypothesis provides another component integrating the various sections of the research process. If no alternative hypothesis is stated, but a research question is implied or made explicit (for instance, "What differences do exist among our groups?"), that question can still provide a framework for interpreting the results.

Developing and Evaluating Hypotheses

The four criteria for writing and evaluating hypotheses are similar to those for analyzing purpose statements. But the second and fourth are unique to the development and evaluation of hypotheses. We will examine these criteria separately and then relate each to a variety of hypotheses.

1. The hypothesis should be stated briefly and clearly.
2. The hypothesis should express the relationship between two variables.

3. The hypothesis should be testable.
4. The hypothesis should be supported by a rationale derived from theory, research, or personal experience.

Brevity and Clarity

The first criterion for developing and evaluating hypotheses demands that they be stated as briefly and clearly as possible. For instance, restating the population in the hypothesis would affect both brevity and clarity. As in the development of the purpose statement, the need to be as clear as possible is also important in the hypothesis. Consider the following:

> We hypothesize that no significant changes will be occurring with fourth graders since it is our belief that if a loss of self-worth is observed due to the achievement level grouping, it will be counterbalanced by an increase, since the fourth grade students probably will be more competitive within the achievement grouped class.

Obviously this hypothesis does not meet the criterion of brevity and clarity. It attempts to embed a rationale for the hypothesis within the hypothesis itself. As we shall see, the rationale accompanies the hypothesis, but not quite that closely. Consider one rewording that might meet our criterion:

> No significant difference will be obtained between the average achievement group and the low achievement group in decreasing level of self-worth.

If we feel strongly that a null hypothesis should be stated in the rewording, we can clearly see the relationship and can now construct a strong rationale to support it.

Relating Two Variables

The second criterion for developing and evaluating hypotheses demands that they express the relationship between two variables. Frequently, a purpose statement expresses the relationship among multiple variables, especially as the problem area becomes more complexly defined. Thus, it is not unusual to have several hypotheses presented, all of which are derived from one main purpose. However, to ensure that readers of our research comprehend the predictions made, we succinctly present each one as an expressed relationship between two variables. Consider the following multiple variables hypothesis:

> High- and low-anxiety male and female psychology students, regardless of achievement level, differ from medium-anxiety psychology students and also differ if they are high or low achievers on measures of statistics, development, and learning knowledge and concepts.

This nondirectional alternative hypothesis predicts several relationships among multiple variables. Presented as a single hypothesis, the expressed relationships are confusing. The various relationships can be more clearly expressed as multiple hypotheses, each presenting the relationship between two variables. Consider the following statement of hypotheses derived from the more complex one above:

> Significant differences will be obtained between the high- and medium-anxiety groups on a measure of: (a) statistics, (b) developmental principles, (c) learning theory.

> Significant differences will be obtained between the low- and medium-anxiety groups on a measure of: (a) statistics, (b) developmental principles, (c) learning theory.

> Significant differences will be obtained between the high-anxiety, low-achievement group and the medium-anxiety, high-achievement group on a measure of: (a) statistics, (b) developmental principles, (c) learning theory.

Each hypothesis predicts a relationship between two variables. The first example predicts that the level of anxiety, high or medium, produces a difference on a measure of statistics. Anxiety level and statistics score are the two variables. Within the first variable, anxiety level, two components are stated. Additional group comparisons within the first variable usually produce confusion. Thus a suggested format for the hypothesis is to state a comparison between two groups or levels of one variable and their relationship to the second variable. Based on the preceding examples, we could state nine different hypotheses.

Given the recommended format, we could encounter duplication and redundancy in our research unless, while developing our hypotheses, we continue to use the condition of a comparison of two components of one variable and their relationship to the second variable. This procedure will facilitate clarity. However, after developing our hypotheses, we can integrate additional variables into one hypothesis if redundancy can be avoided and clarity is maintained. Thus the first three hypotheses could be restated as:

> Significant differences will be obtained between the high- and medium-anxiety groups on measures of statistics, developmental principles, and learning theory.

Writing hypotheses is like writing purpose statements; we have to develop the appropriate general conceptual level for a particular research study. It should be not too specific so as to produce redundancy, nor too general so as to produce ambiguity. Thus, instead of giving nine hypotheses predicting the relationship between two variables, we have three hypotheses, each predicting the relationship between two variables in three different ways.

This idea of expressing multiple hypotheses from one purpose statement is most applicable with those research investigations which have

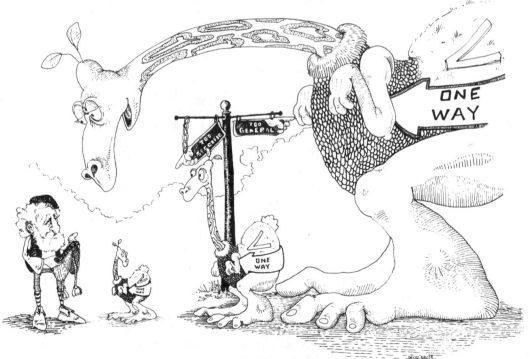

Specifying the Hypothesis

complex purpose statements. Consider the purpose statement from which the previous hypotheses were derived:

> The main purpose of this study is to determine differences among levels of anxiety—high, medium, and low—in psychology students on measures of statistics, developmental principles, learning theory, and research and evaluation concepts. Levels of achievement—high, average, and low—and sex differences are also examined.

We could have predicted all possible combinations of the two variables in our research. Or we could have hypothesized only the relationships we were interested in and for which we could provide a rationale. Or we could decide not to offer any hypothesis but instead to try to determine what relationships existed. The last two options are the ones most frequently used in educational research.

Testing Hypotheses

The third criterion for conducting and evaluating research demands that the hypothesis be testable. This criterion restates an earlier one presented for purpose statements which said that they should be researchable or amenable to empirical investigation. As we proceed in the steps of the research process, the variables and interrelationships set forth at a conceptual or construct level are made more specific and concrete, and thus by the time we reach the Instrumentation subsection they will be fully operationalized. Consider the following two hypotheses:

> Feedback causes improvement.
>
> Positive teacher comments will increase reading comprehension scores when compared to neutral teacher comments.

As stated, the first hypothesis is not testable. The second is just one rewording that expresses the relationship between two levels of one variable, teacher comments—positive or neutral—with a second variable, reading comprehension scores. This rewording enables the variables in the hypothesis to be operationalized and thus to be tested.

Deriving a Rationale

The final criterion demands that the hypothesis be supported by a rationale derived from theory, research, or personal experience.

Professional predictions do not occur in a vacuum isolated from experiences, from educational theories, or from the mass of existing research. Frequently, researchers want to plunge into their project without suitable preparation. They end up remapping the same territory rather than improving on what preceded or charting new unmapped territory.

Generating hypotheses is challenging and fun. Typically, we progress through different stages that vary in their specificity. A first step is usually based on some intuition, experience, or thought we have had. It is, therefore, frequently vague and ill-defined. The second step is a period of incubation that includes gathering information informally and reviewing past theories and research that seem to support our hazy perspective. The last step is one in which we clearly state our prediction and rationale. Specific theoretical principles, research findings, or explicit personal experiences have been manifested which facilitate the development of the initial intuition.

Within the Introduction we may include a review of relevant literature that provides the support or rationale for the hypotheses, as well as the support for the general problem of our research endeavor. As we examine the relationship of the literature review to the purpose and hypothesis, we will delineate a strategy to integrate these three components.

Levels of Hypotheses

As we use the scientific method to develop our research plan, we find we must develop hypotheses in the third step. Ideally, these hypotheses should meet the four criteria for developing and evaluating hypotheses discussed in the preceding section. Frequently, we write or encounter a wide range of hypotheses that vary according to their consistency with the four criteria. The following four different levels of hypotheses are encountered in educational research:

Value-laden or nontestable hypotheses
Implied hypotheses
Partial criteria hypotheses
Complete criteria hypotheses

Value-Laden or Nontestable Hypotheses

Value-laden or nontestable hypotheses are frequently encountered in educational research. As with purpose statements, either an obvious or subtle bias may exist:

We will show that secondary rewards are more effective.

> Busing will be proved to be ineffective for achieving racial desegregation.
>
> What effect, if any, will group study contribute to better achievement?
>
> Our adolescent enrichment program is better than any others in demonstrating the obvious improvements made in personality characteristics.

Not only do these hypotheses not meet our criteria, they all contain instances of bias or value judgments. There is a difference between individuals' professional predictions and their obvious biases. Predictions minimize error in the research process while biases become embedded within predictions and increase the error.

Implied Hypotheses

The second level of hypothesis is an implied one. Frequently, when a hypothesis is not explicitly stated, we may infer one based on the tone of the Introduction. The Introduction may include references to the idea that a certain curriculum or counseling technique is more effective than others, but the hypothesis is not stated directly. Read the following Introduction and generate an explicit hypothesis based on the flow and tone of the review of the literature.

Self Actualization in Marital Enrichment

Robert P. Travis
Patricia Y. Travis

The idea of enhancing one's level of self-actualization through establishing authentic communication between partners in marriage may appear to be an inappropriate aspect of a marriage enrichment program to be evaluated. Perhaps the reason for this is the false assumption that the enrichment of the "relationship" is the goal of such a program, not the "individual partners" in the relationship. However, it is our contention that self-actualization is the primary goal of any type of therapeutic intervention and particularly within the marital health approach.

We designed the Pairing Enrichment Program (PEP) as a research effort in the area of marital health. Marital health is a professional health field with a central focus on teaching, training, counseling, and research concerning the marital dyad separate and apart from child psychology and family dynamics (Vincent, 1973; Bosco, 1973; Mace, 1974; Travis & Travis, 1975a). The approach of marital health is preventive rather than crisis intervention.

The Pairing Enrichment Program is a three-week program offered to married couples who have a mutual commitment to enhance the quality of their unique relationship. Initially the couples go through a weekend retreat where all concepts, techniques, and communication exercises of PEP are discussed and experienced. At the end of the weekend retreat, each couple is given a booklet which contains summaries of each of the sessions and suggestions for exercises to be followed at home for the remainder of the three weeks. For a more detailed description of PEP see Travis and Travis (1975b).

One of the major aspects of the philosophical framework from which PEP originated is that it is not the concept of "two becoming one" in the marriage, but the individuality, self-respect, self-identity, and personal growth which is critical for interpersonal growth and can be appreciated in marriage. "To grow individually together" summarizes this concept.

Maslow (1954, 1962) maintains that there is a basic need for and drive toward self-actualization in every individual. There are four types of lower-order needs (physiological needs, safety or security needs, the needs for love, affection and to belong, and the esteem needs) which must be satisfied before the need for self-actualization becomes very important. Most of these lower-order needs involve human relations and can only be satisfied in interaction with other people; thus, we might think of relationships as the vehicle which carries us toward self-actualization (Fitts, 1970). Consequently, the marriage relationship can be viewed as a vehicle which can move individuals toward self-actualization (Travis, 1975).

A pilot study was done to assess the effectiveness of PEP in this regard (Travis & Travis, 1975a). This study revealed a significant movement toward greater self-actualization on seven of the 12 subscales by both husbands and wives on the Personal Orientation Inventory (POI), and there was a significant gender difference on eight of the scales. The POI is a technique developed by Shostrom (1966) to assess positive mental health as opposed to psychopathology. The POI has been the instrument used to assess the effectiveness of such personal growth methods as individual therapy (Weir & Cade, 1969), transcendental meditation (Seeman, Nidich, & Banta, 1972), marathon encounter group experience (Guinan & Foulds, 1970; Treppa & Fricke, 1972; Young & Jacobson, 1970), sensitivity training (Culbert, Clark & Bobele, 1968), "creative risk taking" training group (Byrd, 1967), and human relations training group (Banman & Capelle, 1972). This is a paper-pencil inventory of 150 two-choice opposite-paired statements of values which consists of 12 scales which measure dimensions of self-actualization.

The Inner Directed (I) scale; which contains 127 of the 150 items, is considered to be the best single estimate of self-actualization (Knapp, 1965) and the most important evidence of the validity of the POI (McClain, 1970).

The exploratory study had several methodological shortcomings. Specifically, there was a lack of control subjects and relevant co-variables were not included in the analysis. The present study attempts to control for these experimental variables.

Based on the tone of the Introduction, in the absence of an explicit hypothesis, we can infer the following alternative directional hypothesis:

> PEP will result in significant increases on twelve subscale measures of self-actualization as compared to no PEP.

The process of developing an explicit hypothesis from an implied one provides a framework for analyzing and interpreting the subsequent results.

Partial and Complete Criteria Hypotheses

The third and fourth levels of hypotheses encountered in the research process are those which meet either some subset of criteria or all of them. Consider this hypothesis:

> Group study contributes to better achievement.

This directional hypothesis is brief, but it is not clear. Two general variables are stated—type of study and achievement—but there is no comparison with group study. Further specificity, such as the type of achievement, would increase clarity. The hypothesis seems testable, and we can analyze whether a strong rationale has been provided by the review of relevant literature. Consider this rewording of the previous hypothesis:

> Group study increases G.P.A. when compared to self-study.

The reworded hypothesis better meets our first three criteria, and we can determine if a rationale has been provided.

Not only can we determine the presence of a strong rationale, but we can analyze whether the variables are consistent with the purpose statement and the variables operationalized in the Instrumentation subsection. The relationship among the variables conceptualized in the purpose and hypothesis with those operationalized in the Instrumentation subsection is an important way by which we can weave and interrelate the various components of the research process into a coherent and integrated entity.

——— SUMMARY ————————————————————

We have discussed three types of hypothesis, the *null,* the *alternative nondirectional,* and the *alternative directional* hypotheses, together with the five most frequently found forms of hypotheses used in educational research. The theoretical, educational, or scientific hypothesis presents the relationship between variables at a concept or construct level. The research hypothesis presents the relationship between variables which have been operationally defined, while the statistical hypothesis presents the relationship symbolically, using the Greek letter μ for the population mean. We have also examined four criteria for developing hypotheses and discussed the levels of hypotheses found in the research literature, including suggestions for writing a concise, complete hypothesis.

——— OBJECTIVES ———

In Chapter 3 we have examined the second component of the research article, the *hypothesis*. Confirm your understanding of the material in Chapter 3 using the following objectives:

Analyze any hypothesis on the basis of form, type, and level, and evaluate it using the four criteria presented.

Relate the notion of indirect proof to the use of any hypothesis, and specify its relationship to the other sections of the research article.

Identify an implied hypothesis in an Introduction, and rewrite it as an explicit one.

——— TERMS ———

alternative directional hypothesis
alternative nondirectional
   hypothesis

mu (μ)
notion of indirect proof
null hypothesis

Reviewing
the Literature

What are the four major sources of research information, and what is the purpose of each?

What are the major reference books available, and what is the purpose of each?

What are the five steps that ensure that our search of the literature will be efficient and effective, and how is each implemented?

How is the review of the literature integrated into the Introduction section of the research article?

How is an Introduction section evaluated with the guidelines for developing an integrated Introduction?

Review of the Literature

Steps in the search	Sources	Integrating the introduction	Categories for organization	Result
Obtain secondary source articles reviewing general topic			Related to introduction: to purpose statement generally specifically to hypothesis to population	
Generate additional key words or phrases	Prelim- inary General Specific	General introduction or overview Develop more specifics Specify purpose statement	Related to method: to tests or instruments to procedure or treatment to statistical analysis	Integrated intro- duction
Systematically search *Psychological Abstracts* and *Current Index to Journals in Education*	Primary	Present rationale for hypothesis Specify hypothesis	Related to implications of results	
Search other preliminary sources as needed	Secondary		Related to improve- ments on prior research	
Revise search and inquiry at each step			Not directly related to this research	

The review of relevant literature provides the framework for the statement of purpose and hypotheses. It presents a *general* rationale to support the purpose of the research investigation as well as a *specific* rationale to support any proposed alternative hypotheses. The integration and blending of these three components comprise the Introduction section of the research article. Thus the review of the literature attempts to answer two main questions relating to the statement of purpose and the hypotheses:

1. Why is this problem area the main purpose of my research investigation?
2. Why predict this outcome for my hypotheses?

Attempting to answer these questions in an integrated Introduction section, we rely heavily on the wisdom gained from past theoreticians and researchers. This knowledge is compiled from various sources, which we will examine so that we may take advantage of the successes and failures of others in undertaking our own research. After we have analyzed these sources, we will examine a strategy for integrating the review of literature with the purpose and hypotheses.

Wisdom of Past Travelers

Sources

Preliminary sources are reference works that index or abstract professional articles, books, and such other information as dissertations or theses. Preliminary sources, such as *Psychological Abstracts* and *Current Index to Journals in Education (CIJE),* provide a useful and manageable compilation of previous theoretical or research-oriented investigations that facilitate our search for knowledge pertinent to our problem area.

Primary sources are reference works that contain direct or original theoretical or research investigations. Primary sources are included in many journals, such as *Journal of Experimental Psychology: General; Journal of Educational Psychology; Child Development;* or *American Educational Research Journal.* These present the original results of researchers' inquiries using the scientific method. Primary sources may also include books, such as textbooks.

Secondary sources are reference works that summarize, review, and/or evaluate primary source material. Secondary sources, such as the *Annual Review of Psychology* and *Review of Research in Education,* as well as most textbooks review, summarize, and interpret original theory or research; that is, they review primary sources. We shall elaborate further on these sources of information.

Preliminary Sources

For our purposes, preliminary sources may be separated into two main categories: *general preliminary sources* and *specific preliminary sources.* A general preliminary source includes major abstracts or indexes that review a broad field of specialization such as psychology and education. A specific preliminary source includes abstracts or indexes whose focus is a particular content area within the broader field, such as the *Exceptional Child Education Resources.* Examples of these sources are described in the next two sections.

General preliminary sources.   We shall describe these four general preliminary sources:

Psychological Abstracts
Current Index to Journals in Education (CIJE)
Education Index
Mental Measurements Yearbook

Psychological Abstracts, published by the American Psychological Association (APA) from 1927 to the present, contains monthly summaries of primary research in the following sixteen areas of psychology: general psychology, psychometrics, experimental psychology (human), experimental psychology (animal), physiological psychology, physiological intervention, communication systems, developmental psychology, social processes and social issues, experimental social psychology, personality, physical and psychological disorders, treatment and prevention, professional personnel and professional issues, educational psychology, and applied psychology. Many of these major categories also contain subdivisions. Each issue contains a "key to the text" that is useful in understanding and using the abstracts.

Also published by the American Psychological Association is the *Thesaurus of Psychological Index Terms,* 2nd ed. (1977), which compiles the vocabulary and jargon used in psychology, education, and related fields. It is useful for finding terms or words related to our areas of inquiry. For instance, if our scientific investigation examines inductive or deductive reasoning, we will find in the relationship section two terms that are related: convergent thinking and syllogistic reasoning; three terms that have a broader meaning: cognitive processes, reasoning, and thinking; and one term that has a narrower meaning: inference. The *Thesaurus* is a useful tool for obtaining additional or related key words or terms.

Two specific preliminary sources that abstract a particular field are also published by the American Psychological Association: *PsycSCAN: Clinical Psychology* and *PsycSCAN: Developmental Psychology.* Both are quarterly publications containing abstracts from selected journals in their respective fields.

Current Index to Journals in Education (CIJE) is one of the major abstracting sources published by the Educational Resources Information Center (ERIC). Monthly since 1969, *CIJE* has abstracted articles from the field of education and related fields. The *CIJE* is organized into four major sections: main entry section, subject index, author index, and journal contents index. The main entry section summarizes entries organized by the sixteen ERIC clearinghouses: Adult, Career, and Vocational Education; Counseling and Personnel Services; Reading and Communication Skills; Educational Management; Handicapped and Gifted Children; Languages and Linguistics; Higher Education; Information Resources; Junior Colleges; Elementary and Early Childhood Education; Rural Education and Small Schools; Science, Mathematics, and Environmental Education; Social Studies/Social Science Education; Teacher Education; Tests, Measurement, and Evaluation; and Urban Education. Each issue provides an "Organization of *CIJE*" section that is useful in finding the numerous entries.

Perhaps the most useful approach to using *CIJE* is through its subject index, which lists every major descriptor and major identifier for each issue. These descriptors and identifiers are derived from the *Thesaurus of ERIC Descriptors* (1980) published by Oryx Press, a useful source for identifying similar or related terms as well as broader or narrower terms for your topic. Similar to the *Thesaurus* from APA, it helps you to develop a context for your inquiry area as you seek additional information.

Also developed from the ERIC system is the preliminary source *Resources in Education* (RIE), published monthly since 1966. It is organized in a way similar to that of *CIJE,* but it differs in the content it abstracts and indexes. Mainly it summarizes unpublished reports of research in progress and completed research that is funded by numerous federal agencies.

Education Index, published monthly by H. W. Wilson Company since 1929, is a cumulative author and subject index for more than 300 major educational periodicals. Unlike *CIJE, Education Index* does not abstract or summarize the entries. Rather, under each key word it presents only the reference for the periodical. Since 1969, when *CIJE* was first published, *Education Index* has overlapped significantly with the *CIJE* entries. Thus the main use of *Education Index* today is for a literature search of educational and related periodicals before 1969.

Mental Measurements Yearbook (MMY) indexes and reviews almost every educational, psychological, and vocational test published in English. Edited by Buros, eight yearbooks from 1938 to 1978 comprise the series. Each *Mental Measurements Yearbook* builds on the previous one by reviewing tests published since the last *Yearbook.* For each test included, one or more reviewers critique the test. A comprehensive reference list of publications that used the test is included, as well as norming information and descriptive information—such as publisher, forms, and prices.

Additional sources that contain indexes and reviews of tests include: *Measures for Psychological Assessment* (Chun, Cobb, and French, 1975); *Tests and Measurements in Child Development: A Handbook* (Johnson and Bommarito, 1971); *Tests and Measurements in Child Development: Handbook II* (Johnson, 1976); *Personality Tests and Reviews* (Buros, 1970); *Tests in Print II* (Buros, 1974); *A Sourcebook for Mental Health Measures* (Comrey, Backer, and Glaser, 1973); and *Measures of Social Psychological Attitudes* (Robinson and Shaver, 1973). Almost every college or university library contains these basic reference texts that supplement and expand on those presented in the *Mental Measurements Yearbook.*

Specific preliminary sources.   We shall describe these six specific preliminary sources:

> *Child Development Abstracts and Bibliography*
> *Deafness Speech and Hearing Abstracts*
> *Educational Administration Abstracts*

Exceptional Child Education Resources
Language and Language Behavior Abstracts
Resources in Vocational Education

Child Development Abstracts and Bibliography, published quarterly since 1927, is an official publication of the Society for Research in Child Development (SRCD). It indexes books and periodical articles in child development and related areas. Abstracts are organized under these six major sections: Biology, Health, Medicine; Cognition, Learning, Perception; Social Psychological, Cultural, and Personality Studies; Educational Processes; Psychiatry, Clinical Psychology; History, Theory, and Methodology.

Deafness Speech and Hearing Abstracts, published since 1960 by Gallaudet College in Washington, D.C., abstracts material from 350 international journals in medicine, sociology, psychology, and other fields that publish studies about hearing. Approximately 2,500 abstracts are issued each year, organized into five subject headings. An annual author-subject index is provided and the literature reviewed is summarized annually.

Educational Administration Abstracts, published quarterly since 1966 by the University Council for Educational Administration in Columbus, Missouri, abstracts 104 English-language journals in educational administration. It includes abstracts of such areas as administrative processes, futurology, long-range planning, organization, programs for educational administrators, and societal factors influencing education. Preferences are given to related abstracts published under different headings. An author-journal index is also included in each issue.

Exceptional Child Education Resources, published quarterly since 1968 by the Council for Exceptional Children, is the ERIC clearinghouse for programs in the exceptional child area. Including areas on both handicapped learners and gifted children, it reviews more than 255 journals as well as doctoral dissertations, texts, and reports and surveys. Abstracts are included in numerical order and a computerized author, subject, and title index is available.

Language and Language Behavior Abstracts, published quarterly since 1967, abstracts approximately 1,000 journals from thirty-two languages with thirty major headings. It is used predominantly in the fields of linguistics, psycholinguistics, educational psychology, sociolinguistics, hearing pathology, and the communication sciences.

Resources in Vocational Education, published bimonthly since 1967 by the Center for Vocational Education from Ohio State University, was known previously as *Abstracts of Research and Related Materials in Vocational and Technical Education.* It is similar to *Resources in Education,* and includes vocational and technical reports as well as instructional materials. Approximately 1,200 abstracts are searched annually. It also contains a subject, author, and institution index. A Projects in Progress section contains research and curriculum developments. All documents abstracted are available through ERIC in microfiche and in standard copy.

Other specific preliminary sources—such as the *Physical Education Index,* the *British Education Index,* and the *Canadian Education Index* —also are available in most major university libraries.

Primary Sources

As we have said, primary sources are journals, final reports, or books that contain original research investigations, theoretical analyses, and/or practical applications. There are many journals in the field of education that contain primary-source articles.

These journals differ in a variety of ways. Some are *refereed* and others are *nonrefereed.* A refereed journal is one having an editorial board that reviews an article and decides whether to publish it verbatim, to revise and then publish it, or not to publish it at all. Usually, two or three members of the editorial board review it. Frequently this procedure results in a more objective review. An additional procedure used by some journals is the *blind review.* A blind review also attempts to reduce the subjectivity of the evaluation by omitting the names of the authors of submitted articles.

Some journals publish primary sources that are predominantly research based. Examples include:

American Educational Research Journal
American Journal of Mental Deficiency
Child Development
Educational Leadership
Education and Training of the Mentally Retarded
Gifted Child Quarterly
Journal of Comparative and Physiological Psychology
Journal of Consulting and Clinical Psychology
Journal of Educational Measurement
Journal of Experimental Education
Journal of Experimental Psychology (all 4 sections)
Journal of Learning Disabilities
Journal of Personality and Social Psychology
Journal of Research on Science Teaching
Journal of Teacher Education
Reading Research Quarterly
Research in the Teaching of English
Science Education

Several journals contain primary sources based on theory or application, as well as empirical research articles. Examples include:

Journal of Abnormal Psychology
Journal of Applied Psychology
Journal of Counseling Psychology
Journal of Creative Behavior
Professional Psychology
Psychological Review

Some journals, such as *Psychological Review* or *Psychological Bulletin,* may confuse the categorical distinctions we have made above, since they may contain some articles that are original theoretical or methodological analyses (and thus are a primary source), while other articles review previous theoretical or methodological advances (and thus are a secondary source).

Secondary Sources

We shall describe the following secondary sources:

Annual Review of Psychology
Handbook of Research on Teaching
Psychological Bulletin
Review of Educational Research
Review of Research in Education

Annual Review of Psychology, published annually since 1949, contains review articles across a wide range of topics. Examples of review areas from Volumes 31 and 32 include: consciousness in contemporary psychology, life-span developmental psychology, brain functions, perception, social motivation, evaluation research, experimental psycholinguistics, biological psychopathology, and multidimensional scaling.

Handbook of Research on Teaching, published by Rand McNally (Gage, 1963), was a project of the American Educational Research Association. It was followed in 1973 by the *Second Handbook of Research on Teaching* (Trayers, 1973). These handbooks provide comprehensive reviews of specific topics in education. For instance, in the Gage (1963) handbook examples of chapter topics include: paradigms for research on teaching, measuring classroom behavior by systematic observation, testing cognitive ability and achievement, measuring noncognitive variables in research on teaching, analysis and investigation of teaching methods, teacher's personality and characteristics, social interaction in the classroom; also separate chapters on research on teaching nursery school, elementary school reading, social studies, composition and literature, secondary school mathematics, science, foreign languages, and visual arts; and teaching at the college and university level.

Psychological Bulletin publishes evaluative reviews and interpretations of methodological problems and issues in psychology. Original research is published only when it illustrates a methodological or substantive issue in research literature. Examples of areas analyzed include: moral cognition and moral action, effects of stress on performance and social behavior, primary process thinking and creativity, visual masking, environmental cognition, and fluid and crystallized intelligence.

Review of Educational Research, published quarterly by the American Educational Research Association, contains integrative reviews and interpretations on substantive and methodological issues in the educational research literature. Examples of issues analyzed include: item-writing technology, cooperative learning, criterion-referenced tests, test anxiety, evaluation models, educational planning, and teacher training.

Review of Research in Education, published annually since 1973 by the American Educational Research Association, reviews substantive problems as well as technical and methodological developments in education. Examples of areas reviewed include: instructional development, social learning, organizational change in schools, history of education, multivariate analysis in educational research, problem solving and decision making, comparative education, and teacher effectiveness.

Preliminary, Primary, and Secondary Sources

Literature as a Source of Ideas

Perhaps the best source for topics that might interest you, and might be researchable and meaningful as well, is your own professional experience in the classroom. The intuitions that lead you to do the right thing without knowing why are important areas for further exploration. For those of you who do not already have classroom or administrative experience, and for those who have but prefer to explore other areas, I recommend exploring the research topics listed in the article at the end of Chapter 1. Also the topic headings summarized under the preliminary, primary, and secondary sources may give you some initial ideas. Useful sources for generating ideas for topics are the secondary sources that review a body of research in a particular topic; sources such as the *Annual Review of Psychology* and the *Review of Research in Education* include numerous research reviews that may suggest interesting problem areas for you.

Some Suggestions

The following list of topics may help to suggest problems from which a research plan, purpose, and hypothesis may eventually be developed.

1. Open versus traditional education
2. Microcomputers
3. Mastery learning
4. Motivation and learning
5. Programmed instruction
6. Year-round versus traditional schools
7. Team teaching
8. Advance organizers on learning
9. Discussion versus lecture
10. Questioning strategies for facilitating comprehension
11. Retention versus passing students who are failing
12. Evaluation of programs, projects, and materials
13. Public versus private schools
14. Basal readers
15. Classroom management
16. Leadership in the classroom
17. Gifted/talented programs
18. Learning styles—mentor, independent study, and small group
19. Teacher burn-out
20. Values and moral development
21. Influence of the home environment
22. Teacher accountability
23. Tutoring and its effectiveness
24. Teaching characteristics and effect on learning

25. Television as an instructional aid
26. Handwriting methods for the elementary grades
27. Grading systems and policies
28. Individual and group testing
29. Cognitive styles—impulsive and reflexive
30. Locus of control—internal and external
31. Popularity and achievement
32. Effectiveness of teacher aides
33. Advanced Placement (AP) programs
34. Self-concept, self-esteem
35. Career counseling
36. Crisis intervention
37. Juvenile delinquents and learning disabilities
38. Elementary counselors
39. Teaching children at home
40. Parents in the classroom
41. Test development and evaluation
42. Memorization and learning
43. Transfer of learning
44. Individualized educational plans (IEPs)
45. Sex-education and myths
46. Foreign-language instruction
47. Effectiveness of counseling programs
48. Truancy and absenteeism
49. Multicultural texts and programs
50. Guided imagery and learning
51. Teacher evaluations
52. Meditation, biofeedback, and yoga in academic achievement
53. English as a second language (ESL)
54. Leadership and administration
55. Effect of preschools on later achievement

Advances in technology and its impact on education is also an area in which research is needed. For instance, research on the effects of the microcomputer in the classroom and its influence on achievement and learning is in its infancy.

As you narrow your choice of topics, you may want to locate review articles on that topic so that you can develop a more complete research context for your potential problem.

A Search Strategy

There are a number of strategies that can be used to review the educational research systematically in a problem area. Let us look at one such strategy that is particularly useful in facilitating your search. As you conduct your own reviews, you will begin to adapt and modify this strategy to tailor it into your own systematic search procedure. There are five main steps in the search strategy:

Obtain secondary source articles reviewing your general topic.
Generate additional key words or phrases.
Systematically search *Psychological Abstracts* and *Current Index to Journals in Education.*
Search other preliminary sources as needed.
Revise your search process and inquiry at each step.

Each of these steps contains additional suggestions that should be useful; thus we will discuss each briefly.

Using secondary sources.   The first step is to obtain secondary source articles reviewing your general topic. A main goal in conducting research within an area of inquiry is to obtain a context or overview within which your research is embedded. Secondary source articles that review your topic help provide the necessary framework.

These review articles will help you gain a perspective for your research endeavor as well as provide an initial data base for the subsequent steps in your search strategy. For instance, if you are interested in different problem-solving strategies for gifted and talented elementary school children, you may find review articles related to problem solving and decision making, or gifted and talented education. More specific reviews are usually generated from the initial ones.

Generating key words or phrases.   The second step is to generate additional key words or phrases. In generating additional key words or phrases you might consult the appropriate thesaurus to find related terms. You can also find the names of investigators who have researched the problem. You can obtain books related to your area from the subject section of the card catalogue. You can compile articles or references collected from your experiences that now seem to relate to your present research endeavor. You can also obtain useful input from your colleagues.

The relatively unsystematic input gathered above should further expand or revise your key words or phrases. You may decide to obtain more specific reviews of your topic prior to conducting a systematic search of the literature. Regardless, the context and framework for your analysis is being expanded and refined. You are acquiring a knowledge base or foundation that will be developed further by the next two steps.

Using preliminary sources.   The next two steps are to systematically search *Psychological Abstracts, Current Index to Journals in Education,* and other preliminary sources as needed. Usually *Psychological Ab-*

stracts and *CIJE* are systematically searched from the most recent or latest issue backward to the earliest. The key words and phrases generated previously are then related to the various subject areas and those areas are systematically reviewed. If, after reading the reference title and abstract, the reference seems to relate directly to your topic, you record it so that you can obtain and evaluate it once your search is completed.

Other preliminary sources such as *Education Index* or *Resources in Education* should be reviewed as appropriate. For instance, if a large amount of research in your area has been generated by federally funded projects, you will want to search *RIE*. If research into your problem area precedes 1969, you may want to search *Education Index*. At the very least, you should exhaustively search *Psychological Abstracts* and *CIJE* to ensure a comprehensive analysis and evaluation.

Historically, these two steps have required the greatest amount of time to accomplish. Depending on your topic, you can actually spend from two days to six months systematically searching the literature. However, today most college and university libraries offer computerized literature searching services that can replace your own search in a fraction of the time.

A typical procedure is to meet with a reference librarian to discuss your topic and to obtain information on the appropriate data bases; for instance, a search of ERIC. Key words are prepared and costs are anticipated. The advantages of searches through computerized retrieval systems like *Bibliographic Retrieval Systems, Inc. (BRS)* or *Dialog-Information Retrieval Service* are that any key word(s) and desired combinations of key words can be entered. Then the title of the reference and the abstract is searched, and if a key word or combination is obtained, the reference is read out. Thus the current computerized searches duplicate the process we once had to go through individually. The earliest computer searches were limited by the key words provided in the particular thesaurus, and frequently would feed out material totally unrelated to the specific problem area. Today, computerized searches can achieve in two hours what used to require six months.

Perfecting the process.   The last step is to revise your search process and inquiry at each step. It is not unusual to generate key words or phrases that are either too general or too specific. If your topic area was problem-solving strategies, *reasoning* would be a general word and *syllogistic logic* would be specific. With the first key word, you will get too many references and with the second, too few. Thus you will need to build into your search strategy an evaluative feedback loop wherein you revise your key words, phrases, and topic statements as you collect new information.

After the search is completed, you will need to obtain the references, read them, and begin to evaluate their appropriateness to your research.

You may want to revise, modify, or expand your statement of purpose based on your elaborated knowledge of the area. You may find research that can be used to support a hypothesis, a procedure, an instrument, or statistical analysis. You will have begun to categorize references. Many will relate to the Introduction section; others will be reserved for subsequent sections; still others will form a reject pile for this research investigation.

Integrating the Literature and the Introduction Section

One useful way to organize the theory, research, and applications you have obtained is to form categories of materials related to your investigation. It is important to remember that for any research endeavor some categories may not be used, but the following headings may make useful categories. You should adapt them as needed to make them most meaningful to your situation.

Related to the Introduction
    General statement of purpose
    Specific statement of purpose
    Prediction/hypothesis
    Population

Related to the Method
    Tests or instruments
    Procedure or treatment
    Statistical analysis
Related to the implications of results
Related to improvements on prior research
Not directly related to the research

The outcome desired from using these categories is the succinct conceptualization of the theory and research related to your specific research investigation. By grouping into smaller, related categories, a larger body of knowledge and information can be processed, integrated, and organized.

Typically, an Introduction section is developed in either of two ways —a general to specific flow, or a specific to specific flow. Let us consider the general to specific flow:

General introduction or overview
    History, definitions, or overview of the general topic of study is
        stated.
Develop specifics
    Treatment, procedure, variables, or population are related to the
        purpose statement.
Specify the purpose statement.

Integrating the Introduction

Present the rationale for the hypothesis.
Specify the hypothesis.

The last two steps should be repeated for multiple hypotheses.

A specific to specific flow is frequently used when a large body of literature has been established in a research area; for example, reinforcement or motivation. In these situations the general step is omitted and the investigators focus directly on the specific variables related to the study's purpose.

Evaluating the Introduction

In reading the following hypothetical Introduction section of a research article, analyze the flow of the review and evaluate the rationale to see if there is sufficient support for the statement of purpose.

The Use of Token Systems in Increasing Achievement

Token reinforcement or similar operant reinforcement programs have been used successfully in a number of different settings for increasing achievement (Lachowicz, 1972). The positive results in achievement shown by the use of token programs have been consistently demonstrated. Thus the token reinforcement method is continuing to be refined and modified in the light of current research (McReynolds and Coleman, 1972; Ribes, Galesso-Coaracy, Durán, 1973).

In a token reinforcement system, stimuli such as gold stars or poker chips are established as conditioned or secondary reinforcers by being paired with privileges, activities, candy, money, or other primary reinforcers. The main advantage of the token reinforcement system is that the token can more conveniently be made an immediate consequence of the behavior to be reinforced as compared to the primary reinforcer. Thus the gap between the desired behavioral response and the primary reinforcers can more easily be bridged (Lachowicz, 1972).

The effects of a token system where the total amount of potential reinforcement was varied were investigated by Lachowicz (1972). Important events presently existing in the environment were used as primary reinforcers. Ten female high school dropouts, between the ages of 16 and 21, were randomly selected from a population of 23 Neighborhood Youth Corps workers. A classroom group received token reinforcement in the form of wage adjustments for correct work done in class and a job group received full wages. Achievement was measured by a pre- and post-administration of the California Achievement Test (CAT). The classroom group had an average increase of 1.3 years from pre to post on the CAT while the job group had an increase of 0.2 years. The researchers concluded that the use of a token system seemed effective in increasing the academic skills of the girls. Due to the small number of subjects employed in the study, caution should be used in generalizing the results beyond the immediate population.

Lahey and Drabman (1974) also examined the effectiveness of token reinforcement in improving performance. They studied the effect of a token reinforcement program on sight-word vocabulary. Sixteen second grade students were drawn from the middle level reading group of a rural community school. Twice a week for five weeks, four subjects were taken from the regular classroom to a room where they were presented Basic Sight Vocabulary Cards. During the training sessions, the students were divided into two groups, those receiving token and verbal reinforcement for the correct identification of word cards and those receiving only verbal reinforcement. At the conclusion of the five-week training session, the students were given a retention test to measure achievement. The researchers concluded that the results depicted the importance of token reinforcement on the retention of vocabulary words. However, since the tokens were presented concurrently with verbal reinforcement, the interaction between the two types of reinforcement may have influenced the results as compared to a treatment in which the only reinforcement presented was tokens.

In a token reinforcement system the relative importance of token presentation must be examined. Ribes et al. (1973) studied the effect of token reinforcement separately from the effects produced with social reinforcement. Four retarded and learning disabled children were each exposed to four different treatments. The conditions were: social reinforcement paired with tokens having value, social reinforcement paired with tokens having no value, social reinforcement independent of tokens with value, and social reinforcement independent of tokens without value. The results indicated that the effects of tokens depend on the social reinforcement concurrently provided. The small number of subjects involved in the treatments, one per treatment, and the interaction of types of reinforcement may have confounded the results.

Thus in order to improve on past research and to determine the effectiveness of token reinforcement, the main purpose of this study was to compare the effects of four reinforcement conditions in increasing the acquisition and retention of scientific facts in potential high school dropouts. The four reinforcement conditions were: token, social, token and social, and no reinforcement. Based upon the findings of the Ribes et al. (1973) study, it was predicted that the token and social reinforcement condition would produce significant gains in acquisition of scientific facts as compared to the other three conditions.

In analyzing an Introduction section, a useful strategy for developing or determining the flow is to outline or to make a table of the relationships among the research literature and the variables proposed in the study. An outline of the above Introduction might look like this:

I. <u>General</u>	Variables	Population

1. Lachowicz (1972)
McReynolds and
    Coleman (1972)
Ribes, Galesso-
    Coaracy, Durán (1973)
	Rationale for:
	X. Token
	   reinforcement
	Y. Increasing
	   achievement	

2. Lachowicz (1972)	Definition of: X. Secondary reinforcers	
II. <u>More specific</u>		

3. Lachowicz (1972)	X. Specific secon-
	   dary reinforcers
	   (wage adjustments)
	Y. Increasing
	   academic achievement
		P. Female high
		   school dropouts

4. Lahey and
   Drabman (1974)
	X. Token and verbal
	   reinforcement and
	   verbal reinforce-
	   ment
	Y. Vocabulary
	   achievement
		P. Second graders

5. Ribes et al. (1973)	X. Token reinforce-
	   ment with or
	   without value
	   paired with social
	   reinforcement
	Y. Other variable
	   omitted
		P. Retarded and
		   learning
		   disabled
		   children

III. <u>Specify purpose</u>		

6. Purpose statement	X. Token, social,
	   token and social,
	   none
	Y. Acquisition and
	   retention of
	   scientific facts
		P. Potential high
		   school dropouts

IV. <u>Rationale for hypothesis</u>		
7. Based upon Ribes et al. (1973)		
V. <u>Specify hypothesis</u>		
8. The token and social reinforcement condition will produce an in- crease in acquisition of scientific facts		

A major advantage of a table picturing an entire Introduction section is that we can better analyze, integrate, and evaluate the rationale provided. As you gain further experience in developing and evaluating research, an external picture probably will not be necessary. Rather, as you read an Introduction section, you will learn to do similar analyses in the margin of the article or in your head. However, the visual organization that the table provides has proven to be a useful tool to reach that point. It also provides a context to further analyze the Introduction.

Reexamine the table and compare the variables labeled X, those labeled Y, and the populations. Take a few minutes to do so before reading further.

The flow found in this Introduction is derived from elaborating and specifying token reinforcement. It is the main variable of interest in this research investigation. Other than relating discrete types of achievement, no flow can be found for the variables under the Y category. Also, there does not appear to be a relationship among the diverse populations examined. Only the Lachowicz (1972) study relates to a similar population.

The only rationale provided in the Introduction is for the token reinforcement variable. Since no rationale is given for the other variable and it has no apparent face validity, serious questions arise:

Why study the acquisition and retention of scientific facts in potential high school dropouts?

What degree of cooperation, motivation, and participation will that population bring to the research process?

Why not analyze the effect of different token reinforcement conditions in areas more meaningful or useful to them; for instance, decreasing absenteeism or participating in a counseling group designed around their needs?

We are not attempting to limit the variables or groups a researcher should study. Rather, we are stressing that a main goal of the Introduction should be to present a rationale for examining the variables and their interrelationships. The absence of a rationale leads to confusion. Thus the goal of the Introduction is to relate the review of literature not just to one of the main variables but to the interrelationship of variables and, we hope, to the population as well.

Additional questions you might have generated in this Introduction could include:

Why were such a narrow time span, 1972–74, and number, 4, of studies presented? They may not accurately represent the current state of the art in that area.

Why not select or review research directly related to token reinforcement and dropouts or potential dropouts? Ambiguous findings
may be attributed to diverse populations.

Since the prior research is critiqued for a particular weakness, how is
this study specifically going to improve on the research which preceded?

Why is each reviewed study given in such detail? If a particular study
is crucial to your current investigation, it is frequently given in
greater detail. However, it should be stated why it is integral to your
current research.

After examining the Introduction above, we should be aware of the
organizational format for our research as well as the need to provide a
rationale for the major variables we shall examine. Using the outline
format to develop and examine our own Introductions is a useful strategy prior to, as well as after, writing, as we constructively attempt to refine and improve our research endeavor.

Example of an Introduction

The following Introduction is from a study by Ashby and Wittmaier
(1978) that examined attitude changes in children after listening to
stories about women in traditional and nontraditional occupations. The
abstract is presented first so that you will have an overview or broader
context to the entire study. Each paragraph of the Introduction then
follows and is preceded by comments to facilitate your understanding of
the organizational format for this first major research component, the
Introduction section.

Previous research has demonstrated that children's literature frequently presents girls and women only in limited, "traditional" roles, with the result that
girls exposed to such literature may limit their own self-perceptions and aspirations. In an experiment with fourth graders, 29 girls were read two stories
with women in traditional roles or two with women in nontraditional roles.
Attitude changes were measured by a picture-choice test, two job checklists,
and two adjective checklists. As predicted, girls who heard nontraditional
stories rated traditionally male jobs and characteristics as appropriate for females more than girls who heard traditional stories. These results underline
the importance of nonsexist books and textbooks in widening girls' aspirations
and self-images.

A general introductory statement in paragraph 1 relates the male and
female models from books to what is perceived as appropriate behavior
by children. A basic principle of modeling from social learning theory

serves as the transition to the specific application of modeling, that is, role models within books.

> Much attention has been given in recent years to the issue of sexism in children's books. Social learning theory predicts that children learn what constitutes sex-appropriate behavior from the sex role expectations and role models they observe around them. The books they read, both in and out of school, provide a major source of role models (Frasher & Walker, 1972). If these models show women in limited, stereotyped roles, girls may tend to limit their own aspirations.

The general premise from paragraph 1 that children's books provide inappropriate sex roles for girls begins to be examined in the literature in paragraph 2.

> Stull (Note 1) examined books that appeal to older children, including Newbery award winning books. She found that many, but not all, of the books presented girls and women only in limited, traditional roles. Newbery award winners were no better in this respect than books that had won no awards. Older books were more likely than recent books to present sexist images of females.

A study on the number of female and male characters in books historically is examined in paragraph 3. The paragraph seems incomplete because it does not flow logically either from the preceding or to the subsequent paragraph. A further statement or two elaborating the results of the Hillman study should provide the necessary linkages to the rest of the Introduction; otherwise, the paragraph should be omitted.

> A study by Hillman (1974) compared children's books written in the 1930s and in the 1970s. She found that books written in the 1970s have more female characters than those written in the 1930s, but female characters are still greatly outnumbered by males.

More specific information in paragraph 4 supports the premise that models in books provide inappropriate sex roles. More female models work at home, spend more time indoors, engage in quiet activities, and are not in leadership positions in the family.

>   Frasher and Walker (1972) examined widely used reading textbooks and found that males outnumber females by a large majority. Few of the females work outside the home, and those who do hold only traditionally female jobs. Fathers hold the position of family leadership. Fathers are shown mainly outdoors, while mothers are indoors. Girls are shown engaged in more quiet activities than boys.

Additional specific information is presented in paragraph 5 from two studies suggesting that positive outcomes in children's behavior or achievement result when a model's behavior is changed. This is an initial rationale for the hypotheses that will be proposed in the last paragraph.

>   A large number of studies point out the widespread sexism that exists in children's books and predict that this influences girls' self-images and aspirations. There is evidence that positive outcomes result from exposing children to nonstereotypical stories. Litcher and Johnson (1969), using multiethnic reading textbooks, succeeded in changing the attitudes of white school children toward blacks. McArthur and Eisen (1976) obtained more achievement behavior from nursery school girls who had heard a story about an achieving girl than those who heard about an achieving boy. This suggests that the content of reading books is important in influencing children's attitudes. By changing the content of the books children are exposed to, one may hope to change their attitudes toward themselves and others.

The last paragraph presents the purpose statement in the first sentence and two hypotheses in the last two sentences. The purpose statement is incomplete because we do not know what variables will be affected by the stories. Rereading the abstract, we know several attitude change measures were to be used; these variables should be presented explicitly. Also, from the abstract we know that books with women in nontraditional roles as well as books with women in traditional roles were read by the female fourth graders. Thus, the purpose statement omitted the traditional role condition as well as the population. The review of literature provides a rationale for examining the traditional and nontraditional role expectations.

> The current study was undertaken to determine the effects on girls of stories that portray women in nontraditional occupations. It was predicted that girls who were exposed to such women would perceive typically male jobs as more attractive than girls who were read stories about women in traditional occupations. It was also predicted that these girls would judge typically male adjectives to refer to both males and females more than girls read traditional stories.

Based upon our knowledge of purpose statements from Chapter 2 and the additional information provided in the Abstract, we can rewrite the purpose so that it meets the four criteria. The original purpose stated:

> The current study was undertaken to determine the effects on girls of stories that portray women in nontraditional occupations.

One rephrasing of the purpose statement states:

> The current study determines differences among fourth-grade girls exposed to children's literature with women in traditional and nontraditional roles on five attitude measures.

This statement meets our criteria for a complete purpose statement. We could elaborate on it with a sentence presenting the conceptual level variables for the attitude measures as well. The two hypotheses are alternative directional hypotheses predicting that girls who were exposed in stories to women in nontraditional occupations would select male jobs as being more attractive as well as perceive that male adjectives referred to both sexes when compared to girls who read traditional stories.

The two hypotheses are completely stated. Only a general rationale for the hypotheses is presented in paragraph 5, namely, attitudes and achievements can be influenced by the models in stories.

Even though the two hypotheses contain the complete information, they can be rewritten to reveal more directly the form of the hypothesis. You should be able to state this type of the hypothesis based upon your experience from Chapter 3. Consider the first hypothesis:

> It is predicted that girls who are exposed to such women will perceive typically male jobs as more attractive than girls who are read stories about women in traditional occupations.
>
> Significantly more male jobs will be selected by girls exposed to women in nontraditional occupations as compared to traditional occupations.

Now consider the second hypothesis:

> It is also predicted that these girls will judge typically male adjectives to refer to both males and females more than girls who read traditional stories.
>
> Girls exposed to women in nontraditional occupations as compared to those exposed to women in traditional occupations will select significantly more male adjectives as referring to both sexes.

You are right if you stated that these hypotheses were alternative directional hypotheses.

A table outlining the Introduction of this study would depict the following:

I. General	Variables	Population
1. Frasher and Walker (1979)	X. General rationale for books being a source for role models	P. Children
II. More specific		
2. Null (Note 1)	X. Books being a source of non-traditional and traditional role models for girls	P. Older children

3. Hillman (1974)	X. Rationale for number of female and male characters presented in books	P. Books
4. Frasher and Walker (1972)	X. Specific statement of difference between male and female portrayal in reading textbooks	P. Reading textbooks

IV. Rationale for hypothesis

5. Litches and Johnson (1969)	Y. Rationale for nontraditional text producing an attitude change of white children toward blacks	P. White school children
6. McArthur and Edison (1976)	Y. Rationale for nontraditional role producing an achievement change	P. Nursery school children

III. Specify purpose

7. Purpose statement	X. Stories of women in nontraditional occupations	P. Girls
	Y. Effects on...	

V.

8. Specify hypotheses	X. Stories about women in traditional and nontraditional roles	P. Girls
	Y. Male jobs as attractive and male adjectives as referring to both sexes	

Thus, from this Introduction, we can see that the three research components—purpose, hypotheses, and review of literature—are partially integrated. The review of literature provides only a rationale for one main variable, namely, the prevalence and possible negative effect of traditional female roles. In addition, the rationale for the two hypotheses is presented ahead of the purpose statement. The statement of purpose is incomplete with only one level of the main variable given, namely, stories of women in nontraditional occupations. The other level of that variable—women in traditional occupations—is omitted, plus any statement of the conceptual level variable, such as attitude or achievement changes, that will be affected by it. The population—girls —should be further specified as fourth-grade girls. Only in the two alternative directional hypotheses are two other variables mentioned. We do not know from the Introduction whether these are the only other variables or if several are examined but only these two relationships are predicted. A complete purpose statement would resolve any confusion about the number of variables examined.

We hope that, from this Introduction and the hypothetical one previously analyzed, the need to specify clearly not only a purpose statement but also any hypotheses has been demonstrated. In addition, these should be integrated into a pertinent review of the literature. The Introduction, which is the first key component of the research process, serves as an important conceptual analysis for the research undertaking.

SUMMARY

We have reviewed the major preliminary, primary, and secondary sources in educational and psychological research and have distinguished between general and specific preliminary sources. We have introduced ideas for generating a topic for research and have described a search strategy for systematically reviewing a problem area. Finally, we have developed a strategy for organizing an integrated Introduction by using a hypothetical Introduction and applying it to an example of an actual Introduction.

OBJECTIVES

In Chapter 4 we discussed the review of the literature as well as strategies for developing an integrated Introduction section. Confirm your understanding of the material in Chapter 4 with the following objectives:

Identify any reference used by a researcher as to type of resource.
Select and refine a topic for research.
Integrate a review of the literature with a statement of purpose and a hypothesis.
Construct a table or other visual device outlining the Introduction section using the guidelines.
Evaluate any Introduction section using the guidelines.

TERMS

Annual Review of Psychology
Child Development Abstracts and Bibliography
Current Index to Journals in Education
Deafness Speech and Hearing Abstracts
Educational Administration Abstracts
Education Index
Exceptional Child Education Resources
general preliminary source
Handbook of Research on Teaching
Language and Language Behavior Abstracts
Mental Measurements Yearbook
preliminary source
primary source
Psychological Abstracts
Psychological Bulletin
Resources in Education
Resources in Vocational Education
Review of Educational Research
Review of Research in Education
secondary source
Second Handbook of Research on Teaching
specific preliminary source

PART 2

Developing the Method Section of the Research Article

As we discovered in Chapter 1, the Method section of the research article typically includes three subsections: Sampling or Subjects, Procedure, and Instrumentation. The goal of the Method section is to transform conceptual level statements of what is to be studied and why, as delineated in the Introduction section, into explicit operational statements of how the study is developed and implemented. The Method section corresponds to the fourth and fifth steps of the scientific method: Develop techniques or instruments to obtain information related to the problem and hypotheses, and collect data or information. Specifically, the Method section attempts to answer three main questions:

1. What sample from what population is analyzed in the present research?
2. What are the specific steps followed in the research process?
3. What specific instruments are used to obtain the information?

Chapter 5 contains different sampling techniques and suggestions for developing the sample for your research investigation. It is an attempt to answer the question: What sample from what group does the present research process analyze?

Chapters 6 and 7 present guidelines for constructing the procedure for your research. Chapter 6 includes specific distinctions made among the types of variables, and there we consider numerous threats to the validity of the research process. In Chapter 7 we examine various types of research designs used in educational research and present recommendations for developing and evaluating a Procedure section. These two chapters are an attempt to answer the question: What are the specific steps followed in the research process?

Finally, Chapter 8 contains suggestions for developing and evaluating an Instrumentation section in order to obtain the necessary data for your study. It is an attempt to answer the question: What specific instruments are used to obtain the information?

Developing the Sample

What is the purpose of the Subjects section?

What is a sample, and what are the four steps in constructing a sample?

How is the population defined in order to be consistent with the statement of purpose?

What are the major demographic characteristics of a population?

How do we determine the sample size and its defining characteristics?

What are random sampling procedures, and how are they used to select representative people from the population?

What is biased or nonrandom sampling, and how does it contribute to misrepresentation of the population?

What are the other main sources of sampling error and bias?

What is the distinction between random selection and random assignment?

How is a Subjects section developed and evaluated?

Subjects

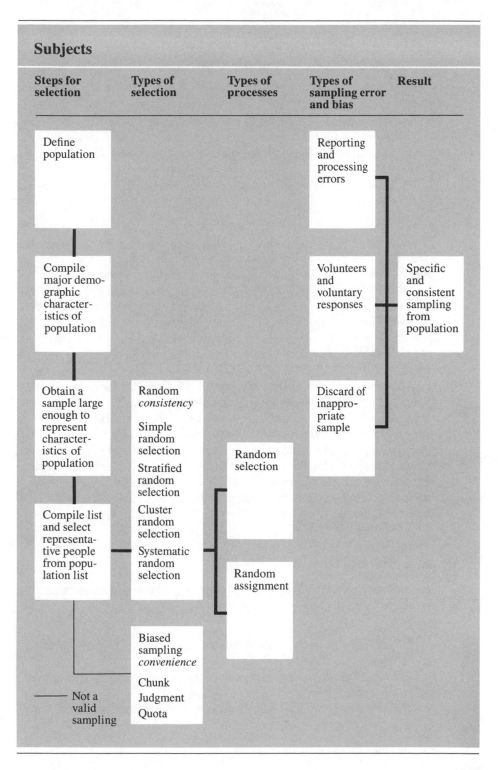

Steps for selection	Types of selection	Types of processes	Types of sampling error and bias	Result
Define population			Reporting and processing errors	
Compile major demographic characteristics of population			Volunteers and voluntary responses	Specific and consistent sampling from population
Obtain a sample large enough to represent characteristics of population	Random *consistency* Simple random selection Stratified random selection Cluster random selection Systematic random selection	Random selection	Discard of inappropriate sample	
Compile list and select representative people from population list		Random assignment		
—— Not a valid sampling	Biased sampling *convenience* Chunk Judgment Quota			

As the publication manual of the APA (1974) recommends, the Subjects subsection of the Method section of a research-based journal article should answer three main questions:

1. Who participated in the study? Present major demographic characteristics.
2. How many subjects participated? Present subgroup numbers as well.
3. How were the subjects selected? Describe assignment to groups also.

The Subjects subsection attempts to operationalize the population presented in the purpose. This process converts conceptual level descriptions of a population into an operationally defined set of subjects and relates to the definitions of *population* and *sample,* as given in Chapter 1. There, a *population* is defined as a complete set of individuals or objects having some common observable characteristic. A *sample* is defined as any subset of a population. The main reason for making a distinction between a population and a sample is that it is rarely possible to gather information from the entire population, largely because of time, money, and available resources. The entire population may be inaccessible unless it is very narrowly defined; for example, students currently enrolled in your section of this research course. The alternative is to select or construct a subset of the population, that is, a sample. In constructing a sample, four steps typically are involved. After we discuss these four basic steps, we shall analyze several sources of bias which can operate in the sample. This sampling bias frequently occurs when we cannot obtain a sample which accurately represents the population. Several examples of different types of Subjects subsections will then be presented.

Steps in Constructing a Sample

In constructing or selecting a sample that is derived from a population, the researcher typically follows four steps:

1. Define the population.
2. Compile the major demographic characteristics of the population.
3. Obtain a sample large enough to represent the characteristics of the population.
4. Compile a population list and select representative people from it.

Let us examine each of these steps.

Sampling the Population

Define the Population

Based on your purpose statement, hypotheses, and review of the literature, you will have stated a conceptual level description of your population, such as graduate counseling majors, elementary school children, and so forth. The major purpose of this first step is to determine how broadly or narrowly you will define the population. For instance, you can define the population as all the children currently enrolled in first through sixth grades—(a) throughout the country, (b) in this geographical region, (c) in this state, (d) in this county, (e) in this school district, (f) in year-round schools in this district, (g) in these two elementary schools because they are trying out a new curriculum, (h) in this elementary school because you know the principal, (i) in this elementary school because it has particular demographic characteristics—and so forth. Based upon your specific knowledge of the population, you need to define a population that will be further revised through the remaining steps.

You also need to consider how you are defining the tentative statement of the population. Are you selecting schools, groups, or individuals that are convenient, or are you defining the population as consistently as possible with your statement of purpose? In research, consistency supersedes convenience. What the question above should elicit is the researcher's rationale for selecting a particular population. This rationale, similar to the one provided for hypotheses, should be grounded firmly in theory, prior research, or reliable personal experience. In the present example, let us define the population as children in grades one through six in the eight elementary schools in School District #11. We selected this school district in our county as being the most representative of the population of school children in urban school districts throughout the country. After defining the population and presenting an initial rationale, you should proceed to compile and describe the major demographic characteristics of the population.

Compile the Major Demographic Characteristics

In a way, we have already started to define the particular characteristics in the population we want to include in the sample. In our previous example, we included two main delimiting characteristics, children and schools. We stated that we are interested in elementary school children in grades one through six. Therefore, that eliminates everyone else; namely, all the people living in your school district, all the people voting in the last school board election, families with school children, mothers and/or fathers of students, students in kindergarten, junior high students and senior high students, business owners, participants in service clubs, teachers, administrators, academic or nonacademic support staff, and so forth.

A second defining characteristic was the statement that we would use children in elementary schools in School District #11. That eliminates all other schools, the high schools and junior high schools in District #11. Our statement also excludes all other schools from surrounding school districts.

In determining additional variables for describing and understanding a population, the following list should be useful. Obviously, not all the variables would be pertinent to every study.

    age
    sex
    ethnicity
    marital status of parents
    socioeconomic status
    grade level/college level
    occupation
    level of education completed
    religious affiliation
    level of income
    parent(s) of school children

geographic region
voters in school elections
type of community members
number of children in school
graduate of local school district
community interest groups and clubs
business organizations
academic and nonacademic support staff in schools
teachers in school system
political affiliation
parent of handicapped child

Some possible resources that may assist you in defining characteristics of a sample include:

student class lists
school/college/university admission and test records
school parents lists
community census lists
voter registration lists
yellow pages of phone books

Another important resource you can use in defining your sample is the information you obtained from your review of the literature. Based on theory or research, you should have compiled additional variables that seem to affect the research results as well as provide a rationale for your population; for example, the sex or age of children for your research. Examples of additional variables that you may discern from the research which can affect your study include:

level of intelligence
level of achievement
reading level
cognitive style
cognitive developmental level

Many other variables can affect your research results; they should be delineated for each particular research investigation. Upon completion of this second step, you should have a fairly specific statement of the population characteristics from which you will derive your sample. For example:

> Male and female, first, third, and sixth graders from four elementary schools in School District #11 will be assessed. Eight elementary schools, Bates, Adams, Carver, Fremont, Keller, King, Pike, and Grant, were selected for

> our population site based on similar size of student population (range 600–750 students), geographic location, and rural representativeness. In addition, schools were considered only in District #11 since it is the central school district serving the town.

The specifics of our population are now detailed.

Obtain a Sufficiently Large Sample

The third step in constructing the sample requires that we obtain a sample large enough to represent the characteristics of the population. As you define the major demographic characteristics of your population you need to determine how many subjects will comprise your population. One way to organize your Subjects subsection is to set up a design of all your groups and variables. Based on the previous example, a partial design of only four schools might look like Table 5.1. Here the numbers of subjects for each of your groups are entered as you obtain them.

Depending upon the nature of your scientific investigation, you might be even more specific; for instance, smaller groups based on the number of classrooms at each grade level, or each child's achievement based on test scores. Thus your design can easily become quite complex; how complex depends directly on the complexity of your purpose statement.

If you do not have enough subjects, bias may operate so that it will be difficult to generalize valid results to the population. If you sample a high proportion from the population, although bias and error may be minimized, other practical considerations of time, money, and available resources may affect your research project.

There are a number of formulas (e.g., Winer, 1971; Cohen, 1977) for determining appropriate sample size. These formulas take into account the size of the differences predicted among your groups, the *effect size,* and *power.* Power is the probability of rejecting a null hypothesis when it is indeed false. A simple explanation of the relationship between the size of the sample and the effect size and power is this: As your sample size increases, the probability also increases that you will be able to reject a false null hypothesis. Either Winer (1971) or Cohen (1977) is recommended for determining the size of your sample based on effect size and power.

Additional strategies for determining sample size vary according to whom you read. Variations from 9 to 50 subjects for each subgroup may be recommended. As an initial strategy, 15 to 25 subjects per group is recommended as a minimum range. Based on the earlier example, we

Table 5.1 Population Characteristics of Four Schools

School	Grade	Sex	Number
Bates	1	M	85
		F	94
	3	M	70
		F	81
	6	M	104
		F	102
Adams	1	M	70
		F	64
	3	M	55
		F	60
	6	M	72
		F	71
Pike	1	M	89
		F	97
	3	M	72
		F	85
	6	M	68
		F	92
Grant	1	M	90
		F	108
	3	M	110
		F	84
	6	M	78
		F	85

would select 15 male first graders from Bates, 15 female first graders from Bates, 15 male third graders from Bates, and so on. Based on 15 per subgroup, we would have a sample of 720 students.

Obviously, the more subgroups we include, the more variables we will have, and the more subjects we will need. A rationale based on theory, research, or experience should be stated in the Introduction to support the addition of variables in your study. As a rule, the more subgroups and thus variables you have, the fewer subjects you will need in each subgroup. Conversely, the fewer subgroups and variables you have, the more subjects you will need for each. In the former situation you might include 10 to 20 subjects per subgroup, and in the latter you might have 25 to 50 subjects, or more.

In the strategy above, the total number of subjects per group or cell is adjusted according to the number of variables, as well as the number of levels of each variable. If you wish a cookbook recommendation for conducting research, then take *20 subjects for each cell.* Regardless of the number of groups, for instance 2 for the sex variable, or 48 in the previous school example, you would obtain 20 subjects for each group, resulting in 40 or 960 subjects respectively. Twenty subjects is large enough to ensure that you are measuring group differences and small enough to test without extensive resources. Keep in mind, however, that most research you review will not adhere to this rigid scheme; rather it is an initial strategy for planning your own research. Most of the published research articles select the total number of subjects based on the number and level of variables mentioned above.

Select Representative People from the Population

After you have decided how many subjects should accurately represent the population characteristics, you must then select representative people from the population list. The fourth step is to compile a population list and select representative people from it. The procedures for selecting representative people from the population are the various types of random and biased sampling described in the next sections. The best procedure is to select randomly since that should ensure that every person in the defined population has an equal probability of being selected for the sample. A biased sample is usually: (a) selected for convenience, (b) more prone to sampling bias, and (c) an inappropriate procedure. We shall discuss four types of random selection procedures and three types of biased sampling:

> simple random sampling
> stratified random sampling of two kinds:
> > proportional and equal size
> cluster random sampling
> systematic random sampling
> biased sampling of three kinds:
> > chunk, judgment, and quota

Simple random sampling. This type of sampling enables every individual in the defined population to have an equal chance of being selected in the sample. For instance, if we define our population as the students currently enrolled in this research course, we might have a population of 32 students. We could obtain a random selection of 15 students for our sample by giving a number to each person, putting that number into a jar or envelope, and selecting 15 numbers from the container. Every person, as long as his or her number is included, has an equal chance of being chosen for the sample. If we take the first 15 persons through the door, that is not a simple random procedure. It is biased, since not all 32 students in the population have an equal chance of being selected.

Another strategy involves the use of a table of random numbers. For example, suppose we have a population of 500 parents with varying educational backgrounds who have children in a secondary school, and we want to determine the average years of parent education for our study of attitudes toward year-round schools. We could hire someone to go through the entire parent list obtaining the years of education for the parents; alternatively, we could select about 200 parents from the list at random, determine the years of education, and divide the total by the number of parents. If the parent years of education on the list are evenly dispersed, the sample should yield an acceptable result. Again, the important thing to remember is that *every parent should have the same chance of being selected in the sample.*

To see how this would operate on a small scale, let us draw a simple random sample of 6 parents out of a population of 18, the 18 consisting of 3 parents with high school diplomas or less, 6 parents with some college education, and 9 parents with a college degree or more. Let us number the 18 parents and assign a hypothetical year of education to each (see Table 5.2).

Table 5.2 Years of Education of 18 School Parents

Parents with high school diploma or less		Parents with some college education		Parents with a college degree or more	
Parent number	*Years of education*	*Parent number*	*Years of education*	*Parent number*	*Years of education*
1	12	4	13	10	20
2	10	5	15	11	18
3	9	6	15	12	16
		7	14	13	16
		8	14	14	17
		9	14	15	16
				16	20
				17	19
				18	16
Total	31		85		158
Average	10.3		14.1		17.4

Years of education

Grand total (18 parents) = 274 years
Grand average   = 15.2 years

Random Sampling

In order to make a random selection of 6 out of 18 parents, we will use the list of random numbers in Table 5.3. We could also use the random number table in Appendix D. Close your eyes and point to any number. Decide to go up, down, right to left, left to right, or diagonally, and select the first six different numbers between 1 and 18.

In this example, let us assume we had decided to go down each column starting from the first number selected and had pointed to number 19. Then the first six parent numbers after 19 are listed in Table 5.4.

Table 5.3 List of Random Numbers

28	77	13	92
19	48	50	21
16	65	02	96
88	96	98	17
03	18	32	63
93	28	16	04
35	09	57	11
23	12	26	35
15	85	37	41
48	82	62	15

Table 5.4 Simple Random Sample

Parent number		Years of education
16		20
3		9
15		16
18		16
9		14
12		16
	Total	91
	Average	15.1[a]

[a] Compared with 15.2 for all 18 parents.

This is but one of 18,564 possible samples of six each for the population of 18 parents. It can be proved mathematically that the average years of education of the 18,564 random sample averages amount to 15.2 years—the same as the average of the original 18 parents in our population. However, an undesirable feature of simple random samplings is that we may happen to select one whose average is rather far from the true average. Thus, instead of the sample we actually drew (average years 15.1), we might have come up with either of the two samples in Table 5.5.

If random sampling occurred and the sample mean is significantly different from the population value, as in these two examples, *sampling error* has occurred. We shall explain the difference between sampling

Table 5.5 Two Examples of Sampling Error Operating

Sample A				Sample B		
Parent number		*Years of education*		*Parent number*		*Years of education*
1		12		10		20
2		10		11		18
3		9		14		17
5		15		15		16
7		14		16		20
8		14		17		19
	Total	74				110
	Average	12.3[a]				18.3[a]

[a] Compared with 15.2 for all 18 parents.

error and sampling bias in the next section. Thus we have not obtained representative sample estimates of the average education of our population of 18 parents from either Sample A or Sample B. Although the risk of selecting such a poor result is small, there is a sampling technique that minimizes the selection of such misleading results. This technique, called *stratified random sampling,* is described next.

Stratified random sampling.   One way to improve the representation obtained through simple random sampling would be to arrange our population of 18 parents into strata or layers. An obvious method of stratification would be to group the parents into their three educational levels: high school diploma or less, some college, and college degree or more. We can then take a random sample from each stratum or subgroup. Stratified random sampling consists of setting up homogeneous strata or subgroups, then independently and randomly selecting subjects from each stratum. For instance, in the earlier example of eight elementary schools, three grade levels, and student sexes, we had used those three variables for stratification to produce 48 subgroups. We can then randomly select from each stratum. Two types of stratified random selection are commonly used: *proportional* and *equal size* stratified sampling. We shall explain each briefly.

In *proportional stratified sampling,* using the school parent population to obtain a sample of six, we can select *one* of the three parents with high school diploma or less; *two* of the six parents with some college education; and *three* of the nine parents with a college degree or more; that is, *one third* of the parents in each stratum. We can use the short list of random numbers given previously to select the first number between 1 and 3; the first two between 4 and 9; and the first three between 10 and 18. We can also use the expanded table of random numbers in Appendix D. The sample would look like Table 5.6.

Since each parent had the same chance of selection in our sample (one in three), we do not need to weight the separate strata results to find the average years of education for the six parents. Thus, the definition of a *proportional stratified selection* is that an equal proportion of subjects from each stratum is randomly selected.

One would intuitively expect—and rightly so—that we have a better estimate from this stratified sample than from a simple random sample of any six parents. The reason is that we are certain to have parents of each variety in our stratified sample, thereby avoiding such extreme samples as six parents all with a college degree or more. In the stratified sampling method, there are 3,780 possible samples of six each, compared to the 18,564 samples of six each possible in simple random sampling.

Equal size stratified sampling would include the selection of *two* parents with a high school diploma or less, *two* parents with some college

Table 5.6 Proportional Stratified Sample

Educational level or stratum	Parent Number	Years of education
Parents with a high school diploma or less	3	9
Parents with some college education	9	14
	4	13
	16	20
Parents with a college degree or more	15	16
	18	16
	Total	88
	Average	14.6[a]

[a] Compared with 15.2 for all 18 parents.

education, and *two* parents with a college degree or more. Thus equal size stratified selection would involve obtaining an equal number of subjects randomly from each stratum or subgroup, and then weighting the results of each. Once again we will use the list of random numbers to select the parents in each stratum.

Obviously, if we select ⅔ of the parents with high school diploma or less in the population, ⅓ of the parents with some college education, and ⅖ of the parents with a college degree or more, we must adjust for these varying proportions to obtain an acceptable result. The so-called *weighting factor* included in Table 5.7 is the inverse of the sampling

Table 5.7 Equal Size Stratified Sample

Stratum	Parent number	Years of education	Weighting factor	Weighted totals
Parents with high school degree	3	9		
	2	10		
Total		19	3/2	28.5
Parents with some college education	9	14		
	4	13		
Total		27	6/2	81.0
Parents with a college degree or more	16	20		
	15	16		
Total		36	9/2	162.0
Grand total				271.5
Weighted average (total ÷ 18)			15.1[a]	

[a] Compared with 15.2 for all 18 parents.

Stratified Random Sampling

proportion; that is, we selected ⅔ of the parents; hence, our weighting factor is ³⁄₂. One obvious disadvantage of this sampling technique is the need for the extra step to weight each level of your variable. However, having equal numbers of subjects in your subgroups is a definite advantage when selecting appropriate statistical analysis, as we shall see in Chapters 9 and 10.

Cluster random sampling. Cluster random sampling is the random selection of areas, groups, or clusters such as schools, classrooms, areas of city; then individuals within these clusters or areas are selected. Each cluster or group must have the same mixture of characteristics as any other group. If this heterogeneous balance does not exist, cluster random sampling would be inappropriate since there would be no accurate representation of defining characteristics from population to sample.

Another way of selecting a sample of six parents from our population would be to group the 18 into heterogeneous groups. We can do this by making up three clusters, each cluster containing one parent with high school diploma or less, two parents with some college education, and three parents with a college degree or more.

Again using the short list of random numbers, the first number between 1 and 3 turns out to be 3, hence Cluster 3 is selected for our sample. The average years of education of the parents in this sample is 15.3, compared with the population average of 15.2.

In general, the most precise results under cluster sampling are obtained when each cluster contains as heterogeneous a grouping as possible and when each heterogeneous cluster is as nearly like the others as possible. The reason the cluster sample estimate in Table 5.8 is so good is that the parents in each cluster are all combined, and each of the three clusters resembles the others closely; that is, each has the same number of parents across clusters.

Cluster sampling is often feasible in preparing sample estimates from data contained in a large number of punch cards. If the cards are stored in several drawers, each drawer can be considered a cluster. Then, several drawers can be picked at random, and either all or a designated fraction of the cards from each drawer can be selected for the final sample.

Systematic random sampling. Systematic random sampling specifies that every *n*th individual of a population listing or roster is selected; the

Table 5.8 Cluster Random Sampling

Cluster 1		Cluster 2		Cluster 3	
Parent number	*Years of education*	*Parent number*	*Years of education*	*Parent number*	*Years of education*
1	12	2	10	3	9
4	13	6	15	8	14
5	15	7	14	9	14
10	20	13	16	16	20
11	18	14	17	17	19
12	19	15	16	18	16
Total	97		88		92
Average	16.1		14.7		15.3

*n*th element is selected randomly. For instance, if we define a population as the 32 students currently enrolled in this research course, and we want to obtain a sample of 10 students, we should randomly select *one* number from our table of random numbers. If, for instance, the number 5 is selected, then the 5th, 10th, 15th, 20th, 25th, 30th, 3rd, 9th, 16th, and 22nd student would be selected. After we go through the list once, we continue to take every fifth person remaining.

We also want to ensure that the first number which was randomly selected allows everyone in the sample an equal chance of being selected. For instance, if we randomly selected 1, 2, or 3, we would have obtained our sample of 10 before we had gone through the entire list of 32. Thus we need to set a minimum limit of random numbers acceptable for the particular population. In this example, we would not accept any number less than 4 nor larger than 9 for purposes of efficiency.

Returning to our parent population of 18, we can select a sample of six parents in the following way. First select at random a number between 3 and 9. Let us select 4 for example. We then include parent number 4 and every fourth parent thereafter in our sample. Our sample would consist of parent numbers 4, 8, 12, 16, 2, and 7. Systematic random sampling is used frequently because it is simple, direct, and inexpensive. When a list of names or items is available, systematic random sampling is often an efficient approach. In selecting a sample of punch cards from drawers full of cards, a ruler is sometimes used to select, say, one card per inch. The sample thus obtained may be treated as a systematic random sample for all practical purposes.

Finally, in specifying a representative sample from our population, we might express it like this:

> A sample of 720 male and female first-, third-, and sixth-grade children from eight elementary schools were randomly selected. The sample was selected using a stratified random procedure based on four schools, three grade levels, and sex. Thus, 48 strata were obtained, and 15 children were drawn from each level. The schools were selected based on geographic location, urban setting, and comparable size student populations from the main school district which serves the city area.

Biased sampling.   A frequent source of bias in sampling is the purposeful selection of a sample which is convenient or biased. There are three types of these inappropriate samples: chunk, judgment, and quota.

Chunk samples selected for convenience fall into this category. Selecting your fifth-grade class, your junior high, your neighborhood, your family, and so forth, because they are accessible is a biased procedure. You cannot generalize beyond that particular chunk. If you select the student union pub to conduct a study on temperance, you may be accused of highly biased chunk sampling.

Judgment samples, although sometimes yielding good results, can encounter error and bias since even the judgment of experts varies considerably in the selection of representative samples. Selecting your boss, your colleagues, your close friends, your enemies, and so forth, will also produce error and bias.

Quota samples also possess the defect of depending on the researcher rather than on random selection. Such a sample might specify that the researcher obtain data from 50 males, ages 35–55, with incomes from $7,000–$11,000. Although these demographic variables restrict the researcher to some degree from making a thoroughly unrepresentative selection, he or she may elect to conduct the interviews during a double-header at the local baseball stadium.

All these procedures represent sampling bias. Additional sources of sampling bias are possible. First we will consider the distinction between *sampling error* and *sampling bias;* then we will consider several procedural flaws which can produce both bias and error. Additional sources of bias are examined in the threats to internal and external validity section in the next chapter.

Sampling Error and Bias

Sampling bias, first encountered in Chapter 1, is the result of not accurately representing the salient parameters of the population in the sample. All the biased sampling techniques discussed are prone to this sampling bias. Possible confounding variables which influence the sample and which are not representative of the population parameters will also produce sampling bias. For instance, if our population had an equal percentage of males and females but our sample contained 80 percent males and 20 percent females, the results may be biased because they do not accurately represent a population characteristic in our sample. Thus, the sex of the subject becomes a possible confounding variable. Sampling bias is usually caused by poor planning.

Differentiating Error from Bias

Sampling error differs from sampling bias in that sampling error is not under the control of the researcher; that is, it is due to the particular random sample obtained. Specifically, *sampling error* is the discrepancy, due to random sampling, between the true value of the population parameter and the sample estimate of that parameter. A misunderstanding exists among many practitioners who believe that the sample is an exact replica of the population, containing the identical characteristics in the same proportion. For example, if everyone in your class selected random samples of 100 teachers from the population of teachers in your city, the mean of the samples would not all be identical. As we saw from the examples given in the section on simple random sampling, some estimates of the mean would be high, some would be low, although most would cluster around the mean of the population parameter being measured. This variability in the sample means that, in their attempt to estimate the population mean, there is sampling error. As mentioned above, this error is not due to the researcher or the process of random selection used, but reflects chance variations that occur whenever a number of randomly selected sample means are calculated.

However, the expected size of this sampling error can be estimated. It is a statistic called the *standard error of the mean,* and is derived from a principle known as the *central limit theorem.* The important conclusion from this theorem, for our purposes, is that the larger the sample, the smaller the standard error of the mean.

If a random selection design is chosen, it is possible to predetermine the size of sample needed to obtain a specified degree of precision. For instance, Winer (1971) can be examined. The standard error of the mean of random samples makes it possible to keep sampling error within desired limits. The following paragraphs—by no means exhaustive—state some of the more important types of errors we should be concerned about when gathering data. Further distinctions of bias are explained in Chapter 6 in the section dealing with threats to internal and external validity.

Identifying Types of Errors

Reporting and processing errors.   One type of error is a result of the capriciousness of human perspective. It is a well-known paradox, for instance, that the average age of women over forty, as reported by the ladies, is under forty, and that the average height of men under five feet five inches, as reported by the gentlemen, is more than five feet five inches. For equally esoteric reasons, a grapefruit picker may report his occupation as citrus grower. Some people may even report different figures for the same variable, such as personal income as listed on a credit application and as reported on the income tax form. Because human beings are human, reporting errors do occur. Processing errors can also be a problem. Basic facts may be entered incorrectly, copied erroneously, coded improperly, manipulated ineptly, or omitted completely. Again, the human factor operates at times against the scientific method.

Volunteer and voluntary responses.   Sometimes the assessment situation encourages bias. One type of bias comes from volunteers and voluntary responses. A person planning an assessment may reason as follows:

> I don't see how this method of selecting these businesses, these families, or these students will have any bearing on the characteristics to be determined from the sample. Therefore, there is no reason to believe that those selected are different from those not selected, and therefore there should be no bias.

Such reasoning is common in situations where little or no planning has occurred. Volunteers may differ from nonvolunteers on important variables, such as motivation, interest, and so forth, which can influence the results. In the case of mailed questionnaires, the argument may be that, since there is *no apparent reason* why any of those who respond will differ from those who do not, the ones who do happen to respond will constitute a random sample of the population. Sometimes a response is obtained from a very high percentage of people in the sample, as high as 85–95 percent. In such instances reliable results may be expected. But with a lower rate of return, the risk of increasing bias results. For instance, if you receive only a 50 percent return of answered questionnaires from the selected sample, the individuals who return the questionnaire may have defining characteristics different from those who have not responded. The various defining characteristics may include age, sex, or occupation groups. If you wish to sample families who do not have children in school as well as those who do, the ones with children in school could make up a large percentage of the 50 percent returns. Therefore, in reporting results, you will need to correct for possible bias, because they may not actually reflect the opinions and/or concerns of your stated sample originally to be tested, namely, families with both school and nonschool members. In such ways, voluntary responses may cause bias.

Discard of inappropriate sample.   One flagrant bias is caused by the decision to select an alternative sample after looking at sample results. An obvious way to arrive at biased results is to examine the returns from an initial sample to see whether they appear acceptable; if they do, you use the results as they are; if they do not, you discard the sample results and draw upon a new sample in the hope that your results will more nearly conform to those you expected. Such an approach can be used to obtain almost any results desired; it could be used to "prove" any hypothesis, even when unbiased methods of selecting the sample and making individual estimates are used.

This is not to suggest that you should refrain from questioning the results when you find that they contradict other data. Often the results of compilations, from samples or censuses or other sources, err for various reasons. The errors could have resulted from mistakes in computation, compilation, interviewing technique, and so on. Obviously, the results should be checked thoroughly. Administrative controls should be established to avoid such errors; verification procedures and error correction should be carried through whether or not the results appear to show what you expect.

Some of the areas of sampling bias relate to particular procedures that should be, but are not, systematically followed. The next chapter on constructing a procedure will expand on these distinctions. Prior to presenting an example of a Subjects subsection, we need to understand the distinction between random selection and random assignment.

Random Selection and Random Assignment

Differentiating Selection from Assignment

Random selection is the process of obtaining a sample from a defined population. We have discussed four types: *simple, stratified, cluster,* and *systematic random.* All our earlier discussions have centered on the notion of random selection.

Random assignment is the process of assigning or dividing subjects from the sample into treatment groups; for example, experimental and control groups. For most types of studies, this assigning of subjects is very desirable to further minimize error. Subjects are assigned to groups using similar random procedures such as names or numbers in a jar. Figure 5.1 illustrates the process.

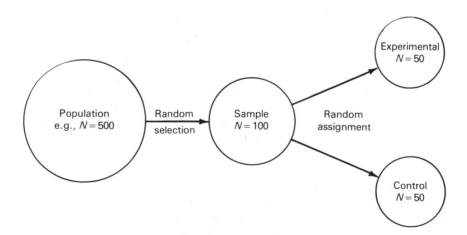

Figure 5.1 Random Assignment

Depending upon the type of research study, you could have:

random selection and random assignment
no random selection but random assignment
random selection and no random assignment
no random selection and no random assignment

If the subjects have already been placed in groups, such as a classroom or counseling group, then random assignment may not be possible. In such situations random selection may occur without random assignment. Many studies may also be able to randomly assign subjects to treatment but initially could not randomly select from the population. Obviously, the situation to avoid because of possible error and bias is when neither random selection nor random assignment is possible.

It is important to remember this distinction between random selection and random assignment, since both should be considered in the Subjects subsection. In addition, types of research will vary because of the presence or absence of random assignment. We will further analyze this distinction when we discuss the types of research in Chapter 7.

Examples of Subjects Subsections

As we said at the beginning of this chapter, the Subjects subsection should answer three basic questions: Who? How many? and How were they selected? In addition, the number assigned to each treatment or condition should be stated. The type, number, and reason for those who dropped out of the study should be given. Payments and promises made should also be stated; and the location of the study should be included, by both geographic region and institution (Publication manual of APA, 1974).

The following Subjects subsection reported by Zimmerman and Kinsler (1979) contains the major components listed above:

Subjects
Fifty-four boys and 54 girls were selected in equal numbers from kindergarten and first-grade classes at a New York City public school located in a lower-class area of Harlem. The first graders ranged in age from 6 years 0 months to 7 years 6 months, and were comparable in age to the 6-year-olds in the Walters and Parke (1964) study. The kindergarteners ranged in age from 5 years 1 month to 6 years 0 month and were comparable in age to the 5-year-olds in the Walters et al. (1963) study.

> The children were of either black or Hispanic origin. Within each age group, the children were randomly assigned to treatment condition.

We can conclude from the first sentence that a stratified random selection by grade level occurred. From the last sentence, we can also conclude that assignment from the two grades to the particular treatment conditions was random. The additional information presented seems to answer the questions we posed earlier. The Subjects subsection by Moore (1979) also seems to answer these basic questions.

> *Subjects*
> The tasks to measure the transitive relation within seriation problems were administered to a sample of 88 male children in a suburban middle-class elementary school. The sample was a stratified random selection from 16 classrooms, four at each grade level from kindergarten through third grade. Thus, 22 children were drawn from each grade level. Sample size was determined following Winer's (1962) procedure. With a moderate-effect size and a .05 significance level, a sample size of 22 gives a power of .90. Age ranged from 65 months to 122 months, with mean ages of 72.4, 82.4, 95.6, and 109.5 months for the four grades.

In this example random assignment was not conducted because of the purpose of this study. It assessed transitive performance by grade level and thus no treatment condition was employed.

The Foulds and Hannigan (1976) study also seems to meet these basic questions.

> *Subjects*
> The subjects were 72 college students who volunteered to participate in a 24-hour marathon Gestalt workshop at the university counseling center. The volunteers responded to announcements in the campus newspaper and/or to the word-of-mouth communications of participants in previous marathon groups. Such groups had been offered to students as personal growth experiences on a regular basis for several years, and the subjects were selected from the top of a waiting list (of over 100 individuals) for such an event. The first 36

males and 36 females who were available on the designated weekends were selected to participate. They ranged from freshmen to first-year graduate students and from 18 to 28 years of age ($\overline{X}$ = 20.1 years). All volunteers participated in a 20–30 minute pregroup interview with one of the workshop leaders to screen for severe psychopathology, to describe the purpose and goals of the workshop and the types of techniques and methods that would be used, to share assumptions regarding the responsibilities of workshop members and leaders, to explain the design of and request the person's cooperation in the research study, and to provide an opportunity for the exploration and expression of thoughts and feelings concerning the event and for making a personal decision with commitment regarding participation. Agreement to participate in research is a well-known and usual condition for acceptance into marathon workshops at this center. The subjects were informed of the purpose of testing and the amount of testing they would be contracting to participate in.

You should start to generate your own concerns from this study, however, about conditions that might affect its results, such as an all-volunteer sample, lack of random assignment, extended age range, prior knowledge of testing purpose interacting with marathon workshop and later testing, and so forth. These limiting conditions need to be taken into account when analyzing and generalizing implications from the results.

SUMMARY

We have examined the four basic steps for selecting a sample: (1) Define the population, (2) Compile major demographic characteristics of the population, (3) Obtain a large enough sample to represent the characteristics of the population, and (4) Compile a population list and select representative people from it. We have discussed four types of random selection sampling techniques for selecting representative subjects: simple random, stratified random, cluster random, and systematic random. We have also described three types of biased sampling: chunk, judgment, and quota. Important distinctions between random assignment and random selection were also made. Finally, we examined examples of Subjects subsections.

—— OBJECTIVES ————————————————

In Chapter 5 we have looked at the steps in selecting the sample from our population. We have discussed how the population is defined, how the number is determined, and how the subjects are selected. In addition, we have explored the ways in which sampling error and bias can creep into our work. Confirm your understanding of the material in Chapter 5 using the following objectives:

Identify the characteristics of the population, how the number is determined, and how the subjects are selected.

Evaluate the total selection process for specificity and consistency.

Analyze the Subjects subsection for the possibilities of sampling error and/or bias.

Differentiate between random selection and random assignment.

—— TERMS ————————————————

biased sampling
chunk sampling
cluster random sampling
effect size
equal size stratified sampling
judgment sampling
population
power
proportional stratified sampling
quota sampling

random assignment
random selection
sample
sampling bias
sampling error
simple random sampling
standard error of the mean
stratified random sampling
systematic random sampling

Constructing a Procedure:
Types of Variables

What are the types of variables, and what is their relationship to each other?

What are the threats to internal validity, and how does each operate?

What are the threats to external validity, and how does each operate?

Procedure

Types of variables	Threats to validity	Types of research designs*	Result
Independent and dependent	Internal	Experimental Quasi-experimental Descriptive Single-subject Historical Meta-analysis	Replicable procedure
Control	History Maturation Testing Instrumentation Statistical regression Differential selection Attrition Interaction between selection and maturation		
Extraneous and confounding	External		

External

Population
Interaction of personological variables and treatment effects
Comparison of accessible population and target population

Ecology
Explicit description of independent variable
Multiple-treatment interference
Hawthorne effect
Novelty and disruption effects
Experimenter effect
Pretest sensitization
Posttest sensitization
Interaction of history and treatment effects
Measurement of independent variables
Interaction of time of measurement and treatment effects

*Details in Chapter 7

The Procedure subsection of the research article should present a concise and specific summary of each step of the research process. It should be written with sufficient clarity and specificity to allow other researchers to replicate the study. Thus, such key features as how instructions were given to subjects, how groups were formed, what special manipulations were unique to the study, and what other procedures were used to minimize error should be succinctly delineated. In a way similar to the specific statement of the subjects discussed in the previous chapter, the Procedure subsection should present the operational definitions of the independent variables as well as the "How?" of the specific steps in implementing the research investigation.

Constructing a Procedure involves not only keeping a comprehensive record of the research process—it also involves discriminating among the variables in the specific research study. Careful discrimination facilitates the entire research process, including the Procedure subsection, the statement of purpose and hypotheses, as well as the statistical analyses that follow.

In this chapter we will discuss four main types of variables encountered in educational research and will consider numerous threats to a study's validity. Chapter 7 will cover the variety of research designs encountered in educational research. At its conclusion, we shall examine several Procedure subsections to show the relationship between variables and various types of research designs.

Types of Variables

The variables already discussed in our statement of purpose and hypotheses can be divided into four types:

> independent variables
> dependent variables
> extraneous or confounding variables
> control variables

One reason for discriminating among the types of variables is that it helps in accurately selecting the appropriate statistical analysis. It also enables us to construct a valid research design. We may thus be able to apply the scientific method so as to minimize any error or bias. Because of their relationship to each other, we shall discuss the first two types of variables together and the remaining two types separately.

Independent and Dependent Variables

We shall introduce these two types of variables by considering a simple purpose statement from Chapter 2:

> The main purpose of this study is to compare the effectiveness of two reading methods, sight and phonics, in increasing the reading comprehension of second graders.

There are two variables here: *reading method* at two levels, sight and phonics, and *reading comprehension*. The investigator has chosen to study the effect of the first variable—reading method at two levels, sight and phonics—on the second variable—reading comprehension.

Distinguishing between the two.   The one or more variables that the experimenter selects or manipulates in order to determine its effect on other variables is called the *independent variable.* The independent variable is independent of any subject's behavior; it is a situation, characteristic, or phenomenon within which the subject functions. In addition, any independent variable must have at least two levels, values, or groups to compare. Thus the two values or levels of reading methods which the experimenter chooses to examine are sight and phonics. These two groups are independent of any subject control. The effect of subjects being placed into each particular group will be assessed by some reading comprehension measure or score, which is a dependent variable.

A *dependent variable* attempts to measure the effect or the results of the treatment of the independent variable(s). A dependent variable depends upon the independent variable and varies as a function of the independent variable. More specifically, the dependent variable varies according to a subject's behavior or performance within a particular level or group of the independent variable. In our example, reading comprehension is the dependent variable because the score is dependent upon the type of reading method received, sight or phonics (the independent variable).

Further clarification.   To further clarify our understanding of a dependent variable, recall the distinction in Chapter 1 between a concept or construct and an operational definition. A concept or construct is an abstraction derived from some aspect of human behavior that varies among individuals. In this example, the dependent variable, reading comprehension, is a concept. We may operationalize the concept in many ways in order to obtain a measure or score for each subject. For instance, we could select one of several standardized tests, some with an essay format and some with a multiple-choice format. In each case we would be generating a different operational definition for the concept of reading comprehension. Thus, differences in the results of a study would vary according to how we have operationally defined the con-

Independent Variable Operating on the Dependent Variable

cept. However, the concept *reading comprehension* remains the dependent variable and *reading comprehension score* (in this example, the *reading comprehension subtest score on the Iowa Tests of Basic Skills (ITBS)*) becomes a measurement type of operational definition of the dependent variable. Usually the operational definition of the dependent variable is expressed as some kind of score. It may be as simple as scores on a standardized test, or it may be expressed less obviously as a frequency or head count, a rating, or as the number of seconds required for a task.

It is possible for a researcher to get a different result in a study by using a different operational definition. This is why it is so important to distinguish between a variable as a concept and the operational definition of it. The relationship between a variable as a concept and its operational definition holds true for the independent variable. If we are studying the effect of two reading methods upon reading comprehension, then, just as the concept of reading comprehension is the dependent variable, so the concept of reading method is the independent variable. Thus, reading method must still be given an operational definition; namely, what is the sight method used and what is the phonics method used in the research study? More specifically, an experimental type of operational definition must be given. If three publishing companies each publish a separate phonics series, then each of these series is an operational definition of the concept called *phonics reading method.*

In research studies, the Procedure subsection of the Method section should contain the operational definitions of the independent variables while the Instrumentation subsection should contain the operational definitions of the dependent variables.

A closer look at independent variables.   The distinction between the two types of operational definitions—the experimental type and the measurement type—relates directly to two main types of independent variables that we shall delineate. (Other authors, such as Borg and Gall (1979), delineate five types; however, two distinctions seem adequate.) Recall from Chapter 1 that an experimental type of operational definition specifies or defines how a researcher will manipulate a variable, and a measurement type of operational definition describes how a concept will be assessed or measured. These two types of operational definitions relate directly to the two types of independent variables.

The two types of independent variables are: (1) those in which the investigator has manipulative control and (2) those which have already occurred, so that there is no manipulative control over the independent variable(s). The former is an *experimental* type and the latter is a *measurement* type of operational definition.

Examples of independent variables where the investigator usually has manipulative control include:

type of incentive at three levels: praise, token, and no incentive.
counseling at four levels: Gestalt, rational-emotive, desensitization, and no counseling.
type of learning at three levels: self-study, computer assisted, and small group.

Usually, with all these examples, the researchers have manipulative control over the type of variable and the particular levels to be examined. They select the counseling therapies or the different incentives to be examined. We may hope the manipulations or levels selected have a firm rationale grounded in theory, research, or practical experience.

We should be precise in stating our independent variables. In the three examples, we would be technically incorrect if we stated that the independent variables for a particular study were types of incentive, counseling, and learning groups. For every independent variable the values or levels must be clearly specified. This will increase clarity and facilitate the interrelationship among various research components. For instance, type of counseling could vary from as few as two levels—counseling and no counseling—to several. In addition, the same two (or more) levels for one study can be and usually are defined differently from one study to another. For instance, type of counseling at two levels can be expressed in several ways: counseling and no counseling, TA and traditional, and behavior modification and Gestalt. This could go on almost indefinitely. Thus, as we increase the precision in our research process, we decrease the amount of error operating in it.

The other type of independent variable has already occurred so that the experimenter has no manipulative control over it. All these variables will receive measurement types of operational definitions. These variables include the *environmental settings* of the subjects, such as:

socioeconomic status
geographic region
classroom style
grade level/college level
urban/rural location

It also includes *personological* (or subject) *characteristics,* such as:

age
sex
ethnicity
marital status
religious affiliation
years of education
grade point average

Remember that, if any of these are being used as independent variables, at least two levels will have to be specified. The levels we select will depend upon the personological parameters in the population for a specific research study.

Various personological characteristics of subjects are used by researchers as independent variables. For instance, if you wanted to determine how a person's level of creativity varied as a function of the type of anxiety (high, average, or low), you might first administer an anxiety test. Once you obtained the range of scores for your sample, you would stratify the scores into high, average, or low with one-third in each grouping. Even though test scores were obtained, anxiety is not a dependent measure. Rather, the test scores were used to form groups for an independent variable: type of anxiety (high, average, or low). The dependent variable, creativity, will be examined to see how it varies according to level of anxiety.

Thus, we cannot automatically conclude that any measurement type of operational definition is a dependent variable. Some researchers will use test scores to form groups of an independent variable. How the test scores are used subsequently in the research design then becomes an important additional consideration. Most often they will be used as dependent measures, but they can also be used to eventually form levels of an independent variable. That independent variable, here anxiety at three levels (high, average, and low), then is a measurement type of operational definition for a nonmanipulated independent variable because the subject's level of anxiety has already occurred. We are just measuring and grouping it rather than experimentally manipulating it. Thus, an independent variable can be operationalized either as a measurement type or an experimental type, while a dependent variable is operationalized as a measurement type of operational definition.

Extraneous or Confounding Variables

The third type of variable we shall delineate is the extraneous or confounding variable. *Confounding variables* are either unknown or not controlled by the researcher and may systematically influence the results obtained from the dependent measure. When taken into account by the investigator, a possible confounding variable can become either an independent or a control variable. A confounding variable can affect the independent variable, the dependent variable, or both.

For instance, suppose we are interested in determining the effect of three counseling techniques—rational-emotive, gestalt, and no counseling—in lowering anxiety levels of volunteer clients at a local mental health facility. However, we neglect to screen our subjects for severe psychopathology. Instead of having just average neurotics in the counseling group, a paranoid psychotic is included in the rational-emotive group. At the conclusion of the study, anxiety level scores are significantly higher in a posttest of that group when compared to the others. Even the control group maintains its anxiety level, or perhaps even decreases it slightly. What do you conclude? If you realize what has happened, that the group members' anxiety score is not just dependent upon the independent variable—type of counseling—but dependent upon the confounding variable—type of psychopathology—then your results can be explained. The paranoid psychotic could have influenced the anxiety level of the other group members as well as disrupted the treatment. Thus, the particular confounding variable has influenced both the independent and the dependent variables. The results obtained for that group will have little meaning and questionable validity for determining the effectiveness of the rational-emotive type of counseling treatment.

Other less obvious examples may produce confounding variables that influence the results of the dependent measures. A less obvious example might include: subjects who varied systematically instead of randomly on some demographic characteristic, such as a disproportionate percentage of males to females in the groups; or we might collect the majority of our data through mailed questionnaires and the rest through phone interviews. In these instances, the results would depend not only on the independent variable, but on the sex of the subjects or the type of assessment procedure, respectively. When a possible confounding variable is not taken into account by the investigator, it threatens either the internal validity or the external validity of the study.

Control Variables

A possible confounding variable that is taken into account by the investigator in the research is called a *control variable*. Typically, control variables are independent variables not under manipulative control by the researcher but included in the research design to prevent error from occurring or to account for any error operating. Thus, a control variable is a possible confounding variable which may influence the results of the study and which is taken into account by the researcher when planning and implementing the research process.

Controlling Variables

The influence of a possible confounding variable on the dependent variable(s) can be controlled or minimized in three ways:

Build the control variable into the research design.
Examine only one level of the control variable.
Statistically remove the effects of the control variable.

We shall discuss each type of procedure briefly.

Build the control variable into the research design. The first way to minimize the effects of a possible confounding variable is to build it into the research design. It then becomes an added independent variable. For example, if we know from past theory, research, or experience that boys score lower than girls on reading comprehension tests, we can measure the influence of sex by incorporating it into the design as a second independent variable. Thus, our results on the dependent measure, *reading comprehension scores,* will be analyzed by both sex and reading method, not just by reading method. Our new design is shown in Table 6.1. This gives a total of four groups, called *cells,* in each of which the score will depend upon the subjects' sex—male or female—and reading method—sight or phonics. The effect on the dependent measure due to sex (as well as reading method) can then be assessed.

Examine only one level of the control variable. A second way to minimize the effects of a possible confounding variable is to examine only one level of the control variable. For instance, if a variable such as sex has been found from past theory, research, or experience to influence the results, then instead of building it into the research design as a separate independent variable, we could assess only one level, that is, test only females or only males, not both. If we were determining only one

Table 6.1 Reading Comprehension Scores

Reading method	Sex	Reading comprehension score
Sight ($N = 30$)	Male ($N = 15$)	$S_1, S_2, S_3, \ldots, S_{15}$ Scores
	Female ($N = 15$)	$S_{16}, S_{17}, S_{18}, \ldots, S_{30}$ Scores
Phonics ($N = 30$)	Male ($N = 15$)	$S_{31}, S_{32}, S_{33}, \ldots, S_{45}$ Scores
	Female ($N = 15$)	$S_{46}, S_{47}, S_{48}, \ldots, S_{60}$ Scores

level of a variable characteristic such as sex, we should delineate the controlling features in the Sample or Subjects subsection of the research article. The disadvantage of assessing only one level of a variable is that it limits the ability to generalize the results. Instead of generalizing to the entire population of third graders, you would be able to generalize only to either the male or female third graders.

Statistically remove the effects of the control variable.   A third way to minimize the effects of a possible confounding variable is to account for the effects of the variable statistically after the research has been conducted. Two statistical techniques frequently used to achieve this are: analysis of covariance and partial correlation. Simply stated, both of these techniques remove the linear effect of a possible confounding variable from the results obtained for the dependent measure. The adjusted results are then analyzed and interpreted. For instance, we could statistically remove the effect of sex on verbal comprehension scores and then analyze the adjusted scores to determine if differences still exist as a function of the type of reading method. Chapter 10 will discuss these techniques further.

Variables in the Research Literature

I have attempted to simplify the many types of variables by discussing four main types. In the educational research literature, you will encounter many other names that refer to the four distinctions we have made. For instance, independent and dependent variables are frequently referred to as *predictor* and *criterion* variables respectively, especially in regression analyses. The goal is to determine which subset of predictor variables best defines or predicts scores for the criterion variable. Control variables may also be labeled *concomitant, covariate,* or *blocking* variables. *Concomitant* variables or *covariates* are any variables that are correlated with (or that covary with) the dependent variable. These terms are most frequently used with the statistical test, analysis of covariance. When used in this context, it is the variable whose effect on the dependent variable is statistically controlled. Recall from our previous discussion of control variables that this procedure is the third way to minimize the effect of confounding variables operating. *Blocking variables* are environmental or personological variables that have been built into the research design. You will encounter this term with research designs that are called block designs; specific types you will encounter are randomized block designs and incomplete block designs. It is the first way to minimize error discussed in the control variables section.

There are still other labels which represent confounding or extraneous variables. *Nuisance* and *limiting* variables are two more labels used to represent these terms. When possible confounding or extraneous variables are not controlled, the effect these variables produce on the scores of the dependent variable may also be called by other names. We have called this effect *bias* or *error;* recall our earlier discussion of sampling bias. *Bias* is any systematic deviation from a true value. Other terms such as *contamination* or *artifact* may also be used. *Contamination* refers to the introduction of confounding variables or random error into a set of data such that the results are distorted or influenced. An *artifact* generally refers to artificial data produced by the procedures used in the study which are not the result or effect of the independent variable.

Whether the term used is *bias, error, contamination,* or *artifact,* all refer to the effect of possible confounding or extraneous variables operating. Further distinctions of types of confounding variables have been made in the educational literature. These distinctions are called *threats to internal and external validity.*

Threats to Internal and External Validity

Campbell and Stanley (1963) differentiated possible confounding variables according to whether they pose threats to internal or to external validity. Later, Bracht and Glass (1968) expanded Campbell and Stanley's (1963) analysis to make additional distinctions of threats to external validity. Basically, internal validity concerns the internal fitness or rigor of the research design. Our study increases in internal validity as we control for the possible effect of confounding variables. As we control confounding variables and thus minimize the operation of error, we can conclude that any observed change in our study is due to the independent variable—not to any extraneous variables that threaten the internal validity.

Threats to external validity concern the degree to which we can generalize our findings to a larger population. That is, with what degree of reliability can we transfer the results from the sample to the entire population? We shall discuss the major threats to both internal and external validity of a study. Following this we shall give several examples of different threats as encountered in the research literature.

Threats to Internal Validity

Campbell and Stanley (1963) delineated eight classes of extraneous or confounding variables that can threaten the internal validity of a research design:

history	statistical regression
maturation	differential selection
testing	attrition
instrumentation	selection-maturation interaction

History.   Since most research studies continue over a period of time, other events may occur in addition to the independent variable or treatment which can account for a change in the dependent measure. For instance, if we have a group of clients receiving therapy over a twelve-week span in order to lower their anxiety level, and we give them a pretest before the treatment and a posttest following it, extraneous variables over the twelve-week span may influence the posttest scores. Some clients may have started individual therapy; some may have undergone a divorce or separation; others may have started a new job, relationship, or graduate school. Any of these possible extraneous variables could have affected their posttest scores. We would not know whether the observed changes in the scores on the two tests were due to the independent variable or to the operation of extraneous variables.

Maturation.   During the course of a research study, biological or psychological processes may operate to produce a change in the individual. Physical, social-emotional, or cognitive changes may occur. Subjects

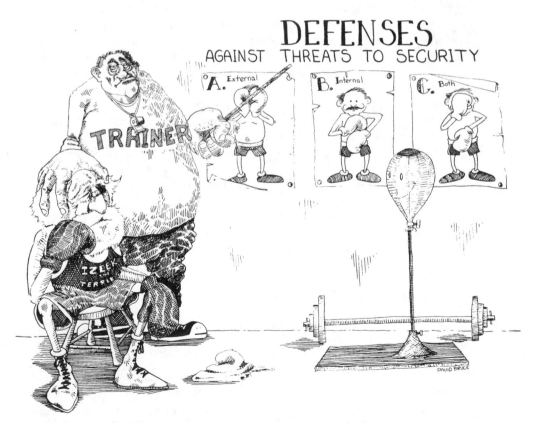

Threats to Internal and External Validity

may become more mature, less egocentric, or more intellectually developed than previously. Subjects may also become more or less motivated, fatigued, or discouraged than when they started. For instance, if over the course of a school year we are examining the effectiveness of a new reading curriculum for increased reading comprehension in grades four through six, maturation rather than the new curriculum may well cause the increases in reading comprehension scores.

Testing.   In many research studies a pretest is administered, the treatment or independent variable operates, and then a posttest is given to measure the effect of the treatment. If the pretest and posttest are identical or similar, subjects may improve scores on the posttest just because of having taken the pretest. Experience with test items, format, and general familiarization or practice on similar tests may improve posttest scores. Thus subjects become more test-wise and perform better not because of the treatment but because of their experience with the pretest. As the time increases between testing, the importance of this extraneous variable usually decreases.

Instrumentation.   If we do try to minimize threats caused by testing, we should also be careful not to increase error brought on by instrumentation. If we change our assessing instrument from pretest to posttest, there may be gains due to the use of a different instrument. For instance, using an easier pretest or posttest, changing the item format from multiple choice to essay, or switching the procedure from mailed questionnaire to phone interview may all cause observed changes in the group. Such changes cannot be attributed solely to the treatment or independent variable. In assessment situations where greater subjectivity may operate, we must take care to minimize it. For instance, when raters or observers are scoring essay measures or rating classroom or client behaviors, the scores or ratings may improve on the posttest because the experimenters *expect* a change to occur. Thus, standardization or uniformity of procedure for scoring should be established to minimize this threat.

Statistical regression.   Statistical regression is the tendency of extremes in a distribution of scores to move closer together, or regress, to the average or mean score upon retesting. This phenomenon is due to the error of measurement contained in extreme scores. The more extreme a score, the larger the error it may contain. Thus, upon retesting, high scores on the average tend to decline and low scores tend to improve.

An analogy from the field of genetics may help. A husband and wife who are extremely tall—for example, six feet four inches and six feet respectively—will tend to have children who are shorter than they are. The child's height will tend to regress toward the average height of the population—five feet seven inches to five feet nine inches—rather than stabilize at about the parent's average height—six feet two inches.

Another example is taken from a classroom setting of thirty children. Based on their reading comprehension test scores, you select the students with the three lowest scores. If you were to retest them, they would tend to score higher on the average then their average scores on the first testing. If, before retesting, you had given nine weeks of remedial reading instruction, you would not be able to tell whether the gains were due to the remedial reading or to statistical regression.

A final example of statistical regression may be seen in many talented and gifted (TAG) programs. Many schools use a high IQ score—greater then 145, which falls at the 99+ percentile—as one selection criterion for their TAG programs. There are many instances in which a group of children are labeled as "gifted" because they have the minimum IQ required on a screening test. Yet, upon subsequent retesting, several score 10 to 20 IQ points lower and are then capriciously "degifted."

Differential selection.   If there is a systematic recruitment of subjects into groups, differential selection may operate. Thus, different scores on subsequent testing may be due to selection rather than to the effects of the independent variable. Comparing the performance of a group of volunteers to that of a control group of nonvolunteers illustrates differential selection. Chapter 5 includes a discussion of volunteers. If groups differed on a demographic characteristic—such as 90 percent males in one group and 80 percent females in another—differences could be attributed to either the treatment or the fact that differential selection occurred with the confounding variable of sex operating. Other examples include convenient or chunk samples, also discussed in Chapter 5. Choosing the first 25 people to come through the door for your experimental group and the next 25 people for your control group illustrates differential selection. The first group may differ in important variables from the second group in such a way as to affect the results; for instance, the first group could be more motivated, more interested, more punctual, or compulsive, and so forth. These systematic differences may affect the scores rather than the treatment itself. The most effective way to control the effects of differential selection is to randomly assign the subjects to treatments. In this way, we may assume that possible systematic differences are randomly distributed between groups.

Attrition or experimental mortality.   If there is a systematic withdrawal in the type of subjects who leave a group, the threat due to attrition may operate. For instance, the lower performing subjects may drop out first; the more disturbed, the less motivated, the more creative, and so forth may systematically leave a particular treatment group. Differences on the dependent measure could then be due not just to the independent variable, but also to attrition. The results of a treatment may be mis-leadingly higher if low achievers leave the experimental group or if high achievers leave the control group. Conversely, lower results may be obtained if high-creative children leave the experimental group or if low-creative children leave the control group. If attrition does occur in a study, the researcher should attempt to measure and explain its possible effects on the results.

Selection-maturation interaction.   Campbell and Stanley (1963) stated that an effect due to interaction of selection and any of the preceding seven threats may operate in a research study. However, the one interaction frequently discussed is that of selection with maturation. Selection-maturation interaction is similar to differential selection except that maturation is the specific confounding variable. That is, a differential assignment of subjects to groups occurs in a way that affects the maturation variable. Children may be assigned to an experimental or control group, for instance, in such a way that the average age differs between the groups, or the two groups may differ in other maturation measures such as physical motor development or cognitive developmental level. Thus, results from the variable may be due to maturation differences rather than the treatment or independent variable.

All eight threats to the internal validity of research designs can be minimized if the experimenter randomly assigns subjects to treatments and incorporates a control group into the research design.

Threats to External Validity: Population

Bracht and Glass (1968) delineated twelve types of extraneous or confounding situations that threaten the external validity of research results. They fall into two broad categories, which Bracht and Glass (1968, p. 438) labeled *population validity* and *ecological validity.* Population validity deals with generalizations to populations of people; that is, what other population of subjects can be expected to respond in the same way as the sample subjects? Two types of threats fall under population validity:

comparison of accessible population and target population
interaction of personological variables and treatment effects

Comparison of accessible population and target population.   The first threat concerns the extent to which the experimenter can generalize from the available population of subjects (the *accessible population*) to the total population (the *target population*). Results of the dependent measure may apply only to the experimentally accessible population from which the subjects were selected and not to the larger target population. In some cases, it may not even be possible to generalize results to the accessible population. This may operate when no inferential statistics are used to analyze the results or when there is no random selection of the accessible population.

The more common threat occurs when generalizing from the accessible population to the target population. For instance, you, the teacher, may have developed a new program for improving reading comprehension in the primary grades. You hope to conclude that your program is better for all first, second, and third graders in the United States (the target population). However, you randomly select your sample from all first, second, and third graders in your school district (the accessible population). In order to generalize your research findings to the target population, you must compare the two populations to determine whether they are similar on all important demographic variables. Frequently, researchers do not randomly select students from the entire district; instead, they select them from the classrooms in one building. Thus the 12 first-through-third-grade classes in Keller Elementary School become the accessible population, and the remaining children in those grades in the district become the target population. If your school is composed mainly of upper-middle-class professional families and the average IQ of your children is 125, generalization of the research findings to all first, second, and third graders in the United States (or even the remaining children in your district) would be highly questionable and pose a serious threat to the external validity of your study.

Interaction of personological variables and treatment effect.   Another threat to the ability to generalize results of a dependent measure is the extent to which personological characteristics of subjects (discussed earlier in this chapter) interact with the treatment or levels of the independent variable. A possible confounding or extraneous variable may operate so as to influence the effects of treatment and thus give results incorrectly generalized to the broader population. For instance, in the previous example, this threat may operate if third graders performed higher and first and second graders performed significantly lower. You cannot generalize for first, second, and third graders that your reading program is effective; you can generalize only for third graders. Thus, grade level (a personological variable) interacted with the treatment (your reading program) to produce a gain for only one level of the personological variable (third grade) rather than for all levels. The best way to minimize the probability of personological variables interacting with the effects of treatment is to build those possible influencing variables into the research design and measure their relative effects. We discussed this approach earlier in the chapter as one of three considered under the broader category of *control variables.* The field of research which systematically studies these interactions is called *aptitude-treatment interaction* research (see Berliner and Cahan, 1973).

Threats to External Validity: Ecology

Ecological validity deals with generalizations about the environmental setting of the study. That is, under what variations in environmental conditions—such as changes in physical setting, length of treatment, time of day, experimenter, dependent measures, and so forth—can similar results be predicted? Bracht and Glass (1968) delineated ten types of threats which may fall under this heading:

explicit description of the independent variable
multiple-treatment interference
Hawthorne effect
novelty and disruption effects
experimenter effect
pretest sensitization
posttest sensitization
interaction of history and treatment effects
measurement of the dependent variable
interaction of time of measurement and treatment effects

Explicit description of the independent variable.   The independent variable must be specifically delineated in the research study to ensure replication and generalization of the results. Detailed descriptions of the physical setting, of experimenter training, of the independent measures as well as explicit directions should be provided in the Procedure subsection of the research article. If you find significant performance gains for gifted children on one level of an instructional method—for instance, shared inquiry—and not on the second or third level—for instance, discovery approach and mentorship—you must describe in the Procedure subsection what the observations entail, otherwise no generalization or replication by others would be possible. Difficulties will arise when you present concept levels of your independent variables but fail to operationalize them to allow replication, for example, traditional and nontraditional; open-learning and self-contained; team and traditional teaching; counseling and no counseling. If the independent variable is not operationally defined as either a measurement type or an experimental type, replication by others is possible only to the degree to which they can read your mind. Usually such mind reading is asking too much of your colleagues.

Multiple-treatment interference.   If a researcher administers two or more treatments consecutively to the same subject, multiple-treatment interference may occur. It is difficult, if not impossible, to isolate the cause of the results. Are they due to both of the treatments or did one or the other treatment produce the effect? Generalizing the results of multiple treatments to settings in which only one treatment occurred threatens the validity of the results.

Suppose you are in a study and are pretested on knowledge of educational research; then in four-week blocks you are exposed to three learning methods: peer teaching, lecture, and computer-assisted instruction. At the end of each four-week block, you receive a posttest, and you make statistically significant gains using computer-assisted instruction. Because of the research design the investigator cannot generalize the findings to settings in which computer-assisted instruction is administered alone. Its effectiveness may depend on the coadministration of the other two treatments. A strategy that minimizes this threat is to randomly assign only one treatment to each subject. Multiple-treatment interference may also occur when the same subjects participate in more than one study. Each study would be considered an additional treatment.

Hawthorne effect.   Knowing that you are a participant in a study may alter your usual responses. These atypical responses are due to the Hawthorne effect. Because of it, the results cannot be explained based on the manipulation of the independent variable. Instead the effect of the situation on your responses—such as more anxious or more relaxed, more cooperative or more defiant, more attentive or more distracted—will artificially affect the scores of the dependent measure.

Concepts related to the Hawthorne effect are the *John Henry effect* and the *placebo effect*. The John Henry effect refers to situations in educational research in which groups not receiving the treatment—such as control groups using a traditional curriculum or counseling—function higher than they normally do. Frequently, when competing with other levels of the independent variable or treatment, such groups try to avoid being beaten by other groups. Teachers in a control group sometimes perform better for the duration of the study—that is, they are better prepared, organized, and motivated—to prove that their way of teaching is as good as any other. Sometimes teachers in the experimental group deliberately try to sabotage an experimental curriculum because it would require too much time and effort to implement the proposed changes. Traditionally, the Hawthorne effect refers to any positive gains by the experimental group, and the John Henry effect to any positive gains by the control group. However, we recommend that you use the term Hawthorne effect to represent any artificial change in scores of the dependent measure, either positive or negative, produced by subjects from any level of the independent variable who knew they were participating in a research study.

Historically, the placebo effect has mainly been of concern to medical and drug researchers. It is the extent to which the act of taking or participating in a treatment, rather than the treatment itself, influences the result. Giving a placebo—which is an inert substance similar in color, taste, and structure to the experimental drug—is an attempt to separate the social and psychological effects—that is, the attention factor involved in receiving a regularly administered drug—from the drug's predicted physiological or biochemical effect. The physiological effect of the drug or treatment can only be determined by comparing the gains obtained with the treatment, with those obtained with the placebo, and with those obtained from a control group which received no placebo.

In educational research, the placebo effect may operate in control groups that do not receive attention comparable to that given the experimental group. Here you would not know whether it was the treatment or the attention surrounding the treatment that produced gains in the dependent measure. However, if you have two groups and, for example, one receives counseling and one does not, you can set up control procedures in either of two ways. The better alternative is to have the control group come into the counseling center for a comparable amount of time each week—comparable, that is, to the amount of time the experimental group spends at the center. The individuals in the no-counseling group may interact as a group although they receive no formal treatment—that is, they may have an informal bull session. The second alternative, frequently but inappropriately used in the research literature, is to have the control subjects remain at their homes and not interact at all in the study. Other than having them together for a pretest and posttest, no interaction occurs. In the first instance, the experimenter is attempting to minimize the influence of the placebo effect by standardizing the amount of peripheral attention each group receives. In the second instance the peripheral attention cannot be adequately determined; therefore, the placebo effect may operate. The ability to generalize research results should be questioned, and perhaps modified, when comparison groups are constructed in a way which does not consider the placebo effect.

Novelty and disruption effects. A new or unusual treatment may exhibit greater gains in the dependent measure when compared to the traditional treatment primarily because it is novel. As the novelty diminishes with time, the greater gains of the treatment may also diminish or disappear. For instance, some teachers may be very enthusiastic about a new curriculum, and this motivation and novelty contribute to greater gains with the new instructional program than with the old. But it is difficult to determine whether the measurement gains are due to the novelty effect or to the superiority of the curriculum.

The counterpart of the novelty effect is the disruption effect that may operate when a new treatment is sufficiently unfamiliar and different that its true effectiveness is not accurately measured during a first analysis. For instance, if teachers using a new curriculum package are still learning how to use it, the results may be lower than they will be later when the teachers have achieved sufficient competency; later the results may be equal to or greater than those of the traditional curriculum.

It is also possible that both novelty and disruption effects may operate in the same study and counterbalance each other. One way to estimate the effects would be to extend the treatment over a longer time. However, another set of problems may develop if the effects caused changes in the skills or personological characteristics of the subjects.

Experimenter effect.   Levels of the independent variable may be more or less superior due to the effect of the experimenter's behavior on the subjects. The results of the dependent measure, then, cannot be generalized to other studies that may have a different experimenter. Bracht and Glass (1968) cited Rosenthal's (1966) distinction between active and passive experimenter effects. *Active effects* relate to differences in the experimenter's behavior that can influence the subject's behavior—differences reflected in such things as facial expressions, random encouragement, and social reinforcement. Active effects include annoying habits of speech, such as saying "you know?—you know?" or softly repeating the subject's responses.

Passive experimenter effects relate to an experimenter's appearance rather than behavior. Such passive effects as the experimenter's age, sex, ethnicity, height, weight, and so forth, may change a subject's behavior in a study.

The experimenter effect may also operate in observing and recording the behavior, if the experimenter has a preconceived notion of where a subject fits into a theory (Boring, 1962). For instance, if an experimenter has a pretty good idea of where a child fits into Piaget's theory (or whether he fits in at all), there may be a tendency to bend the child's behavior to fit the theory. In other words, if the experimenter has a presupposition that Piaget's theory is true, that assumption may influence the data-gathering process, and thus influence the subsequent perception, observation, and recording of behavior. Thus, interobserver or interrater measures of consistency or reliability should be included in your study.

Pretest sensitization.   In some studies a pretest may interact with the treatment and affect the results of the dependent measure. The pretest may sensitize the subjects in addition to effects of the treatment. You cannot then generalize the results to studies in which no pretest was administered. Pretest sensitization is likely to occur when the dependent variable consists of a self-report measure of personality, attitude, or opinion. The pretest sensitization may facilitate learning and general awareness, or it may clarify the subject's own perspective. Only if the research is designed to control the pretest effect—for instance, two groups receive the treatment and posttest, one with a pretest and the other without—can you determine whether the pretest effect was operating.

Posttest sensitization. The counterpart to pretest sensitization is posttest sensitization. An analogous effect on the dependent measure may result from the administration of a posttest, since the posttest is itself a learning experience. For instance, a posttest assessing the effects of a science curriculum may enable subjects to acquire more knowledge by "putting it all together" beyond the effects of the school curriculum, in which no posttest is administered. Although posttest sensitization may be a threat to external validity, it has not been experimentally studied as has its counterpart, pretest sensitization. In studies where posttest sensitization may affect the results, Bracht and Glass (1968) recommend that the experimenter use valid, unobtrusive measures for assessing treatment effects.

Webb, Campbell, Schwartz, and Sechrest (1966) labeled as *unobtrusive measures* any behavior that does not involve direct observation of an individual and thus is not susceptible to the Hawthorne effect. For instance, you can train observers in a classroom to record teacher responses that may be characteristic of individualized instruction. Or you may collect unobtrusive measures of individualized instruction operating indirectly—such as the number of reading groups, the variety of texts and workbooks, the arrangement of the classroom, the variety of classroom assignments or projects, and so on. The latter procedure may be more valid than direct classroom observation. This is especially true in situations where obtrusive observers, with white lab coat, clipboard, and stopwatch, are going out into the world to "do research."

Interaction of history and treatment effects. The historical conditions or milieu at the time a research study is conducted may affect the results of the dependent measure. These historical conditions may be of short duration, such as a favorite teacher's dismissal, or state football playoffs. Usually, we can determine whether these emotional events have affected the results. Sometimes the historical conditions may be of longer duration, such as the opposition to the Vietnam war, or the low morale of the students. Longer historical events may affect the treatment, and the effect would not necessarily be obvious or measurable. If the interaction of history with the treatment is perceived, replicating or repeating the study over a period of time will enable you to determine its effect.

Measurement of the dependent variable. The ability to generalize results obtained from the dependent measure may be limited to how it is operationalized. The operational definition of the dependent variable requires choosing a measuring instrument that will validly assess the concept under inquiry. Several tests or instruments may be selected for many dependent variables. In a sense, the degree to which tests are comparable determines the ability to apply them to other dependent measures. For instance, could you generalize the results obtained from multiple choice tests to those obtained with an essay format? Other characteristics of tests that may limit their generalizability include: speed tests compared to power tests; group administered intelligence or achievement tests compared to individually administered tests; and monitored tests compared to nonmonitored tests. As mentioned previously, operational definitions of measurements used for dependent variables should be elaborated in the Instrumentation subsection in order to determine to what degree this threat may operate.

Interaction between time of measurement and treatment effects. Posttests administered some time after the first posttest may show different results for the effectiveness of the treatment. In other words, a treatment effect may not appear at the first posttest, but at subsequent testings—say at three-week, six-week, or three-month intervals. The opposite results may also occur. For instance, a significant difference may be observed initially and not persist or be enhanced in later tests. There was one instance in which a weekend study compared the effectiveness of a counseling marathon workshop in raising the level of self-actualization. At the end of the workshop, significant gains on five of the ten subscales were observed. Six months later at a subsequent posttest, the comparable gains seen in the first posttest were no longer evident. In this case, the interaction of time of measurement and treatment effects was operating, and this influenced the ability to generalize the results.

We have discussed above eight threats to the internal validity and twelve threats to the external validity of a research design. Bear in mind that all these are specific instances of possible extraneous and confounding variables operating in a research study. Being aware of the variety of threats that may arise helps us to prepare research designs containing a minimum of errors that may influence our results. It also provides a useful set of categories for evaluating possible sources of error in the research studies we encounter.

Examples of Threats to Internal and External Validity

We shall present four brief paragraphs, each dealing with a separate study. Consider each one carefully, and see if you can determine the major threats to internal or external validity based on the preceding discussion.

A senior high school teacher wishes to find evidence to prove that his course on leadership and communication was valuable in training future leaders. He reviewed the school's records and obtained the names of boys who were active in his classes fifteen years ago. Concurrently, he got the names of boys who were not in his classes. He compared the two groups as to occupations, salaries, and so forth at the time, and found that his students were doing significantly better than the others. He concluded that the result was due to the impact of his courses on the boys he had as students.

If you conclude that the threat to the validity of this study is differential selection, you are correct. The teacher's systematic selection was a biased procedure. We don't know if the groups were initially equivalent in environmental and personological characteristics. His class might have been offered as part of a college-preparatory program. If a higher percentage of his students went on to college compared to those not in his classes, the possible confounding variable—level of education completed—could account for the occupational and salary differences—not his classes at all.

Another researcher designed a study to examine the relationship between level of achievement and performance of a complex learning task. An achievement test was administered to 400 subjects, and the top 10 percent became the high achievement group while the bottom 10 percent became the low achievement group. The complex learning task was then administered and, counter to the researcher's hypothesis, no significant difference in performance between the two groups was observed. The researcher concluded that level of achievement does not affect performance on a complex learning task.

The main threat to internal validity in this study is statistical regression. Due to observing only the extremes of the distribution, a retest with a related measure may yield scores that regress toward the mean. If statistical regression appears to be operating in a study, a better procedure would be to test a broader distribution of subjects.

A professor of counseling at the local university wishes to determine if her three-semester program for training counselors was effective in increasing the personal growth of her students. At the beginning of the core sequence in the summer, she administered to 55 new students a self-concept test, a self-actualization test, and a flexibility test. She gave a posttest at the end of the spring semester using the same measures to the remaining 40 students. She observed significant increases in all measures and concluded that her program brought about the improvements in personal growth.

In this example there is more than one threat to the internal validity of the study. One obvious threat is attrition. We don't know if the fifteen students who dropped out of the program differed significantly from those who remained. Furthermore, there are likely to be threats due to history and maturation. With regard to history, other events in the students' lives may account for the personal improvements. For example, a marriage (or divorce, depending on your perspective) may have taken place which caused a change, rather than the program. With regard to maturation, the students who are 11 months older will have adjusted to graduate school during the interim. Thus, the passage of time alone could have brought about the gains instead of the counseling program. Threats due to testing or instrumentation should not operate here since the measures were administered sufficiently far apart and the same measures were used for posttesting.

> A new talented and gifted (TAG) program at Grant Elementary School was approved on a one-year trial basis for grades 4 to 6. Students were to participate one day a week in a partial pull-out program that was staffed by two teachers. Ms. Mann and Ms. Arnold were responsible for developing the proposal and the curriculum that were subsequently approved and funded by the school board. Pretests and posttests at the beginning and end of the year were to be given to assess achievement and intelligence levels. Throughout the school year, several city and school district dignitaries would visit and observe the students while they were in the program. Posttest scores revealed significant differences in the measures of achievement and intelligence compared to the pretest scores, as well as compared to students not in the program at a different elementary school. The program was considered a great success and plans were approved for implementing it in all schools in the district the next year.

Threats to the external validity of this study include the novelty effect, the Hawthorne effect, and the experimenter effect. The new and exciting treatment may show gains simply because it is novel or new. In addition, the students knew that they were in a program that was special and reinforced by the dignitaries, teachers, and parents, and the added attention may have increased their motivation to achieve and succeed. Finally, the teachers may have contributed to an experimenter effect since their behavior could have positively influenced the students. All three of these threats to the external validity of the study would reduce the ability to generalize the results for the broader population. Similar gains by students in other district schools, involving other teachers, may not occur. There could also be threats to the internal validity of the study. For instance, differential selection may operate since students from different schools were compared.

Discuss these four studies among yourselves to see if you can find other threats to validity and to clarify your understanding of threats to the internal and external validity of the studies. You might also try to identify the independent and dependent variables in each study.

SUMMARY

We have identified four types of variables: independent, dependent, confounding, and control variables. In addition, we have discussed eight threats to the internal validity of a study and twelve threats to the external validity of a study. Finally, we have analyzed studies in terms of the main threats to internal and external validity that could be operating.

OBJECTIVES

In Chapter 6 we have identified four types of variables, and examined those confounding variables which are threats to either the internal or external validity of a study. Confirm your understanding of the material in Chapter 6 using the following objectives:

Identify the independent and dependent variables in any research article.

Specify the procedures or variables that serve as control components in the research process.

Identify and evaluate the threats to internal and external validity of your own research or of research you evaluate.

TERMS

accessible population
analysis of covariance
aptitude-treatment interaction
artifact
attrition
bias
blocking variable
concomitant variable
confounding variable
contamination
control variable
covariates
criterion variable
dependent variable
differential selection
environmental variable
experimental mortality
experimenter effect
external validity
extraneous variable
Hawthorne effect

history
independent variable
instrumentation
internal validity
John Henry effect
limiting variable
maturation
multiple treatment interference
novelty and disruption effect
partial correlation
personological or subject
    variable
placebo effect
posttest sensitization
predicter variable
pretest sensitization
selection-maturation interaction
statistical regression
target population
testing
unobtrusive measures

Constructing a Procedure: Types of Research Designs

What are the three main types of educational research, and how are they distinguished from one another?

What are the reseach designs within each of the types of educational research, and how are they appropriately used?

What are the main types of single-subject designs, and how do they attempt to control sources of invalidity?

What are the two types of educational research found less frequently in the research literature, and what are their key characteristics?

What is the typical organization of a Procedure subsection?

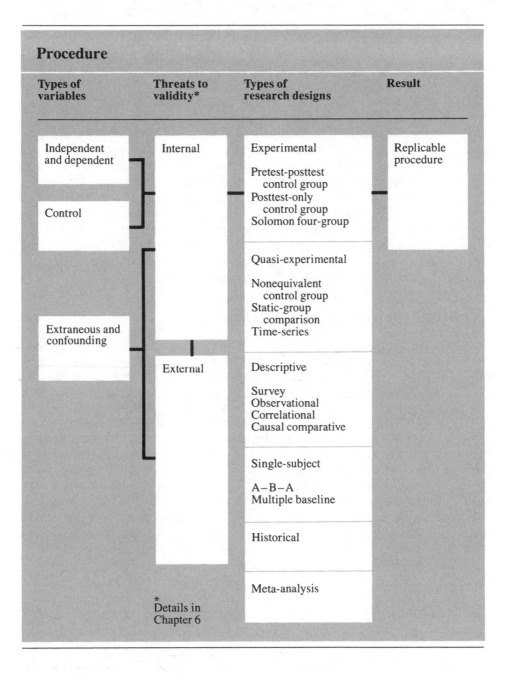

Procedure

Types of variables	Threats to validity*	Types of research designs	Result

Independent and dependent

Control

Extraneous and confounding

Internal

External

Experimental

Pretest-posttest
  control group
Posttest-only
  control group
Solomon four-group

Quasi-experimental

Nonequivalent
  control group
Static-group
  comparison
Time-series

Descriptive

Survey
Observational
Correlational
Causal comparative

Single-subject

A−B−A
Multiple baseline

Historical

Meta-analysis

Replicable procedure

*Details in Chapter 6

Three main types of educational research are encountered in the literature: experimental, quasi-experimental, and descriptive. The distinctions among these three types of research can best be understood by relating them to two concepts previously discussed: the distinction between random assignment and random selection; and the distinction between the two types of independent variables, those which are an experimental type and those which are a measurement type of operational definition. You may wish to reexamine these concepts. The former was discussed at the end of Chapter 5 and the latter at the beginning of Chapter 6. Following the three main types of educational research, we shall examine representative designs of each. Knowing the types of research and the particular research design for any given study should help us to minimize the threats to the internal and external validity of the study and will help us in the statistical analysis of the data.

Multiple-Subject Research Designs

Two criteria determine whether a study falls under the category of experimental research. The first is that the experimenter must have manipulative control over the independent variable; that is, the variable is an *experimental type of operational definition.* The second is that subjects must be *randomly assigned* to levels of the independent variable or to the different treatments. No other consideration is needed to determine if a study is experimental. If either of these criteria is missing, we do not have experimental research. For instance, if an experimenter selects the independent variable and its levels, such as type of incentive at three levels—verbal, token, and verbal and token—and randomly assigns subjects to each of the levels, the study would fall under the category of experimental research. Again, we would not need to know any other information, such as the dependent measure, the number of subjects, and so on.

The same two criteria for experimental research apply to determining whether a study falls under the category of quasi-experimental research. The first criterion is the same as for experimental research: the experimenter must have manipulative control over the independent variable; that is, the variable is an *experimental type of operational definition.* The second criterion is the only condition that distinguishes experimental research from quasi-experimental research: *there is no random assignment of subjects to the treatment.* If a researcher selects the independent variable, for example, type of teaching method at two levels—lecture and group discussion—and chooses two classes that already use that approach, then there is no random assignment of subjects to treatments; that is, the class membership has already been determined. Such a study would fall under the category of quasi-experimental research.

The only criterion used to determine if a study falls under the category of descriptive research is the type of independent variable used. Specifically, if the researcher has no manipulative control over the independent variable, that is, the variable has already occurred, it is then a *measurement type* of operational definition, and it falls under the category of descriptive research. If a researcher stratifies on a personological variable, such as level of intelligence—high, average, and low—no manipulative control would be possible. The subjects' levels of intelligence would already be fixed; they already range from low to high, and all we have done is to measure the level and then categorize it into one of the three levels of the independent variable. Usually, we do not have manipulative control over any personological or environmental variable; all we can do is determine how to measure it. Thus, the study would fall under the descriptive research category.

Frequently, a study will have more than one independent variable; it may contain a combination of independent variables, some of which are under manipulative control and some not. In such cases, we first determine what the main independent variable is (it will usually be the one under the experimenter's manipulative control), then determine whether or not random assignment occurs, and then conclude what type of research it is.

Consider each of the following abstracts from hypothetical research studies and decide what type of research each is:

One study tried to determine whether there are significant differences between elementary school children with learning disabilities and those without in the use of emotional words. Each child was shown four stimulus cards and asked to describe what was taking place in the pictures. Each time a child used an emotional word included in a master list, a tally was made.

Ninety junior high school students were randomly assigned to one of three types of instruction. One group was assigned to a microcomputer individually; one group was assigned to a microcomputer with a partner; and the third group was assigned to a microcomputer in a team of five. At the end of 15 weeks, each group was assessed on a measure of programming ability.

Three teachers of eleventh-grade English agreed to participate in a study examining the effect of classroom learning style on the understanding of literature and its allegorical interpretations. One class was instructed by

Types of Research

lecture only, one by group discussion only, and one by a combination of lecture and discussion.

After examining each of the three partial abstracts, you should be able to identify the independent and dependent variables, and determine the type of research. They are, respectively: descriptive, experimental, and quasi-experimental. In the first study, the independent variable has already occurred; the children are already learning disabled or not; no experimenter manipulation of the independent variable is possible. In the second example, the experimenter randomly assigned, and has manipulative control over, the independent variable, which is type of microcomputer instruction at three levels—self, partner, and team. In the final example, the experimenter has manipulative control over the independent variable but does not randomly assign; the class membership was already determined; thus, it is quasi-experimental research.

pre-exp. is weakest in making causal statements.
quasi next in strength
true exp is strongest

Multiple-Subject Research Designs   165

Experimental Designs

We shall first examine the three kinds of experimental research designs presented by Campbell and Stanley (1963), then discuss the major quasi-experimental designs, and then types of descriptive research. The three experimental research designs are:

pretest-posttest control group design
posttest-only control group design ⌐
Solomon four-group design

These three designs are very powerful and useful in applying the scientific method to educational research. They are the three designs which minimize the amount of error operating in the research process. Fundamental to all research using the scientific method is the process of *comparison* and providing a *context* for comparison. Any research findings that are not derived from comparisons are susceptible to the threats to internal and external validity, as discussed previously. Two main comparisons are useful in a research design; one is the comparison among treatment groups or levels of the independent variable; that is, experimental and control groups; the second is the comparison between pretest and posttest scores. Combined with random assignment to groups, these comparisons minimize the error which may operate in the research. All three of the experimental designs incorporate random assignment. We shall consider each separately.

Pretest-posttest control group design.   Using Campbell and Stanley's (1963) symbols, we can represent this design in this way:

$$R \quad O \quad X \quad O$$
$$R \quad O \quad \quad O$$

The R's represent random assignment. The O's refer to some process of observation or measurement, usually a pretest or posttest on the dependent measure. An X represents the exposure of the group to the experimental treatment. The left-to-right arrangement reflects the temporal order, and the X and O's in vertical columns denote simultaneous events. Finally, the O's and X in a row refer to the same group of subjects; that is, each row represents one level of the independent variable.

The pretest-posttest control group design is one of the most frequently used experimental designs. Four steps comprise the design:

1. Subjects are randomly assigned.
2. A pretest is given to the groups.
3. The experimental group receives treatment; the control group receives nontreatment activities to minimize the placebo effect.
4. A posttest is given to the groups.

Extensions of more than one treatment as well as more than one control group are frequent. The strength of this design is that, if properly conducted, it minimizes the effects of the eight threats to internal validity. Once we have developed a satisfactory procedure, the main threat to external validity would be pretest sensitization—that is, one could not generalize to situations in which no pretest was administered. The remaining threats to external validity would also have to be analyzed to ensure that their effects were minimized, since they relate to the implementation of the procedure rather than the chosen design.

According to Campbell and Stanley (1963), the most widely used and acceptable statistical test involves obtaining for each group a posttest-pretest gain score and calculating a t-test between experimental and control groups on these gain scores. However, they recommend a still more useful and precise test; namely, an analysis of covariance with the pretest scores as a covariate. Campbell and Stanley (1963) also stress that an *incorrect* analysis is frequently used in the educational research literature. This consists of calculating two t-tests, one for the pretest-posttest difference in the experimental group, and the second for the same difference in the control group. If the first is statistically significant and the second is not, then the researcher, without any direct comparison between the two groups, erroneously concludes that the treatment had an effect on the dependent measure.

We have not yet discussed the different statistical analyses mentioned above; they are treated later in Chapters 9 and 10. So you are not expected to understand them completely. However, we include them here in order to more closely integrate each research design with its more widely used statistical analyses.

Variations of the pretest-posttest control group design are frequent in the research literature, but they are *not* experimental designs. Two that we shall consider briefly are called *pre-experimental designs;* both are subject to the operation of error and bias. One very weak variation is the *one-group pretest-posttest design* represented in this way:

$$O \quad X \quad O$$

This design lacks an important feature: a comparison with at least one other group or level of the independent variable. There is no random assignment or control group comparison here. There is only a pretest, a treatment, and a posttest. If significant gains are obtained on the posttest, you would still not have answered the question: "So what?" Interpretation of results will be meaningless since there is no context for comparison, and the threats to internal and external validity are not sufficiently minimized. Only threats due to selection and attrition would be measurable; all other threats could and usually would operate. Obviously, the control group and comparison levels of the independent variable add much to the strength of a study and it thereby becomes an experimental design.

The one-group pretest-posttest pre-experimental design is popular with those who support instructional programs at all educational levels, and who are interested in determining if their program "makes a positive difference in the life of the students." A battery of tests is typically used as a pretest measure for the entering students, they receive the treatment of the program, and prior to moving out of the program, they take a posttest. Believe it or not, posttest gains from pretest scores are found to be statistically significant, whereupon the program is pronounced "worthwhile." It is recommended that the program be continued and given financial support. Meanwhile, five threats to internal validity and twelve threats to external validity may have operated in such a way as to explain the differences!

A still weaker variation of the one-group pretest-posttest design is the *one-shot case study, pre-experimental design,* represented in this way: *2*

$$X \quad O$$

In this design, a single group is studied only once, and an implicit comparison is made with other events ". . . casually observed and remembered" (according to Campbell and Stanley, 1963, p.7). Comparisons are made upon superficial and general expectations of what the data would be if the treatment had not occurred. No explicit comparisons of any kind are made, either pretest or posttest. There are no experimental and control group comparisons. No threats to internal and external validity are minimized. Therefore, no reliable or valid information is obtained. Researchers are advised to avoid these two pre-experimental designs, since the effort expended in the research is not justified by the paucity of useful information obtained.

Posttest-only control group design.   A variation of the pretest-posttest control group experimental design is the posttest-only control group design. It is similar to the former except that no pretest of the dependent measure is administered to any levels of the independent variable; that is, to the experimental and control groups. Three steps comprise the design:

1. Subjects are randomly assigned to groups.
2. The experimental group receives the treatment while the control group receives activities to minimize the operation of the placebo effect.
3. A posttest is given to both groups.

Extensions of additional experimental and/or control groups are also frequent in this design. When pretest sensitization may operate as a threat to external validity, the recommended design is represented in this way:

$$R \quad X \quad O$$
$$R \qquad\quad O$$

The usefulness of this design rests on the validity of the assumption that random assignment into similar groups is effective. In rare instances, random assignment will not be effective, due to the low probability of accurately distributing personological and environmental characteristics of subjects randomly to the groups. If random assignment is not effective, then pretest scores and/or information about possible confounding variables for each subject will be needed. This information is used in the subsequent statistical analyses to determine the degree of confounding or artificial effect. However, having a larger number of subjects in the study—fifty or more—will help to ensure that random assignment is effective.

Using this design in order to minimize the threat to external validity due to pretest sensitization requires the assumption, as mentioned above, that random assignment is effective. In trying to control for pretest sensitization, this design may produce a different threat due to the interaction of personological variables with the treatment. Stratification on pretest scores may have revealed a differential effect of the treatment for subjects at different levels.

Attrition may also operate. The pretest of the dependent measure will enable us to determine if attrition produced an effect if subjects dropped out of the study prior to taking the posttest. The other major threats to internal validity are minimized by this design. Other than the two just mentioned, other threats to external validity will also have to be analyzed to determine their effect for a particular research study.

Campbell and Stanley (1963) stated that the simplest statistical analysis for this research design would be a *t*-test calculated by comparing the posttest scores. They also recommended that an analysis of covariance on the posttest scores, with pertinent personological and environmental variables, such as GPA, grade, sex, and so forth, used as the covariate(s), would increase the power of the statistical analyses.

Solomon four-group design.   The final type of experimental research is the Solomon four-group design. It explicitly considers the effect due to testing as well as that due to pretest sensitization. It is a combination of the two prior experimental designs and is represented in this way:

$$R \quad O_1 \quad X \quad O_2$$
$$R \quad O_3 \qquad\quad O_4$$
$$R \qquad\quad X \quad O_5$$
$$R \qquad\qquad\quad O_6$$

According to Campbell and Stanley (1963), the effect of the treatment can be measured in four ways: $O_2 > O_1$, $O_2 > O_4$, $O_5 > O_6$, and $O_5 > O_3$. Four statistical directional hypotheses can be created to test these comparisons. For example, H_1: $\mu_2 > \mu_1$, H_1: $\mu_2 > \mu_4$, and so on. Four steps comprise this design:

1. Subjects are randomly assigned to groups.
2. Two of the groups (O_1 and O_3) are pretested.
3. The first and third groups receive the treatment while the second and fourth groups (the control groups) receive activities to minimize the placebo effect.
4. All four groups are posttested.

The Solomon four-group design is probably the most powerful experimental design, powerful in the sense of minimizing all the threats to internal validity and of enabling assessment of pretest sensitization as

Not All Research Designs Are Created Equal

well. The remaining threats to external validity must still be determined for each particular research study.

The main trade-off in using this design is the larger sample needed and the additional time and resources demanded from the researcher because of the four groups. Another difficulty is that there is no one statistical test that uses all six sets of scores simultaneously. Campbell and Stanley (1963) recommend that the researcher analyze the four posttest scores with a simple 2 (pretest) × 2 (treatment) analysis of variance design. The Solomon four-group design is used mainly when there is pretest sensitization and the researcher wishes to study its effect. In other situations, either of the first two experimental designs would be preferred.

These types of experimental design have focused on the use of one independent variable at two or more levels. Research, however, is commonly more complex, involving multiple independent variables or having multiple dependent measures. Studies that incorporate multiple independent variables are called *factorial designs* and have several subdistinctions; for instance, they can be a nested design, a blocked design, or a Latin squares design. Those who wish to explore the relationship between factorial designs and analysis of variance are referred to Kirk (1968). We shall discuss analysis of results that incorporate multiple independent variables in Chapter 10.

Quasi-Experimental Designs

Campbell and Stanley (1963) discussed fourteen variations of quasi-experimental research. You are referred to their study for a complete elaboration of these designs. However, we shall describe only three designs widely used in educational research:

> nonequivalent control group design
> static-group comparison design
> time-series design

Nonequivalent control group design. This is similar to the pretest-posttest control group experimental design except for one important feature: there is no random assignment to groups; indeed, none is possible. Thus, equivalence between the experimental and control groups cannot be assumed. Rather, the groups usually are intact units, such as classrooms or counseling groups. The experimenter is assumed to have manipulative control over whichever group receives the treatment. Also, the accessible target populations are assumed to be similar but not so similar as to eliminate the need for a pretest. It may be represented in this way:

$$\frac{O \quad X \quad O}{O \qquad O}$$

The dashed line represents nonequivalence or the absence of random assignment. The major difficulty with nonequivalent groups is that, since there is no random assignment, the possible interaction of selection with other internal threats—such as history, maturation, or testing —rather than the independent variable or treatment, may be able to explain differences in the dependent measure. Threats to external validity need to be individually examined as well.

The more similar the groups are, and the more this similarity is confirmed by the pretest scores, the more effective the control group becomes (Campbell and Stanley, 1963, p. 48). There are ways of ensuring similarity of groups even though there is no random assignment of subjects to treatments. One way to increase the similarity in characteristics is to *choose intact groups,* such as classrooms or school buildings that have similar characteristics. These would have similar socioeconomic status, similar urban/rural location, similar size, and so forth.

A second way to increase the similarity of groups is to *randomly assign the intact units to each treatment,* since random assignment of subjects to treatments is impossible. For instance, if we take as our sample ten classrooms from one school (the accessible target population), we can randomly assign each classroom to either the experimental or control group. The intact unit, the classroom, can then become the *experimental unit,* and we can analyze class differences rather than individual differences.

A third way is to *test statistically whether there were initial differences among the groups.* As we discussed in Chapter 6 in the section on control variables, if we determine that the groups were not equivalent on the pretest measures we could control for these differences statistically. For instance, an analysis of covariance could adjust the posttest means by removing the effect of any possible extraneous variables.

Static-group comparison design.   Campbell and Stanley (1963) considered this to be a pre-experimental design. However, for our purposes we shall think of it as a variation of quasi-experimental research. In this design, one group or level of the independent variable receives the treatment and the other does not; then both are posttested. We may represent it in this way:

$$\frac{X \quad O}{O}$$

As the dashed line shows, there is no random assignment here. It is similar to the posttest-only control group design except for the lack of random assignment.

The main threats due to internal validity are that posttest differences on the dependent measure can be attributed to differential selection and to interaction of selection with maturation. That is, the groups were not initially equivalent for such pertinent variables as pretest scores or environmental or personological variables. Attrition may also explain the posttest scores if there is a differential dropout of subjects from the groups. All the threats to external validity must also be considered.

The static-group comparison design is relatively weak compared to others because of neglecting to control for threats to internal and external validity. If the researcher should add a pretest, it becomes a non-equivalent control group design; then differences in the posttest can more confidently be attributed to the operation of the independent variable or treatment.

Posttest mean scores from this design may be analyzed by the t-test. If more than two groups comprise the independent variable, you can conduct an analysis of variance.

Time-series design.   The time-series design periodically obtains measurements or observations of a single group of subjects; the treatment is administered between two of these observations. It may be represented in this way:

$$O_1 \quad O_2 \quad O_3 \quad O_4 \quad X \quad O_5 \quad O_6 \quad O_7 \quad O_8$$

This is an elaboration of the one-group pretest-posttest pre-experimental design discussed earlier in this chapter. The added observations or scores derived from the dependent variables increase the validity of this design over the earlier one. Internal validity threats due especially to history but also to instrumentation may still be present. In the former, the comparison group is omitted; in the latter, if human observers are used who are aware of the study's purpose, artificial support for the hypothesis may result from the experimenter effect or from observer bias. Major threats to the external validity of the design may also be present.

An important improvement in the time-series design is the addition of a similar intact unit that does not receive the treatment. If one group receives the treatment and the other does not, the latter serves as a control group. We can increase the similarity between intact groups or units in the ways mentioned above in the section on the nonequivalent control group design.

The addition of the intact group with multiple observations is called by Campbell and Stanley (1963) a *multiple time-series design;* it may be represented in this way:

$$O \quad O \quad O \quad O \quad X \quad O \quad O \quad O \quad O$$

$$O \quad O \quad O \quad O \qquad O \quad O \quad O \quad O$$

This is one of the stronger quasi-experimental designs since it minimizes all the threats to internal validity. One threat to external validity may operate due to pretest sensitization. Others may or may not operate according to the implementation phase of each particular research study. Statistical analyses appropriate for a time-series design are variations of an analysis of variance or trend analysis.

In discussing earlier the threats to internal and external validity, and in discussing the relative strengths and weaknesses of these quasi-experimental designs, we do not mean to convey a feeling of hopelessness or frustration in your attempts to design high-quality research. We hope that these discussions of threats and research designs will make you more aware of variables and factors that should be considered in designing and evaluating research. The goal is not to inhibit research but to encourage better research and provide a better understanding of competing explanations for the treatments that can affect posttest scores. There is no intention here to discourage quasi-experimental research designs. Rather, as Campbell and Stanley (1963) put it, quasi-experimental designs should be used only in those realistic field situations "... *where better designs are not feasible"* (p. 34). In other words, under whatever realistic restrictions the researcher may operate, the best available design should be used—not the most convenient one.

To complete this section on quasi-experimental designs, we shall discuss two variations of the random assignment concept. One is the variation of *matching with random assignment.* This may occur with scores on a pretest or on pertinent environmental or personological variables. The total group of subjects available for a study are organized into matched pairs; for example, the two highest scores form one pair and so on until the two lowest scores form the last pair. Individuals from each pair are then randomly assigned to the levels of the independent variable—that is, the experimental and control groups. This procedure usually minimizes possible threats better than random assignment alone. Matching subjects on the basis of one or several pertinent variables *without* random assignment is not recommended (Campbell and Stanley, 1963, p. 49). Even though matching alone does not adequately establish equivalence between groups, this procedure is still inappropriately used in the literature. A simpler procedure to increase the equivalence between groups is to carry out matching along with random assignment, or to conduct an analysis of covariance using pertinent variables as covariates.

The second variation of random assignment relates to the statement made earlier that lack of random assignment of subjects to treatments, given manipulative control of the independent variable, determines whether or not a study is quasi-experimental research. *Random assignment of intact groups or units* may also occur, as in the case of classrooms or counseling groups. If it does occur, the design can be considered either quasi-experimental or experimental research. The distinction depends upon how the scores are analyzed. If there is random assignment of intact groups, yet differences are analyzed on the basis of individuals, it is probably a quasi-experimental design. However, if the scores are analyzed by intact groups—that is, a mean score for the group is used instead of the individuals' scores—and there is random assignment of intact groups, then the study is probably an experimental research design. This distinction also assumes the operation of the other criteria—namely, the researcher has manipulative control over the independent variable and can randomly assign which group receives the treatment.

Descriptive Designs

In studies where random assignment of subjects to treatments and manipulative control of the independent variable are impossible, the independent variable will have already occurred. As already indicated, research which incorporates these nonmanipulative independent variables is categorized as descriptive research. There are over twenty-five variations and distinctions of descriptive research listed among the various educational research texts. We shall discuss these four major types:

survey
observational
correlational
causal-comparative

All these types of descriptive research entail collecting data in an attempt to describe as accurately as possible a subject's behavior, attitude, or values. Predicting and establishing cause-and-effect relationships among variables is not the goal of descriptive research; however, it is the main goal of experimental research. In experimental research, the manipulation of the independent variable(s) with random assignment of subjects to treatment is the only way to assess causal relationships. On the other hand, the purpose of descriptive research is to determine what presently exists with regard to the problem or phenomenon. Descriptive research attempts to accurately portray situations and events, and sometimes to describe their interrelationship in the hope of obtaining useful information, often in order to plan subsequent experimental studies.

Survey The purpose of survey research is to obtain information that describes existing phenomena by asking the individuals their perceptions, attitudes, behaviors, or values. Therefore, it is a *self-report* assessment. It is probably the type of research most widely known to the general public. The Gallup, Harris, and Roper polls, frequently reported in newspapers and electronic media, are three of the best-known surveys for sampling public opinion. Typically, a survey raises a specific problem; for example: Should we increase our defense spending over the next four years? What are the attitudes toward year-round schools compared to nine-month schools? After a problem is clearly specified, a desired population is randomly selected. Results of attitudes or behaviors asked by the survey are frequently grouped by environmental variables to determine if differential behavior or attitudes exist. For instance, results may be given according to the population's age, sex, race, political party, or religious affiliation.

Within the field of education, many kinds of surveys are conducted, including community surveys, pupil surveys, interview surveys, job surveys, market surveys, teacher-rating surveys, and needs assessments, or preliminary planning of evaluation studies. Typically, surveys are conducted using a questionnaire or interview format. They may be mailed to subjects, or administered individually, or by phone. The key to conducting quality survey research is similar to that of experimental and quasi-experimental research. There should be an attempt to minimize the threats of possible confounding variables that could influence the survey results. Random selection and the stratification of results by levels of environmental or personological variables help to prevent these threats from operating. Another technique to ensure validity is the use of neutral, unbiased questionnaires or interviews.

Observational. Self-report measures often used in survey studies may contain bias, misinformation, or inaccurately remembered information. Use of the observational method in descriptive research can minimize the limitations inherent in self-report methods if it is properly implemented. If a researcher observes relatively simple behaviors and is not required to infer complex constructs from them, observational research can yield objectively observed and recorded information. For instance, observing the number of disruptive behaviors in a classroom, or the total time students spend asking questions of their teachers, is usually observed and recorded more objectively than observing evidence of anxiety in a classroom, or self-concept in a teacher. Regardless of the level of behavior observed, if they are not operationalized behaviorally, there will be difficulty in establishing adequate interobserver consistency. *Interrater reliability* (or *interscorer reliability* or *interobserver reliability*) is a measure of the consistency of observers recording the desired behavior. The degree of agreement between two observers of one comparison is expressed as a value from 0.00 to +1.00. The closer the value to +1.0, the greater the agreement. Typically, interrater reliabilities ranging above 0.80 are expected. Studies reporting data collected from observational procedures should always include the interrater reliability. This is a special use of the correlational coefficient explained in Chapter 9.

Accuracy in observing and recording behavior is reduced if an observer is required to watch several subjects or the entire class simultaneously. More consistent results are usually obtained when an observer watches one subject, such as the teacher, while another observer watches the students' reactions to the teacher. It is difficult for one observer to do both, and should not be attempted.

Another threat to an observational study is the degree to which the observer's presence in a particular setting changes the behavior being observed. For instance, the observer in a classroom setting may alter the behavior of both the teacher and the class. Using one-way viewing screens is one way of minimizing the observer effect. Also, having an observer visit the classroom several times prior to observing the desired behavior may enable a class to adapt to the observer's presence and to react normally—that is, as if no observer were present.

The use of adequately trained observers will also minimize the recording of errors. The tendency of an observer to rate subjects high, or average, or based on first impressions, and having a knowledge of the subject's performance on another variable—such as a pretest—all introduce error into the research. All these errors in rating subjects would constitute threats to the external validity of the research due to experimenter effects. More specifically, when we permit our ratings of subjects to be influenced by our initial impressions of the subjects, we have what is called the _halo effect_. When we are aware of a subject's performance on another variable, or even are aware of what treatment group the subject is in, this knowledge can influence or contaminate our observation and subsequent recording of the subject's behavior. This is an example of _contamination_, described in Chapter 6. In order to determine the possible experimenter effects, not only is an interrater reliability measure desirable, but a complete account of the observer's training should be included in the Procedure subsection. In some research studies where experimenter effects are not adequately minimized, the use of _unobtrusive measures_ (Webb et al., 1966)—mentioned earlier—may be more appropriate.

Correlational. Studies that attempt to determine the degree or strength of relationship between two variables fall under the category of correlational research. Many correlational studies attempt to describe these relationships; others attempt to predict relatonships through the use of sophisticated correlational statistics, such as multiple regression, discriminant analysis, factor analysis, or canonical correlation. The simplest correlational studies are those which try to describe the interrelationship among a number of variables compared two at a time. Frequently in such studies distinctions among independent and dependent variables are never made. Interest is directed toward determining and describing interrelationships or intercorrelations among variables without making distinctions among the types of variables.

In describing the strength of relationships, care must be taken not to confuse a relationship with a cause-and-effect relationship. Only experimental designs can measure causal relationships. Correlational research may provide useful information about the strength of a relationship between two variables; the more sophisticated correlational studies can also predict relationships between variables. Both types of studies can provide information among variables which may be causal and which would have to be tested subsequently by means of an experimental design. Correlational research that describes the relationship among variables makes use of descriptive statistics, such as the Pearson product moment correlation, also called the Pearson _r,_ or the Spearman Rho. All these statistics produce a _correlational coefficient_ that has common characteristics across the different types of statistical tests, as we shall see in Chapter 9.

Correlational research not only attempts to describe interrelationships which may subsequently, in an experimental design, reveal causal relationships, but they may also yield spurious or false relationships. Spurious correlations, such as a positive relationship between the size of the big toe and the level of intelligence, may be due to chance or to error operating in the study. Any relationship between two variables (X and Y) can be explained in one of four ways: (1) X is a determinant of Y; (2) Y is a determinant of X; (3) a third variable (Z) determines the relationship between X and Y; or (4) X and Y are spuriously related.

An example of a positive relationship is the correlation between the weight of elementary school students and academic achievement. Is weight a determinant of achievement? Do we feed children more to increase their achievement? Or is this a spurious relationship? It is not spurious, because in this case a third variable, the child's age, can be shown to be related to both weight and achievement.

Although correlational coefficients are used predominantly in correlational research, as a type of descriptive statistic such as the Pearson r, they are routinely calculated along with two other descriptive statistics —the mean and the standard deviation—in other research designs in order to describe more accurately and completely the characteristics of, and the relationships among, the variables.

Causal-comparative. Causal-comparative or _ex post facto_ research involves at least two levels of a nonmanipulated independent variable; that is, the variable is a measurement type of operational definition. Intact groups usually comprise each level of the independent variable. The comparison on the dependent measure is an attempt to discover possible causes or reasons for differences due to the subject differences in the environmental or personological variable. For example, in the field of medical research, smokers versus nonsmokers is a personological independent variable that is not manipulated by the researcher. It is compared in terms of a dependent measure, the frequency of lung cancer. The observation that a significantly higher probability of lung cancer is found in smokers than in nonsmokers does not prove that smoking causes lung cancer. You can only conclude that, within a particular degree of probability, you are more likely to develop lung cancer if you smoke. Causal-comparative research does not isolate a cause. Rather, like correlational research, results may suggest possible causal relationships. In this example, a hypothetical Z factor may influence the relationship; a chemical used in the tobacco-curing process may be the cancer-producing agent. If it were omitted in the curing process, there would be no observable difference between smokers and nonsmokers in the frequency of lung cancer.

The many threats to internal and external validity may operate as possible confounding variables. For instance, if the intact groups compared are not homogeneous, there may be differential selection operating as a main threat. Information on other pertinent environmental or personological variables may also be important. You might have to determine the age, sex, social class, and so on, in order to minimize the threat due to the interaction of personological variables and the treatment. In this instance, the treatment is another personological variable.

Frequently in educational research, experimental designs are not appropriate or ethical, and causal-comparative research definitely is justifiable. Comparing juvenile delinquents and nonjuvenile delinquents, or high-creative and low-creative students, may be useful in uncovering possible causal relationships that could be examined in subsequent experimental research. The same four relationships between two variables discussed under correlational research apply to examining variables in a causal-comparative study. For instance, high-creative students perform significantly higher when compared to low-creative students on measures of academic achievement, including reading comprehension, mathematical reasoning, and figural reasoning. Possible rival hypotheses that might explain the differences include the following: Did the high-creative group achieve higher because they were creative? Were they already high achievers before they were labeled creative? Were they labeled high-creative because they were high achievers? Did a third variable, such as high intelligence level or IQ, cause the relationship between creativity and achievement? You can see that researchers conducting causal-comparative studies should attempt to measure additional variables and discuss rival hypotheses that may explain the observed results.

Single-Subject Research Designs

In the preceding discussions of experimental, quasi-experimental, and descriptive research designs, we have pointed out the need for an adequate number of subjects for each design. However, in educational research—or more specifically in research on behavior modification—single-subject designs may be used effectively. Previous research designs that omitted a comparison group could be used with a single-subject design of greater sophistication that enables cause-and-effect relationships to be determined. These are variations of experimental designs. As mentioned in the discussion of characteristics of experimental research, the strength or power of research designs lies in their ability to make comparisons, either with a comparison group or with comparison scores; for example, comparing a pretest with a posttest. The principle of comparison is incorporated into the two single-subject designs we shall consider, but with a slight variation from the two comparisons above. Refer to Hersen and Barlow (1976) for a complete discussion of single-subject designs and for appropriate statistical techniques. The two types we shall discuss are *A–B–A* designs and multiple-baseline designs.

A–B–A Designs

In *A–B–A* designs, the letter *A* stands for the baseline condition, and *B* stands for the treatment. This is similar to a time-series design, but with an important variation in the expectations of the posttest, or second *A* in the design. This is also called a *reversal design,* since *A* is repeated. For instance, if we have a child in the classroom who exhibits inappropriate and disruptive behavior—meaning he starts fights—we might use an *A–B–A* design. We must first establish a baseline for the behavior we wish to study. Such behavior as number of classroom fights started might be observed daily for four or five weeks. This is analogous to a pretest on the dependent measure. Next, the treatment *B* is initiated. For instance, you might initiate a primary or secondary reinforcement system like this: For every class session the student goes without starting a fight, he will receive five tokens. These tokens may be traded for privileges. Twenty-five tokens will earn him a movie ticket; twenty tokens will earn a lunch at McBurger's; fifteen tokens will earn the use of his bike to ride to school for a week; and so on. This treatment constitutes one level of the independent variable. Now the dependent measure is observed and recorded until it achieves a new stable level of responding. As part of the third phase of the design, the treatment is removed so that the baseline environmental conditions are restored. In behavior modification terms, extinction is initiated. In terms of a research design, the second *A* is analogous to a posttest of the dependent measure. Observation and recording of the response must again be conducted until a stable pattern of responding is obtained. If the pattern of responding is similar in the two *A* conditions but the *B* condition produced a significant decrease in response, we have support for the claim that the independent variable or treatment caused the decrease in the dependent measure. If, however, the second *A* response pattern is not similar to the first baseline condition, further experimental control is necessary before we can establish a causal relationship.

Numerous variations of the *A–B–A* design are possible. For instance, if for practical or ethical reasons the treatment should be restored, you can conduct an *A–B–A–B* design. Thus, if the treatment is effective and causal, there should be a comparable response rate under the second *B* treatment when compared with the first. A weaker variation is the *A–B* design. Many threats to the design due to possible confounding variables may occur to explain the results other than the treatment itself. The greater threats are due to the lack of comparisons in the design.

Multiple-Baseline Designs

In situations where reversal designs are not possible or desirable, we may establish multiple baselines simultaneously. The treatment, or one level of the independent variable, is introduced to each baseline behavior, or dependent measure, separately, one at a time. For instance, continuing with our earlier example, suppose that, in addition to cutting down on fighting, we wish to reduce the number of truant days and to lower the number of verbally disruptive behaviors. We must first obtain a stable baseline for each and continue it until the treatment is introduced for all three dependent measures. After we have established a baseline over a period of five weeks, we introduce the token reinforcement system for one behavior, or dependent measure, and obtain a response rate for the next five weeks. After the second five-week period, we introduce the treatment to the second behavior and observe the response rate for five more weeks. Finally, after another five weeks, we introduce the treatment to the third behavior and observe the response rate over the next five weeks. Concurrently, we are continuing the treatment and recording its effects on the other two behaviors as well. Corresponding shifts or changes in the response rates for each of the dependent measures with each introduction of the treatment establishes a relationship, inferred to be causal, between the independent and dependent variables. The *Journal of Applied Behavior Analysis* is one journal that publishes single-subject designs.

In all the types of research we have discussed—experimental, quasi-experimental, descriptive, and single-subject designs—threats to internal and external validity may operate. We have seen that different threats may arise due to the particular design selected. As a general strategy, we should not select a research design on the assumption that we don't have to be concerned with a particular threat—rather, we should critically analyze each possible threat to the study, no matter what the design. Be an active critical participant, either as a researcher or as a reader, and select that research design which is most feasible rather than the one which is most convenient. Then, critically analyze the study to minimize the operation of confounding variables.

Historical and Meta-Analysis Research

Two other less frequently used research methods found in the educational literature are historical research and meta-analysis of research. Historical research has long been available as a research technique while meta-analysis research is a relatively new technique. We shall discuss both briefly.

Historical Research

Historical research is the study of a problem in the past that requires collecting information from the past, which serves as the data to be interpreted in the study. Primary source material is important in historical research in order to establish the authenticity and credibility of the findings. _External criticism_ is the process of determining the authenticity of the sources. How, when, where, and why did the document or relic originate? The possibility of recording errors and perpetrating frauds or forgeries must always be considered. _Internal criticism_ is an attempt to determine the meaning of the information obtained. Thus the treatment of the data in historical research consists of the interpretation of the data obtained. The interpretation should be derived from a competent understanding of the information, from clearly specified relationships in the data, and from valid conclusions (the interpretation) that are arrived at objectively without any experimenter bias. For instance, one type of bias that may operate is the imposition of the modern _zeitgeist_ (meaning spirit of the times or thought patterns of the day) upon an earlier time that one is interpreting. Historical researchers use a format similar to the scientific method consisting of these six steps:

1. Identifying and isolating the problem
2. Developing a hypothesis
3. Collecting and classifying source materials, and determining facts by internal and external criticism
4. Organizing facts into results
5. Forming conclusions
6. Synthesizing and presenting the research in organized form

Thus, instead of data being collected from contemporary human or animal subjects, the data and subsequent verification are obtained from predominantly primary or secondary source materials (step 3). The library, public school records, census data, computer records, and other depositories are the main sources of historical research in education. The relationship among these facts or variables must be determined (step 4). Valid interpretations or conclusions are then generated (step 5). Finally, the research article is assembled, which typically is organized by time, geographical regions, or subject areas. Similar components for writing the research article are followed except that between the method and results sections, there must be an elaboration of the data or evidence (Hopkins, 1980, pages 249–268).

One journal that contains primarily historical research is the *History of Education Quarterly;* others that publish historical research are the *Journal of Educational Research* and *Educational Horizons.* Two examples of historical research are studies by Hillman (1974) and Lee (1968). Hillman (1974) analyzes male and female roles in children's literature in two time periods; namely, the 1930s and from the mid-1960s to the mid-1970s. Lee (1968) examines the interrelationships among the concepts about the nature of the preadolescent child with teaching theories and the culture in which they appear in the United States in the progressive era between 1900 and 1914.

Meta-Analysis Research

Meta-analysis is the statistical analysis of a larger set of analyses obtained from separate research studies. The purpose of meta-analysis is to statistically integrate the findings from a broader population of individually conducted studies. Glass (1976) proposed meta-analysis as a "rigorous alternative to the casual, narrative discussion of research studies" (p. 3) that have typified the educational field. A main goal of meta-analysis is to statistically integrate the findings of many studies; in fact, one statistic used is the magnitude of the effect of the treatment. This *effect size (ES)* is the mean difference between the treatment ($\overline{X}_T$) and control subjects ($\overline{X}_c$), divided by the standard deviation of the control group (s_c):

$$ES = \frac{\overline{X}_T - \overline{X}_c}{s_c}$$

Thus, an effect size of ". . . +1 indicates that a person at the mean of the control group would be expected to rise to the 84th percentile of the control group after treatment" (Smith and Glass, 1977, p. 753).

In the analysis of results from individual studies, more than one effect size may be obtained. Different effect sizes may be calculated for one specific outcome or for varied dependent measures which, at a broader conceptual level, represent a unified outcome. In the Smith and Glass (1976) meta-analysis that analyzed psychotherapy outcome studies, the

Combining Past Research to Determine Effect Size

researchers used both procedures and calculated 833 effect sizes from 375 studies. These effect sizes then became the dependent variables in the design, and 16 independent variables were examined. Across all of the 10 measured outcomes, the average study exhibited a +0.68 standard deviation unit superiority of the treatment group over the control group. Thus the ". . . average client receiving therapy was better off than 75 percent of the untreated controls" (Smith and Glass, 1977, p. 754). The effect size is only one measure used to integrate the findings from numerous studies; other statistical techniques such as regression analysis have also been employed.

Meta-analysis is a promising new approach to data analysis that provides significantly more information than a typical review of the literature. As of this writing, based on a computerized search of the ERIC and *Psychological Abstracts* data bases, there have been 75 references dealing with meta-analysis since 1976. Meta-analysis research has been conducted on such topics as: (1) the effects of desegregation on academic achievement (Krol, 1981); (2) the relationship of class size to classroom processes, teacher satisfaction, and pupil effect (Smith and Glass, 1980); (3) the effect of individualized instruction in science (Aiello and Wolfle, 1980); (4) the effects of television viewing on prosocial and antisocial behavior (Hearold, 1980); and (5) the relationship between the level of teacher questioning and student achievement (Redfield and Rousseau, 1981).

There has been dialogue among researchers as to what meta-analysis entails (see Cook and Leviton, 1980; Cooper and Arkin, 1981; and Leviton and Cook, 1981), as well as critiques and evaluation of the Glass and Smith (1979) meta-analysis on the relationship of class size to achievement (see Hess, 1979; Glass and Smith, 1979; Simpson, 1980; Cohen and Filby, 1979; and Glass, 1980).

What type of research is meta-analysis? Some researchers might classify it as causal-comparative. Can you see why? Since meta-analysis is a new technique for analyzing research results, others tend to let it stand by itself to undergo the scrutiny and review that all new procedures and methods are subject to in psychological and educational research.

All the types of research previously considered—experimental, quasi-experimental, descriptive, single-subject, historical, and meta-analysis —can be used to assess learning or development either longitudinally or cross-sectionally. A *longitudinal* study is conducted over an extended period of time during which the same subjects are retested. Typically used to assess developmental measures, the Terman study of genius (Seagoe, 1975), mentioned in Chapter 1, is a classic example of a longitudinal study. A *cross-sectional* study investigates development by comparing different age groups at one point in time instead of following the same group through a long period of time. For instance, one could construct age groups of 4 to 6, 7 to 9, and 10 to 12 years of age, test them on a set of measures, and infer how the 4- to 6-year-olds might function based on another comparable group performance at ages 10 to 12. Obviously, error can creep into the results if the groups are not comparable in pertinent personological or environmental variables. The advantage of the longitudinal approach is that any potential error related to nonequivalent groups is eliminated since the same subjects are retested over time. The main disadvantage is the added cost, time, and resources needed to conduct a longitudinal study. These factors probably explain why so many cross-sectional studies are implemented while so many longitudinal studies wait for the necessary state, federal, or private money needed to initiate projects of this magnitude.

This completes our discussion of the different types of research designs covered in this chapter, as well as the different types of variables and the possible threats to the internal or external validity of the study covered in Chapter 6. Our purpose in delineating these topics was to discriminate sufficiently among the variables and research so that we have a firm foundation for developing or evaluating the Procedure subsection of the Method section of the research journal article. As previously indicated, the Procedure subsection includes an operational definition of each independent variable in the research, while the Instrumentation subsection delineates an operational definition for each dependent variable. The next section will apply the knowledge we've gained from the last two chapters to understanding how a Procedure is formulated and developed.

Examples of a Procedure Subsection

Typically, a Procedure subsection contains an operational definition of each independent variable in the research study. Also included should be the specific research design used. If the dependent variables are stated in this section, they are usually given at a conceptual level and then operationalized in the next section. The Procedure subsection includes all the key features of the study needed for replication: the formation of groups, training of researchers, instructions to subjects, accurate and complete description of the treatment and other levels of the independent variables, a sequential but usually temporal summary of each key step in the implementation phase of the study, and special procedures implemented to minimize error. In other words, the Procedure subsection should report the actual steps and problems encountered in implementing the research study rather than the ideal steps usually proposed in designing the study. The goal of the Procedure subsection is to describe accurately the independent variables, the research design, and the implementation phase of the study so that any experienced researcher can read it and replicate the study. An experienced researcher may not replicate the study exactly. For instance, the researcher may try to avoid any errors and pitfalls that you encountered. However, the goal remains the same; it should be an accurate reflection of the fundamental details or the "How?" of the research study.

Consider the Method section from the Zimmerman and Kinsler (1979) study.

Method

Subjects

Fifty-four boys and 54 girls were selected in equal numbers from kindergarten and first-grade classes at a New York City public school located in a lower-class area of Harlem. The first graders ranged in age from 6 years 0 months to 7 years 6 months and were comparable in age to the 6-year-olds in the Walters and Parke (1964) study. The kindergartners ranged in age from 5 years 1 month to 6 years 0 months and were comparable in age to the 5-year-olds in the Walters et al. (1963) study. The children were either of black or Hispanic origins. Within each age group, the children were randomly assigned to treatment condition.

Task

The experiment was conducted in two adjoining rooms of a public school. The wall connecting the two rooms was equipped with a one-way mirror. In one room, a 3 × 8 ft. (.9 × 2.4 m) table was placed with a chair at one end. A pictureless psychology textbook was put on the table near the chair. Eight toys were placed on the table: a toy camper, a tea set, 15 alphabet blocks, a toy gun, a white and a black doll, two toy cars, a coloring book and crayons, and two children's picture books. These toys were selected to be attractive to boys and girls of this age.

A high resolution television monitor and a Sony 3600 videotape deck were placed on a moveable steel stand located behind the chair. This equipment was used to show the videotaped episodes.

Videotapes

Two videotapes were created that were identical in length, sequence of events, child model, and setting. Only the identity of the adult varied between the two videotapes. Two black women in their twenties served as the adult models in the videotapes. A black 8-year-old girl served as the child model in both videotapes.

In each tape, the woman told the child that she had to leave the room to retrieve a forgotten item, and during her absence, the child should look at the book that was placed before her on the table. The same eight toys described above were also located on the table. The woman informed the child that she would close the door so the child would not be disturbed and would knock before reentering. Shortly after the adult's departure, the child put the book aside and proceeded to play with the toys for approximately 2 minutes. Upon hearing a knock at the door, the child vainly tried to replace the toys in their original positions. When the adult reentered the room, she began to chastise the child for playing with the toys that didn't belong to her. The videotape ended with the child being spanked and depicted as crying.

Procedures

One of the two black women who performed on the videotape also served as experimenter during the study. She escorted each child from the classroom to the experimental room and seated the child in the chair beside the table. Children in the *videotape* condition were told by the experimenter, "I am going to show you a movie." The child's chair was turned toward the television monitor, and the experimenter started the videotape. After the episode was shown, the experimenter turned the child's chair back toward the table and gave the child one of three types of instructions. In the *strong-prohibition* condition, the experimenter said, "In this room, there are some toys. They belong to another child. You are not to touch or play with them." In the *mild-prohibition* condition, the experimenter said, "In this room there are some toys. They belong to another child. I would prefer that you don't touch or play with them." In the *no-prohibition* condition, the experimenter said, "In this room, there are some toys. They belong to another child." For all prohibition groups, the experimenter continued, "In a little while, I am going to read you a story, but I have forgotten something and must go get it. Sit in this chair and look at this book while you are waiting for me." At this point the experimenter handed the child the psychology textbook to the child and said, "I am going to close the door so no one will bother you. I will knock when I return so you will know it's me." Children assigned to the *no-videotape* condition were given one of the three types of prohibition immediately upon entering the room.

The child was left alone and was observed for 15 minutes by the experimenter and in some cases a reliability coder from an adjoining room. Upon returning, the experimenter knocked and waited for 15 seconds before the experimenter entered the room. As the experimenter walked in, she said, "That took much longer than I thought. Now I don't have time to read you a story as I planned. But I'll come back in a week. Then we can read the story." The experimenter returned the child to the classroom. This completed the *posttest phase* of the experiment.

After 1 week, the experimenter returned to the children's classroom and again brought them individually to the experimental room for a *retention-test phase*. The child was again seated at the table. The toys and book were situated in the same positions as in posttesting. This time the experimenter didn't mention the toys or give any further instructions about playing with them. After seating the child, the experimenter began to search through some papers she was carrying. Pretending to have misplaced the child's consent slip, she said, "I seem to have lost your consent slip. I must have it for you to be here with me. You wait here and I'll get it." The child was left alone for 15 minutes. Upon returning, the experimenter said, "I found it. Now I can read you a story as I promised." The child was asked to select one of the story books from the table to be read. After reading the story, the experimenter returned the child to his or her classroom.

Scoring

As in the original Walters and Parke (1964) study, the experimenter recorded the times at which the children touched and ceased to touch the toys on a specially prepared form. The time was read from a stopwatch. From this record, the children's latency of first touch, the number of touches, and the total time spent touching the toys were calculated. All analyses reported in the present article are based on the latter measure for a number of reasons. This measure was the most comprehensive of the measures, has been found to be highly correlated with other measures in prior research, and has been used most extensively in prior studies. Our analyses of the present data based on the other two measures revealed them to be less sensitive to treatment variations but to otherwise yield similar results. Thus all findings reported in this article are based on the total time the child spent touching the toys during the observation periods.

A second observer, a white male, coded approximately one fourth of all children for reliability purposes. The second observer was naive concerning the hypotheses governing the study. The product-moment correlation between the two observers was .97.

The Task, Videotapes, and Procedures sections all encompass what we are describing as the Procedure subsection. The Scoring section corresponds to the Instrumentation subsection. Procedural steps in the implementation of the research are clearly presented. However, the specific independent and dependent variables used in the study are unclear; they are left to the reader to infer since they are not made explicit. For this study the relationship among independent variables is finally presented in the Results section.

Next, consider the Method section from the Huber, Treffinger, Tracy, and Rand (1979) study. The PCTP refers to the Purdue Creativity Training Program, a set of programmed materials of twenty-eight audiotaped stories and presentations, each with exercises to facilitate verbal and figural creative thinking abilities.

Method

Subjects

Six hundred forty-eight subjects from six school buildings in Grades 4, 5, and 6 were selected from an urban public school system. Three hundred nine subjects were enrolled in self-contained classes for intellectually gifted students, and 339 were enrolled in regular classrooms in the same attendance centers. Eighteen classes, consisting of one gifted and one regular class at each grade level in each of three schools, were randomly designated as experimental groups. The remaining 18 classes received no experimental instructional program. The number of students for each cell is presented in Table 1.

Table 1
Distribution of Subjects by Cell

	Experimental		Control	
Grade	Gifted	Regular	Gifted	Regular
4	55	64	49	52
5	47	60	51	46
6	52	63	55	54

The school population was representative of those in other cities of its size (200,000–300,000). The schools in the sample were comparable in socioeconomic status and distribution of sex and race of students and were substantially representative of the total school population in the city.

The gifted program provides an enriched learning environment for pupils of high academic potential. Specific criteria for eligibility for this program include the following: (a) academic excellence in the regular program, prior to selection; (b) IQ score of 125 on an individual test, and at least 2 years above grade level on standardized achievement tests; (c) good emotional, social, and personal development, as evaluated by the professional staff.

Research Design

A $2 \times 2 \times 3$ multivariate analysis of variance (MANOVA) was employed. The independent variables were instructional program or no program (PCTP vs. control), class type (gifted vs. regular), and grade (four, five, or six). The six dependent variables were the verbal and figural fluency, flexibility, and originality scores from the Torrance Tests of Creative Thinking (Torrance, 1974a). Pre- and posttest score differences (posttest minus pretest score) were computed, and the unit of analysis was the gains of individual students.

There were unequal numbers of subjects in each cell of this research design (Table 1). The computer program used for this research (BMD $\times$ 64), was modified by E. B. Cobb of the University of Kansas Department of Mathematics to handle MANOVA designs and unequal cell sizes; therefore, no effort was made to randomly equalize group sizes.

Instruments and Scoring

A battery of tests from the Torrance Tests of Creative Thinking (TTCT; Torrance, 1974a) were used as criterion measures. As operationally defined for this study, creative thinking abilities consisted of verbal and figural fluency, flexibility, and originality. Fluency was defined as the number of relevant responses to the test tasks. Flexibility was the number of different approaches or categories used in producing responses.

Originality was measured by summing the response weights provided by the scoring manual; these weights reflect the statistical infrequency of responses. All scoring was conducted by trained scorers following the procedures described by Torrance (1974b).

Five subtests of the TTCT, three verbal and two figural, were employed. The verbal tests were Product Improvement, Just Suppose, and Unusual Uses; the figural subtests were Repeated Figures and Incomplete Figures. Alternate forms of these tests were administered as pre- and posttests. Scores for each of the verbal and figural tasks were analyzed separately, yielding six dependent variables. Rater reliabilities ranged from .85 to 1.0 for the six variables.

Reliability and Validity of the TTCT

Numerous studies were cited by Torrance (1974b) supporting the reliability of the Torrance Tests of Creative Thinking. Of particular interest was the report by Torrance (1972b) concerning the predictive validity of the TTCT for both short-range and long-range studies. The evidence presented was highly supportive of the ability of the TTCT to predict creative behavior on a wide range of criterion measures.

Although the TTCT are not comprehensive in the measurement of all facets of creative behavior, Torrance (1974b) contended that the tests sample a wide range of the abilities in such a universe. Treffinger, Renzulli, and Feldhusen (1971) proposed that measures of divergent thinking such as the TTCT may be viewed as necessary and useful, but not a sufficient component in the assessment of creative potential. Treffinger and Poggio (1972) suggested that divergent thinking tasks would be correlated with a more comprehensive measure of creative functioning but that the more comprehensive measure would also be related to other cognitive abilities.

Data Collection Procedures

Prior to placing the PCTP in the classrooms, two meetings were held with the teachers whose classes received the treatment. The nature and purpose of the research were outlined and discussed. Mimeographed instructions were distributed that included a description of the PCTP and suggestions for individualizing the program. The instructions asked the teachers to avoid examples of specific responses to the exercises, avoid evaluations of students' responses to exercises, provide opportunities for students to use the PCTP at their own discretion, and permit as much time as possible for a student to complete the exercises before listening to the next tape.

Five subtests from the TTCT, Form B, were administered to all students before the instructional period with the PCTP began in the experimental groups.

Three verbal and two figural tasks were administered, with 8 minutes allowed for each task. The tests were administered by trained members of the research staff in the students' regular classrooms.

The students in the experimental classes used the PCTP over a 12-week period. There were a variety of program implementation strategies observed during this period. These included use of a specific, scheduled time period during the day; a free-time activity option; a free-choice activity for students upon completion of their regular class work; and a free-choice activity any time during the school day. Records of the amount of time spent with specific tapes were not uniformly kept across all experimental groups. The classes in the control group continued normal activities with no special instructional treatment during these same 12 weeks. At the end of the 12-week instructional period the corresponding five subtests from TTCT, Form A, were administered to all students.

Treatment of Data

The data were analyzed using a $2 \times 2 \times 3$ multivariate analysis of variance for unequal cells. The independent variables were class type (gifted or regular), treatment (PCTP or control), and grade (four, five, or six). The six dependent variables were verbal and figural fluency, flexibility, and originality. Analyses were conducted using simple gain scores (posttest minus pretest).

A multivariate analysis of variance was conducted; where significant values occurred for Wilks's (1932) lambda criterion (λ) univariate analyses (ANOVAs) were conducted for each dependent variable. The significance of Wilks's lambda was tested using the table in Timm (1975, p. 635). When significant Fs were obtained on the ANOVAs, appropriate Scheffé post hoc contrasts were conducted. The .05 level of significance was the criterion for all tests.

The Research Design, Data Collection Procedures, and Treatment of Data sections comprise the Procedure subsection, while the Instruments and Scoring and Reliability and Validity of the TTCT sections comprise the Instrumentation subsection. Although the major components of the Procedure subsection are present, including a statement of the independent and dependent variables, the section is poorly organized. For instance, the Treatment of Data section is redundant to most of the Research Design section. Both of these two subsections also omit any discussion of control features to minimize the operation of any possible confounding variables.

The Alexander, Frankiewicz, and Williams (1979) study contains a fairly well organized and complete Procedure subsection.

Method

Subjects

The subjects were 270 fifth-, sixth-, and seventh-grade students from five elementary schools and two junior high schools. The schools were located in middle-class neighborhoods, and the students were predominantly white. The subjects (122 males and 148 females) were randomly selected and transported from their schools for the expressed purpose of participating in a multicultural instructional program. Because time away from the classroom limited each student's participation to only one instructional program, subjects were randomly assigned, within grade level, to one of five experimental conditions. The five conditions involved four types of cognitive organizers and a control condition in which no organizer was presented.

Material

The oral instructional material consisted of presentations on only one of the cultures: Africa, China, Germany, India, and Mexico. The subjects were provided specific information about one of these five cultures by a teacher well-versed in that culture. Presentations for each of the organizer treatment groups were 40 minutes in duration; an additional 10 minutes was allocated for presentation of the appropriate organizers. For the control-group subjects the presentation was extended to 50 minutes to equate the time they spent on the instructional material to the time spent by each of the treatment groups on the organizer and the instructional material together.

The instructional material from each of the five cultures was content analyzed to establish high-level, superordinate concepts. These concepts, then, coupled with particular attributes of the subjects, became the basis for construction of the advance and post organizers. The format of the visual advance and visual post organizers consisted of photographic slides specifically selected and arranged to illustrate several high-level concepts. For example, the notion that the Earth is small in relation to the universe was depicted by one set of slides, which proceeded to emphasize its tremendous diversity through a display of colors along several comprehensive global and flat-surface map features. Another series of slides utilized nondescript stick figures to focus on the general idea that people are different, yet essentially the same. Basic needs common to various primitive and more advanced communities were illustrated by a variety of other slides.

The oral–interactive advance and post organizers consisted of two basic elements. First, an oral presentation provided general ideas about culture and how it emerges. Proceeding from the notion that all communities have certain basic needs, culture was characterized as the outcome of a community's attempts to satisfy those needs. Members of a community then utilized those implements and commodities at their disposal to satisfy their needs, thus accounting for similarities and differences across communities and cultures. The second element in the oral–interactive organizers was a discussion structured to generate specific, high-level concepts that comprise a notion of culture. For example, in one set of discussion questions, students were asked,

What are some basic needs that all humans have? What are some ways in which primitive people attempted to satisfy those needs? Do you think primitive people satisfied those needs the same way in all communities? Or do you think they satisfied them differently? Why?

Each of the organizers was constructed according to the criteria specified by Ausubel. They were more general and inclusive than the instructional material and, by making subsumption under specifically relevant propositions possible, provided optimal anchorage to the meaningful instructional material. According to Ausubel et al. (1978) such a process promotes both initial learning and later resistance to obliterative subsumption.

Instrumentation

Five evaluative instruments, each capable of measuring the acquisition and retention of the oral instruction imparted in the five separate cultural instructional programs, were developed for this study. In developing each of the instruments, a pool consisting of 30 questions was written and submitted to the appropriate one of the five competent teachers of the cultures involved to determine how well the test reflected its intended objectives (the content of the oral instruction). A particular item was retained if the five teachers were in unanimous agreement that the item reflected objectives imparted in the oral instruction. The final format of these instruments consisted of 20 multiple-choice items, with one correct answer and three distractors per item. This procedure assured the content validity of the items in each of the five instruments.

In a pilot study conducted with a group of 18 subjects, each of the five instruments was administered to all subjects immediately following the respective cultural presentation. Presentation sequences were randomized for this group of subjects. The one cultural-specific instrument exhibiting the most variance among the five cultural tests was selected as the metric into which the remaining four cultural instruments were transformed. Inspection of the bivariate frequency distributions resulted in designation of a linear transformation in all cases. Accordingly, the African cultural instrument was regressed upon each of the remaining four cultural instruments. The four resulting linear regression equations were used to transform the administration of both learning and retention of the appropriate cultural instrument into the common metric of the African cultural instrument.

This is an exceedingly conservative procedure in that not all of the reliable variability of each cultural instrument is employed in establishing treatment differences. The advantage is generalizability across several distinct cultural presentations. Essentially, any treatment difference detected employing this strategy would be more dramatic had only one culture been studied. However, such a situation was impossible due to the limited time students were permitted to be away from the classroom.

In conjunction with the aforementioned pilot study, the evaluative instruments were tested for reliability. Coefficients of reliability were computed on the tests for learning and retention using the Kuder–Richardson 21 formula. This procedure yielded an r of .74 for learning and .90 for retention.

Procedure

When random assignment of the subjects to organizer treatment conditions had been completed, the subjects were again randomly assigned to receive oral instruction on only one of the five cultures. Subjects assigned to advance organizer groups received oral instruction immediately following the administration of the advance organizer. Those assigned to post organizer groups received post organizers immediately following the oral instruction. Students assigned to the control group received no advance or post organizer in conjunction with the oral instruction.

Two administrations of the instrumentation were undertaken in order to assess the effects of the independent variable, type of organizer, on the two dependent variables, learning and retention. The first administration, measuring learning, took place immediately following treatment; retention was measured by a second administration of the same instrument 2 weeks following treatment. A standard set of instructions for taking the test was read at each administration. No time limit was given for completion.

Two independent variables, grade level and type of organizer, were arranged in a 3 × 5 factorial design. A two-way, mixed-effects, multivariate analysis of variance was used to analyze the effects of the independent variable, type of organizer, on the dependent variables, learning and retention. No test of significance for main effect for grade level or interaction between grade level and treatment condition was necessary. Interest in this variable was for control purposes only. Blocking on grade level deliberately confounded the mean square for error and type of organizer, thus increasing the precision of the significance test for organizer treatments.

In the Alexander et al. (1979) study, the sections headed Material and Procedure comprise the broader Procedure section that we have discussed. The instructional materials are spelled out completely; example questions and a temporal summary of the research implementation phase are included. Specification of the independent and dependent variables, as well as the control or blocking variables, is also delineated. Replication of the study should be possible.

SUMMARY

We have delineated three main types of multiple-subject research designs: experimental, quasi-experimental, and descriptive. Additional research designs were distinguished within each major type. Three types of experimental designs are: pretest-posttest control group; posttest-only control group; and Solomon four-group. Three types of quasi-experimental designs are: nonequivalent control group; static-group comparison; and time-series designs. We then examined the four most frequently used types of descriptive studies: survey; observational; correlational; and causal-comparative.

We next introduced two types of single-subject research designs: the A–B–A and the multiple-baseline designs. Next we briefly described two less frequently used types of research: historical research; and meta-analysis research. Finally, we reprinted three examples of different Procedure subsections in order to delineate those key components which should be included in a replicable procedure.

OBJECTIVES

In Chapter 7 we have examined the numerous types of research designs that are employed in the educational literature. Check your understanding of the material in Chapter 7 using the following objectives:

Identify the main types of research design: experimental, quasi-experimental, and descriptive.

Identify the specific type of research design for each, and evaluate the appropriateness of the design to a research problem.

Evaluate the specific research design in terms of its threats to internal and external validity.

Identify the two types of single-subject designs: *A–B–A* and multiple-baseline.

Identify the types of research called historical and meta-analysis.

Develop and evaluate a Procedure subsection.

──── TERMS ────

A–B design
A–B–A design
A–B–A–B design
causal-comparative research
correlational research
cross-sectional study
descriptive research
effect size
experimental research
ex post facto research
external criticism
historical research
internal criticism
longitudinal study
meta-analysis
multiple-baseline design
multiple time-series design

nonequivalent control group design
observational research
one-group pretest-posttest design
one-shot case study
posttest-only control group design
pre-experimental design
pretest-posttest control group design
quasi-experimental research
reversal design
single-subject design
Solomon four-group design
static group comparison design
survey research
time-series design

Evaluating
the Instruments

What are the main differences between standardized and
nonstandardized tests?

What is the difference between norm-referenced and criterion-
referenced tests?

What are the different categories of tests, and what is the
purpose of each?

What are the four types of questionnaire or interview scales,
and how do they differ?

What are the different types of reliability, how do they differ,
and what is the appropriate use of each?

What are the different types of validity, how do they differ, and
what is the appropriate use of each?

What are the different types of scores, and how do they differ?

What are the main responsibilities of users of standardized tests?

What key information should an Instrumentation section
contain?

How should a Method section be integrated?

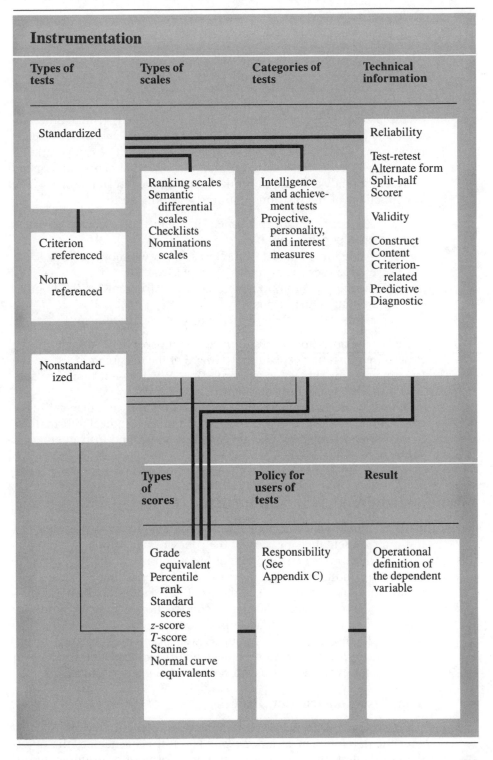

Instrumentation

Types of tests	Types of scales	Categories of tests	Technical information
Standardized			Reliability
	Ranking scales	Intelligence and achieve- ment tests	Test-retest Alternate form Split-half Scorer
	Semantic differential scales	Projective, personality, and interest measures	Validity
Criterion referenced	Checklists Nominations scales		Construct Content Criterion- related Predictive Diagnostic
Norm referenced			
Nonstandard- ized			

Types of scores	Policy for users of tests	Result
Grade equivalent Percentile rank Standard scores z-score T-score Stanine Normal curve equivalents	Responsibility (See Appendix C)	Operational definition of the dependent variable

The main purpose of the Instrumentation subsection of the Method section of a research article is to present the measurement type of operational definition for each dependent variable used in the study. Each dependent variable, first introduced at a concept level in earlier sections of the article, should now be operationally defined so that other researchers can evaluate as well as replicate the study and thereby determine the validity and generalizability of results. An operational definition of each dependent variable increases the clarity and specificity of the study and also minimizes error in the research process. The key functions of the Instrumentation subsection are to:

1. Describe the test or instrument as well as subtests used to assess each dependent variable
2. Provide sample items, if the test is not well known
3. Describe the type of scores obtained from the test
4. Describe the appropriateness of the instrument for the population; that is, the norms
5. Describe the reliability and validity of the instrument

Just as the operational definitions of the independent variables in the Procedure subsection explain the "How?" of the research process, so the Instrumentation subsection presents the "What?"—meaning the specific instruments used in conducting the research project.

In this chapter we shall discuss these five functions and then apply the characteristics of tests and their scores, and other technical information, by reviewing examples of the Subjects, Procedure, and Instrumentation subsections of the Method section.

Standardized and Nonstandardized Tests

Tests are the principal instrument for assessing human performance. A test is a representative measure of the behavior of a sample of a population. A *standardized test* is one that has a consistent and uniform procedure for administering, scoring, and interpreting the subject's behavior. Tests that are not standardized have not established a consistent procedure nor gone through a construction process to minimize error. Examples of nonstandardized tests are those constructed by teachers for use in the classroom as well as many developed by researchers for a research study. Nonstandardized tests typically are not available for evaluation or use in replicating a study's results.

The Test-Construction Process

Constructing a standardized test involves a lengthy process starting with the development of a *test plan.* The test plan includes the objectives of the test, the item scoring and item format (for example, multiple-choice or essay), the target population, and any other pertinent information. In a sense, the test plan is a comprehensive content outline developed from the specifically stated objectives. After the test plan is laid out, test items are written and revised. Following the item-writing phase, specific directions are developed for administering, scoring, and interpreting the test. Throughout the process of test construction, an evaluation and revision feedback loop is incorporated. For instance, items and directions might be field tested several times to weed out poor items or to revise potentially good ones. The difficulty level of items may also be determined at this time. This revision process helps to minimize error.

After the items and directions are established, another step in the test-construction process is to determine the test's reliability and validity. The *reliability* of a test refers to its consistency. Regardless of what concept a test purports to measure, does the test measure it consistently? Three types of reliability measures are typically obtained; they are the consistency (1) from one time of testing to another; (2) among the items or content of the test; and (3) as scored by different individuals.

The validity of a test is perhaps the most important indicator of its quality. *Validity* attempts to determine whether a test measures what it says it measures. If different tests state that they measure an individual's level of anxiety, self-concept, or intelligence, do they indeed measure that concept? In other words, does the test accurately measure the specified concept-level of the dependent measure? This aspect of validity concerns either the content or the concept the test attempts to measure. Other aspects of validity involve determining whether the test can predict or diagnose a subject's performance on another measure. For instance, can this test predict whether the subject is likely to become schizophrenic? Or can this test diagnose whether a person has a reading problem?

Such technical information is derived by assessing a *standardization sample* or *norm group*. To standardize a test, it must be administered to a large, representative sample of subjects for whom it was designed. The group of subjects becomes the standardization sample, and *norms* are calculated from the group's performance. Norms are scores obtained by comparing the subjects' performances. Such scores as percentile ranks, stanines, standard scores, and mean and standard deviations of the distribution of scores are calculated from the sample to obtain a comparison group for interpreting scores. The technical information obtained from this standardization sample—norms, item difficulty, reliability, and validity—is incorporated into the test manual for any particular test. The test manual also includes the information about administering, scoring, and interpreting the test. The test manual and the test comprise the basic source for determining a test's appropriateness for your subjects and your study's purpose. As mentioned in Chapter 4, re-

Standardized Tests Can Help Protect Reliability and Validity

views of various kinds of useful tests may be found in preliminary sources such as *Mental Measurements Yearbook*.

Obviously, not all standardized tests are well constructed and adequately normed. Misuses and abuses do occur; the American Psychological Association has published *Standards for Educational and Psychological Tests* (1974), a useful set of guidelines to "standardize standards" and minimize error and abuse. It was developed by a joint committee from the American Psychological Association, the American Educational Research Association, and the National Council on Measurement in Education, and sets up three levels of standards—essential, very desirable, and desirable—for guidance. These are useful not only to test constructors, but also to those who may wish to evaluate tests for various purposes.

The main reason for using standardized tests and for following the standards for developing tests is to minimize error operating in testing situations. Nonstandardized tests are more susceptible to error. Usually greater information about nonstandardized tests should be provided in the Instrumentation subsection than is required for the standardized measures we are familiar with. Nonstandardized measures also limit the ability to generalize findings and do not facilitate replication by others.

Even though published tests may be well constructed and standardized, they can still be misused by researchers and practitioners. For instance, Gronlund (1981) stated five misuses of published tests in education:

1. Failure to consider the educational objectives measured
2. Failure to consider the limited role tests play in evaluation
3. Failure to interpret realistically the test results
4. Failure to consider the appropriateness of the test for the group intended from the group tested
5. Use of the standardized test score to evaluate teacher effectiveness

Thus, error may arise not just because of the type of test selected but also because of misuse or incorrect administration, scoring, or interpretation of the test.

Norm-Referenced and Criterion-Referenced Tests

Standardized tests are subdivided into norm-referenced and criterion-referenced tests. A *norm-referenced test* or interpretation compares a subject's performance to that of others who have taken the same test. The norm group to which the subjects are compared has similar environmental and/or personological characteristics, such as age, sex, grade, geographical region, and ethnicity. The types of scores derived from a normative comparison include grade equivalents, normal curve equivalents, percentile rank, stanines, and standard scores.

A *criterion-referenced test* or interpretation describes a subject's performance without reference to the performance of others. In this case, a comparison is made to some criterion of performance rather than to a set of norms. Typical criteria used in a criterion-referenced interpretation include *time to task completion* (for example, a puzzle is completed without error in 20 seconds); *precision of task completed* (for example, a puzzle is completed with two errors or less); and *percentage of task items correct* (for instance, 80 percent of a group of puzzles are completed correctly). The percentage correct score is the most widely used of these. Such tests as the Stanford Achievement Tests attempt to combine the elements of both a norm-referenced and a criterion-referenced interpretation. That is, norm-referenced information, such as the stanine, can be sought; also, an item analysis can be requested that analyzes performance by items on test objectives—a criterion-referenced interpretation.

Both norm-referenced and criterion-referenced tests are widely used in schools. For group district-wide testing on measures of intelligence or achievement, norm-referenced tests and scores are generally obtained and reported. A few far-sighted districts may request a criterion-referenced interpretation of test scores as well, to provide instructional assistance to classroom teachers. Norm-referenced tests are used predominantly for the identification, labeling, or comparison of students; criterion-referenced tests are used to get information for developing programs for the instructional needs of students.

Standardized tests are classified according to the concept or construct which the test purports to measure. We shall briefly describe three different classes of such tests. For more detailed descriptions of some of the tests refer to Appendix A.

Intelligence and Achievement Tests

Typically, with intelligence tests we try to measure a subject's current level of ability. Tests designed to measure intelligence may be administered individually or in groups. Concepts frequently tested for in intelligence tests include measures of vocabulary, comprehension, verbal and figural analogies, quantitative or arithmetic reasoning, and even performance measures like block designs or picture arrangements. Two individually administered intelligence tests widely used in schools are the Wechsler Intelligence Scale for Children–Revised (WISC–R), and the Stanford-Binet Intelligence Scale. Three frequently used group intelligence tests are the Cognitive Abilities Test (CAT), the Otis-Lennon Mental Ability Test (OLMAT), and the Test of Cognitive Skills (TCS).

Achievement tests attempt to measure the specific accomplishments of a student after a period of learning in order to determine the level of achievement attained. Most group achievement tests are used to assess student learning over a broad field of knowledge. Most are used by school districts as part of their district-wide testing plans to assess student growth. Areas assessed by such tests include reading, vocabulary, spelling, capitalization, punctuation, word usage, work study, mathematics concepts, problem-solving, and computation. Other content areas, such as science or social studies, may also be assessed. Examples of group achievement tests include Comprehensive Tests of Basic Skills (CTBS), Iowa Tests of Basic Skills (ITBS), Metropolitan Achievement Tests, SRA Achievement Series, and the Stanford Achievement Tests.

Projective, Personality, and Interest Measures

Personality tests encompass both projective and interest measures. Generally speaking, personality tests are measures used to assess attitudinal, emotional, motivational, or social characteristics rather than general intellectual abilities or achievement. Except for the projective tests, these include paper-and-pencil, self-report inventories, or questionnaires administered either individually or in groups.

Projective techniques set out a relatively unstructured task permitting a number of possible responses. In addition, projective testing provides a type of covert psychological interpretation in the sense that the subject is usually not aware of the interpretation made of the responses. Projective techniques have been heavily criticized for being filled with error and bias due to the potential for misinterpreting responses. Such techniques require extensive training in interpreting responses and are used predominantly by clinical psychologists. Perhaps the two most popular projective tests are the Rorschach and the Thematic Apperception Test (TAT).

Personality measures tend toward two extremes: those used to obtain a broad personality profile, and those used to measure a specific aspect of personality. Most are paper-and-pencil, self-report inventories that may be influenced by the error of a subject's misrepresenting an event, emotion, or attitude. However, such personality measures as the Minnesota Multiphasic Personality Inventory (MMPI) can measure this error. Examples of concepts for which personality tests have been constructed include anxiety, dogmatism, flexibility, self-concept, creativity, self-actualization, and leadership.

Interest inventories are designed to determine one's attitude or interest toward a concept. Several compare the subject's perception to the interests expressed by numerous norm groups. One of the most widely used in research studies is the Strong-Campbell Interest Inventory (SCII). It seeks a subject's interest in or attitude toward different occupations, school subjects, activities, amusements, types of people, and their preference between two activities.

In the event that a standardized test does not meet your particular research needs, you may have to develop your own questionnaire, interview, or even your own test.

Questionnaires and Interview Scales

The process of constructing teacher-made tests or researcher-made tests is beyond the scope of a research and statistics textbook. Three comprehensive texts that focus on the test construction and evaluation process are by Gronlund (1981), Thorndike and Hagen (1977), and Tuckman (1975). Thus, we shall not consider further the test construction and validation process or the types of items, such as short answer/ completion, true-false or alternative response, matching, multiple-choice, or essay types, which are used in a test.

However, the education research literature contains numerous questionnaires and interviews that employ a variety of observational and attitudinal scales. We shall briefly describe each of the following four

Concepts and Their Operational Measurements

scales so that you will be aware of the variety of measurement procedures available. They are: (1) ranking scale; (2) semantic differential; (3) checklist; and (4) nominations scale.

Ranking scale.   Perceptions, attitudes, values, and behavior are frequently sought out by using observational or self-report measures. In order to assess these more subjective and intangible components in research, we construct a numerical and a descriptive scale to rate or rank a perception. Even though a numerical scale is employed, it is used primarily to organize responses and to minimize the subjectivity inherent in this type of measurement. The procedure still lacks the desired precision found in other assessments. Variations of a ranking scale look like the following:

Directions: Circle the number that best indicates the degree to which the researcher considered the various threats to internal and external validity. The numbers represent the following values: 5 — outstanding; 4 — good or above average; 3 — average; 2 — poor or below average; and 1 — unsatisfactory.

1. To what extent does the research article consider threats to its internal validity?

1   2   3   4   5

2. To what extent are the threats that are considered pertinent to the research design employed?

1   2   3   4   5

This first scale is a *numerical rating scale.* The one that follows is an example of a *graphic rating scale.*

Directions: Place an X along the horizontal line where it indicates the degree to which the researcher considered the various threats to internal and external validity.

1. To what extent did the research article we evaluated consider threats to internal validity affecting its design?

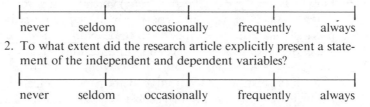

never   seldom   occasionally   frequently   always

2. To what extent did the research article explicitly present a statement of the independent and dependent variables?

never   seldom   occasionally   frequently   always

The third scale is a variation of the graphic rating scale. Called a Likert scale, it is one of those most frequently used to measure attitudes or perceptions. Consider these two formats for expressing the same questions.

Directions: Please circle the letter below to indicate your perception about each statement. If you *strongly agree,* circle *SA;* if you *agree* with the statement, circle *A;* if you *neither agree nor disagree,* circle *U* for *undecided;* if you *disagree,* circle *D;* and if you *strongly disagree,* circle *SD.*

1. The instructor was organized for class.   SA A U D SD
2. Class discussion was pertinent to the topics considered.   SA A U D SD

or this format:

1. The instructor was organized for class.

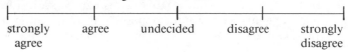

strongly   agree   undecided   disagree   strongly
agree   disagree

2. Class discussion was pertinent to the topics considered.

|————————————|————————————|————————————|————————————|

strongly   agree   undecided   disagree   strongly
agree   disagree

The numerical scoring for a Likert scale usually assigns a 5 = SA, 4 = A, 3 = U, 2 = D, 1 = SD. If a negatively worded item is used, the scale is reversed: 1 = SA, 2 = A, 3 = U, 4 = D, 5 = SD. This procedure would apply to the two following statements, one worded positively, the other negatively:

The instructor was interesting.

or

The instructor was boring.

Following this procedure enables you to add up the item scores to determine how positive the attitudes were toward the concept being rated.

Semantic differential scale. The semantic differential scale, also known as the bipolar adjective scale, typically is a seven-point scale that pairs an adjective with its opposite. It is used to describe or evaluate a particular situation or experience. In developing a semantic differential scale, the main task is to select appropriate adjectives. The developers of the scale (Osgood, Suci, and Tannenbaum, 1957) list a large group of adjectives from which adjective pairs can be selected. The example below is from the Tuckman Teacher Feedback Form (Tuckman, 1975).

Place an X in that one space of the seven between each adjective pair that best indicates your perception of the teacher's behavior. The closer you place your X toward one adjective or the other, the more you think that adjective better describes the teacher than the other.

(1)	ORIGINAL ____:____:____:____:____:____:____	CONVENTIONAL
(2)	PATIENT ____:____:____:____:____:____:____	IMPATIENT
(3)	COLD ____:____:____:____:____:____:____	WARM
(4)	HOSTILE ____:____:____:____:____:____:____	AMIABLE
(5)	CREATIVE ____:____:____:____:____:____:____	ROUTINIZED
(6)	INHIBITED ____:____:____:____:____:____:____	UNINHIBITED
(7)	ICONOCLASTIC ____:____:____:____:____:____:____	RITUALISTIC
(8)	GENTLE ____:____:____:____:____:____:____	HARSH

To score, positive and negative items can be scored from 7 to 1, with negative items scored in the opposite direction, similar to the scoring on the Likert scale. Or, as Tuckman (1975) recommends, positive and negative items can both be scored from 7 to 1, and then the score of the negative items can be subtracted from the score on the positive items to derive a total score.

Checklists.   Whereas rating scales are an attempt to determine the degree to which a behavioral characteristic is present or the frequency with which a behavior occurs, checklists usually ask for a simple "yes–no" judgment (Gronlund, 1981). They have been used successfully to evaluate specific behavioral or performance skills. A specific type is the *adjective checklist* in which a list of adjectives for describing or evaluating a situation is presented to the subject, and the directions ask the subject to check all those which apply. For instance:

1. This research study was ＿＿informative
                              ＿＿well constructed
                              ＿＿worthwhile
                              ＿＿incomprehensible

or

2. I am ＿＿happy
        ＿＿noisy
        ＿＿helpful
        ＿＿lazy

The adjective checklist is a useful tool to help individuals learn to use adjectives to describe their feelings. A score is obtained by adding the number of positive adjectives checked and subtracting from the total number of negative adjectives checked. The resulting total score is an indicator of the positiveness of the attitude. An example is the Adjective Checklist (ACL) published by Consulting Psychologists Press.

Nominations scale.   With this scale subjects are asked to name one or more things, people, or situations that best correspond to a category. The procedure has been used extensively with students and teachers to nominate children who exhibit a variety of social or academic characteristics in the classroom. A current use is to incorporate a nominations procedure into the selection procedure for choosing students for gifted and talented programs. Peer, teacher, and parent nominations have been employed. Questions such as the following have been used:

1. Name the three students who are best in math.
   (A) ＿＿＿＿＿, (B) ＿＿＿＿＿, (C) ＿＿＿＿＿
2. Who always asks the best questions?
   (A) ＿＿＿＿＿, (B) ＿＿＿＿＿, (C) ＿＿＿＿＿
3. Who is good at making things up, like stories, games, jokes, and pictures?
   (A) ＿＿＿＿＿, (B) ＿＿＿＿＿, (C) ＿＿＿＿＿

4. Who has a lot of different ideas?
   (A) —————, (B) ——————, (C) ————
5. Who can talk to grown-ups easily?
   (A) —————, (B) ——————, (C) ————
6. Who plays table games the best? (Games like Monopoly, chess, dungeons and dragons, backgammon)
   (A) —————, (B) ——————, (C) ————

Scoring for the nominations procedure is relatively easy. Students get one point every time they are nominated in a particular category. As the scores are totalled, students with the highest scores in each category become the nominees. The researcher should always specify the context for the nominations in order for the procedure to have some validity.

So far in this chapter we have discussed what a standardized test is and how it differs from a nonstandardized test. We have also presented the different categories of tests and discussed the four main scales which are used in the research literature. Another characteristic of standardized tests we shall consider is the technical information available from the standardization sample. This discussion on reliability and validity will be followed by an interpretation of the numerous test scores obtained from the instruments used in educational research.

Reliability and Validity

The technical quality of a test depends upon its reliability and validity. As we have said, the reliability of a test refers to its consistency. Regardless of what the test measures, does it do so consistently? We shall analyze three types of reliability: the consistency of a test from one time of testing to the next; the consistency of the test items or content; and, the consistency of scoring among different observers or raters. Validity, on the other hand, attempts to determine whether a test measures what it says it measures. After a separate discussion of reliability, we shall focus on these three types of validity: construct validity, content validity, and criterion-related validity, both diagnostic and predictive.

Reliability

There are two major components of any obtained test score: *true score,* and *error. True score* reflects the individual's actual performance or ability level, while *error* reflects the limitations of the test, the circumstances of the testing situation, or the human errors of the tester or testee. The goal in testing is to minimize the error and increase the probability that the obtained test scores accurately reflect the subject's true ability. For every obtained score, we may have either a large degree of

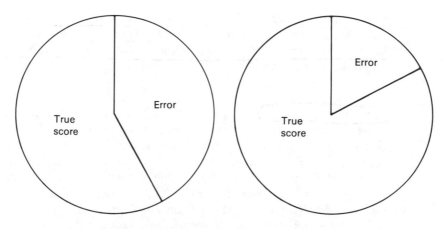

Figure 8.1 Major Components of a Test Score

error or a minimum of error; but we can never eliminate it, as illustrated in Figure 8.1.

The error component is divided into four types: (1) error due to time of testing, (2) error due to the items or the content of the test, (3) error due to scoring, and (4) unexplained error. Thus, we can revise the graph to look like Figure 8.2.

The main types of reliability attempt to measure the degree of consistency of the test scores, or conversely, to measure the degree of error operating from each of the principal sources. We can indicate the degree

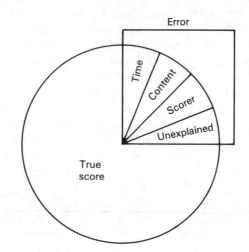

Figure 8.2 Kinds of Test Error

of reliability by using a value ranging from 0.0 to +1.0. The closer the value approaches +1.0 the more reliable or consistent a test score is. Reliability coefficients above 0.80 generally indicate good consistency. As the value approaches 0.0, error is maximized and consistency is minimized.

Test-retest reliability. Test-retest reliability measures the consistency of test scores over time. The same test is given twice to the standardization sample with a time interval typically ranging from a few days to a year or more. The obtained test scores are correlated, and the reliability coefficient obtained indicates how stable or consistent the test scores are over time. For instance, if it is above 0.80, subjects tend to obtain similar, though usually not identical, scores in the two test administrations.

Test-retest reliability coefficients should be examined in such situations as pretest-posttest designs in which the same test is readministered. An important point to consider is the time interval for the test-retest measure. If only a few days or a week separate testing times, the coefficient may be misleadingly high due to subjects recalling items. If the period is as long as a year or more, the coefficient may not accurately reflect the consistency of the test, since subjects will have matured, and other confounding variables may spuriously affect the reliability coefficient.

Alternate-form reliability. Also called *equivalent-form reliability, alternate-form reliability* measures the consistency of the test due to its content. It measures the degree to which two forms of the same test are measuring similar aspects of behavior. Two forms of the test are administered to the norm group, frequently back-to-back, or with only a short interval, and the obtained test scores are correlated. The resulting reliability coefficient is interpreted in a way similar to that for the test-retest method. Researchers who use different forms of the same test should consider the alternate-form reliability. Test developers also should report the reliability coefficients in the test manual along with the other coefficients.

Sometimes the alternate-form method is administered after a time interval. In this situation the reliability coefficient provides a measure of consistency due to time as well as due to the content or equivalence of items. In these cases, as in the test-retest procedure, the length of time between the two forms should be considered. For a longer time period, we would expect to obtain a smaller reliability coefficient.

There are two other reliability procedures frequently used to determine the consistency of test scores due to the content or test items. One is the *split-half reliability* procedure in which the test is given only once and is divided in half to score. The typical procedure is an odd-even one in which one score is obtained for the even-numbered items and one for the odd-numbered items. The two scores for each subject are correlated, and the resulting value provides a *measure of internal consistency* of the test. The split-half reliability coefficient represents the degree to which the two halves of the test are equivalent or consistent in terms of its items. Since the original coefficient was based on two scores from *half* the test, it needs to be adjusted to obtain the reliability coefficient for the *entire* test. To estimate the reliability of scores for the whole test, the Spearman-Brown Prophecy formula should be employed and reported in the test manual or research study. The Spearman-Brown formula is:

$$\text{Reliability of entire test} = \frac{2 \times \text{reliability of } \frac{1}{2} \text{ test}}{1 + \text{reliability of } \frac{1}{2} \text{ test}}$$

If the original coefficient is .70 based on half the test items, then:

$$\text{Reliability of entire test} = \frac{2\,(.70)}{1 + .70} = \frac{1.40}{1.70} = .82$$

In this case, the corrected reliability coefficient is 0.82 for the entire test, based on the Spearman-Brown Prophecy formula, as compared to the smaller reliability coefficient of 0.70 based on half the test items.

The second method used to estimate the reliability of the content of a test is the Kuder-Richardson (K–R) formulas. Two of the most frequently used are the *K–R 20* and *K–R 21.* Both provide a measure of the internal consistency of the test. They are most appropriate when tests are untimed or when the speed of work is not a factor influencing test scores. The earlier method should be used if reliability for speed tests is sought.

Scorer reliability. The third basis for estimating the reliability of a test is the accuracy of scoring. For many tests that are computer scored, there is no need to determine this reliability. However, when subjects are being rated on numerous dimensions or observed on various attributes, this reliability is essential. Whenever multiple interpretations of a subject's performance on a test are possible, scorer reliability should be obtained. Scorer reliability also is known as *interobserver reliability, interrater reliability, or interscorer agreement.* Basically, a group of raters, scorers, or judges each scores a number of tests. For instance, four raters may all score ten tests. Then correlation coefficients are calculated for all possible pair-wise raters, and this represents the strength of the scorer agreement. With four raters we might generate the coefficients shown in Table 8.1.

Table 8.1 Interrater Reliability for Four Raters

	Rater 1	Rater 2	Rater 3	Rater 4
Rater 1	1.00	0.94	0.97	0.80
Rater 2		1.00	0.95	0.79
Rater 3			1.00	0.75
Rater 4				1.00

In this case the rater agreement ranges from 0.75 to 0.97. Upon further inspection we see a high scorer reliability among raters 1, 2, and 3; but rater 4 shows a lower agreement. Rater 4 may not have been as well trained or may not have been as accurate in interpreting the scoring system. Also, experimenter bias may have been operating with rater 4.

We have examined the three main types of reliability used in determining a test's consistency in educational research. However, there is another important reliability concept that is used to meaningfully interpret individual test scores. This is the *standard error of measurement,* which we will now briefly describe.

Standard error of measurement. Unlike the previous indicators that estimate the reliability of the entire test, the standard error of measurement (SEM) estimates the error of an individual's test score and is used to interpret it.

Using the SEM, a person's *true* score will fall in a range of plus or minus one standard error on each side of the test score 68 percent of the time. For instance, if we have an obtained IQ score of 130 and the SEM is 5 IQ points, then the range about the obtained score of 130, within which the true score would fall 68 percent of the time, would be an IQ range from 125 to 135.

If we had a range of plus or minus 2 SEM, a person's true score would fall within that range about the obtained score 95 percent of the time. And, if we had a range of plus or minus 3 SEM, 99 percent of the time the true score would fall within that range. However the range may become so large that it loses its practical meaning. For ± 2 SEM in the previous example, the range would be from 120 to 140, and for ± 3 SEM the range would be from 115 to 145.

All test manuals should state the standard error of the particular test and it should be reported by the researcher. It is derived from the reliability coefficient; the higher the reliability coefficient, the smaller the standard error; conversely, the lower the reliability coefficient, the greater the standard error. The use of the standard error minimizes the preoccupation and potential for misinterpretation of one particular score and emphasizes the need to consider the ranges of error within a particular test score. The result should be a more thoughtful and rational basis for interpreting test scores.

Validity

The validity of a test is probably the most important indicator of its quality. As we have said, validity indicates whether a test measures what it says it measures. If a test claims to measure creativity, does it, as the operational definition of the creativity concept, accurately measure that particular concept? Or, if a test claims to diagnose schizophrenia, can it, as the operational definition, really diagnose that concept? The three types of validity are: construct, content, and criterion-related validity. We shall discuss each of these individually.

Construct validity. Construct validity is the broadest type and actually includes the other types we shall discuss. It attempts to determine the degree to which a particular test measures a theoretical construct or trait. For instance, all the following are hypothetical constructs: self-actualization, intelligence, anxiety, creativity, self-concept. They are hypothetical constructs because they are not directly observable behaviors but are inferred from their effect on behavior. In other words, construct validity attempts to determine whether a test measures the construct it says it measures. We shall discuss three frequently used techniques for establishing construct validity.

Age differentiation is a validity technique used to determine whether there is increasing performance with increasing age. Useful with intelligence and achievement measures where cognitive development or reasoning increases with age, it has only limited use with personality measures.

Correlations with other tests is a validity technique used with new tests. For instance, if you have just developed a new intelligence test, you may have your standardization sample of subjects take it, along with two or three other available intelligence tests, plus a creativity test, and perhaps a self-concept test or anxiety test. Ideally, you would want your new test to correlate only moderately well with the other intelligence tests. Too high a correlation might indicate that yours is a redundant version of what is already available. In addition, you may want your test to correlate negatively (or low) with the self-concept or anxiety test, since you did not develop your test to measure those constructs. Finally, you may want a positive correlation with the creativity test scores, since the two constructs do relate in past research; but you will not want the relationship to be as high as those with the other intelligence measures. With these comparisons, you may be able to conclude that your test does seem to measure intelligence as a construct as measured by the other tests.

The third procedure uses a statistical technique called *factor analysis* that is used to validate hypothetical constructs. This is a statistical procedure to identify those items which seem to relate most to each other, and which then form separate traits or factors. This procedure also is called *factorial validity.*

Content validity. The degree to which a sample of test items represents the area of content the test is designed to measure is *content validity.* For instance, if you stated that your test measures arithmetical reasoning, and the test items are mainly computational, your test would have a low content validity. No numerical coefficient similar to reliability coefficients is obtained with content validity. Instead, a professional with expertise in the respective field is asked to examine the test. Frequently, half of a group of professionals is given the test and asked to analyze it to determine what the test measures. The other half is given the test and objectives and told: "This test is an attempt to measure arithmetical reasoning. Please examine it and evaluate it to determine if it seems to measure what we think it measures." These two procedures are known as *face validity.* Face validity is a professional appraisal of what appears to be valid for the content the test attempts to measure.

A second type of content validity is known as *sampling validity.* Sampling validity is the degree to which a test measures a sufficient sample of the total content that it purports to measure. For instance, for an achievement test, does it cover a representative sample of curricular materials? By examining the test objectives and the number and quality of items in each subject area, some decision about its sampling validity can be made.

Content validity is most useful with intelligence, ability, achievement, and skill and proficiency tests. For personality measures, content validity is inappropriate and can be misleading, since questions may bear no obvious relationship to the personality domain being tested. Actually, the questions may be derived through statistical procedures to validate their relationship to a particular construct such as factor analysis.

Criterion-related validity. The degree to which a test is effective in predicting or diagnosing an individual's behavior in specific situations is *criterion-related validity.* Performance on the test is compared to an external criterion. The criterion is an independent measure of that which the test is designed to predict or diagnose. There are two types *predictive* and *diagnostic.* Criterion-related predictive validity attempts to estimate or predict future outcomes. For instance, the question may be:

> Is the subject likely to: (a) become schizophrenic; (b) succeed in college; (c) become depressed; (d) succeed in job training?

In other words, the criteria are all future oriented rather than immediate. *Criterion-related diagnostic validity,* on the other hand, attempts to determine or diagnose the existing state of a subject. The question may be:

> Is the subject: (a) schizophrenic; (b) learning disabled; (c) mentally retarded?

Thus the only difference between these two types of criterion-related validity is the immediate or future nature of the external criterion.

An example of criterion-related predictive validity is the comparison or correlation of Scholastic Aptitude Test (SAT) scores with either the external criterion of college grade-point average (GPA), or more simply, the criterion of whether the subject completed or did not complete college. Thus the size of the validity coefficient obtained, which ranges from 0.0 to +1.0, indicates the strength of the prediction. Validity coefficients of 0.40 or 0.50 are considered high.

Validity and Reliability Protecting the Hypothesis

An example of criterion-related diagnostic validity is the procedure of comparing or correlating scores on the Minnesota Multiphasic Personality Inventory (MMPI) with the immediate criterion of whether the subjects are institutionalized schizophrenics, or whether the subjects are members of an average college student population. In other words, one could hypothesize that institutionalized schizophrenics would have a different MMPI profile from a college population. Thus, diagnostic information about the criterion of being schizophrenic or not is obtained by the profile of scores for that particular test. Validity coefficients of 0.40 and 0.50 again are considered high for criterion-related diagnostic validity.

In selecting or evaluating a test, you should not only consider its practical qualities—such factors as ease of administration, length of time to give it, functional appearance, and so on—you should also evaluate it for its technical qualities. These technical qualities include its reliability, its validity, and the type of norms available. The following section will interpret the scores most frequently derived from the standardization sample.

Interpreting Types of Scores

Many types of scores can be obtained from any one test. For each type, the interpretation and meaning of that value will vary. The most basic score obtained from any test is the *raw score.* This is the first and most frequently used score in teacher-made tests. For instance, if a sample of 25 students takes a 50-item multiple-choice test, the total number of items answered correctly by each subject would be his or her raw score. In this case the range of raw score values could conceivably run from 0 to 50. The raw score is the basic performance score obtained from a test prior to transformation into some other score. Percentile rank scores are derived by transforming raw scores. Thus a *derived score* is a numerical score obtained by transforming a raw score. The derived score must be based on some norm scale that has meaning. The specific types of derived scores which are norm based and which we will consider are:

> grade equivalent norms
> age equivalent norms
> percentile ranks or norms
> standard score norms: *z*-scores, *T*-scores, stanines, and normal curve
>   equivalents (NCEs).

Typically, the extent of interpretation of raw scores available to a teacher or researcher is obtained by first ranking the scores from highest to lowest and making a general decision as to whether a subject has performed in the high, average, or low range of the distribution. It doesn't matter what the percentage of correct items was, such as 80 or 50 percent, since it will not affect the subject's relative standing in the distribution. The advantage of most derived scores over raw scores is that they allow for more extensive and meaningful interpretation and comparison. However, some are prone to so much misinterpretation that their use is no longer recommended. For instance, in the *Standards for Educational and Psychological Tests* (APA, 1974) it is recommended that:

> Interpretive scores that lend themselves to gross misinterpretation, such as mental age or grade equivalent scores, should be abandoned or their use discouraged (p. 23).

Grade Equivalent Norms

Grade equivalent norms are constructed by giving a test to a standardization sample at the grade levels for which the test is developed. First, the *average raw score,* or the average number of correct items for students at each grade level, is calculated. The average raw score is then assigned the corresponding grade-level value. This in turn becomes the *grade-equivalent score.* For instance, on a 50-item reading comprehension subtest designed for grades 3 through 8, we may obtain the following information:

Average raw score	12	18	27	31	37	43
Grade level	3.1	4.1	5.1	6.1	7.1	8.1

The grade level is reported with the .1 because the norm group was tested in the first month of a 10-month school year. (In some test manuals the grade level is reported without the decimal, such as 31, 41, and so forth.) Intermediate grade equivalent values for raw scores between each of the above values are calculated by interpolation. Interpolating would result in an expanded set of scores as in Table 8.2.

Interpretation of grade equivalent (GE) norms can be deceptive. In any norm-based interpretation you must always keep in mind that comparisons are made to the subject's norm group. For instance, Johnny, who is a fifth grader, received a GE = 5.1. Susie, also a fifth grader, received a GE = 3.1, and Janna, also a fifth grader, received a GE = 8.1. What do we infer from these scores? We can interpret the following:

Compared to *other fifth graders,* Johnny performed at the average level.
Compared to *other fifth graders,* Susie performed below average.
Compared to *other fifth graders,* Janna performed above average.

Table 8.2 Grade Equivalents for Raw Scores

Raw score	Grade equivalent	Raw score	Grade equivalent
10	2.8	29	5.6
11	3.0	30	5.9
12	3.1	31	6.1
13	3.2	32	6.3
14	3.4	33	6.5
15	3.6	34	6.7
16	3.8	35	6.9
17	4.0	36	7.0
18	4.1	37	7.1
19	4.2	38	7.4
20	4.3	39	7.6
21	4.4	40	7.7
22	4.5	41	7.9
23	4.6	42	8.0
24	4.8	43	8.1
25	4.9	44	8.3
26	5.0	45	8.5
27	5.1	46	8.7
28	5.3	47	8.9

For many of the achievement tests on the market, this is the most we can conclude about a student's performance. We *cannot* state that:

Susie performed at a third-grade reading comprehension level, or two years below grade level.

Janna performed at an eighth-grade reading comprehension level, or three years above grade level.

For most tests, we also cannot conclude that Susie scored the same as the *average performance* of third graders in their first month of school, or that Janna scored the same as the average performance of eighth graders in their first month of school. The reason is very simple, yet ignored by many test developers. In the standardization of the test, children at different grade levels do not receive the same test or the same items to answer. Most tests have children taking a different level at each grade, where only a fraction of the items overlap. For instance, a fourth grader may start a test halfway or two-thirds of the way into where the third grader will stop, and will end his test one-third into where a fifth grader started his test. And so, in this instance, similar items across each grade may overlap only one-third of the time. Thus, the fifth grader is answering different and harder items than the fourth grader, and the fourth grader is answering different and harder items than the third grader. We cannot conclude, therefore, that a fifth grader, like Janna, scored at the average level of eighth graders in their first school month. The eighth graders are usually asked harder and more appropriate eighth-grade items; they are taking another level of the same test. Janna's performance is based on mastery of fifth-grade knowledge—not on the ability to do eighth-grade work. *If, and only if, they answered the same test items could we make the comparison to the average performance of a norm group other than the fifth graders.*

Some tests have separate test booklets or levels for every two or three grades. For instance, level 1 for grades 1 to 3, level 2 for grades 4 to 6, and so on. Only if children took the same level test—that is, the same test items for that level—would comparison to the average performance of another grade be valid. Otherwise, the most we can say about GEs is that, compared to other students in the same grade, the child performed average, below average, or above average. It does not mean that Janna is ready for eighth-grade work, nor should Susie be placed into third-grade work.

Another frequent misinterpretation of grade equivalents is to make comparisons and interpretations across subtests using GEs. In other words, grade equivalents from one school subject to another are not comparable, because growth occurs at different rates in different subject areas. Other derived scores, such as percentile ranks, or standard scores, would be more valid for comparing performance across school subjects.

It is not clear why grade equivalents continue to be widely used. I have conducted workshops, minicourses, and graduate courses for more than a thousand teachers, parents, counselors, and administrators, and in surveying them before the course, have found only about 2 of every 100 people who correctly interpreted a GE. I suspect the reason they are still used is based on shared misinterpretation. That is, nearly everyone misinterprets them in the same way, and so no one raises questions since they are all consistently wrong. The counselor misinterprets GEs to the teacher, and the teacher to the parent; but since they all agree and are satisified, they assume that they have interpreted the scores correctly, instead of being consistently wrong. A serious concern is that this procedure is propagated in standardized test manuals that also misinterpret and recommend using only grade equivalents. Thus, school district personnel may confidently cite a test manual as their authority, yet still be incorrect.

Age Equivalent Norms

Age equivalent norms are developed in a way similar to that used for grade equivalents and are subject to similar misinterpretation. The *age equivalent score* is the average score of subjects of a particular age. It is obtained by testing a representative standardization sample of 5-year olds, 6-year olds, 7-year olds, 8-year olds, and so on. The criticism of age equivalent norms is similar to that of grade equivalents: Is a year's growth a standard equal unit? For instance, is the growth from age 6 to age 7 equal to the growth from age 10 to age 11? Or with grade equivalents, is a gain from 4.1 to 5.1 the same as a gain from 7.1 to 8.1? Not at all, for most concepts being examined. It has been found to be of most use in infancy, early childhood, and the primary grades—particularly to score the physical characteristics such as height and weight, and general intelligence of children.

Because of the widespread misinterpretation of both grade and age equivalents, it is urged that, if these scores must be obtained, they be converted to percentile ranks, or standard scores, or other derived scores that are more accurately interpreted.

Percentile Ranks or Norms

A widely used and easily understood derived score to describe test performance is the percentile rank. A *percentile rank* (Pr) describes the subject's position in a relative distribution of scores in terms of the percentage of subjects who scored *equal to or lower than* a given score. Thus if Janna had a Pr = 90th percentile, we would know that 90 percent of the students in her norm group, the fifth grade, scored equal to or lower than her score. Remember that a person's performance should always be referred to the respective norm group. We could conceivably compare her performance to that of any norm group; for instance, compared to fourth graders, her Pr might equal 99+, and compared to eighth graders, her Pr might equal 60. Typically, however, a subject's performance is reported in terms of his or her relative standing to a meaningful group, such as grade, age, sex, ethnic group, or type of curriculum studied.

Here is a simple formula for determining the percentile rank of any given score:

$$\text{Pr} = \frac{\text{cum } fX + \frac{1}{2} fX}{N}$$

where Pr   is the percentile rank,
  cum fX is the cumulative frequency of scores below the score X,
    $\frac{1}{2} fX$ is one-half of the frequency of scores that score X, and
    N is the total number of scores.

For instance, if we want to calculate the percentile rank of a score of 42 for Greg on a reading comprehension test in a class of 35 students, we note that four students in the class scored 42, including Greg, and 22 students scored lower than 42. In this case,

$$\text{cum } fX = 22$$
$$\tfrac{1}{2} fX = \tfrac{1}{2}(4) = 2, \text{ and}$$
$$N = 35.$$

Substituting into the formula, we have:

$$\text{Pr} = \frac{22 + 2}{35} = 24/35$$
$$\text{Pr} = 0.6857$$
$$\text{Pr} = 69\text{th percentile}$$

Thus Greg's reading comprehension score, rounded to the nearest whole number and compared to his third-grade classmates, is at the 69th percentile.

The main limitation of percentile norms is that the percentile units are not equal on all sections of the scale. That is, they fall on an ordinal measurement scale rather than on an interval scale. For instance, a percentile difference of ten units about the 50th percentile, from $\text{Pr} = 45$ to $\text{Pr} = 55$, represents a smaller discrepancy in test performance than the same ten-unit difference at the ends of the distribution—say from 5 to 15, or from 85 to 95. This is because more subjects usually perform near the average, the 50th percentile, and fewer subjects perform at the low or high extremes. This finding follows from the properties of the *standard normal distribution*, or the *normal curve* with which you are no doubt familiar. Two implications of the unequal unit nature of percentiles should be remembered. One is that percentile ranks that are averaged arithmetically—by calculating a *mean score*—do not result in a meaningful value, hence should be discouraged. As we shall see in Chapter 9, the *median* is the most appropriate average value when summarizing performance using percentile ranks. The second implication is that small differences in percentile rank scores near the middle of the distribution are not very meaningful. Similar differences toward the extremes of the distribution, though, are meaningful, because in order to increase his score by 10 percent of the distribution, the subject must increase his raw score by a large amount, since there are so few subjects near the extremes of the distribution.

Standard Score Norms

The remaining types of norms are called *standard score norms* because they are derived from the properties of the normal curve, or standard normal distribution. These standard scores express performance in terms of standard deviation units above or below the mean. The mathematical properties of the standard normal distribution will first be explained. *If you do not have a good understanding of the mean and standard deviation, read the appropriate sections in Chapter 9 before continuing this discussion.* After delineating the properties of the standard normal distribution, we will consider four types of standard scores.

Standard normal distribution.   The standard normal distribution, also called the *normal curve,* is a symmetrical, bell-shaped curve whose mathematical properties are useful for test interpretation. The normal distribution is divided into equal intervals denoted by $\overline{X}$ and s; between every two portions of the distribution, a particular percentage of scores will fall (see Figure 8.3).

Thus, between the $\overline{X}$ and +1 s, 34.13 percent of the scores will fall; between +1 s and +2 s, 13.59 percent of the scores will fall; and between +2 s and +3 s, 2.14 percent of the scores will fall. Since the distribution is symmetrical, what occurs above the mean also occurs below the mean. Thus between −3 s and +3 s, 99.74 percent of the scores in a distribution will fall.

For instance, if we had a distribution that was standardized on $\overline{X}$ = 100 and s = 15, as the WISC–R is, the curve would look like Figure 8.4. Thus, a full scale IQ = 115 would fall one standard deviation above the mean, and an IQ = 70 would fall two standard deviations below the mean. Rounding the percentage of scores between every two sections in Figure 8.3, we can determine the percentage of scores that fall below the IQ of 115. Thus, 84 percent of the scores (50 percent below the mean plus 34 percent between the mean and +1 s) fall below an IQ of 115. The score is equal to the 84th Pr for an IQ of 115 when standardized on $\overline{X}$ = 100 and s = 15. A score of 70 would fall at the 2nd percentile since 2 percent of the scores fall below −2 s.

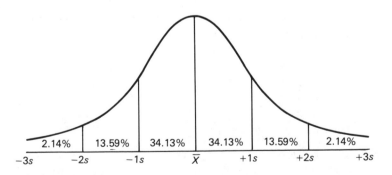

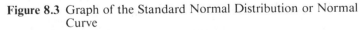

Figure 8.3 Graph of the Standard Normal Distribution or Normal Curve

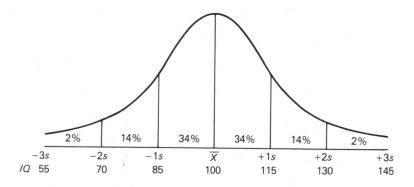

Figure 8.4 Distribution of IQ Scores on the Normal Curve

z-Score.   The *z*-score is one of many standard scores used in testing; it is the most basic standard score and is the one from which others are derived. The *z*-score expresses raw score performance in terms of the number of standard deviation units above or below the mean. It is standardized on $\overline{X} = 0$ and s = 1. In a sense we have already introduced the *z*-score in discussing the properties of the normal distribution. For instance, the IQ = 115 fell at +1 s above the mean, and the IQ = 70 fell at −2 s below the mean. These values, +1.0 and −2.0 respectively, are *z*-scores. More specifically, the formula for calculating the *z*-score expresses systematically the information we obtained intuitively with the two *IQ* scores.

$$z = \frac{X - \overline{X}}{s}$$

where *z* is the *z*-score value,
      X is any particular score,
      $\overline{X}$ is the arithmetic mean of a distribution of scores, and
      s is the standard deviation of that same distribution.

With the two *IQ* examples, a *z*-score is calculated for each.

$$z = \frac{115 - 100}{15} \qquad z = \frac{70 - 100}{15}$$

$$z = 15/15 \qquad \text{and} \qquad z = -30/15$$

$$z = +1.0 \qquad z = -2.0$$

Knowing the *z*-score of any score enables us to determine the percentile rating of the score by comparing it to the properties of the standard normal distribution (see Table 8.3). However, when a *z*-score does not

Table 8.3 Comparison of z-Scores with
Percentile Ranks

z	Pr
−3.0	1
−2.0	2nd
−1.0	16th
0.0	50th
+1.0	84th
+2.0	98th
+3.0	99th

round off nicely to either the mean or one of the standard deviation units, visual inspection of the distribution will not yield exact values.

For instance, the Pr for an IQ of 110 will give a $z = +0.67$, as this calculation shows:

$$z = \frac{110 - 100}{15}$$

$$z = 10/15$$

$$z = +0.67$$

We know that the IQ score fell two-thirds of a standard deviation above the mean. To arrive at the specific Pr for that z, or others that fall between the values above, a table giving the percentage of scores which fall below a particular z-score value must be consulted. Table 2 in Appendix D gives these corresponding values. Thus a $z = +0.67$ has 74.86 percent of the scores which fall below it. Rounding to the nearest whole number gives a $Pr = 75$th percentile. To use the table you go down the rows until you find 0.6 and across the columns until you find .07. The intersecting value is .2486. As the table explains, for a positive z-score you add 50 percent to it (.5000 + .2486 = .7486), then move the decimal two places to the right to convert from proportion to percentage (or multiply the proportion by 100), and round to the nearest whole number to obtain the percentile rank. Thus, for a $z = 0.67$ from an IQ score $= 110$ (standardized on a $\overline{X} = 100$ and $s = 15$), the score falls at the 75th percentile. For a negative z-score, the intersecting value is subtracted from 50 percent and rounded to the nearest whole number to obtain the percentile rank (e.g., $z = 0.53$, .5000 − .2019 = .2981, .2981 × 100 = 29.81%, $Pr = 30$th).

T-score. The *T-score* is another of the most widely used standard scores. It is standardized on $\overline{X} = 50$ and $s = 10$. For instance, the SCII and the MMPI, mentioned earlier, report results in terms of T-scores. The T-score is found by multiplying the z-score by 10 (the new T-score standard deviation) and adding the result to 50 (the new T-score mean). Thus

$$T\text{-score} = 50 + 10(z)$$

Like the z-score, any T-score can be directly interpreted since we know the $\overline{X}$ and s. For instance, converting the three z-scores obtained from the IQ scores of 70, 110, and 115, respectively, we get these results:

(1) $IQ = 70$ T-score $= 50 + 10(-2.0)$
      $z = -2.0$ $= 50 - 20 = 30$

(2) $IQ = 110$ T-score $= 50 + 10(+.067)$
      $z = +0.67$ $= 50 + 6.7 = 56.7$

(3) $IQ = 115$ T-score $= 50 + 10(+1.0)$
      $z = +1.0$ $= 50 + 10 = 60$

A T-score also is directly interpretable. For instance, a T-score $= 60$ always means that the score fell $+1$ s above the mean, and the Pr would always be at the 84th percentile. By transforming the T-score formula algebraically, we can also convert a T-score to a z-score.

$$z = \frac{T - 50}{10}$$

These formulas give us a lot of flexibility for comparing test scores and for obtaining the Pr or the most appropriate values for our research.

Stanine.   A *stanine* value also is reported in the norm tables of some test manuals. Stanines are standardized on $\overline{X} = 5$ and $s = 2$. Stanine values range from 1 to 9. Stanines divide the normal distribution into nine parts; in fact the word stanine comes from <u>sta</u>ndard <u>nine</u> point scale. Stanine 5 is located in the center of the distribution and includes the middle 20 percent of scores; the percentile ranking range of a stanine of 5 would include $Pr = 41$ to 60. The subsequent stanines are distributed symmetrically on either side of stanine 5. Stanines 4 and 6 each encompass 17 percent of the scores; stanines 3 and 7 each encompass 12 percent of scores; stanines 2 and 8 each encompass 7 percent and stanines 1 and 9 each encompass 4 percent of the scores in a distribution. Compared to the z-score that represents performance in terms of standard deviation units, each of the stanine units represents one-half of a standard deviation. The relationship between each stanine, with the percentile rank range and the standard deviation units it includes, is given in Table 8.4.

Table **8.4** Comparison of Stanines, Percentile Ranks, and z-Scores

Stanine	Percentile rank	z-score
9	97–99.99	+1.75 and above
8	90–96	+1.25 to +1.75
7	78–89	+0.75 to +1.25
6	61–77	+0.25 to +0.75
5	41–60	−0.25 to +0.25
4	24–40	−0.75 to −0.25
3	12–23	−1.25 to −0.75
2	5–11	−1.75 to −1.25
1	1–4	−1.75 and below

The advantage of stanines is that they represent performance in terms of broader categories which minimize the focus upon a particular score. However, for such purposes as staffings and evaluating research results, the stanine is not precise enough, and a more appropriate standard score should be used.

Normal curve equivalent.   The last standard score we shall consider is the most recent, the *normal curve equivalent* (NCE). It was developed to alleviate the problem inherent in the percentile rank, that of unequal intervals between values. The NCE is an equal interval scale standardized on $\overline{X} = 50$ and $s = 21.06$. Like percentile scores, NCE values range from 1 to 99. For the values of 1, 50, and 99, NCE and Pr scores are identical. Because of its interval nature, any difference, such as 5 NCE's has the same meaning regardless of the part of the scale one is concerned with. Currently, its major use is evaluating the effectiveness of Title I programs. Since NCE scores have the advantage of equal units, unlike the ordinal scale nature of percentiles, they are preferred over percentiles for statistical analysis. Table 3 in Appendix D presents a conversion table from percentiles to normal curve equivalents.

We could also convert a z-score to an NCE or vice versa, based on a modification of the T-score formula. For instance, you could convert any z-score to an NCE using:

$$NCE = 50 + 21.06(z)$$

Consider an example of a $z = +2.0$. We know the score falls two standard deviations above the mean and it would have a $Pr = 98$th percentile. The T-score for a $z = +2.0$ would be a $T = 70$. Substituting the z-score into the formula above we obtain an NCE = 92.

$$NCE = 50 + 21.06(+2.0)$$
$$= 50 + 42.12$$
$$= 92.12 = 92$$

To convert from an NCE to a z, we follow a formula similar to the T-score conversion, but with the appropriate mean and standard deviation inserted:

$$z = \frac{NCE - 50}{21.06}$$

If we start with an NCE = 92.12 and work in reverse, we should obtain a $z = +2.0$.

$$z = \frac{92.12 - 50}{21.06}$$
$$z = \frac{42.12}{21.06}$$
$$z = +2.0$$

Thus, if we know the basic z-score, we have maximum flexibility for converting to any other type of norm to obtain useful comparable information.

Figure 8.5 gives a comprehensive graphic comparison of all of the standard scores we have considered.

All the scales we have discussed, except for grade equivalent and age equivalent scores, relate to the properties of the standard normal distribution. The equivalence of the different scales are portrayed in Figure 8.5. We can easily convert from one norm score to another and compare performance on different tests by converting to one scale, the z-score. We can also convert standard scores to percentile ranks to facilitate parental or teacher understanding of any test scores. Regardless of the type of standard score reported, it should be derived from a representative and relevant standardization sample that is not outdated. All scores reported should be comparable to each other, and the norms should be adequately described in terms of the method and procedure. Important environmental and personological variables should also be clearly delineated.

Responsibilities of Users of Standardized Tests

We have considered several types of tests, the technical information—reliability and validity—and ways of interpreting the many scores available from standardized tests. Whether as an educator or researcher, we have a responsibility to use wisely standardized tests and the information they provide. Not only should we have a thorough understanding

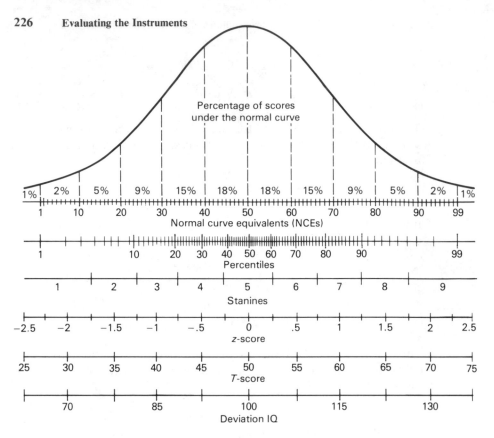

Figure 8.5 Comparison of the Various Standard Scores

of all this information, but we should be aware of the broader policy for the responsible use of tests. In Appendix C we reprint the policy statement of the American Personnel and Guidance Association (APGA) on the responsibilities of users of standardized tests. The article is organized into major sections on test selection, qualifications of test users, test administration, scoring of tests, test interpretation, and communication of test results. Each section offers pertinent information to standardizing the test process, minimizing the influences of possible confounding variables, and providing accurate test interpretations to concerned individuals. Every teacher and researcher should be familiar with this policy.

Examples of Instrumentation Subsections

The purpose of this chapter has been to provide a solid base for developing and evaluating the Instrumentation subsection of the Method section of a research article. The main purpose of the Instrumentation subsection is to present the measurement type of operational definition for each dependent variable used in the study. A sufficiently detailed operational description is required so that other researchers can evaluate and/or replicate the study to determine the validity and generalizability of results. In addition, an adequate operational definition of each dependent variable clarifies the study and minimizes error in the research process. An Instrumentation subsection should provide adequate information on each of these seven points:

1. What test or instrument is used to assess each dependent variable? Include subtests if any.
2. If the test is not well known, provide sample items.
3. What type of score is used, and what range of values is found for each instrument in the study?
4. For what population is the test appropriate? Describe norms available as needed.
5. If appropriate, what is the scorer reliability?
6. If appropriate, what is the reliability due to content, time, or form?
7. What is the validity of the instrument for the purpose for which it was intended?
8. If a researcher-developed instrument was used, are enough examples provided? Is the test-construction phase adequately described? Is information related to points 1 through 7 provided for the instrument?

Consider the Instrumentation subsection of the Huber et al. (1979) study that we first examined in Chapter 7 as an example of one type of Procedure section.

Instruments and Scoring

A battery of tests from the Torrance Tests of Creative Thinking (TTCT; Torrance, 1974a) were used as criterion measures. As operationally defined for this study, creative thinking abilities consisted of verbal and figural fluency, flexibility, and originality. Fluency was defined as the number of relevant responses to the test tasks. Flexibility was the number of different approaches or categories used in producing responses. Originality was measured by summing the response weights provided by the scoring manual; these weights reflect the statistical infrequency of responses. All scoring was conducted by trained scorers following the procedures described by Torrance (1974b).

Five subtests of the TTCT, three verbal and two figural, were employed. The verbal tests were Product Improvement, Just Suppose, and Unusual Uses; the figural subtests were Repeated Figures and Incomplete Figures. Alternate forms of these tests were administered as pre- and posttests. Scores for each of the verbal and figural tasks were analyzed separately, yielding six dependent variables. Rater reliabilities ranged from .85 to 1.0 for the six variables.

Reliability and Validity of the TTCT

Numerous studies were cited by Torrance (1974b) supporting the reliability of the Torrance Tests of Creative Thinking. Of particular interest was the report by Torrance (1972b) concerning the predictive validity of the TTCT for both short-range and long-range studies. The evidence presented was highly supportive of the ability of the TTCT to predict creative behavior on a wide range of criterion measures.

Although the TTCT are not comprehensive in the measurement of all facets of creative behavior, Torrance (1974b) contended that the tests sample a wide range of the abilities in such a universe. Treffinger, Renzulli, and Feldhusen (1971) proposed that measures of divergent thinking such as the TTCT may be viewed as necessary and useful, but not a sufficient component in the assessment of creative potential. Treffinger and Poggio (1972) suggested that divergent thinking tasks would be correlated with a more comprehensive measure of creative functioning but that the more comprehensive measure would also be related to other cognitive abilities.

How does this Instrumentation section compare to the seven questions? The test is specified, and operational definitions of the dependent measures are provided. The population for the test is not specified. The type of scores obtained are mentioned in the operational definitions. Rater reliabilities are given for the six variables, but we do not know how many raters were used, or the average rating. Reliability coefficients are not provided, although a reference is cited to support the overall reliability of the test. The criterion-related predictive validity of the test was found to be highly supportive, but there were no validity coefficients or information on the population from which the validity evidence was obtained. Finally, the last paragraph summarizes theoreticians who commented on whether the test has adequate content validity as an assessment of the concept of creativity.

Consider the Instrumentation subsection of the Alexander et al. (1979) study, also examined in Chapter 7. It is an example of a researcher-developed instrument for that study. Compared to other published research articles, this one describes in depth the instrument development phase.

Instrumentation Sections Should Facilitate Accurate Replication

Instrumentation

Five evaluative instruments, each capable of measuring the acquisition and retention of the oral instruction imparted in the five separate cultural instructional programs, were developed for this study. In developing each of the instruments, a pool consisting of 30 questions was written and submitted to the appropriate one of the five competent teachers of the cultures involved to determine how well the test reflected its intended objectives (the content of the oral instruction). A particular item was retained if the five teachers were in unanimous agreement that the item reflected objectives imparted in the oral instruction. The final format of these instruments consisted of 20 multiple-choice items, with one correct answer and three distractors per item. This procedure assured the content validity of the items in each of the five instruments.

In a pilot study conducted with a group of 18 subjects, each of the five instruments was administered to all subjects immediately following the respective cultural presentation. Presentation sequences were randomized for this group of subjects. The one cultural-specific instrument exhibiting the most variance among the five cultural tests was selected as the metric into which the remaining four cultural instruments were transformed. Inspection of the bivariate frequency distributions resulted in designation of a linear transformation in all cases. Accordingly, the African cultural instrument was regressed upon each of the remaining four cultural instruments. The four resulting linear regression equations were used to transform the administration of both learning and retention of the appropriate cultural instrument into the common metric of the African cultural instrument.

This is an exceedingly conservative procedure in that not all of the reliable variability of each cultural instrument is employed in establishing treatment differences. The advantage is generalizability across several distinct cultural presentations. Essentially, any treatment difference detected employing this strategy would be more dramatic had only one culture been studied. However, such a situation was impossible due to the limited time students were permitted to be away from the classroom.

In conjunction with the aforementioned pilot study, the evaluative instruments were tested for reliability. Coefficients of reliability were computed on the tests for learning and retention using the Kuder–Richardson 21 formula. This procedure yielded an r of .74 for learning and .90 for retention.

An example of face and sampling validity is given in the first paragraph. The second and third paragraphs discuss the test development and standardization processes. The last paragraph contains reliability coefficients based on the internal consistency of the item (KR–21).

Example of a Method Section

Chapters 5 through 8 have considered the three subsections of the Method section: Subjects, Procedure, and Instrumentation. The purpose of the Method section is to define the sample and to provide operational definitions of the independent, dependent, and control variables. These explicit statements are derived from the concept-level statements of the variables and population in the Introduction. Thus, the goal of the Method section is to operationally define the independent and dependent measures, to describe the "How?" of the research process so that it can be adequately evaluated and, if necessary, replicated. Read the following Method section from the Zimmerman and Kinsler (1979) study. The Subjects subsection is correctly labeled; the Task, Videotapes, and Procedures subsection comprise the Procedure. The Scoring section is the Instrumentation subsection.

Method

Subjects

Fifty-four boys and 54 girls were selected in equal numbers from kindergarten and first-grade classes at a New York City public school located in a lower-class area of Harlem. The first graders ranged in age from 6 years 0 months to 7 years 6 months and were comparable in age to the 6-year-olds in the Walters and Parke (1964) study. The kindergartners ranged in age from 5 years 1 month to 6 years 0 months and were comparable in age to the 5-year-olds in the Walters et al. (1963) study. The children were either of black or Hispanic origins. Within each age group, the children were randomly assigned to treatment condition.

Task

The experiment was conducted in two adjoining rooms of a public school. The wall connecting the two rooms was equipped with a one-way mirror. In one room, a 3 × 8 ft. (.9 × 2.4 m) table was placed with a chair at one end. A pictureless psychology textbook was put on the table near the chair. Eight toys were placed on the table: a toy camper, a tea set, 15 alphabet blocks, a toy gun, a white and a black doll, two toy cars, a coloring book and crayons, and two children's picture books. These toys were selected to be attractive to boys and girls of this age.

A high resolution television monitor and a Sony 3600 videotape deck were placed on a moveable steel stand located behind the chair. This equipment was used to show the videotaped episodes.

Videotapes

Two videotapes were created that were identical in length, sequence of events, child model, and setting. Only the identity of the adult varied between the two videotapes. Two black women in their twenties served as the adult models in the videotapes. A black 8-year-old girl served as the child model in both videotapes.

In each tape, the woman told the child that she had to leave the room to retrieve a forgotten item, and during her absence, the child should look at the book that was placed before her on the table. The same eight toys described above were also located on the table. The woman informed the child that she would close the door so the child would not be disturbed and would knock before reentering. Shortly after the adult's departure, the child put the book aside and proceeded to play with the toys for approximately 2 minutes. Upon hearing a knock at the door, the child vainly tried to replace the toys in their original positions. When the adult reentered the room, she began to chastise the child for playing with the toys that didn't belong to her. The videotape ended with the child being spanked and depicted as crying.

Procedures

One of the two black women who performed on the videotape also served as experimenter during the study. She escorted each child from the classroom to the experimental room and seated the child in the chair beside the table. Children in the *videotape* condition were told by the experimenter, "I am going to show you a movie." The child's chair was turned toward the television monitor, and the experimenter started the videotape. After the episode was shown, the experimenter turned the child's chair back toward the table and gave the child one of three types of instructions. In the *strong-prohibition* condition, the experimenter said, "In this room, there are some toys. They belong to another child. You are not to touch or play with them." In the *mild-prohibition* condition, the experimenter said, "In this room there are some toys. They belong to another child. I would prefer that you don't touch or play with them." In the *no-prohibition* condition, the experimenter said, "In this room, there are some toys. They belong to another child." For all prohibition groups, the experimenter continued, "In a little while, I am going to read you a story, but I have forgotten something and must go get it. Sit in this chair and look at this book while you are waiting for me." At this point the experimenter handed the psychology textbook to the child and said, "I am going to close the door so no one will bother you. I will knock when I return so you will know it's me." Children assigned to the *no-videotape* condition were given one of the three types of prohibition immediately upon entering the room.

The child was left alone and was observed for 15 minutes by the experimenter and in some cases a reliability coder from an adjoining room. Upon returning, the experimenter knocked and waited for 15 seconds before the experimenter entered the room. As the experimenter walked in, she said, "That took much longer than I thought. Now I don't have time to read you a story as I planned. But I'll come back in a week. Then we can read the story." The experimenter returned the child to the classroom. This completed the *posttest phase* of the experiment.

After 1 week, the experimenter returned to the children's classroom and again brought them individually to the experimental room for a *retention-test phase*. The child was again seated at the table. The toys and book were situated in the same positions as in posttesting. This time the experimenter didn't mention the toys or give any further instructions about playing with them. After seating the child, the experimenter began to search through some papers she was carrying. Pretending to have misplaced the child's consent slip, she said, "I seem to have lost your consent slip. I must have it for you to be here with me. You wait here and I'll get it." The child was left alone for 15 minutes. Upon returning, the experimenter said, "I found it. Now I can read you a story as I promised." The child was asked to select one of the story books from the table to be read. After reading the story, the experimenter returned the child to his or her classroom.

Scoring

As in the original Walters and Parke (1964) study, the experimenter recorded the times at which the children touched and ceased to touch the toys on a specially prepared form. The time was read from a stopwatch. From this record, the children's latency of first touch, the number of touches, and the total time spent touching the toys were calculated. All analyses reported in the present article are based on the latter measure for a number of reasons. This measure was the most comprehensive of the measures, has been found to be highly correlated with other measures in prior research, and has been used most extensively in prior studies. Our analyses of the present data based on the other two measures revealed them to be less sensitive to treatment variations but to otherwise yield similar results. Thus all findings reported in this article are based on the total time the child spent touching the toys during the observation periods.

A second observer, a white male, coded approximately one fourth of all children for reliability purposes. The second observer was naive concerning the hypotheses governing the study. The product-moment correlation between the two observers was .97.

Although the independent and dependent variables are not explicitly stated, they are given in this Method section. One independent variable is the videotape condition at two levels—videotape and no videotape. A second independent variable is the type of prohibition at three levels—strong, mild, and none. A third independent variable is test phase at two levels—posttest and retention test. The only dependent variable entered into the subsequent data analysis is total time spent touching the toys. The task, specific videotape directions, general procedure, and scoring were explained in sufficient detail to replicate the study. Although the technical information on validity was not given, a rationale for using the dependent measure was provided. In addition, rater reliability was obtained.

It is not clear whether random selection was used with the subjects or not; the authors said "selected" but failed to state what sampling technique was used or if it was random. Random assignment, however, did occur. The number of children, age range, and ethnicity were also indicated.

Although some information could be explicitly stated and certain sections reorganized for greater clarity, the Method section does seem to convey the "How?" for this research study. The next two chapters will focus on analyzing the scores obtained from the dependent measures described in the Instrumentation section.

——— SUMMARY ———————————————————————

We have delineated the differences between standardized and non-standardized tests, and between norm-referenced and criterion-referenced tests. We have also described intelligence and achievement tests, as well as projective, personality, and interest measures. Then came four scales for questionnaires or interviews: ranking, semantic differential, checklists, and nominations. Then followed four types of reliability: test-retest, alternate form, scorer, and the standard error of measurement. Three types of validity were next delineated: construct, content, and criterion-related (predictive or diagnostic). The variety of scores available from standardized tests were interpreted: grade equivalents and percentile ranks; followed by standard score norms, z-score, T-score, stanine, and normal curve equivalents. You were referred to the APGA policy statement in Appendix C that describes the responsibility of users of standardized tests. Finally, we examined examples of an Instrumentation subsection and a Method section to help integrate the Methods section of the research-based journal article.

OBJECTIVES

In Chapter 8 we have presented a variety of information about tests: kinds of tests, their reliability and validity, the types of scores available, the responsibilities of tests users as well as examples of an Instrumentation and Method section. Confirm your understanding of the information in Chapter 8 using the following objectives:

Specify the differences between a standardized and nonstandardized test.

Specify the differences between a norm-referenced and a criterion-referenced test.

Identify the major categories of standardized tests, and describe the major purpose of each.

Describe the four scales used for questionnaires or interviews.

Evaluate the reliability and validity of a test used in the research process.

Interpret the scores of any test.

Evaluate an Instrumentation subsection, and determine whether it provides sufficient information.

Evaluate a Method section and determine whether it provides sufficient information.

TERMS

achievement test
alternate-form reliability
checklist
construct validity
content validity
criterion-referenced test

criterion-related validity
derived score
diagnostic criterion-related validity
face validity
factorial validity

grade equivalent
intelligence test
interest inventory
interobserver reliability
interrater reliability
Kuder-Richardson 20 (KR–20)
Kuder-Richardson 21 (KR–21)
measures of internal consistency
nominations scale
nonstandardized test
norm
normal curve equivalent
norm group
norm-referenced test
percentile rank
personality test
predictive criterion-related
  validity
projective test
ranking scale

raw score
reliability
sampling validity
scorer reliability
semantic differential scale
Spearman-Brown prophecy
  formula
split-half reliability
standard error of measurement
standardization sample
standardized test
standard normal distribution
standard score norms
stanine
test plan
test-retest reliability
true score
T-score
validity
z-score

PART **3**

Analysis of the Results Section

In Chapter 1 we found that the third major component of the research-based journal article is the Results section. This section corresponds to the sixth step of the scientific method: Analyze the data or information. In it we attempt to answer the question: What are the major findings of the study? In other words, the Results section uses different statistics to summarize, describe, and generalize the results of the study to the population. In Chapter 9 on descriptive statistics we shall investigate ways to summarize the scores obtained from the instruments used. The study of inferential statistics in Chapter 10 will apply statistics and other supporting information to test hypotheses and to determine if inferences to the population can be derived from the sample's results. Descriptive and inferential statistics comprise the means by which we analyze the data obtained in the research study.

Descriptive Statistics

What are the different measurement scales for variables?

What are the measures of frequency, proportion, and percentage, and how are they used in tables and graphs?

What are the measures of central tendency, and how are they used in the Results?

What are the measures of variability, and how are they used in the Results?

What are the measures of relationship, and how are they used in the Results?

What is the relationship between the measurement scales and the descriptive statistics?

Descriptive Statistics

Relationship to measurement scales

	Nominal	Ordinal	Interval	Ratio	Result
Measures or techniques for tables or graphs	Frequency Proportion Percentages	Frequency Proportion Percentages	Frequency Proportion Percentages	Frequency Proportion Percentages	Succinct summarization and description of data
	Bar graphs	Bar graphs			
			Frequency polygons	Frequency polygons	
Measures of central tendency	Mode				
		Median			
			Mean	Mean	
Measures of variability			Range	Range	
			Variance	Variance	
			Standard deviation	Standard deviation	
Measures of relationship		Spearman rho			
			Pearson r	Pearson r	
			r^2	r^2	

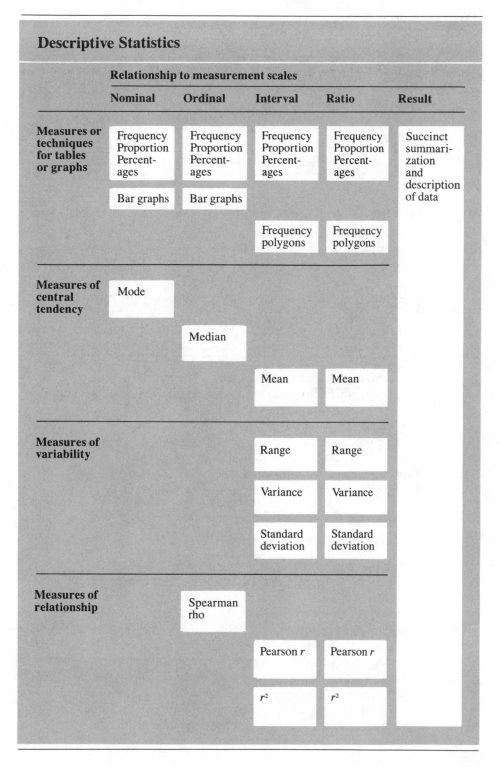

The Results section should present a succinct summary of the data analyses. This summary requires statistics to determine the effect of the independent variable on the dependent variable. Well-written Results sections should include five key components in logical sequence:

1. Overview of the statistics used
2. Statement of the results of the descriptive statistics
3. Discussion of the assumptions for the inferential statistics
4. Statement of the results of the inferential statistical analysis
5. Statement of the results of the supporting inferential statistical analysis

If the Results section includes multiple analyses, steps 3, 4, and 5 are repeated in sequence until all analyses are included. Variations of this plan are obviously possible. However, this format is the one most frequently found in well-organized Results sections. Using these five steps, the Results section presents the major findings of the research study.

Developing or evaluating a Results section requires a basic understanding of the descriptive and inferential statistics. As we have said in Chapter 1, there is no mystery or magic about the proper statistic to use in a particular context. We need only a knowledge of two main concepts in order to accurately select the appropriate statistic. The first is an understanding of which measures are the independent variables and which are the dependent variables in the study. The second is the type of measurement scale the variable falls on for a particular study. By understanding these two concepts, you will be able to choose the correct statistical analysis for the research you are developing or evaluating. Before we take up the individual descriptive statistics, we shall delineate four types of measurement scales.

Types of Measurement Scales

We can operationally define the independent variable as being either an experimental or measurement type, and the dependent variable has a measurement type of operational definition. The measurement type of operational definition gives us a score, or numerical value. With the experimental type of operational definition, we will have to represent, or code, each value (or level) of the independent variable. We can code the variables alphabetically, numerically, or in a combination; that is, *alphanumeric.* For instance, with the two levels of the variable *sex,* we could code each level as: M, F; 1, 0; or, M2, F1. However, since most statistical analyses are performed by computer, it is simpler and more efficient to represent each value of the variable numerically.

Numerals and Numbers

Knowing the distinction between *numerals* and *numbers* will help us to understand these choices above, as well as the four types of measurement scales. *Numerals* are figures, letters, or words—that is, *symbols*—which are used to represent or denote numbers. Examples of numerals include: a zip code, a social security number, a telephone number, a serial number on a library book, and so forth. Numerals may be used for different purposes and not always to indicate amount or quantity.

Numbers are a special case of numerals with distinct properties; specifically, any two numerals, such as 2 and 3, are numbers only if you can apply the mathematical operations of addition, subtraction, multiplication, and division and obtain a meaningful value. For instance, you cannot divide your social security number by your friend's and obtain a meaningful value. Instead, numerals are used mainly to represent categories or a position in a series.

The first two types of measurement scales we will discuss are special uses of numerals; each will be considered separately. They are: *nominal scale* and *ordinal scale*. The other two types of measurement scales are special uses of numbers; because of their similar properties we shall discuss them together. They are: *interval scale* and *ratio scale*.

Nominal scale.   The *nominal scale* uses numerals to represent categories or levels of a variable. The numerals assigned to each category do not represent any quantitative distinction. Examples of nominal variables include: sex, ethnic group, social security number, and marital status. For the nominal variable, sex, we can assign a 0 to the female level and a 1 to the male level. The numerals 1 and 0 represent only which category each subject is in. You cannot add, subtract, multiply, or divide the distribution of 0's and 1's and get a value that is meaningful. Furthermore, the assignment of numerals is arbitrary; we can assign any value to any level—a 1 to males and 2 to females, or a 15 and 30, and so on.

Ordinal scale.   The *ordinal scale* uses numerals to represent relative position or order among the values of a variable. The numerals assigned to each position in a series represent only the order in that series—not any quantitative distinction. Examples of ordinal variables include: percentile rank, social class, high school or college class rank, mental age, and grade equivalent scores. High school class rank may be coded, for example, from 1 to 500, with a rank of 1 representing the valedictorian and the rank of 500 representing the person with the lowest grade point average of the graduating seniors. The numerals represent a particular position or order in a larger series. Here again, applying the mathematical operations would not be meaningful.

Interval and ratio scale.   Both of these scales use numbers to represent quantity. The mathematical operations can be applied to both to obtain meaningful values. The key characteristic of the interval scale is that *numbers represent equal units or intervals.* These numbers describe the magnitude of the differences among the variables measured. The only difference between variables on the interval scale and those on the ratio scale is that in the ratio scale numbers represent equal units from an *absolute or true zero point.* Interval level measurement enables the researcher to study differences among levels of a variable but not their proportionate magnitudes, as is the case with the ratio scale. Examples of interval variables are: years A.D. and Fahrenheit temperature. Examples of ratio variables are: time, weight, distance, height, and Kelvin temperature. The years measured since A.D. are on an *interval scale* since equal units occur (1984 is 50 equal units greater than 1934), but there is no true zero point. A year approximate to the birth of Jesus Christ is selected as the zero point rather than a true zero point of something like the beginning of time. Time is an example of a variable on the *ratio scale;* a specific use of time in educational research is the number of seconds taken to complete a task. In this case, both a true zero point and equal intervals operate.

In educational research, true interval-level measures are difficult to find. Most educational and psychological tests do not have true equal intervals. Usually, those which do have a fixed equal unit also have a true zero point. Those measures which don't usually *assume* equal intervals in order to apply more powerful statistics developed for a higher level of measurement. To be more exact, they fall into a transition category between the ordinal and interval scale, a kind of *quasi-interval* scale.

The ordering of scales from nominal and ordinal to quasi-interval, interval, and ratio is purposeful. This progression represents a movement from less refined to more refined measurement procedures and statistical analyses—that is, from a lower to a higher order.

Measurement Scales and Statistics

We have said that measurement scales relate to the various types of statistical analyses. Thus, if you know the measurement scale for the variables in a research study, the guesswork and hassles over which statistics to use will be minimized. For instance, if you have *one nominal independent variable,* such as marital status at four levels—married, di-

Types of Measurement Scales

vorced, separated, and widowed—and *one interval level dependent variable,* such as a self-report anxiety score, then the analysis of variance is an appropriate statistic to use to determine if there are significant differences. We shall further elaborate this relationship between measurement scale and statistical analyses in this and the next chapter.

An important relationship between measurement scales and statistics is that statistics developed for one scale of measurement can always be used with variables measured on a higher scale, but not with variables on a lower measurement scale. For instance, the median and Spearman rho presume an ordinal level of measurement, but they can also be used meaningfully with interval or ratio scale variables. However, they cannot be meaningfully applied to variables measured at the nominal level.

The corollary to this is that variables at a higher measurement scale can always be expressed at any of the lower scales, but the opposite is not possible; that is, a variable on a lower measurement scale cannot be expressed at a higher level. For instance, the variable *height,* normally a ratio scale variable, can be expressed on all three lower levels:

1. Ratio—absolute height of a student; measured from zero inches to maximum height in class
2. Interval—height of a student measured from table top; requires an arbitrary zero point and equal intervals
3. Ordinal—relative height of students measured from tallest to shortest; requires the value of the tallest position in the series
4. Nominal—the height of students categorized into three groups: tall, average, short; requires the value of 3, 2, and 1 for each group

A variable at a lower measurement scale, such as sex or marital status, which are nominally scaled variables, would have difficulty being expressed at a higher level, and would not be useful at such levels:

1. Nominal—male and female; 0 for female, 1 for male
2. Ordinal—rank of femaleness to maleness; range from +10 to −10
3. Interval—quantity of maleness and femaleness; would a 6 be three equal units above a 3?
4. Ratio—proportional differences of maleness to femaleness. Is a 10 twice as female as a 5? What would be a true zero point?

Thus, knowing the measurement scale for the variables facilitates our task of accurately selecting appropriate statistics to analyze our results. We shall discuss this important relationship further after we consider the various kinds of descriptive statistics.

Descriptive Statistics

We have already discussed several descriptive statistics while interpreting types of scores in the previous chapter. Specifically, the z-score, T-score, percentile rank, stanine, and normal curve equivalent are all examples of descriptive statistics. In the first chapter, we said that descriptive statistics describe or summarize in a convenient, usable form the data of a study. Every statistic has a special role or purpose; the ones we use depend upon the type of variables, their measurement scale, and the purpose of the study. There are five categories of descriptive statistics, each of which contains specific statistical techniques. Since we have previously considered the derived score measures, they are included here only to complete the listing of descriptive statistics. The remaining four will be considered separately. The five categories are:

1. Measures for tables or graphs
   a. frequency
   b. percentage
   c. proportion
2. Measures of central tendency
   a. mean
   b. median
   c. mode
3. Measures of variability
   a. standard deviation
   b. variance
   c. range
4. Measures of relationship
   a. Spearman rho correlation
   b. Pearson product-moment correlation
5. Derived score measures (already considered)
   a. grade and age equivalents
   b. percentile rank
   c. z-score, T-score, stanine, and normal curve equivalents

Measures for Tables and Graphs

It is not unusual to include tables or graphs in the Results sections of many research articles. The tables will usually include at least one of the following statistics to summarize the data: *frequency, proportion,* and *percentage.* The distinctions among the three are easy to understand. Consider the following example:

In a class of 200, there are 80 males and 120 females.
1. What is the *frequency (f)* of women in the class?
   frequency = headcount; so $f = 120$
2. What is the *proportion (p)* of women in the class?
   proportion of women $= \dfrac{\text{subgroup}}{\text{total group}}$;
   so $p = 120/200 = 0.60$
3. What is the *percentage (%)* of women in the class?
   percentage of women = proportion $\times$ 100; so
   percentage of women $= .60 \times 100 = 60\%$

Thus, *frequency* is the number of subjects in a particular category. *Proportion* is the ratio of a subgroup to the total group, expressed as a decimal value from 0.0 to 1.0. *Percentage* is the proportion of a subgroup to the total group, expressed as a value from 0% to 100%.

Results in a table are reported typically with the frequency and percentage of response under each category. For instance, a table like Table

9.1 might appear in a Results section. Of a total number of 50 students in the class ($N = 50$), each rated each item of the questionnaire from strongly disagree (SD) to strongly agree (SA). Thus, not only do we know the frequency of students who marked each scale point but also the relative percentage. This example totals up nicely, since $N = 50$. However, most data do not. Also, it is quite usual to have some subjects omit answering some questions; therefore, the frequency value by itself could be misleading. Table 9.1 summarizes the relative frequency and percentage at each scale value. We could easily add to the interpretability of the results by adding the mean and standard deviation to the right-hand column as well.

Bar graphs and frequency polygons are two common ways of graphically presenting results. *Bar graphs* are used with nominal or ordinal scale variables; *frequency polygons* are used with interval or ratio scale variables. The horizontal *x*-axis represents the variable and the vertical *y*-axis represents the frequency. Bar graphs are not widely used in journals today because of the extra cost and space needed to reproduce them. Unless the relationship is complex, it is usually included in the narrative of the Results.

Frequency polygons are similar to bar graphs, but, since they use interval or ratio scale variables, they form a *continuous value* on the horizontal axis compared to the nominal and ordinal variables that form *discrete or separate categories.* When there is a continuous interval scale, the points are joined together. Review the bar graph and fre-

Table 9.1 Frequency and Percentage of Course Evaluation Items

	SD		D		A		SA	
Question	f	%	f	%	f	%	f	%
1. Instructor prepared for class	7	14	8	16	15	30	20	40
2. Course content well structured	6	12	4	8	25	50	15	30
3. Assignments valuable as learning experience	20	40	11	22	14	28	5	10
4. Sufficient feedback provided on student performance	7	14	21	42	17	34	5	10

$N = 50$

quency polygon in the journal article in Chapter 1 so that the distinctions between the two are clear.

Measures of Central Tendency

The *mean, median,* and *mode* are the three descriptive statistics that measure the central value in a distribution of scores. The *mean* is used with interval or ratio scale variables. The *median* is used with ordinal scale variables, but is also appropriate with interval or ratio scale variables. The *mode* is used with nominal variables and can be used with the three higher scales as well. Data in most distributions usually cluster around a central value that can be specified quantitatively.

Mean.   The *mean* is the arithmetical average that is obtained by adding all the scores in a distribution and dividing by the number of scores. The formula for calculating the mean is:

$$\overline{X} = \frac{\Sigma X}{N}$$

where $\overline{X}$ is the mean score,
Σ is a summation sign, so that
ΣX means the sum of all the X scores, and
N is the total number of scores.

Symbols other than $\overline{X}$ have been used to represent the mean; for instance, M and μ (the Greek mu for the population mean). A simple example will help to clarify the meaning of the mean score. Consider this example:

$$\underline{X}$$
19
14
14
13
13
13
11
9
7
7

Here we have a distribution of ten scores from subjects on a quiz that ranged from 0 to 20 points. We need only one additional piece of information to calculate the mean score, the ΣX. We already know that $N = 10$. Thus:

$$\underline{X}$$
$$19$$
$$14$$
$$14$$
$$13$$
$$13$$
$$13$$
$$11$$
$$9$$
$$7$$
$$\underline{7}$$
$$\Sigma X = 120$$
$$N = 10$$

Then: $\overline{X} = \dfrac{\Sigma X}{N} = \dfrac{120}{10}$

$$\overline{X} = 12.00$$

Thus, the mean score in this distribution is 12.00.

Median.   The *median* is that single score (or potential score) in a distribution of scores above and below which 50 percent of the scores fall. In other words, it is the score that falls at the 50th percentile. In distributions with an odd number of scores, the median is the middle score. Look at this set of 15 scores:

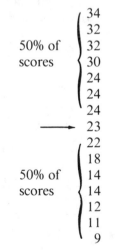

In this example, the median is the eighth score, since 7 of the scores fall above it and 7 fall below it. Since the eighth score is 23, therefore the median equals 23.

When a distribution has an even number of scores, the median is found by averaging the two middle scores. For instance:

$$
\begin{array}{r}
50\% \text{ of} \\
\text{scores}
\end{array}
\left\{
\begin{array}{l}
29 \\
26 \\
24 \\
24
\end{array}
\right.
$$

$$
\longrightarrow
\left.
\begin{array}{l}
22 \\
20
\end{array}
\right\}
\begin{array}{l}
\text{two middle} \\
\text{scores}
\end{array}
$$

$$
\begin{array}{r}
50\% \text{ of} \\
\text{scores}
\end{array}
\left\{
\begin{array}{l}
19 \\
18 \\
14 \\
12
\end{array}
\right.
$$

Thus, the median $= \dfrac{(20 + 22)}{2} = \dfrac{42}{2}$

median $= 21$

An important characteristic of the median is that it is insensitive to extreme scores. The mean, even though more stable than the median, is more susceptible to extreme scores when the distribution does not represent a symmetrical curve, like the normal distribution discussed in Chapter 8. For instance, consider the mean scores of these two distributions of five scores each:

X_1	X_2
18	52
14	18
12	12
11	11
9	9
$\Sigma X_1 = 64$	$\Sigma X_2 = 102$
$N_1 = 5$	$N_2 = 5$
$\overline{X}_1 = \dfrac{64}{5}$	$\overline{X}_2 = \dfrac{102}{5}$
$\overline{X}_1 = 12.8$	$\overline{X}_2 = 20.4$

A change of only one extreme score in the distribution significantly affects the mean value, as seen in the second case. When extreme scores may affect the mean score in a research article, both the mean and median are usually reported. In the two examples above, the median has a value of 12. As we can obviously see in the second example, the median score more accurately reflects the central value in the distribution. When a distribution of scores is symmetrical, the mean and the median will be identical, and the mean will be used. When a distribution is *skewed* or nonsymmetrical, like the second case, the mean may be a

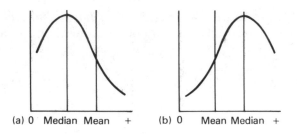

(a) 0 Median Mean   +   (b) 0   Mean Median +

Figure 9.1 Comparison of Mean and Median Values on Two
Skewed Curves

misleading estimate of the central value. In that event, the mean and the median should be reported, and the median score should be used.

The mean is always drawn in the direction of the extreme score(s). Consider the skewed distributions in Figure 9.1 (a) and (b). In (a), the mean is pulled in the direction of the extreme high scores in the distribution; this curve is a *positively skewed* distribution. In (b), the mean is pulled in the direction of the extreme low scores in the distribution; this curve is a *negatively skewed* distribution.

Mode.   The *mode* is the most frequent score in a distribution of scores. It is used today as a crude estimate of the average value, but is seldom reported in the research literature. What is the modal score of the following distribution?

> 79
> 60
> 55
> 54
> 54
> 54
> 51
> 51
> 43
> 42
> 42
> 38

If you answered 54 you are correct, since 54 occurred most frequently in the distribution; the frequency, $f = 3$.

Comparison of mean, median, and mode.   Table 9.2 summarizes the main points of comparison among the three measures of central tendency. Any of these measures, depending on the purpose of the study,

Table 9.2 Comparison of Mean, Median, and Mode

Mean	Median	Mode
1. Used for interval or ratio data	1. Used for ordinal data and above	1. Used for nominal data and above
2. Most stable measure, but affected by extreme scores	2. Insensitive to extreme scores	2. Least stable
3. Uses all mathematical operations	3. Uses a few mathematical operations	3. Cannot use mathematical operations

may be appropriate to use. Usually, however, the mean is calculated and used; if the distribution is skewed, the median is also obtained and used in place of the mean value.

Measures of Variability

The *standard deviation, variance,* and *range* are three measures of variability or dispersion of scores that we shall discuss. There are measures that we will not discuss, since they are infrequently used in the research literature: the *interquartile range* and *mean deviation.*

Standard deviation. This measure describes how scores vary about the mean score. It is a measure of deviation expressed in standard units about the mean score, hence the name *standard deviation.* In our earlier example of the mean, the score was found to be 12.00, but scores varied about it from a low of 7 to a high of 19. The standard deviation systematically measures this dispersion, or variability. Mathematically, the standard deviation is equal to the square root of the sum of the squared deviations about the mean divided by the total number of scores. The formula is:

$$s = \sqrt{\frac{\Sigma(X - \overline{X})^2}{N}}$$

where s is the standard deviation,

$\sqrt{}$ indicates the square root,

$\Sigma(X - \overline{X})^2$ stands for the sum of the squared deviations about the mean, and

N is the number of scores.

The most important concept in this formula is the term:

$$(X - \overline{X})$$

which stands for the mean score subtracted from a given score in the distribution; the resulting value is called a *deviation score.* For instance, if the raw score in the above distribution is 19, the deviation score would be 7:

$$X - \overline{X} = 19 - 12 = 7$$

The deviation score is basic to understanding the standard deviation, as well as many other statistics you will encounter. The deviation score is a measure of how a given score deviates from the mean score. It is the foundation upon which the standard deviation is built.

The four steps in obtaining the standard deviation are:

1. Calculate the deviation score for all raw scores and list them in a column
2. Check to see if the sum of this column equals zero: $\Sigma(X - \overline{X}) = 0$
3. Square each deviation score: $(X - \overline{X})^2$
4. Calculate the sum of the squared deviations for the entire set of scores: $\Sigma(X - \overline{X})^2$

These steps are shown in Table 9.3.

Table 9.3 Steps in Calculating the Standard Deviation

X	(1) $(X - \overline{X})$	(3) $(X - \overline{X})^2$
19	7	49
14	2	4
14	2	4
13	1	1
13	1	1
13	1	1
11	−1	1
9	−3	9
7	−5	25
7	−5	25
$\Sigma X = 120$	(2) $\Sigma(X - \overline{X}) = 0$	(4) $\Sigma(X - \overline{X})^2 = 120$
$N = 10$		
$\overline{X} = 12.00$		

We now have all the data needed to calculate the standard deviation:

$$s = \sqrt{\frac{\Sigma(X - \overline{X})^2}{N}}$$

$$s = \sqrt{\frac{120}{10}}$$

$$s = \sqrt{12} = 3.46$$

Keep in mind that the conceptual foundation for the standard deviation is the deviation score, $X - \overline{X}$, which is calculated for each score in the distribution. The other basic concept is that the value is divided by the number of scores, N. As in the formula for the mean, the total N is divided into the deviation score to get a measure of the average deviation for the entire distribution of scores. The use of this formula for calculating the standard deviation is called the *deviation score method* and it is the better way to obtain a conceptual understanding of the standard deviation.

Another formula used to calculate the standard deviaton is the *raw score method*. This is easier to calculate but conceptually more difficult to understand, since the essence of the standard deviaton, the deviation score $X - \overline{X}$, is not explicitly included in the formula. The raw score method for calculating the standard deviation is given by the formula:

$$s = \sqrt{\frac{\Sigma X^2}{N} - \overline{X}^2}$$

where ΣX^2 stands for the sum of the squares of the raw scores,
      $\overline{X}^2$ is the square of the mean score, and
      N is the total number of scores.

Table 9.4 illustrates how this formula is used to calculate the standard deviation for an example of a distribution of nine scores. This raw score method requires one less step than the preceding deviation score method.

In Chapter 8, we pointed out the relation between the mean and standard deviation; namely their relationship to the mathematical properties of the standard normal distribution. A second relationship concerns the size of the standard deviation. Consider two studies that have

Table 9.4 Alternative Method of Calculating
the Standard Deviation

X	X^2
15	225
13	169
12	144
11	121
10	100
9	81
8	64
8	64
4	16
$\Sigma X = 90$	$\Sigma X^2 = 984$

$$N = 9.0$$

$$s = \sqrt{\frac{\Sigma X^2}{N} - \overline{X}^2}$$

$$s = \sqrt{\frac{984}{9} - 100}$$

$$s = \sqrt{109.34 - 100}$$

$$s = \sqrt{9.34} = 3.06$$

the same mean score, yet the standard deviation values are very different:

$$\overline{X}_1 = 100 \qquad \overline{X}_2 = 100$$
$$s_1 = 5 \qquad s_2 = 25$$

What does this relationship tell us about the respective populations from which the sample of scores was obtained? In the first example, the distribution of scores is grouped closely about the mean. Thus, the distribution reflects a more homogeneous distribution of scores of the measured variable. In the second example, the scores are widely dispersed about the mean and reflect a more heterogeneous distribution. If we relate this back to the relationship of the standard deviation to the percentage of scores included in the normal distribution curve, we recall that 68 percent of the scores will fall between ± 1 s. Thus, in the first example, the distribution of ± 1 s scores will range from 95 to 105; and in the second example, the distribution of ± 1 s scores will range from 75 to 125.

Variance.   The variance (s^2) is directly related to the formula for the standard deviation. It is the value prior to extracting the square root in the standard deviation formula. Thus, the *variance* is the sum of the squared deviations about the mean divided by the number of scores.

<table>
<tr><td align="center">*Deviation score method*</td><td align="center">*Raw score method*</td></tr>
<tr><td align="center">$$s^2 = \frac{\Sigma(X - \overline{X})^2}{N}$$</td><td align="center">$$s^2 = \frac{\Sigma X^2}{N} - \overline{X}^2$$</td></tr>
<tr><td align="center">$$s = \sqrt{\frac{\Sigma(X - \overline{X})^2}{N}}$$</td><td align="center">$$s = \sqrt{\frac{\Sigma X^2}{N} - \overline{X}^2}$$</td></tr>
</table>

In the earlier example in which we calculated the standard deviation, $s = 3.06$, using the raw score method, the variance also was calculated: $s^2 = 9.34$. The standard deviation enables a researcher to make a more useful interpretation of scores within a distribution because of its relationship to the mean and normal distribution. The variance is part of the computational system for calculating inferential statistics, such as the analysis of variance. Thus, in educational research it is not reported frequently by itself, but it is often included in the inferential statistics used to calculate whether there is statistical significance among groups. Like the standard deviation, the foundation of the variance is also the notion of the deviation score, $X - \overline{X}$. It is simply manipulated differently in the latter formula.

Different symbols are used to represent the standard deviation and variance. You will encounter all of the following in the educational research literature.

<table>
<tr><td align="center">*Standard deviation*</td><td align="center">*Variance*</td></tr>
<tr><td align="center">s</td><td align="center">s^2</td></tr>
<tr><td align="center">S</td><td align="center">S^2</td></tr>
<tr><td align="center">SD</td><td align="center">σ^2 (Greek sigma</td></tr>
<tr><td align="center">σ (Greek letter
sigma)</td><td align="center">squared)</td></tr>
</table>

Technically, the appropriate value to represent the standard deviation and variance is the lower case s and s^2. The Greek letter *sigma* (σ) is appropriately used when measuring the population standard deviation or variance (σ^2). In general, the use of a Greek letter represents an attempt to measure a population parameter. However, when one is obtaining an unbiased estimator of the population statistic, the denominator of the formula should be adjusted from N to $N - 1$. This change in the denominator value helps to ensure that an unbiased estimate of the population value derived from the sample is obtained. This means that the estimate in the long run is not systematically larger or smaller than the value it is estimating. It is an adjustment to the standard deviation formula to account for the operation of sampling error. Recall that we discussed sampling error in Chapter 5.

Range.   The most unstable and crudest measure of variability of scores within a distribution is the *range.* By itself it does not allow for the interpretation of a score within the distribution; it is instead an index of the range of scores in that distribution. To calculate the range, we subtract the lowest score from the highest score; that is, range = top score − bottom score. Some texts also recommend the inclusive formula; it is, range = (highest − lowest) + 1. Whichever is used, the range is still a crude measure of variability and is seldom reported today. Consider these five scores:

$$9 \quad 11 \quad 12 \quad 18 \quad 52$$

The range would equal 52 − 9 = 43.

Measures of Relationship

We turn now from the statistical techniques used to describe the distribution of scores for one variable to the various measures that enable us to determine the degree of relationship between two variables. The quantitative degree of relationship between two variables is given by a *correlation coefficient.* The values of the correlation coefficient, no matter what the specific type, always vary between −1.00 and +1.00. These two values represent the extremes of perfect relationship; a value of $r = 0.0$ represents the absence of any relationship.

A *perfect positive* relationship is denoted by a correlation coefficient of $r = +1.00$. It means either of two relationships: first, as scores on one distribution (X) increase, scores on the other distribution (Y) also increase; or second, as scores on one measure (X) decrease, scores on the second measure (Y) also decrease. Thus, the closer the value of r is to $+1.0$ the stronger the positive relationship.

A *perfect negative* relationship is denoted by a correlation coefficient of $r = -1.00$. This also means either of two relationships: as scores on the X measure increase, scores on the Y measure decrease; or conversely, as scores on the X measure decrease, scores on the Y measure increase. Thus the closer the value of r is to -1.0, the stronger the negative relationship.

A *perfect zero* relationship is denoted by $r = 0.0$. Scores around 0.0 mean there is little or no relationship between the two measures as determined by that particular type of correlational coefficient.

The reliability and validity coefficients discussed in the last chapter are all variations of the correlation coefficient, except that they differ in ranging only from 0.0 to +1.0. The decision to use a particular correlational technique is based mainly on the type of measurement scale each variable is expressed on—whether a nominal, ordinal, interval, or ratio type—and whether the scores are distributed in a linear or nonlinear relationship. Basically, all correlational techniques measure the relationship in either of two situations: either we have two sets of measures from the same subject, or we have a measure obtained from individuals who are matched on some criteria. Examples of the first situation include correlating high school G.P.A. with college G.P.A., correlating creativity scores with intelligence scores, and so on. An example of the second situation is illustrated when pairs of subjects are matched on some criterion, such as anxiety level, then randomly assigned to either a treatment or control group, and then tested to obtain a self-actualization score. The self-actualization scores are correlated between the two groups.

Examples of correlation coefficients found in the research literature are included in Table 9.5.

A frequent misinterpretation found in the research literature is to infer that the observed relationship derived from a correlation coefficient is a causal one. Correlation coefficients do *not* measure causal relationships; they measure the strength or degree of a relationship.

With any two variables X and Y, X may cause Y, Y may cause X, or a third variable Z may influence the relationship between X and Y, or the

Table 9.5 Correlation Coefficients for Several Variables

Variable	Correlation coefficient
Intelligence test scores of identical twins reared together	0.91
Height versus weight of 10-year-olds	0.60
Intelligence test scores compared to parents' occupational levels	0.30
Height versus Stanford-Binet IQ scores	0.06
Artists' interests versus bankers' interests	−0.64
Intelligence test scores of unrelated children reared together	0.23
Intelligence test scores of unrelated children reared apart	0.00
Rank in high school class versus teachers' ratings of work habits	0.73

relationship may be a *spurious* relationship. This means that the two variables are related only by chance—not due to a conceptual or causal relationship. An example of a spurious relationship is the low positive correlation between shoe size and level of intelligence, or the low negative correlation between women's bust size and level of intelligence. A spurious relationship may occur but it will be due to chance rather than to a meaningful conceptual or causal relationship.

We shall discuss two types of correlational techniques: the *Spearman rho* correlation and the *Pearson product-moment* correlation. The Spearman rho is used with ranked or ordinal data; the Pearson *r* is used with interval or ratio data. Both statistics measure the strength of the linear relationship between two variables.

Spearman rho correlation.   The formula for the Spearman rho is:

$$\text{Spearman rho} = 1 - \frac{6\Sigma D^2}{n(n^2 - 1)}$$

where D is the difference between each ranked pair of scores,
ΣD^2 is the sum of the squares of the differences *(D)*, and
n is the number of pairs of scores.

Suppose a researcher is attempting to determine the relationship between perceived leadership in class and perceived intelligence level as ranked by the classroom teacher. Table 9.6 shows how two ordinal scale variables are used to calculate the Spearman rho. Thus, the Spearman rho correlation coefficient between leadership and intelligence ranked by the classroom teacher is 0.36, a moderately positive relationship.

Pearson product-moment correlation.   The Pearson product-moment correlation, also called the Pearson *r,* is a second correlational technique we shall examine. Used with interval or ratio scale variables to measure linear relationships, the formula is:

$$\text{Pearson } r = \frac{N\Sigma XY - (\Sigma X)(\Sigma Y)}{\sqrt{N\Sigma X^2 - (\Sigma X)^2} \cdot \sqrt{N\Sigma Y^2 - (\Sigma Y)^2}}$$

where ΣXY is the sum of the XY cross products,
ΣX is the sum of the X scores,
ΣY is the sum of the Y scores,
ΣX^2 is the sum of the squared X scores,
ΣY^2 is the sum of the squared Y scores, and
N is the number of pairs of scores.

This complex-looking formula is really quite easy to calculate. All we have to do is to arrange in parallel columns the first five sets of infor-

Table 9.6 Spearman rho Correlation Between Leadership and
Intelligence

Leadership rank	Intelligence rank		
X	Y	D	D^2
1	2	−1	1
2	7	−5	25
3	1	2	4
4	3	1	1
5	9	−4	16
6	4	2	4
7	10	−3	9
8	8	0	0
9	6	3	9
10	4	6	36
			$\Sigma D = \overline{105}$

$$\text{Spearman rho} = 1 - \frac{6\Sigma D^2}{n(n^2 - 1)}$$

$$= 1 - \frac{6(105)}{10(10^2 - 1)} = 1 - \frac{630}{10(100 - 1)} = 1 - \frac{630}{10(99)}$$

$$= 1 - \frac{630}{990} = 1 - 0.636 = 0.364$$

Spearman rho $= 0.36$

mation above; we usually already know N. Consider Table 9.7, which
shows ten pairs of scores obtained by a researcher calculating the correlation between self-actualization and achievement level.

After we insert the appropriate values into the formula, calculating
the Pearson r value requires only simple mathematical computations.
With a hand calculator, the steps are really not difficult. Solving for the
Pearson r value gives:

$$\text{Pearson } r = \frac{111610 - 110670}{\sqrt{45380 - 44100} \cdot \sqrt{285030 - 277729}}$$

$$= \frac{940}{\sqrt{1280} \cdot \sqrt{7301}} = \frac{940}{(35.78)(85.45)}$$

$$= \frac{940}{3057.40} = 0.307 = 0.31$$

Deterring the Direction of Causation

This shows that the correlation coefficient for the hypothetical data between self-actualization and achievement test scores is a moderate positive relationship, where $r = 0.31$. In other words, as one's self-actualization score increases, achievement test scores tend to increase to a moderate degree.

As mentioned previously, both the Spearman rho and Pearson r measure the *linear* relationship of two variables, X and Y. If X and Y are perfectly linearly related, the points on a graph, or *scatterplot,* will all fall on a straight line. A perfect linear relationship could be either a *perfect positive* or a *perfect negative* correlation, as seen in Figures 9.2 and 9.3.

If points vary or are distributed above and below a straight line, a high, moderate, or low positive linear relationship of X and Y will exist,

Table 9.7 Calculating the Pearson r Correlation for Ten Scores on Two Variables

Self-actualization score (range 0–30)		Achievement score (range 20–80)		
X	X^2	Y	Y^2	XY
28	784	50	2500	$1400 = (28 \times 50)$
24	576	58	3364	$1392 = (24 \times 58)$
23	529	64	4096	$1472 = (23 \times 64)$
23	529	47	2209	$1081 = (23 \times 47)$
22	484	70	4900	$1540 = (22 \times 70)$
20	400	44	1936	$880 = (20 \times 44)$
19	361	53	2809	$1007 = (19 \times 53)$
19	361	48	2304	$912 = (19 \times 48)$
17	289	41	1681	$697 = (17 \times 41)$
15	225	52	2704	$780 = (15 \times 52)$

$\Sigma X = 210$ $\Sigma X^2 = 4538$ $\Sigma Y = 527$ $\Sigma Y^2 = 28503$ $\Sigma XY = 11161$
$N = 10$ $N = 10$
$\overline{X} = 21.0$ $\overline{Y} = 52.7$

Step 0: pair each set of scores, one for X and the other for Y.
Step 1: calculate the ΣX and the ΣY.
Step 2: calculate the square of each X and the square of each Y.
Step 3: add up the X^2 and add up the Y^2 columns.
Step 4: multiply each X by its paired Y.
Step 5: add up the XY column.
Step 6: substitute the appropriate values in the formula and solve for the Pearson r. Thus:

$$\text{Pearson } r = \frac{10(11161) - (210)(527)}{\sqrt{10(4538) - (210)^2} \cdot \sqrt{10(28503) - (527)^2}}$$

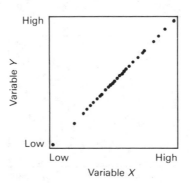

Figure 9.2 A Scatterplot Showing a Perfect Positive Relationship, $r = +1.0$

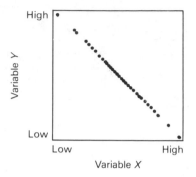

Figure 9.3 A Scatterplot Showing a Perfect Negative Relationship, $r = -1.0$

as seen in Figure 9.4. If we are inspecting a scatterplot and the points approach a circular arrangement, no linear relationship will exist. This lack of relationship is shown in Figure 9.5 where $r = 0.0$

If points vary above and below a curved line, a *curvilinear* relationship may exist, as shown in Figure 9.6. Since the r and rho correlation coefficients measure the strength of linear relationship, the value of these correlations will *underestimate* the degree of curvilinear relationship. Thus, most researchers will inspect a scatterplot of variables to determine whether a given observed relationship approximates a linear one. The correlation ratio, *eta squared* (η^2), is frequently used to measure the degree of nonlinear relationships. Glass and Stanley (1970) supplied the calculation of the η^2 for determining curvilinear relationships.

There are other types of correlational techniques found in the research literature. However, the Pearson r and Spearman rho comprise more than 90 percent of the correlation coefficients reported (Hopkins and Glass, 1978, pp. 112–116).

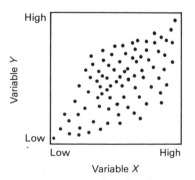

Figure 9.4 A Scatterplot Showing a High Positive Relationship, $r = +0.70$

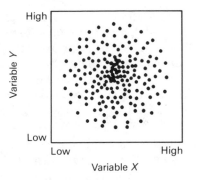

Figure 9.5 A Scatterplot Showing No Relationship, $r = 0.0$

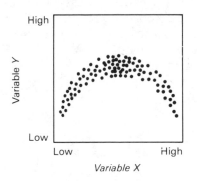

Figure 9.6 A Scatterplot Showing a Significant Curvilinear Relationship

Coefficient of determination.   A variation of the correlation coefficient is the *coefficient of determination, r^2.* The r^2 value indicates the *proportion of total variability of scores explained by the relationship between the two variables.* When $r = 0.0$ then $r^2 = 0$ percent, and when $r = 1.0$, then $r^2 = 100$ percent. Thus, the variance in test scores can be explained by the r^2 relationship.

r	r^2
0.00	0%
.10	1%
.20	4%
.30	9%
.40	16%
.50	25%
.60	36%
.70	49%
.80	64%
.90	81%
1.00	100%

Even with such a moderate positive relationship as $r = .50$, only 25 percent of the variability of test scores is explained by the relationship between the two variables. This means that 75 percent of the variability remains to be explained by relationships to other variables. Thus, even though a correlation coefficient may be statistically significant, the percentage of variance, or variability explained, may still be low, as seen above. Only high correlations of 0.70 or above explain even half of the variability of scores (when $r = 0.70$, $r^2 = 49$ percent). As reviewers and evaluators of educational research encountering correlation coefficients which either may or may not be statistically significant, we can square the r value to more accurately estimate the percentage of variance or variability of scores explained by the two measures.

The reliability coefficients discussed in Chapter 8 can be further understood by this r^2 concept. For instance, if we had a test-retest reliability coefficient equal to 0.80, we could square it ($r^2 = 64$ percent). We could then state that 64 percent of the variability in test scores can be explained by the time of testing. This means that 36 percent remains to be explained by such other sources as the reliability due to content or error in testing.

Statistical Evolution

Table 9.8 Measurement Scales and Statistics

Type of statistic or technique	Nominal	Ordinal	Interval or ratio
Techniques for tables or graphs	bar graphs	bar graphs	frequency polygon
Measures of central tendency	mode	median	mean
Measures of variability			standard deviation variance
Measures of relationship		Spearman rho	Pearson r
Measures of derived scores		percentile rank	z-score T-score stanine normal curve equivalent

Relationship of Measurement Scale to Statistics

We have completed our discussion of the important descriptive statistics encountered in educational research. The decision to use a particular statistic rests mainly on the type of measurement scale the variable falls on—whether it is nominal, ordinal, interval, or ratio. This is true of all the inferential statistics we will encounter. However, we must also know which are independent and which are dependent variables.

At this point, a summarizing table (Table 9.8) integrating the main descriptive statistics with their appropriate measurement scales should be a useful tool as you consider the educational research in your field of interest. Frequencies, proportions, and percentages can be obtained for all these variables.

—— SUMMARY ——

We have explained four types of measurement scales: nominal, ordinal, interval, and ratio, and seen how they relate to descriptive statistics. Measures or techniques for use with tables or graphs include: frequency, percentage, proportion, bar graphs, and frequency polygons. Measures of central tendency include: the mean, median, and mode. Measures of variability include: the standard deviation, variance, and range. Measures of relationship include: the Spearman rho and the Pearson product-moment correlation. Finally, Table 9.8 summarizes the relationship between descriptive statistics and the type of measurement scale.

——— OBJECTIVES ———————————————

In Chapter 9 we have analyzed the variety of descriptive statistics encountered in research. We have also examined their relationship to the types of measurement scales. Confirm your understanding of the material in Chapter 9 using the following objectives:

Distinguish among the four types of measurement scales.
Distinguish among frequency, percentage, and proportion.
Distinguish among the three measures of central tendency.
Distinguish among the three measures of variability.
Distinguish between the two measures of relationship.
Calculate the values of each of the descriptive statistics.
Identify the type of measurement scale for which each descriptive statistic is appropriate.

——— TERMS ———————————————

bar graph
coefficient of determination
continuous
correlation coefficient
curvilinear relationship
deviation score
discrete
eta square
frequency
frequency polygon
interquartile range
interval
mean
mean deviation
median
mode

negatively skewed distribution
nominal
numbers
numerals
ordinal
Pearson product-moment
    correlation
percentage
positively skewed distribution
proportion
range
ratio
scatterplot
Spearman rho
standard deviation
variance

Inferential Statistics

What are the levels of statistical significance, and how do we use them to understand the results from any statistic?

What is a Type I or Type II error, and how are they related to decisions for accepting or rejecting the null hypothesis?

What are the four assumptions used in determining whether an inferential statistic should be used with a particular distribution of scores?

What are parametric and nonparametric statistics, and how do we distinguish one from the other?

What is the Chi-square statistic, and how is it calculated?

What are the two types of *t*-tests, and how is each calculated?

What is the one-way analysis of variance, and how is it calculated?

What is the main difference between a priori and a posteriori tests, and how is a Tukey test calculated?

What is a factorial analysis of variance?

What is an analysis of covariance?

What are multivariate statistics, and how do they differ from univariate statistics?

How are data prepared and used in a computer analysis?

What are the five steps for integrating the information into the Results section of the research article?

Inferential Statistics

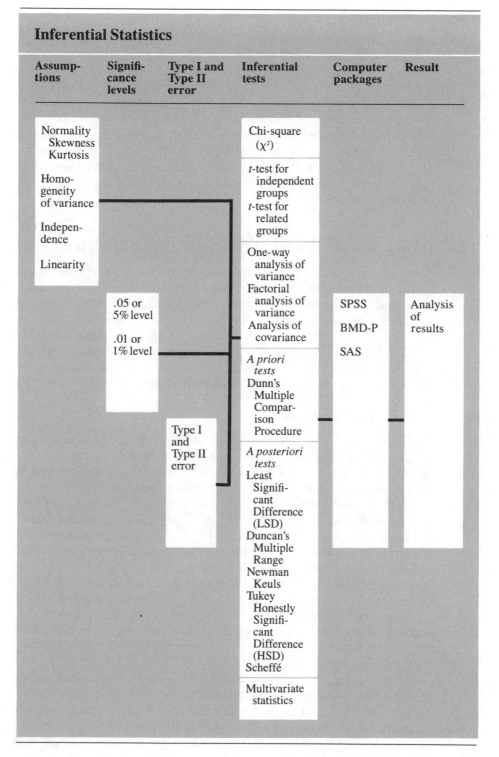

Assumptions	Significance levels	Type I and Type II error	Inferential tests	Computer packages	Result
Normality Skewness Kurtosis			Chi-square (χ²)		
Homogeneity of variance			*t*-test for independent groups *t*-test for related groups		
Independence	.05 or 5% level		One-way analysis of variance Factorial analysis of variance Analysis of covariance	SPSS	Analysis of results
Linearity	.01 or 1% level	Type I and Type II error	*A priori tests* Dunn's Multiple Comparison Procedure	BMD-P SAS	
			A posteriori tests Least Significant Difference (LSD) Duncan's Multiple Range Newman Keuls Tukey Honestly Significant Difference (HSD) Scheffé		
			Multivariate statistics		

Now that we understand the main types of descriptive statistics, we shall consider inferential statistics. First, however, we shall discuss three important supporting concepts: (1) probability and the level of significance; (2) Type I and Type II errors; and (3) assumptions for the use of inferential statistics. After considering the main inferential statistics, we will discuss the different computer packages for statistical analysis and data preparation for computers. Finally, we shall relate the material of Chapters 9 and 10 to developing and evaluating a Results section using the five steps for organizing a Results section introduced at the beginning of Chapter 9.

Probability and the Level of Statistical Significance

Recall from Chapter 3 that a null hypothesis states that no difference between the variables is predicted. In other words, any difference that is observed is due to chance or error. When a researcher states a null hypothesis, he or she anticipates that there is a difference and expects that the sample will reject the null hypothesis. As you may recall, a null hypothesis is usually set forth in order to be rejected. When a null hypothesis is rejected, the researcher's alternative hypothesis (either directional or nondirectional) can then be accepted.

Level of Significance

The decision to reject or accept a null hypothesis is based on a value of probability called the *level of significance.* Probability values are used since we are dealing with only a sample. Thus, there may be sampling error that results in incomplete information. The level of significance is also called *alpha;* alpha is the probability of rejecting the null hypothesis wrongly, should it in fact be true. The particular significance level, which is selected by the researcher ahead of the data collection phase, depends on the nature of the research problem. It is the main criterion for determining whether the null hypothesis will be rejected. In rejecting the null hypothesis, the researcher is stating that a significant difference exists; that is to say, the results are not due to sampling error. Typically in education, the level of significance is set at .05 or .01. In a few instances, it may be set at .10. The researcher must decide, by examining the problem and the consequences of being wrong, what the level of significance should be for the study.

Understanding the concept of level of significance and how it is used is the key to understanding the results derived from most statistics. Regardless of the statistical analysis used to arrive at the results, the obtained statistical value is always converted to a decision as to whether or not the level of significance was reached; that is, whether one can reject or accept the null hypothesis.

As we have said, the level of statistical significance is typically set at .05 or .01. We indicate the 5 percent level as either $p = .05$ or $p < .05$, where p stands for the probability. What this means is that the probability is fewer than five times out of one hundred that the obtained results are due to chance or error. In other words, if we were to conduct the study 100 times, the *same* differences between groups would be attributed to significant differences 95 times out of a hundred. However, five times out of a hundred ($p < .05$), those same differences would be attributed to chance or error.

A similar interpretation exists when $p < .01$, only the level of error the researcher is willing to accept is smaller. Thus, $p < .01$ means that the probability is fewer than one time out of one hundred that the obtained results are due to chance. Repeating the study 100 times, these same differences between variables would be attributed to significant differences existing 99 times out of a hundred. Still, one time out of a hundred ($p < .01$), the same differences would be due to chance.

If we selected $p < .05$ as the level of significance, then any value greater than 5 percent would mean we had not obtained statistical significance. We would then accept the null hypothesis of no differences. Levels of significance greater than 5 percent are represented in the research literature as either $p > .05$ or at the actual level of significance. The symbol, $p > .05$, means that the probability is *greater than* five times out of a hundred that the obtained results are due to chance or error. This is a greater error than the researcher is willing to accept. Sometimes the values greater than the 5 percent level are reported; these are indicated by $p > .05$ and upward: $p > .06$, $p > .07$, $p > .08$, $p > .09$, $p > .10$, and so on to $p > .99$.

All these levels of significance mean that error is occurring more than five times out of a hundred. For instance, $p > .11$ means that the obtained differences are due to chance or error. Thus, there is more error (11 out of 100 compared with 5 out of 100) than the researcher is willing to accept.

Some researchers, after setting their level of significance at $p < .05$, may report that a statistical result "approached statistical significance," and cite the corresponding significance level, e.g., $p = .12$. Most researchers, however, argue that a result is either statistically significant or not. They argue that we should not attempt to legitimize a nonsignificant result by stating that it "approached significance."

We have considered the instance of values greater than the set level of significance. Now if a statistic reports a corresponding level of significance equal to or less than the set significance level, such as $p = .05$, a statistically significant difference has occurred. That is, the level of error is less than 5 out of 100 times. These levels of significance include: $p < .05$, $p < .04$, $p < .03$, $p < .02$, $p < .01$; also, $p < .009$ to $p < .001$, and $p < .0009$ to $p < .0001$. The level of significance reflects the particular prob-

The Struggle for Significance

ability of error or chance operating: less than 5 in 100 ($p < .05$); less than 1 in 100 ($p < .01$); less than 1 in 1000 ($p < .001$); to less than 1 in 10,000 times ($p < .0001$). Thus, the probability is increased that the obtained results, having reached a particular level of significance, represent or can be attributed to significant differences between the groups as the probability of chance or error operating is decreased. Understanding this concept of level of significance will help you to determine for any study, regardless of the statistic used, whether or not a comparison attained statistical significance.

Keep in mind that statistical significance is only a baseline decision for determining the theoretical or applied implications of the results. We must first have statistical significance to ensure that error or chance is sufficiently minimized before we can determine the practical significance of the results. Otherwise, we would waste time determining the practical implications of results which would not be statistically significant. Practical significance includes the implications of results in terms of theoretical or educational importance as well as the implications for future research. Practical significance may also include considering such criteria as time, money, resources, and staff in the decision-making process. For instance, a school board may wish to put into effect a new curriculum because it raises reading comprehension scores over the old curriculum at statistically significant levels. However, the mean score difference between the two curricula may be only five points (say, a half standard deviation difference). In considering the practical significance of this small difference in terms of text purchases, staff training and time, and staff and student attitudes (the overwhelming majority may prefer the old curriculum!), the school board probably would not recommend the change even though there was a statistical significance. Thus, we need to consider not only the statistical significance but, more importantly, the practical significance of our results.

Regardless of the level of significance set for a particular study, when we reject the null hypothesis, there is always some probability that we are making a mistake. That is, regardless of the probability level selected, some degree of error will always operate. In the next section we will discuss the types of mistakes or errors that might occur.

Type I and Type II Errors

When we reject the null hypothesis, we can never know for certain whether the differences are real ones or whether they were caused by chance or error. With any level of significance, such as $p < .05$, some element of error will always occur. This is due to the nature of the scientific inquiry, which is grounded in probability rather than some set of absolutes. Thus, in testing hypotheses we can make two types of error.

In a *Type I error,* we reject the null hypothesis when no differences exist. In a *Type II error,* we accept the null hypothesis when differences do exist. The probability of making a Type I error is the actual level of significance set by the researcher, such as $p = .05$. In this case we are willing to reject the null hypothesis and accept the chance of being wrong 5 out of 100 times.

Making a Type I error implies that a researcher is making a new claim or assertion for a relationship among variables that does not really exist. The implication of a Type II error is that: "I should have concluded that differences existed, but I didn't; I accepted the null of no differences when I should have rejected it." In general, researchers would rather make a Type II error than a Type I error, since they do not want to conclude that a phenomenon exists, when it does not. And, if the phenomenon does indeed exist, they might not observe it now but, with continued research, the phenomenon or relationship may be discovered.

Defenses Against Type I and Type II Error

A related concept, briefly alluded to in Chapter 5, is power. *Power* is the probability of making a correct decision to reject a null hypothesis when differences do exist. In order to set a level of power, the size of the sample and the effect size—whether small, moderate, or large—that you wish to observe should be considered. Winer (1971) or Glass and Stanley (1970) give the necessary calculations.

In developing or evaluating the Results section, it is very important to clearly understand the levels of significance and types of error which may operate as the researcher decides to reject or accept the null hypothesis.

Assumptions for Inferential Statistics

As we have seen in Chapter 1, inferential statistics are used to make inferences about population characteristics; such inferences are derived from the data obtained from the sample. In other words, inferential statistics are concerned with generalizing the results from the sample back to the population. In deciding to select a particular inferential statistic, we must decide whether or not the distribution of scores meets the various assumptions for its correct use. There are four main assumptions; however, not all assumptions apply to each statistic. As we discuss each inferential statistic in the following section, its corresponding assumptions will be identified. The four main assumptions are: (1) normality, (2) homogeneity of variance, (3) independence, and (4) linearity.

Normality

The assumption of *normality* concerns the degree to which a distribution of scores approximates the standard normal distribution, or normal curve. Two statistics are used to calculate the two related aspects of normality: *skewness* and *kurtosis.*

Skewness. *Skewness* measures deviation from a symmetrical normal curve. We have already discussed in Chapter 9 positively skewed and negatively skewed distributions. A positively skewed distribution implies very few high scores and the bulk of the scores being average and low, thereby producing a *floor effect.* Figure 10.1 is a graph illustrating this distribution.

A negatively skewed distribution implies very few low scores and the bulk of the scores being average and high. For instance, a test that is too easy would have many students scoring high and few scoring low, thus producing a *ceiling effect.* Figure 10.2 is a graph illustrating this distribution.

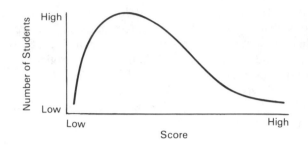

Figure 10.1 A Positively Skewed Distribution

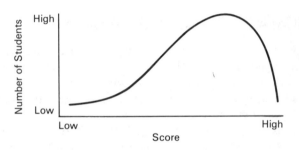

Figure 10.2 A Negatively Skewed Distribution

The assumption of normality means that the set of scores does not significantly deviate from a symmetrical distribution, or is not significantly skewed. Accordingly, we frequently make a scatterplot of the data and calculate a coefficient of skewness. For example, the values of the coefficient of skewness for the formula used by the *Statistical Package for the Social Sciences* (SPSS) (Nie, Hull, Jenkins, Steinbrenner, and Bent, 1975, p. 185) range from zero, for a completely symmetrical distribution, to positive values indicating positively skewed distributions, to negative values indicating negatively skewed distributions.

Kurtosis.   *Kurtosis* is a measure of the steepness or flatness of the symmetrical curve, based on the distribution of scores. There are three typical shapes of kurtosis: a *mesokurtic curve* is the standard normal distribution; a *leptokurtic curve* is a steep and sharp symmetrical curve; and a *platykurtic curve* is a flat symmetrical curve. Figure 10.3 illustrates these three types of curves.

The values of kurtosis calculated by the SPSS program (Nie et al., 1975, p. 185) range from zero for a normal mesokurtic distribution, to positive for the steeper leptokurtic distribution, to negative for the flatter platykurtic distribution.

Other researchers calculate the coefficient of skewness and kurtosis using the analysis of Snedecor and Cochran (1967, pp. 86–90), where

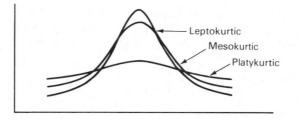

Figure 10.3 Three Kurtosis Curves

tables are provided to test the statistical significance of either skewness or kurtosis. Others, such as the χ^2 *(chi-square) goodness of fit test* (Snedecor and Cochran, 1967, p. 84), or *Geary's test of normality* (D'Agostino, 1970, pp. 138–140), are also found in the research literature as tests of the assumption of normality. When you encounter these statistics, you may be sure the investigators are trying to determine the degree to which the scores are normally distributed.

Homogeneity of Variances

The assumption of *homogeneity of variances* indicates the degree to which variances from each treatment group or level are similar or homogeneous to each other. The preferred result when testing this assumption is that *variances are homogeneous and thus are not statistically significant from each other.* Two tests frequently used to determine whether the assumption of homogeneity of variances is met are the *F-test* (Nunnally, 1975, pp. 214–215) and the *F-maximum test for homogeneity of variances,* or the *F-max test* (Kirk, 1968, p. 62).

F-test. The *F*-test is used when two samples comprise the study. If the obtained *F*-test value is significantly greater than the tabled *F* values, then the assumption is *not* met; that is, the groups would be statistically significant from each other and not homogeneous. The formula is:

$$F = \frac{s_1^2}{s_2^2} \qquad df_1 = n_1 - 1 \qquad df_2 = n_2 - 1$$

where s_1^2 is the largest variance between the two groups,
s_2^2 is the smallest variance between the two groups,
df is the degrees of freedom for the numerator and denominator,
$n_1 - 1$ is the number of subjects in group 1 minus 1, and
$n_2 - 1$ is the number of subjects in group 2 minus 1.

If we find variances for our two groups of $s_1^2 = 23.04$ and $s_2^2 = 16.81$, while $n_1 = 25$ and $n_2 = 51$, then the values obtained from the formula would be:

$$F = \frac{23.04}{16.81} = 1.37 \qquad df = 24/50$$

In the special case of testing the assumption of the homogeneity of variances, the significance level must be doubled in Table 4 of Appendix D, which presents the tabled F-ratio values. Thus, the significance levels in Table 4, which are .05 and .01, are adjusted to .10 and .02, respectively. The reason we have to double the probabilities in this special case only is that we arbitrarily placed the larger variance in the numerator and the smaller in the denominator. Keep in mind that, in order to meet the assumption of homogeneity of variances, or similar variances, we don't want statistical significance; instead, we want the F value to be less than the appropriate tabled value. Thus, looking across the columns with the degrees of freedom for the numerator ($df = 24$), we locate the appropriate column. Next we locate the appropriate row by using the degrees of freedom for the denominator ($df = 50$). The two tabled F values are .10 = 1.74 and .02 = 2.18. Thus, the value $F = 1.37$, $df = 24/50$ obtained is not equal to or greater than the tabled F values, so there is no statistical significance. Therefore, we have met the assumption of homogeneity of variances since no significant differences were obtained.

F-max test.   To determine whether the variances of more than two sets of scores meet the assumption of homogeneity of variances, we calculate the *F-max test*. In this case the formula is:

$$F \max = \frac{s_L^2}{s_S^2} \qquad \begin{aligned} df_L &= k \\ df_S &= n - 1 \end{aligned}$$

where s_L^2 is the largest of the variances in the study,
      s_S^2 is the smallest of the variances in the study,
      df_L for the numerator is k, the total number of variances, and
      df_S for the denominator is $n - 1$, where n is the number of scores within each treatment level.

The assumption of homogeneity of variance is accepted if the F-max obtained is less than the tabled F-max. Again, we are not concerned with statistical significance, so we don't want a value equal to or greater than the tabled value. Consider the study in which we had four groups with an $n = 8$ in each group. Here the variances are:

$$s_1^2 = 8.40$$
$$s_2^2 = 6.00$$
$$s_3^2 = 4.80$$
$$s_4^2 = 2.00$$

Taking the largest variance from among the four, $s_1^2 = 8.40$, and the smallest variance, $s_4^2 = 2.00$, we can find the F-max as follows:

$$F\text{-max} = \frac{8.40}{2.00} = 4.20$$

Thus we get an F-max = 4.20 with $df = 4/7$. Locating the F-max values in Table 5 of Appendix D, we find by going across to the $df = 4$ column and down to the $df = 7$ row that the values of .05 and .01 in the table are, respectively, 8.44 and 14.50. We find that the F-max value we obtained is less than the tabled F-max value; hence, the assumption of homogeneity of variances for the four groups has been met: F-max (4,7) = 4.20, $p > .05$.

Independence

The assumption of independence is met only if an individual's score is independent of every other score. It is expected that each subject's score will not be influenced by the scores of other subjects. In other words, the scores are not correlated, matched, or paired in any way. If this assumption of independence is not met, the probability of making a Type I or Type II error is significantly increased. An example of scores that are correlated or dependent is given in the case of a pretest-posttest design in which subjects receive both measures. If a study were to match and then randomly assign subjects to treatments, interdependence would also be obtained. If you use a design in which you do not maintain independence of scores, you will have to use appropriate statistical tests. For instance, a researcher can calculate either a *t-test for independent groups* or, if the scores are not independent, a *t-test for correlated groups.*

Other threats to the independence of scores must be considered as one attempts to minimize the possibility of extraneous or confounding variables operating in the study. For instance, if cheating occurred, scores would not be independent; or if one psychotic in a counseling group made the other subjects so nervous and anxious that they all performed poorly on the measure, independence of scores again would not be assured. There is no statistical measure by which to test the assumption of independence. It is by the choice of the design and the ability to control possible confounding variables that independence either is or is not obtained.

Linearity

Finally, there is the assumption of linearity. We briefly considered linearity in the discussion of the Pearson r correlation coefficient. Basically, the use of some inferential statistics as well as some descriptive statistics, such as the Pearson r, depends on whether the underlying distribution of scores is linear; that is, whether or not the assumption of linearity is met. An inspection of scatterplots of the variables will generally determine whether or not the relationship is linear. In some research a *polynominal regression* equation (Nie et al., pp. 371–373) is used to determine the number of "bends" or changes in direction there are in a curved regression line in order to fit the data. Such a formula helps determine whether or not the distribution of scores is linear; and if it is not, how many significant changes in direction, or bends, there are in the distribution. Sometimes, the original variables can be transformed to restate the relationship between variables into a linear form. Four of the most common *transformations* used in the research literature are the *reciprocal, square root, square,* and *natural log functions.* In these transformations, each score X is recalculated and then analyzed as $1/X, \sqrt{X}, X^2$, or Ln (X), respectively (Nie et al., p. 371). One problem in converting scores into these transformed scores is that it may be difficult to accurately interpret the results and implications of findings derived from the transformed values. This procedure is not generally recommended for the novice researcher.

Parametric and Nonparametric Decisions

Generally speaking, if the particular assumption for the use of a statistic was violated, then nonparametric statistics were recommended and desirable. *Nonparametric statistics* make fewer of the underlying assumptions about the nature of the distribution of scores. More specifically, most nonparametric tests do assume the independence of scores, but not the three other assumptions. Neither the shape of the distribution curve nor the variance of the scores are important concerns of nonparametric statistics. Seigel's (1956) work on nonparametric statistics is one of the best-known texts.

In the last two decades, there has been a growing body of literature suggesting that the inferential tests are "robust" with respect to violating the assumptions. For instance, in the *t*-test and the analysis of variance, the identical assumptions apply: normality, homogeneity of variances, and independence of observations or scores in the population. A review by Glass, Peckham, and Sanders (1972) reports that violations of these assumptions are inconsequential; that is, the *t*-test and ANOVA are "robust" with respect to violations of the assumption of homogeneity of variances *provided equal subjects in each comparison group are main-*

tained. Thus, there is a big advantage in having the same number of subjects in our groups when we sample. Several perspectives have since emerged.

In the past, if there were significant violations of assumptions, non-parametric statistics were consistently recommended. However, as a result of the research into violations during the last two decades, it is suggested that, even with violations of assumptions, the inferential (or parametric) statistic is still preferred to the nonparametric statistic. One reason for this preference is that they are more powerful and make possible advanced mathematical analysis. With interval data, some researchers may still choose to use parametric statistics, even with significant violations to the assumptions of normality and homogeneity of variances. Their rationale includes these three points: (1) Departures from the assumptions have little effect on the value of the inferential statistic; (2) Nonparametric tests are less powerful (that is, in order to reject a false null hypothesis, more subjects must be tested to obtain the same level of statistical significance); and (3) The nonparametric tests are more complicated and difficult to calculate. Regardless of the reasons for or against the effect of violations of the assumptions of inferential statistics, both nonparametric and parametric analyses continue to be conducted.

Today we can perceive three main strategies in the educational research literature. One is the use of nonparametric statistics when violations occur. The second is the use of inferential (parametric) statistics whether or not the tested assumptions are violated. The third is the use of inferential statistics and the testing of assumptions for their use that are not considered by the researcher and are ignored or omitted from the Results section. The third strategy is the one most frequently found in the literature today. Although it is more frequent, this strategy is not the most useful, since information about the violation of assumptions is never determined or provided. Subsequent reviews to test the effect of violation of assumptions are not facilitated. Also, the basic awareness of the presuppositions for the use of various statistics is minimized, and more sloppy, careless research may result. The decision to use a particular statistic may depend on what the researcher knows how to calculate or to program on a computer, rather than on which is the appropriate statistical test for the variables examined. Thus, as we now consider the following inferential statistics, we shall include several of the parallel nonparametric tests.

Inferential Statistics

We shall examine the following six types of inferential statistics that are frequently encountered in the research literature: (1) chi-square (χ^2), (2) *t*-test for independent and related groups, (3) one-way analysis of variance, (4) a priori and a posteriori tests, (5) factorial analysis of variance, and (6) analysis of covariance.

Chi-square (χ^2)

Chi-square (χ^2) has been considered as either a parametric or non-parametric statistic; it is a test of significance appropriate for such nominal data as head counts or frequency counts. It has also been used with percentages and proportions. The main assumption in using χ^2 is the independence of scores. This means that an observation cannot occur simultaneously in two or more categories; rather, each frequency or head count must be in a mutually exclusive category. Conceptually, a χ^2 test compares the observed frequencies with the expected frequencies to determine if they are significantly different from each other. Consider a study in which parents are asked to respond *yes* or *no* to the question of whether they prefer year-round schools over traditional 10-month schools for their children. Of 220 parents responding, 80 say *no* and 140 say *yes*. This is the observed frequency. The expected frequency would be the average of the total responses divided by the number of categories; that is, $(140 + 80)/2 = 220/2 = 110$. Thus we have:

Attitude toward year-round schools

	Yes	*No*
Observed	140	80
Expected	110	110

The formula for χ^2 requires that $df = k - 1$, where k equals the number of categories:

$$\chi^2 = \Sigma \left[\frac{(f_o - f_e)^2}{f_e} \right]$$

where f_o is the observed frequency,
        f_e is the expected frequency, and
        Σ means the sum of the values in the brackets
        for each cell or level of the variable.

When we insert the values from the table, we get:

$$\chi^2 = \left[\frac{(140 - 110)^2}{110} \right] + \left[\frac{(80 - 110)^2}{110} \right] = \left[\frac{(30)^2}{110} \right] + \left[\frac{(-30)^2}{110} \right]$$

$$= \frac{900}{110} + \frac{900}{110} = 8.18 + 8.18 = 16.36,$$

$$\text{where } df = k - 1 = 2 - 1 = 1$$
$$df = 1$$

If there were more than two cells, we would calculate the bracket value for each additional cell. For instance, if we had three categories (such as yes, sometimes, no), we would have included the third value within brackets in calculating our χ^2 value. From Table 6 in Appendix D, we can see that with $df = 1$, the obtained value required for statistical significance at three levels is:

$$.05 = 3.84$$
$$.01 = 6.64$$
$$.001 = 10.83$$

Thus, our obtained $\chi^2 = 16.36$ is equal to or greater than all three of the values from the table. Therefore, the difference in responding either *yes* or *no* is statistically significant at the highest level reported; namely, $\chi^2(1) = 16.36$, $p < .001$. Many other variations of the basic χ^2 formula are possible. You should consult a basic text, such as Siegel (1956) or Hopkins and Glass (1978), for variations in the use of χ^2.

t-test

The *t*-test is used to determine whether there is statistical significance between the means of two groups. It is used with interval and ratio scale variables where the populations are normally distributed and have homogeneity of variances. In using the *t*-test for independent groups, independence of observations or scores is necessary. Otherwise, the *t*-test for related groups is calculated. Departures from the assumption of normality do not greatly affect the results with sample sizes of 30 or more (Hays, 1973). Violations of the assumption of homogeneity of variances also have little effect on the *t*-test value when sample sizes are equal. If the sample sizes are very small and of unequal numbers, however, there is a significant effect on the *t*-ratio. Two options are available, either to use equal numbers or to use a nonparametric test instead of a *t*-test. In order to minimize the effects of violations of the assumptions of normality and homogeneity of variances, equal sample sizes with at least 30 in each of the two groups should be constructed.

t-test for independent groups. There are a variety of formulas for the *t*-test for independent groups. We shall examine one of the more useful formulas and calculate a problem.

$$t = \frac{\overline{X}_1 - \overline{X}_2}{\sqrt{\dfrac{\left[\Sigma X_1^2 - \dfrac{(\Sigma X_1)^2}{N_1}\right] + \left[\Sigma X_2^2 - \dfrac{(\Sigma X_2)^2}{N_2}\right]}{N_1 + N_2 - 2} \cdot \left(\dfrac{N_1 + N_2}{N_1 \cdot N_2}\right)}}$$

Here $\overline{X}_1$ is the mean of group 1,

   ΣX_1^2 is the sum of the squares of the individual scores for group 1,

   $(\Sigma X_1)^2$ is the square of the sum of the individual scores for group 1,

   N_1 is the number of subjects in group 1,

$N_1 + N_2 - 2$ are the degrees of freedom (df), equal to 2 less than the sum of the number of subjects in groups 1 and 2.

The symbols for group 2 have the same meaning as for group 1. In the formula, the numerator is the observed difference between the means. The denominator is an estimate of error; specifically, it is an estimate of the variability of the difference between the two means. The observed differences (the numerator value) is divided by the variation of differences (the denominator value). Thus, if there are no significant differences between the two groups, the t-ratio will be zero. The greater the value of the t-ratio, the greater the probability of significant differences between the groups.

Conceptually, then, the t-ratio compares the differences between the two groups (the numerator value) with the differences within each group (the denominator value) in order to determine whether the resulting proportion is large enough to indicate significant differences *between* groups after having taken into account the differences of scores *within* groups. Figure 10.4 shows two normal curves overlapping slightly and illustrates this concept. Given the differences of scores within each distribution, are the mean scores between the groups still statistically significant?

This ratio of between-group differences to within-group differences is what the t-test calculates. Thus, if it is statistically significant, the t-ratio will be large; that is, the between-group difference in the numerator will

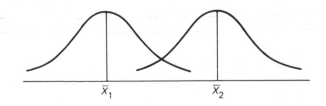

Figure 10.4 Illustrating the t-score Concept

be large compared to the within-group difference. If the t-ratio is not statistically significant, the within-group difference in the denominator will be large compared to the between-group difference.

Let us conceptually examine two sets of independent data and calculate the t-ratio. The purpose of the research was to determine differences between a traditional inservice teacher workshop and a new inservice teacher workshop on a measure of motivation. A group of 20 elementary teachers were randomly assigned into one of the two groups. A posttest only control group design was used. The two sets of ten posttest scores for each group are given in Table 10.1.

We need to find eight numbers from Table 10.1 to substitute into the formula:

1. To find ΣX_1 add the scores in the column headed X_1
2. To find N_1 count the number of scores in the X_1 column
3. To find $\overline{X}_1$ divide the $\Sigma X_1/N_1$
4. To find ΣX_1^2 square each score in the X_1 column and add the scores in the column headed X_1^2
5. Repeat steps 1 to 4 for group 2 to find ΣX_2, N_2, $\overline{X}_2$, ΣX_2^2

We can now substitute these eight numbers into the t-test formula as follows:

$$t = \frac{52.00 - 40.00}{\sqrt{\frac{\left[27,330 - \frac{(520)^2}{10}\right] + \left[16,374 - \frac{(400)^2}{10}\right]}{10 + 10 - 2} \cdot \left(\frac{10 + 10}{10 \cdot 10}\right)}}$$

Table 10.1 Data Gathered for First t-Test Example

Traditional Group 1		New Group 2	
X_1	X_1^2	X_2	X_2^2
60	3600	50	2500
58	3364	48	2304
57	3249	44	1936
56	3136	44	1936
52	2704	40	1600
50	2500	39	1521
50	2500	36	1296
48	2304	35	1225
47	2209	34	1156
42	1764	30	900
$\Sigma X_1 = 520$	$\Sigma X_1^2 = 27,330$	$\Sigma X_2 = 400$	$\Sigma X_2^2 = 16,374$
$N_1 = 10$		$N_2 = 10$	
$\overline{X}_1 = 52.00$		$\overline{X}_2 = 40.00$	

Solving the formula is accomplished by using the basic mathematical operations:

$$t = \frac{12}{\sqrt{\dfrac{\left[27{,}330 - \dfrac{270{,}400}{10}\right] + \left[16{,}374 - \dfrac{160{,}000}{10}\right]}{18} \cdot \left(\dfrac{20}{100}\right)}}$$

$$t = \frac{12}{\sqrt{\dfrac{[27{,}330 - 27{,}040] + [16{,}374 - 16{,}000]}{18} \cdot \left(.20\right)}}$$

$$t = \frac{12}{\sqrt{\dfrac{290 + 374}{18} \cdot \left(.20\right)}}$$

$$t = \frac{12}{\sqrt{\dfrac{664}{18} \cdot \left(.20\right)}}$$

$$t = \frac{12}{\sqrt{36.89 \cdot (.20)}}$$

$$t = \frac{12}{\sqrt{7.378}}$$

$$t = \frac{12}{2.716}$$

$$t = 4.42$$

In order to make a statistical decision, we must now:

1. Find the degrees of freedom: $df = N_1 + N_2 - 2 = 10 + 10 - 2 = 18$.
2. State the obtained t value: $t = 4.42$.
3. Find the tabled t value. Use the t-distribution in Table 7 of Appendix D. Find the df column and go down it until you find the correct df. Find your preset level of significance (.05). Since we did not propose a directional hypothesis (one-tail test), we posed a nondirectional one (a two-tail test); thus we look under the .05 level column for a two-tail test. The tabled value at the .05 level for a two-tail test with $df = 18$ is: $t = 2.101$.

4. If your obtained t value ($t = 4.42$) is equal to or larger than the tabled t value ($t = 2.101$), you do have statistical significance, and you reject the null hypothesis. If your obtained t is less than the tabled t, you accept (or more precisely, you fail to reject) the null hypothesis.

5. If your obtained t value ($t = 4.42$) obtains statistical significance, then you determine the highest level of significance for the value. Thus, with $df = 18$ for a two-tail test, the tabled t values at higher levels of significance looking across the columns are: $t = 2.552$, $p < .02$; $t = 2.878$, $p < .01$; $t = 3.922$; $p < .001$. Since our obtained $t = 4.42$ is larger than any of the tabled values, it is statistically significant at the highest significance level presented, $p < .001$.

Thus, a significant mean difference, $t(18) = 4.42$, $p < .001$, was obtained between the traditional and new inservice teacher workshop on a measure of motivation. The elementary teachers in the traditional workshop group scored significantly higher on a measure of motivation compared to those in the new inservice workshop ($\overline{X}_1 = 52.0$ compared to $\overline{X}_2 = 40.0$).

t-test for related groups. If the measures are related, such as groups that are matched on some variable, then the t-test for related groups is calculated. Here the formula takes into account the interrelationship between the two variables. The difference between each pair of scores is computed and used to estimate the standard error of the difference. This formula is somewhat easier to calculate:

$$t = \frac{\overline{D}}{\sqrt{\dfrac{\Sigma D^2 - \dfrac{(\Sigma D)^2}{N}}{N(N-1)}}}$$

where $\overline{D}$ is the mean of the difference,
    ΣD^2 is the sum of the squares of the differences,
  $(\Sigma D)^2$ is the square of the sum of the differences,
     N is the number of pairs of scores,
  $N - 1$ is the degrees of freedom (df), equal to one less than the number of pairs of scores.

When we calculated the Spearman rho, we also calculated a difference score between each matched pair of scores. We shall do the same thing in calculating the t-test for related groups. This difference score (D) is the way we take into consideration the interrelationship between

Table 10.2 Data Gathered for Second *t*-Test Example

Group 1 posttest	Group 2 posttest		
X_1	X_2	D	D^2
62	60	2	4
61	55	6	36
55	52	3	9
54	57	−3	9
52	52	0	0
49	50	−1	1
		$\Sigma D = 7$	$\Sigma D^2 = 59$

$N = 6$
$\overline{D} = D/N$
$\overline{D} = 7/6 = 1.17$

pairs of scores. We need to make sure, though, that each pair of scores is appropriately lined up in a one-to-one correspondence with each other. Consider the six pairs of scores in Table 10.2.

We need to find four numbers from Table 10.2 to substitute into the formula:

1. To find the ΣD, after listing each corresponding pair of scores, set up a D column, then subtract each value in the second column from its pair in the first column. Then add up the positive numbers ($2 + 6 + 3 = 11$), and add up the negative numbers ($-3 + (-1) = -4$) and add: $\Sigma D = 11 + (-4) = 7$.
2. To find N, count the number of pairs of scores.
3. To find the mean, $\overline{D}$, divide the ΣD by N.
4. To find ΣD^2, set up a D^2 column, square each D value and add up the numbers in the D^2 column.

We can now substitute these four numbers into the formula, and solve for *t*:

$$t = \frac{1.17}{\sqrt{\dfrac{59 - \dfrac{(7)^2}{6}}{6(6 - 1)}}}$$

After the values are correctly entered, the formula is solved with the basic mathematical operations:

$$t = \frac{1.17}{\sqrt{\dfrac{59 - \dfrac{49}{6}}{6\,(5)}}}$$

$$t = \frac{1.17}{\sqrt{\dfrac{59 - 8.17}{30}}}$$

$$t = \frac{1.17}{\sqrt{\dfrac{50.83}{30}}}$$

$$t = \frac{1.17}{\sqrt{1.69}}$$

$$t = \frac{1.17}{1.30}$$

$$t = 0.90$$

In order to make a statistical decision we must now:

1. Find the degrees of freedom for the t-test for related groups, $df = N - 1$, $df = 6 - 1 = 5$.
2. State the obtained t value: $t = 0.90$.
3. Find the tabled t value. Use the t-distribution in Table 7 of Appendix D. Find the df column and go down it until you find the correct df, ($df = 5$). Find your preset level of significance (.05). Since we did not propose a directional hypothesis (one-tail test), we posed a nondirectional one (a two-tail test); thus we look under the .05 level for a two-tail test with $df = 5$. The tabled value is $t = 2.571$ with $df = 5$ at the .05 level.
4. If your obtained t value ($t = 0.90$) is equal to or larger than the tabled t value ($t = 2.571$) you do have statistical significance, and you reject the null hypothesis. If your obtained t is less than the tabled t (as in this example), you fail to reject the null hypothesis.
5. If your obtained t value ($t = 0.90$) is larger than the tabled t, then determine the t value's highest level of significance, using the appropriate df and appropriate one- or two-tail test. The obtained t value is then reported at its highest level of significance. In this example, where $t(5) = 0.90$, $p > .05$, there is no significant difference between the two groups on the posttest measure.

Corresponding nonparametric tests for the two types of *t*-tests with similarly scaled variables are the *Mann-Whitney U Test* and the *Wilcoxon Signed-Rank Test*. The Mann-Whitney U Test determines significance between the medians of two independent samples and is used with ordinal data and when there are significant violations of assumptions to interval data. The Wilcoxon Signed-Rank Test is used if the two sets of scores are correlated or related to each other. Thus, the former corresponds to the parametric *t*-test for independent groups while the latter corresponds to the *t*-test for related groups.

As we have shown, the *t*-test is used to compare two groups. Frequently, however, three or more groups are studied in a research project. In these instances, it is not efficient to make multiple comparisons of two groups at a time. If we had five groups we would have to calculate ten *t*-tests. Calculating ten *t*-tests rather than one analysis also would increase the probability of incorrectly rejecting the null hypothesis; that is, we would increase the likelihood of making a Type I error. Therefore, the statistical analysis used to test three or more groups is the analysis of variance.

One-Way Analysis of Variance

The *analysis of variance* (ANOVA), also called the *F*-test, is used to test one independent variable with three or more groups and one dependent variable. (The ANOVA can also be used with two groups instead of using the *t*-test.) The independent variable is a nominal scale variable and the dependent variable is an interval or ratio scale variable. The purpose of the ANOVA is to test whether the difference or variance among the means of these groups is significant or due to chance alone. Since the groups are tested simultaneously with the ANOVA, it replaces the strategy of calculating multiple *t*-tests.

Assumptions for the use of the ANOVA are normality, homogeneity of variances, and independence of scores. If the sample sizes are equal, the test for homogeneity of variance is not usually necessary (Hays, 1973).

Understanding the F-ratio.   To determine whether a significant difference exists, a preset probability level is selected (usually $p = .05$), and an ANOVA is calculated that results in a value called the *F*-ratio. The basic principle underlying the ANOVA is that the total variability or variance of test scores can be attributed to two sources: the variability *between groups,* due to the treatment or to chance variations; and the variability *within groups,* which is produced by individuals differing within each group. The within-group variation is considered the *error term,* or *error variance.*

As in the case of the t-test, we set up a ratio, called the F-ratio, in which the between-group variance or difference is the numerator and the within-group variance is the denominator. Then, if the treatment difference (or between-group variance) is large enough relative to the error variance (or within-group variance), a statistically significant F-ratio will be obtained. Conversely, if the between-group variance is small relative to the within-group variance, the F-ratio will be small and not statistically significant. Thus the larger the relative difference between the two values, the larger the F-ratio. These two variances comprise the F-ratio value for the ANOVA.

$$F\text{-ratio} = \frac{MS_{between}}{MS_{within}}$$

Here $MS_{between}$ is a measure of the mean square variability between groups, and

MS_{within} is a measure of the mean square variability within groups.

This is the basic formula for the one-way ANOVA. We shall consider a couple of examples to clarify the important relationship of between-group variability to within-group variability or error. We shall then expand on the formula and illustrate how it is used.

$$F\text{-ratio} = \frac{15}{2} \qquad F\text{-ratio} = \frac{1}{2}$$
$$F\text{-ratio} = 7.50 \qquad F\text{-ratio} = 0.50$$

In these two examples, the between-group difference is large in the first case and small in the second, while the error term is the same in both. Thus in the first, the between-group difference is large relative to the within-group variability or error, so that statistical significance results. In the second instance, the between-group variability is small relative to the error term, so that the F-ratio is not statistically significant. Consider two other examples in which the error terms vary and the between-groups variability remains constant.

$$F\text{-ratio} = \frac{20}{4} \qquad F\text{-ratio} = \frac{20}{40}$$
$$F\text{-ratio} = 5.00 \qquad F\text{-ratio} = 0.50$$

Here, the between-group difference relative to the error term, even though the same value in the two examples, produces statistical significance in the first case and not in the second. This is because the within-group term varies from a very small to a very large error. Thus, the calculations for the ANOVA involve obtaining a value for the between-group variance, a value for the within-group variance, and a value for the total variance that is equal to the sum of the other two components.

These values are all generated from the notion of deviation score ($X - \overline{X}$) as previously discussed. Specifically, these values are derived from the sum of the squared deviation scores, $\Sigma(X - \overline{X})^2$, that we used in the calculation of the standard deviation and variance. Recall that the variance is the sum of the squared deviation scores divided by N. The term *sum squares* is a shorter name for the sum of the squared deviation scores. When we calculate the sum squares for the entire distribution of scores, as we have previously done, it is called the *total sum squares,* and represents the total variability, variance, or deviation of scores for the total distribution. The aim of the ANOVA analysis is to calculate this *total sum squares* and separate or partial that value up into two components, the *between-group sum squares* and the *within-group sum squares.*

Keep in mind that the *total sum squares* is always equal to the *sum of the between-group sum squares* and the *within-group sum squares.* In calculating an F-ratio, these latter two values are each divided by the appropriate degrees of freedom. The degrees of freedom for the between-group sum squares is $df = k - 1$, where k is the number of groups. For the within-group sum squares, the degrees of freedom is $df = N - k$, where N is the total number of scores and k is the number of groups. When each of the sum squares is divided by its appropriate degrees of freedom, we obtain *a mean square between-groups* (MS_b) and *a mean square within-groups* (MS_w) value. Thus, working backward from the F-ratio, we get:

$$F\text{-ratio} = \frac{MS_b}{MS_w}$$

This is the same formula presented earlier. Now, since

$$MS_b = \frac{SS_b}{df_b}$$

$$\text{and } MS_w = \frac{SS_w}{df_w}$$

we can rewrite or expand the formula to read:

$$F\text{-ratio} = \frac{SS_b/df_b}{SS_w/df_w}$$

Since the total sum squares (SS_t) is equal to the between-group sum squares (SS_b) plus the within-group sum squares (SS_w), we need only calculate any two of them, and substitute into this formula to find the third value:

$$SS_t = SS_b + SS_w$$

Conceptually, this is what the formula for the analysis of variance determines when calculating an F-ratio. The only other data needed to calculate an ANOVA are the specific values for the SS_t, SS_b, and SS_w.

Example of an ANOVA with two groups.   Let us calculate for illustrative purposes a two-sample example with only four subjects in each group using the data in Table 10.3.

To calculate the ANOVA we use the following steps:

1. Find the values of ΣX_1 and ΣX_2
2. Find the values of N_1 and N_2
3. Calculate the mean values $\overline{X}_1$ and $\overline{X}_2$
4. Calculate ΣX_1^2 and ΣX_2^2

After finding these four values, we can find the total sum squares using the deviation score method:

$$SS_t = \Sigma (X - \overline{X})_t^2$$

We can also use the raw score method:

$$SS_t = \Sigma X_t^2 - \frac{(\Sigma X_t)^2}{N_t}$$

Table 10.3 Data Gathered for Two-Group ANOVA Analysis

Group 1		Group 2	
X_1	X_1^2	X_2	X_2^2
1	1	6	36
2	4	7	49
5	25	9	81
8	64	10	100
$\Sigma X_1 = 16$	$\Sigma X_1^2 = 94$	$\Sigma X_2 = 32$	$\Sigma X^2 = 266$
$N_1 = 4$		$N_2 = 4$	
$\overline{X}_1 = 4.0$		$\overline{X}_2 = 8.0$	

The raw score method saves a step in the calculations, since we don't have to find a deviation score first; we can get the same value directly from the raw score. All we need, then, are three sets of information—N, ΣX, and ΣX^2 for each group and for the total groups combined. We shall use the raw score method throughout, since your conceptual understanding of the deviation score and the relationships of SS_b and SS_w is well established by now.

Since we have already calculated N, ΣX, and ΣX^2 for each group, we need to find their sums for all groups to get N_t, ΣX_t, and ΣX_t^2. And so the next three steps are:

5. Find the value of N_t, where, $N_t = N_1 + N_2 = 4 + 4 = 8$.
6. Find the value of ΣX_t, where $\Sigma X_t = \Sigma X_1 + \Sigma X_2 = 16 + 32 = 48$
7. Find the value of ΣX_t^2, where $\Sigma X_t^2 = \Sigma X_1^2 + \Sigma X_2^2 = 94 + 266 = 360$

These seven steps give us all the information needed to calculate the three components—SS_t, SS_b, and SS_w—in the ANOVA formula. Step 8 then gives us the total sum squares:

8. To find the *total sum squares (SS$_t$)*, we substitute the appropriate values into the formula:

$$SS_t = \Sigma X_t^2 - \frac{(\Sigma X_t)^2}{N_t}$$

which gives us:

$$SS_t = 360 - \frac{(48)^2}{8}$$

$$SS_t = 360 - \frac{2304}{8}$$

$$SS_t = 360 - 288$$

$$SS_t = 72$$

9. To find the *between-group sum squares (SS$_b$)*, we substitute the values into the formula:

$$SS_b = \Sigma \left[\frac{(\Sigma X)^2}{N} \right] - \frac{(\Sigma X_t)^2}{N_t}$$

Where $\sum \left[\dfrac{(\Sigma X)^2}{N} \right]$ means to calculate the value in the brackets for each group and then to sum those values together

$(\Sigma X_t)^2$ is the square of the sum of X for the total group

N_t is the total number (already calculated)

By substituting these values we get:

$$SS_b = \left[\frac{(16)^2}{4} + \frac{(32)^2}{4} \right] - \frac{(48)^2}{8}$$

We have obtained the values for group 1 and group 2 respectively and will add up that value prior to subtracting from it the remaining value. We must repeat the calculation of the value in brackets for as many groups as we have. We then substitute into the formula to obtain:

$$SS_b = \left[\frac{256}{4} + \frac{1024}{4} \right] - \frac{2304}{8}$$

$$SS_b = [64 + 256] - 288$$

$$SS_b = 320 - 288$$

$$SS_b = 32$$

10. To find the *within-group sum squares (SS$_w$)*, we can subtract the between-group sum squares *(SS$_b$)* from the total sum squares *(SS$_t$)*, since $SS_t = SS_b + SS_w$. Or we can calculate SS_w, which gives us a check on our computation. For illustration, we shall show both calculations:

$$SS_t = SS_b + SS_w$$

$$72 = 32 + SS_w$$

$$SS_w = 72 - 32$$

$$SS_w = 40$$

Or we can use the following formula to solve for SS_w:

$$SS_w = [\Sigma X_1^2 - (\Sigma X_1)^2 / N_1] + [\Sigma X_2^2 - (\Sigma X_2)^2 / N_2]$$

Substituting into the formula, we have:

$$SS_w = [94 - (16)^2 / 4] + [266 - (32)^2 / 4]$$
$$SS_w = [94 - 254/4] + [266 - 1024/4]$$
$$SS_w = [94 - 64] + [266 - 256]$$
$$SS_w = 30 + 10$$
$$SS_w = 40$$

If we have more than two groups, the values within the brackets are obtained for each group and summed for all groups.

After these three values, SS_t, SS_b, and SS_w are obtained, we must calculate the values for MS_b and MS_w.

11. To find the *mean square between-groups, MS_b,* recall that:

$$MS_b = SS_b/df_b$$

where df_b is the degrees of freedom between groups
df_b $= K - 1$, where K is the total number of groups
thus df_b $= 2 - 1 = 1$.

$$MS_b = 32/1$$
$$MS_b = 32$$

12. To find the *mean square within-groups, MS_w,* recall that:

$$MS_w = SS_w/df_w$$

Here, df_w is the degrees of freedom within groups
df_w $= N - K$, where N is the total subjects and
K is the total number of groups,
thus df_w $= 8 - 2 = 6$

$$MS_w = 40/6$$
$$MS_w = 6.67$$

13. The last step is to calculate the F-ratio from the formula:

$$F\text{-ratio} = \frac{MS_b}{MS_w}$$

$$F\text{-ratio} = \frac{32}{6.67}$$

$$F\text{-ratio} = 4.80$$

To arrive at your statistical decision you will follow these four steps.

1. Present the obtained F-ratio with its degrees of freedom, $F = 4.80$, $df = 1/6$.
2. Obtain the tabled F-ratio at the preset level of significance (.05). Use the F values in Table 4 of Appendix D. With the $df = 1$ for the numerator value (MS_b), locate column 1. Then look down the rows until you find the sixth row, $df = 6$, for the denominator value (MS_w). The tabled F-ratio at the $p = .05$ level with $df = 1/6$ is the F-ratio $= 5.99$.
3. If the obtained F value is equal to or greater than the tabled F value, significant differences are obtained and the null hypothesis is rejected. If the obtained F value is less than the tabled F value, a significant difference is not obtained and you accept the null hypothesis.
4. If your obtained F value is larger than the tabled F value, determine the highest level of statistical significance for the obtained F value by comparing it to the tabled F value at the other significant level(s) with the appropriate degrees of freedom.

Thus, no significant difference, $F(1,6) = 4.80$, $p > .05$, was obtained between our two groups. We must conclude that any difference between our groups is due to the operation of chance or error. We are not able to reject the null hypothesis of no differences.

Example of an ANOVA with three groups. We shall consider one further example of an ANOVA, this time with three levels of an independent variable. The purpose of this study was to determine the effectiveness of three types of counseling—rational-emotive, gestalt, and no counseling—in increasing level of self-concept in graduate school clients. We hypothesize that significant differences should exist among the three types of counseling on the self-concept measure. Twenty-seven counseling clients were randomly assigned to the three groups. A posttest only control group design was employed. Following a fifteen-week treatment, the subjects were tested on the Self-Concept Inventory in which possible scores range from 0 to 20. Scores on the posttest for all 27 of the subjects in the three groups are tabulated in Table 10.4.

Table 10.4 includes the first four calculations:

1. ΣX for each group: $\Sigma X_1 = 46$, $\Sigma X_2 = 78$, and $\Sigma X_3 = 34$
2. N for each group: $N_1 = N_2 = N_3 = 9$
3. $\overline{X}$ for each group: $\overline{X}_1 = 5.11$, $\overline{X}_2 = 8.67$, and $\overline{X}_3 = 3.78$
4. ΣX^2 for each group: $\Sigma X_1^2 = 292$, $\Sigma X_2^2 = 756$, and $\Sigma X_3^2 = 168$

Next we calculate the totals for all groups combined, ΣX_t, N_t, ΣX_t^2.

Table 10.4 Data Gathered for Three-Group ANOVA Analysis

Rational-emotive		Gestalt		No counseling	
X_1	X_1^2	X_2	X_2^2	X_3	X_3^2
10	100	14	196	8	64
8	64	12	144	6	36
6	36	10	100	5	25
5	25	9	81	4	16
5	25	9	81	3	9
4	16	8	64	3	9
4	16	7	49	2	4
3	9	5	25	2	4
1	1	4	16	1	1
$\Sigma X_1 = 46$	$\Sigma X_1^2 = 292$	$\Sigma X_2 = 78$	$\Sigma X_2^2 = 756$	$\Sigma X_3 = 34$	$\Sigma X_3^2 = 168$
$N_1 = 9$		$N_2 = 9$		$N_3 = 9$	
$\overline{X}_1 = 5.11$		$\overline{X}_2 = 8.67$		$\overline{X}_3 = 3.78$	

5. To find ΣX_t, we use:

$$\Sigma X_t = \Sigma X_1 + \Sigma X_2 + \Sigma X_3$$
$$\Sigma X_t = 46 + 78 + 34 = 158$$

6. To find N_t, we use:

$$N_t = N_1 + N_2 + N_3$$
$$N_t = 9 + 9 + 9$$
$$N_t = 27$$

7. To find ΣX_t^2, we use:

$$\Sigma X_t^2 = \Sigma X_1^2 + \Sigma X_2^2 + \Sigma X_3^2$$
$$\Sigma X_t^2 = 292 + 756 + 168$$
$$\Sigma X_t^2 = 1216$$

These seven pieces of information are all we need to substitute into the formulas used to calculate the *F*-ratio value.

8. Calculate the total sum squares *(SS_t)*:

$$SS_t = \Sigma X_t^2 - (\Sigma X_t)^2/N_t$$
$$SS_t = 1216 - (158)^2/27$$
$$SS_t = 1216 - 24964/27$$
$$SS_t = 1216 - 924.59$$
$$SS_t = 291.41$$

9. Calculate the between-groups sum squares (SS_b):

$$SS_b = \sum \left[\frac{(\sum X)^2}{N} \right] - \frac{(\sum X_t)^2}{N_t}$$

$$SS_b = \left[\frac{(46)^2}{9} \right] + \left[\frac{(78)^2}{9} \right] + \left[\frac{(34)^2}{9} \right] - \frac{(158)^2}{27}$$

$$SS_b = \left[\frac{2116}{9} \right] + \left[\frac{6084}{9} \right] + \left[\frac{1156}{9} \right] - \frac{24964}{27}$$

$$SS_b = [235.11 + 676.00 + 128.44] - 924.59$$

$$SS_b = 1039.55 - 924.59$$

$$SS_b = 114.96$$

10. Calculate the within-groups sum squares (SS_w). We can calculate this most easily by using:

$$SS_t = SS_b + SS_w$$
$$291.41 = 114.96 + SS_w$$
$$SS_w = 291.41 - 114.96$$
$$SS_w = 176.45$$

We can also use the SS_w formula as a check to ensure that we've arrived at computationally correct values.

$$SS_w = \sum[\sum X^2 - (\sum X)^2/N]$$

where $\sum$ means to calculate what's in the bracket for each group and add them together thus:

$$SS_w = [292 - (46)^2/9] + [756 - (78)^2/9] + [168 - (34)^2/9]$$
$$SS_w = [292 - 2116/9] + [756 - 6084/9] + [168 - 1156/9]$$
$$SS_w = [292 - 235.11] + [756 - 676.00] + [168 - 128.44]$$
$$SS_w = 56.89 + 80.00 + 39.56$$
$$SS_w = 176.45$$

We see that the value of the SS_w is the same by both methods.

11. Summarize the values for SS_t, SS_b, and SS_w.

$$SS_t = 291.41$$
$$SS_b = 114.96$$
$$SS_w = 176.45$$

12. Calculate the appropriate degrees of freedom *(df)* for the SS_b and the SS_w. To find df_b:

$$df_b = k - 1$$
$$df_b = 3 - 1$$
$$df_b = 2$$

To find df_w:

$$df_w = N - k$$
$$df_w = 27 - 3$$
$$df_w = 24$$

13. Calculate the between-group mean square *(MS$_b$)*:

$$MS_b = SS_b/df_b$$
$$MS_b = 114.96/2$$
$$MS_b = 57.48$$

14. Calculate the within-group mean square *(MS$_w$)*:

$$MS_w = SS_w/df_w$$
$$MS_w = 176.45/24$$
$$MS_w = 7.35$$

15. Finally, calculate the *F*-ratio:

$$F = \frac{MS_b}{MS_w}$$
$$F = \frac{57.48}{7.35}$$
$$F = 7.82$$

To arrive at your statistical decision you will follow these four steps.

1. Present the obtained *F*-ratio with its degrees of freedom, $F = 7.82$, $df = 2/24$.
2. Obtain the tabled *F*-ratio at the preset level of significance ($p < .05$). Use the *F*-values in Table 4 of Appendix D. With the $df = 2/24$, you go over to column 2 and down to row 24. The tabled *F*-ratio at the $p = .05$ level with $df = 2/24$ is the *F*-ratio $= 3.40$.
3. If the obtained *F* value is equal to or larger than the tabled *F* value, reject the null hypothesis; if not, accept the null hypothesis. In this example we reject the null hypothesis.

Source of variation	SS	df	MS	F
Between-groups	114.96	2	57.48	7.82
Within-groups	176.45	24	7.35	
Total	291.41	26		

Table 10.5 ANOVA Summary Table

4. If significant at the preset level, determine the highest level of significance. With $df = 2/24$ at the $p < .01$ level, the tabled F value is $F = 5.61$. Thus, the obtained F value is significant at the $p < .01$ level.

Thus, there is a significant difference, $F (2, 24) = 7.82$, $p < .01$, between the three counseling groups on the measure of self-concept.

Frequently in educational research, instead of presenting the results in the narrative part of the Results section as we have done—namely, $F (2, 24) = 7.82$, $p < .01$—the results are presented in what is called an ANOVA summary table, as shown in Table 10.5.

The summary table presents the major values in calculating the F—namely, SS_b, SS_w, SS_t; df_b, df_w, df_t; MS_b, MS_w, and the F value. Some research articles omit the SS column, and other slight variations may be made; but you should now be able to understand a summary table, since the values are all derived according to our earlier conceptual and mathematical discussions.

A Priori and A Posteriori Tests

Whenever we have more than two groups in the calculation of an inferential statistic, if we do get statistical significance, as we did in the previous example, we know that we do have an overall significance among the three means; we do not know which specific mean or means are significantly different from the others. If we have statistical significance when we have only two groups, and thus only two means, we can visually inspect the data to determine which group performed better than the other. But when we have three or more groups, we need to investigate specific mean comparisons—that is, specific hypotheses—by statistics that fall into two broad classes of multiple comparisons, *a priori* or planned comparisons, and *a posteriori* or *post hoc* comparisons.

A priori or planned comparisons.   A priori comparisons are used when specific mean comparisons are planned or hypothesized in advance of the data collection. In the case of a priori tests, we do not need to have an overall significant *F*-ratio first. In other words, you present a rationale for predicting a particular outcome or hypothesis in your review of the literature; then, regardless of whether the overall *F* is significant or not, you undertake to investigate a specific mean comparison. Kirk (1968, pp. 73–86) presents several of the frequently used a priori comparisons, such as Dunn's Multiple Comparison Procedure.

A posteriori or post hoc comparisons.   A posteriori or post hoc comparisons are appropriate when a comparison or a directional hypothesis is not presented in advance of the data collection procedure. Five of the frequently used a posteriori comparisons are:

1. Least significant difference (LSD) test
2. Duncan's multiple range test
3. Newman Keuls test
4. Tukey honestly significant difference (HSD) test
5. Scheffé test

Both Kirk (1968, pp. 87–98) and Nie et al. (1975, pp. 427–428) discuss these a posteriori comparisons. The list above is presented in decreasing order of power; that is, the probability of rejecting a false null hypothesis. In other words, the LSD test is the most powerful and the Scheffé test the least. A similar way of conceptualizing this order is in terms of how conservative the test is in concluding that there are significant mean differences. Thus the LSD test is least conservative and the Scheffé test is the most conservative in concluding that differences do exist among the group means. That is, the LSD test is most likely, and the Scheffé test is least likely to make a Type I error.

As a specific example of the use of an a posteriori test, we shall calculate the Tukey HSD test on the data obtained for the previous three-group ANOVA example. Kirk (1968, pp. 88–90) elaborates at some length on the Tukey HSD test. To use the Tukey HSD test, the overall *F*-ratio must be significant and the assumptions should be met. In addition, the subjects in each group should be equal or nearly equal. If the obtained difference equals or exceeds the HSD value, a difference between the two means is significant at a given probability level (called alpha, which is usually the .05 level). Thus:

$$\text{HSD} = q_\alpha \sqrt{\frac{MS_w}{N}}$$

where MS_w is the within-group mean square,

  N is the number of subjects in *each* treatment, and

  q_α is a tabled value for a given level with k (the number of means) and the df_w.

Table 10.6 Tukey HSD Test for Differences Among Means

Group Mean	$\overline{X}_1$	$\overline{X}_2$	$\overline{X}_3$
$\overline{X}_1$ = 5.11	—	3.56	1.33
$\overline{X}_2$ = 8.67		—	4.89
$\overline{X}_3$ = 3.78			—

Using the earlier example of the three-group ANOVA, our *first* step in calculating the HSD is to construct a table showing the means of each group and the mean difference between each pair of means (Table 10.6). The *second* step is to summarize the obtained information needed for the HSD formula.

$$df_w = 24$$
$$k = 3$$
$$MS_w = 7.35$$

The *third* step is to refer to Table 8 of Appendix D to find the q_α value. We have set α in this example at the .05 level.

α	q
.05	3.53
.01	4.55

Here, $q_{.05}$ equals 3.53. The *fourth* step is to substitute into the formula and solve for HSD.

$$HSD = q_\alpha \sqrt{\frac{MS_w}{N}}$$

$$HSD = 3.53 \sqrt{\frac{7.35}{9}}$$

$$HSD = 3.53 \sqrt{.82}$$

$$HSD = 3.53 \,(.91)$$

$$HSD = 3.21$$

Thus, any mean difference of 3.21 points or greater is statistically significant at the .05 level. The *fifth* and last step is to refer back to Table 10.6

Table 10.7 Tukey HSD Test for Differences Among Means

Group Mean	$\overline{X}_1$	$\overline{X}_2$	$\overline{X}_3$
$\overline{X}_1 = 5.11$	—	3.56*	1.33
$\overline{X}_2 = 8.67$		—	4.89*
$\overline{X}_3 = 3.78$			—

*$p < .05$,   HSD = 3.21

and mark the significant mean comparisons with an asterisk as in Table 10.7.

We conclude that two specific mean comparisons are statistically significant; they are $\overline{X}_1$ with $\overline{X}_2$, and $\overline{X}_2$ with $\overline{X}_3$. The mean comparison of group 1 with group 3 is not statistically significant. Referring back to the specific example, we find that Gestalt counseling ($\overline{X}_2$) produced a significantly higher gain on a measure of self-concept than either rational-

Power and Conservatism Are Related Inversely

emotive ($\overline{X}_1$) or no counseling ($\overline{X}_3$). No other significant comparisons were obtained.

Thus, a priori and a posteriori tests are essential when we have more than two levels of an independent variable so that we can determine what specific mean group comparisons are statistically significant and thereby can conclude that we are not measuring differences due to chance or error.

Factorial Analysis of Variance

We have considered in some depth the one-way ANOVA that is used when we have two or more levels of one independent variable and one dependent variable. Frequently, our research purpose is more complex. For instance, it becomes more complex when we include two or more independent variables in the research design with one dependent measure. Whenever we analyze results with two or more independent variables (also called *factors*), we are conducting a *factorial analysis of variance*. We will not go into the calculations in this text. However, you can find complex factorial designs in Kirk (1968) and Nie et al. (1975). We shall focus on a conceptual understanding of factorial ANOVAs so that you will be able to interpret those you encounter in the research literature. Let us consider a two-factor ANOVA with the design given in Table 10.8.

The main factor or independent variable is grade at three levels—first, third, and fifth. The second factor or independent variable is sex at two levels—male and female. The dependent variable is a creativity score. A factorial ANOVA is usually represented in the Results section of the research article as follows:

> A 3(grade) × (read "by") 2(sex) factorial ANOVA was conducted on the dependent measure, creativity score.

Table 10.8 A Two-factor ANOVA

Grade	Sex	Creativity score
First	Male	$\overline{X}_1$
	Female	$\overline{X}_2$
Third	Male	$\overline{X}_3$
	Female	$\overline{X}_4$
Fifth	Male	$\overline{X}_5$
	Female	$\overline{X}_6$

In this way the factor and number of levels of that variable are represented. Based on the statement above, we have all the information necessary to diagram or design the study using a format similar to the two-factor ANOVA design previously presented. We might need to check other sections of the article to identify what the specific levels are, but we would know for sure how many levels there are.

In a factorial ANOVA, an *F*-ratio is usually obtained for each *main effect* and *interaction*. In this example, we would have two main effects and one interaction. There is a main effect for each independent variable. For instance, regardless of differences by sex, is there a significant main effect due to grades? Thus, the factorial ANOVA combines the sex means into three means by grade to determine if there are significant mean differences by grade. Specifically:

$$\overline{X}_{\text{grade 1}} = (\overline{X}_1 + \overline{X}_2)/2$$
$$\overline{X}_{\text{grade 3}} = (\overline{X}_3 + \overline{X}_4)/2$$
$$\overline{X}_{\text{grade 5}} = (\overline{X}_5 + \overline{X}_6)/2$$

Thus, one *F*-ratio would be obtained to test the significance of the main effect due to grade. Another *F*-ratio would be obtained to test the significance of the main effect of sex regardless of the grade level. The means to test sex would be recombined in this way:

$$\overline{X}_{\text{males}} = (\overline{X}_1 + \overline{X}_3 + \overline{X}_5)/3$$
$$\overline{X}_{\text{females}} = (\overline{X}_2 + \overline{X}_4 + \overline{X}_6)/3$$

The only interaction we would find in this study is that between grade and sex. Thus, the means in the smallest cells or groups would be analyzed to determine if there were statistical significance. The interaction would be between:

$$
\begin{aligned}
\text{male first graders} &= \overline{X}_1 \\
\text{female first graders} &= \overline{X}_2 \\
\text{male second graders} &= \overline{X}_3 \\
\text{female second graders} &= \overline{X}_4 \\
\text{male third graders} &= \overline{X}_5 \\
\text{female third graders} &= \overline{X}_6
\end{aligned}
$$

Thus, if an overall significant *F*-ratio is obtained for any of the two main effects or the interaction, a multiple comparison would have to be performed to find out which specific mean group difference comparisons are statistically significant. The exception, again, would be where we have only two levels, such as the sex variable. If we have a significant *F*, we visually inspect the means to determine which group performed

Table 10.9 A 3 (Grade) × 2 (Sex) Factorial ANOVA Summary Table

Factor	SS	df	MS	F
Grade (A)	240.00	2	120.00	44.44*
Sex (B)	110.00	1	110.00	40.74*
A × B interaction	50.00	2	25.00	8.99*
Within-group error variance	150.00	54	2.78	
Total	550.00	59		

$*p < .01$

higher than the other. Table 10.9 is a factorial ANOVA summary table for the above example; it includes hypothetical data.

If each of the *MS* for the two main effects and one interaction is divided by the error term, 2.78, the appropriate *F* values are calculated. We can then check the statistical significance of each of the *F*-ratios in Table 4 of Appendix D. Factor A has a $df = 2,54$; factor *B* has a $df = 1,54$; and the interaction of A × B has a $df = 2,54$. Thus, all our obtained values are greater than the tabled values at the $p < .01$ level. Therefore, there is statistical significance at that level.

We should now be able to interpret most of the ANOVA tables we are likely to encounter. That which will vary as a function of the number of independent variables is the number of main effects and interactions possible. For instance, for three independent variables (A, B, and C) we will have three main effects and four interactions:

A
B
C
A × B
A × C
B × C
A × B × C

An ANOVA summary table would report an *F*-ratio for each. Obviously, then, as we add more factors, the more complicated the study becomes; but the basic strategy will remain; that is, an *F*-ratio will be obtained for each main effect and interaction. If it is significant, a multiple comparison will be conducted (if the variable has more than two levels) to determine what specific mean group comparisons are statistically significant.

Repeated Measures ANOVA

Another variation of the ANOVA that you may encounter in the educational literature is a *repeated measures* or *repeated measurement design*. The most common use of repeated measures design has the same subjects obtaining multiple or repeated scores on the dependent variable. For instance, if the test you used produced a global creativity score, you would analyze just that score, as we've discussed so far. However, a test will frequently have subtests, and you can analyze differences among groups by each subtest score if you wish. Thus you have a repeated measure because you have measures for each subtest. For instance, if you wanted to analyze results by three subtests on a creativity test, you might report the information in this way:

> A 3(grade) × 2(sex) × 3(subtest) factorial
> ANOVA with a repeated measure on the last
> factor will be conducted.

In this instance, you would add another independent variable to your design—namely, subtest at three levels—since each subject's creativity score will depend on the subtest taken as well as on his or her sex and grade level.

This strategy contrasts with the situation where you have three separate scores: an IQ score, a creativity score, and a self-concept score. We shall discuss research designs that incorporate more than one dependent variable in a later section on multivariate decisions.

Analysis of Covariance

In Chapter 6 under the heading of extraneous or confounding variables, we discussed three ways to minimize the influence of possible confounding variables operating on the dependent measure. One way was to incorporate a variable into the design as an additional independent variable. A second way was to examine only one level of the variable in the research. A third way was to statistically control for the influence of an extraneous variable. One of the most frequently used statistics to adjust for the influence of an extraneous variable is the analysis of covariance (ANCOVA). This adjusts the scores on the dependent measure by taking out the linear influence of one or more possible confounding variables. Thus, instead of determining statistical significance among groups based on the original mean score, an adjusted mean score is obtained and used to determine significance among the groups. Recall from the discussion in Chapter 6 that possible confounding variables which are removed from the scores of the dependent measure are called either *concomitant* variables or *covariates*. The statistical procedure involves measuring those concomitant variables that represent a source of variation as well as measuring the dependent variable, all of which are believed to affect the dependent measure. A statistical procedure called a *multiple regression analysis* is then used to remove the variation in the dependent measure due to one or more of the concomitant variables. An analysis of variance is then calculated on these adjusted, or corrected, scores.

The statistical value reported from conducting an ANCOVA is also an *F*-ratio. Similar summary tables and modes of reporting the ANCOVA follow the same modes of reporting as for the ANOVA. What differs is usually the addition of two pieces of information: data describing the covariates and a table giving the original mean scores and the adjusted mean scores. The same strategy for interpreting the ANOVA is used to interpret the ANCOVA results. For factorial designs, if an overall significant *F* is obtained for any main effect or interaction, an appropriate multiple comparison is conducted. Again, if the main effect has only two levels, the visual inspection of the means is sufficient to determine which group performed better than the other.

Multivariate Decisions

We have discussed the main descriptive and inferential statistics you are likely to encounter in the educational research. In presenting the inferential statistics, we have so far focused exclusively on statistical analyses having only one dependent variable. These are sometimes known as *univariate statistics*. Research studies are often more complex in that they have two or more dependent measures as well as two or more independent measures. Statistical techniques that calculate differences among two or more dependent measures are called *multivariate statistics*. They should be used in the appropriate situation when more than two dependent measures are involved.

For instance, a multivariate counterpart to the ANOVA is the *multivariate analysis of variance* (MANOVA). The advantage of calculating a multivariate analysis over a univariate analysis is that the multivariate calculations consider the interrelationship among the dependent measures but the univariate analysis does not. If we had three dependent measures, we could calculate three separate ANOVAs, or we could calculate one corresponding MANOVA. The more useful strategy is to calculate the MANOVA.

The correct use and interpretation of multivariate statistics require a good deal of training and technical sophistication. There are many articles in the research literature in which multiple univariate statistics are calculated rather than a single multivariate analysis; for instance, one article may report 50 *t*-tests rather than one MANOVA. The more statistical tests one conducts, the greater the chance for significance based on calculating more tests of significance rather than due to treatment differences among variables. Multivariate texts such as those by Cooley and Lohnes (1971) and Morrison (1967) are recommended for those who may wish to pursue the topic of multivariate statistics in depth. Other statistical analyses considered to be multivariate procedures (Cooley and Lohnes, 1971) are: canonical correlation, factor analysis, factorial discriminant analysis, multiple covariance analysis, and multiple regression. Each is used with a specific research purpose in mind; thus there is no comprehensive purpose for the use of any one. These are but a few of the more complex multivariate statistics. Their general purpose remains to understand the relationship among variables and, in most cases, to understand and predict the relationship between a set of independent variables and a set of dependent variables.

Statistical Packages for Computer Analysis

Three statistical packages of computer programs are frequently used by educational researchers:

1. Statistical Package for the Social Sciences (SPSS)
   (Nie et al., 1975)
2. Biomedical Computer Programs (BMD-P)
   (Dixon and Brown, 1979)
3. Statistical Analysis System (SAS)
   (Barr, Goodnight, Sall, and Helwig, 1976)

All these computer packages make possible the computational analysis of scores in a fraction of the time required by hand calculations. Depending upon your college or university setting, you may have access to one or all of these packages.

For those who will pursue the field of educational research and statistics in greater depth, a working knowledge of these three computer packages is an essential beginning. A comparison of some of the statistical tests provided by either SPSS, BMD-P, or SAS is given in Table 10.10. Frequently, in the Results section of a research article, the type of computer package and program name are mentioned. Table 10.10 includes many of the programs you will encounter in the research literature.

Data Preparation for Computers

After values of either a measurement type or an experimental type for the independent variables and values of a measurement type for the dependent variables have been obtained from the data collection process,

Table 10.10 Comparison Table of Selected Procedures in SPSS, BMD-P, and SAS

Procedure	SPSS name	BMD-P name	SAS name
Means and standard deviations	CONDESCRIPTIVE	P1D	MEANS
Frequency distribution	FREQUENCIES	P4D	FREQ
Histograms or plots	SCATTERGRAM	P5D	SCATTER
Chi-square	CROSSTABS	P1F	FREQ
Correlation	PEARSON CORR	P6D	CORR
Partial correlation	PARTIAL CORR	P2R	GLM
Multiple regression	REGRESSION	P1R	GLM
t-tests	T-TEST	P3D	T TEST
Analysis of variance	ANOVA	P1V	GLM
Analysis of covariance	ANOVA	P2V	GLM
Factor analysis	FACTOR	P4M	FACTOR

they must be coded and entered into a computer. Most instructions and data are given to either SPSS, BMD-P, or SAS on *computer cards.* These 7⅜ by 3¼ inch cards come in a variety of colors and designs. The important part of these cards is the holes punched into each one, since the computer's *card reader* reads only the holes that have been punched. The card reader electronically senses the holes in each column and translates them into the corresponding electronic impulses. An example of a computer card is shown in Figure 10.5.

Figure 10.5 Example of a Computer Card

Each card has 80 columns and each column can contain a different character such as single digits, letters, or mathematical symbols. Each of the 80 columns has 12 fields or rows in which a hole may be punched. For instance, the letter *A* has one punch in the 12 field and one in the 1 field; the letter *J* has one punch in the 11 field and one in the 1 field. The top two rows are *12* and *11* fields, respectively, and the bottom ten rows are numbered zero through nine.

The machine used to punch information onto the computer cards is called a *keypunch.* Similar to the keyboard of an electric typewriter, it punches holes in blank cards as the corresponding key is pressed. It contains additional switches or buttons to feed the cards into the keypunch. In addition, there are no lowercase letters and the numbers are located in different places. However, it is quite easy to learn how to operate one.

A plan or coding system assigning each variable and value of the variable to a particular column must be developed prior to keypunching the data. Table 10.11 illustrates such a code.

We can continue this coding system for as many variables as there are in our research project. Thus, we can code variables of either a measurement type or an experimental type. If we run out of columns on one card we can continue with additional variables on subsequent cards. The cards for our first three subjects would look like Figure 10.6.

Figure 10.6 tells us that subject one is a male fourth grader with an IQ of 110 and an achievement score of 85. After data are prepared, each of the computer packages has a variety of *control cards* that are specific commands given to the computer (or, more specifically, the central memory of the computer) to tell it how to analyze the data. Storage vehicles other than computer cards are also used, such as magnetic tapes and disk packs. As you become more involved in data preparation for computer analysis, you will want to consult your local computer center

Table 10.11 Typical Coding System for a Computer Program

Computer Card	Variable
Columns 1–3	Subject number (001–999 possible)
Column 5	Sex: 1-male; 0-female
Column 7	Grade level: 1 to 6 for grades one through six
Column 9–11	IQ score: enter appropriate score, range is 088 to 124
Column 13–15	Achievement score: enter appropriate score, range is 060 to 110

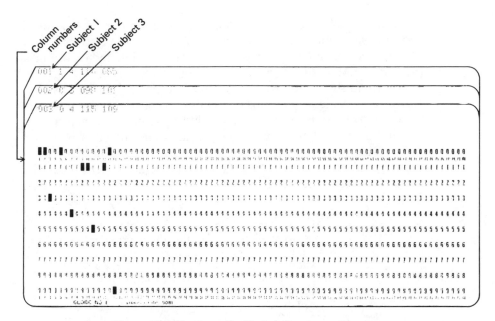

Figure 10.6 Portion of a Coded Computer Program

and one of the statistical packages mentioned—SPSS, BMD-P, or SAS —in order to prepare your data and instructions more completely.

Example of a Results Section

As we have indicated at the beginning of Chapter 9, the purpose of the Results section is to present the results of the descriptive and inferential tests calculated on a distribution of scores. Typically, the Results section is introduced by a paragraph containing an overview or summary of the statistics used. For instance, consider the first two paragraphs of the study by Moore (1979).

Results

For all analyses, the dependent variables were total scores across the eight tasks for the three measures: strategy, explanation, and judgment. The main analysis was a four-group multivariate analysis of variance (MANOVA). The independent variable consisted of four grade levels: kindergarten, first grade, second grade, and third grade. The secondary analysis was a three-group MANOVA. The independent variable was conservation of length,

as indicated by membership in one of the three categories: nonconserver, transitional, and conserver.

Additional analyses for the MANOVA results were computed. An η^2 was obtained for each of the three criteria to determine which measure accounted for the largest percentage of variance among each group (Cooley & Lohnes 1971, p. 234). A Scheffé test for multivariate multiple comparison also was obtained (Morrison 1968, pp. 183–185).

Frequently, this overview paragraph is also found at the end of the Procedure subsection and is used as a transition to the Results section. For instance, reread the Treatment of Data section by Huber et al. (1979) in the Method section at the end of Chapter 7.

The second step in the Results section is to present the results of the descriptive statistics. Often this will consist of two tables summarizing the descriptive results, one of which includes the mean, standard deviation, and intercorrelations of all the measures, and the other presenting the frequency distribution and percentages of responses stratified by the key independent variables. Other tables may include descriptive results stratified by the particular comparisons.

Means, standard deviations, and intercorrelations were obtained for the three criteria and four external measures: grade level, age, conservation of length, and performance on a seriating task. Results are presented in table 1. A correlation of .91 was obtained for strategy with explanation, .79 for strategy with judgment, and .82 for explanation with judgment. In addition, correlations of .40, .47, and .34 were obtained for performance on the conservation-of-length assessment with strategy, explanation, and judgment total scores, respectively. Low, positive correlations (.10, .21, and .11) were obtained with the seriating task and the three criteria: strategy, explanation, and judgment, respectively. The low variability on the seriating task may account for the lack of relationship with the criteria.

TABLE 1

INTERCORRELATION, MEAN, AND STANDARD DEVIATION OF THE THREE CRITERIA AND FOUR EXTERNAL MEASURES FOR THE TOTAL SAMPLE

	Grade	Age	Conservation of Length	Seriating Task	Strategy	Explanation	Judgment
Grade.................							
Age....................	.95						
Conservation of length....	.49	.44					
Seriating task...........	.32	.29	.23				
Strategy...............	.36	.34	.40	.10			
Explanation............	.45	.43	.47	.21	.91		
Judgment..............	.24	.21	.34	.10	.79	.82	
Mean.................	1.50	89.95	.70	.92	12.49	10.53	3.18
SD...................	1.12	14.72	.90	.27	12.83	11.58	2.86

NOTE.—For a sample size of 88, any correlation of .21 or greater is statistically significant at the .05 level.

TABLE 2

MEAN AND STANDARD DEVIATION FOR THREE CRITERIA BY GRADE LEVEL

	EXPLANATION		JUDGMENT		STRATEGY	
GRADE	M	SD	M	SD	M	SD
Kindergarten.......	3.59	8.29	2.73	2.45	6.95	11.15
First..............	7.09	12.13	2.64	2.63	9.82	13.36
Second............	12.00	13.13	3.32	2.78	12.41	13.53
Third.............	19.45	12.78	4.04	3.55	20.77	13.30

NOTE.—N children at each grade level was 22. The range of scores was 0–40 for explanation and strategy and 0–8 for judgment.

TABLE 3

MEAN AND STANDARD DEVIATION FOR THREE CRITERIA BY LEVEL OF CONSERVATION OF LENGTH

	EXPLANATION		JUDGMENT		STRATEGY	
LEVEL OF CONSERVATION	M	SD	M	SD	M	SD
Nonconserver.......	5.52	9.01	2.27	2.39	7.81	10.63
Transitional........	14.90	15.39	3.50	3.21	18.60	15.74
Conserver..........	18.88	14.31	4.46	3.30	19.50	14.80

NOTE.—N children classified into the three conservation levels was 52, 10, and 26, respectively.

TABLE 4

FREQUENCY DISTRIBUTION AND PERCENTAGES OF EXPLANATION AND STRATEGY RESPONSES BY GRADE LEVEL

	GRADE							
	K		1		2		3	
TOTAL SCORE	N	%	N	%	N	%	N	%
	Explanation							
0..........	16	72.7	13	59.1	8	36.4	3	13.6
1–8..........	3	13.6	3	13.6	3	13.6	3	13.6
9–16..........	0	0	2	9.1	5	22.7	3	13.6
17–24..........	2	9.1	1	4.5	2	9.1	3	13.6
25–32..........	1	4.5	1	4.5	1	4.5	6	27.3
33–40..........	0	0	2	9.1	3	13.6	4	18.2
	Strategy							
0..........	14	63.6	11	50.0	8	36.4	3	13.6
1–8..........	2	9.1	2	9.1	3	13.6	2	9.1
9–16..........	2	9.1	3	13.6	3	13.6	2	9.1
17–24..........	3	13.6	3	13.6	4	18.2	5	22.7
25–32..........	0	0	1	4.5	2	9.1	5	22.7
33–40..........	1	4.5	2	9.1	2	9.1	5	22.7

The third step of the Results section presents the violations of assumptions for the use of a particular inferential statistic. This is one of the most frequently omitted steps in the research process. In addition, subgroup means and standard deviations are frequently reported here.

> Means and standard deviations by grade level for the three criteria are presented in table 2. Mean scores increased from kindergarten through third grade for the strategy, explanation, and judgment measures. Raw score means for the four grade levels were inspected and were observed to vary independently of variances for each dependent variable. The assumption of equality of dispersion was met, $F(18,2934) = .83$, $p > .05$. Since the above conditions existed, no transformation would make data more suitable for analysis (Kirk 1968, p. 64).

The fourth step of the Results section usually gives the results of the main inferential statistics. This section usually delineates which overall comparisons obtained statistical significance. In some studies the percentage of variance explained by the measures is also included. If many comparisons have been calculated, an overall summary table may be included. Otherwise, the significance of the results is given in the narrative.

> The set of observed criteria significantly separated the four grades, Wilks $\lambda = .71$, $F(9,199) = 3.35$, $p < .001$. Strategy total score significantly discriminated among the four grades, $F(3,84) = 4.71$, $p < .004$, and accounted for 14% of the variance among the grades. Explanation total score also discriminated significantly among the four grades, $F(3,84) = 7.54$, $p < .001$, and accounted for 21% of the variance. Judgment total score did not significantly discriminate among the four grades, $F(3,84) = 1.68$, $p > .18$, but accounted for 6% of the variance. The three measures also were subjected to analysis simultaneously; the generalized proportion of variance which they explained was 29% (MANOVA $\eta^2 = .289$).

Finally, the fifth step presents the results of any supporting inferential statistics derived from the overall significance in the preceding step, including the results of any multiple comparisons conducted.

> Results of the Scheffé post hoc test at the .10 significance level for multivariate multiple comparisons (Morrison 1968, pp. 183–185) of the four grade levels for each criterion were obtained. Significant mean strategy differences were obtained for the kindergarten and third-grade comparison, and significant mean explanation differences were obtained for the kindergarten and third-grade comparison and the first- and third-grade comparison. No significant mean differences among grades were obtained for the judgment variable.

If additional inferential analyses are conducted on subsequent comparisons, the last three steps are repeated in sequence until all the analyses are completed. Variations of this five-step format are possible; however, this one is most frequently used.

> Means and standard deviations for the nonconserver $(N = 52)$, the transitional $(N = 10)$, and the conserver $(N = 26)$ are presented in table 3 for the three criteria. The assumption of equality of dispersions was not met, $F(12,3172) = 1.89$, $p < .05$. With an unequal number of subjects in each of the three groups, the results of this analysis should be interpreted with the qualification that the assumptions for the use of the MANOVA may be violated, even though the test for the discrimination among groups is fairly robust under departures from its assumptions (Cooley & Lohnes 1971, p. 228).
>
> The three criteria significantly separated the three groups, Wilks $\lambda = 0.7464$, $F(6,166) = 4.36$, $p < .001$. The three measures also were subjected to analysis simultaneously; the generalized proportion of variance among the groups which they explained was 25% (MANOVA $\eta^2 = .2536$). All three measures significantly discriminated among the three groups: strategy, $F(2,85) = 8.81$, $p < .001$; explanation, $F(2,85) = 12.35$, $p < .001$; and

judgment, $F(2,85) = 5.51$, $p < .005$. The explanation total score variable accounted for 23% of the variance among the three groups; strategy and judgment total scores accounted for 17% and 12%, respectively, of the variance among the three groups.

Results of the Scheffé post hoc test at the .10 level of significance for multivariate multiple group comparisons for each criteria also were calculated. A significant mean difference was obtained for the nonconserver- and conserver-of-length comparison for each of the three criteria: explanation, strategy, and judgment. Percentages of type of strategy and explanation used by each grade level are presented in table 4.

Writing the Results section is probably the easiest part of the research article, because it has the most concrete and specific format and information to include. One of the more difficult sections to write is the last one—the Discussion section—which is the focus of the next chapter.

——— SUMMARY ———

We have delineated the important concepts of levels of significance, Type I and Type II errors, and assumptions for the use of inferential statistics. The assumptions of parametric statistics include normality, homogeneity of variances, independence, and linearity. We have distinguished between parametric and nonparametric statistics. The inferential statistics, chi-square (χ^2), t-test for independent and related groups, one-way analysis of variance, and a priori and a posterori tests, have been calculated and conceptually interpreted. In addition, factorial analysis of variance, analysis of covariance, and multivariate statistics have been introduced conceptually. We have given examples of computerized statistical packages: SPSS, BMD-P, and SAS, and suggestions for data preparation. Finally, we presented an organizational format and an example of a Results section.

——— OBJECTIVES ———

In Chapter 10, we have analyzed the statistics encountered in the research process. We have examined their assumptions and the concepts of level of significance and types of error encountered in their use. Finally, we have examined the format for a Results section. Confirm your understanding of the information in Chapter 10 using the following objectives:

Understand and use the levels of statistical significance in calculating or evaluating a statistic.
Interpret a Type I and a Type II error.
Identify and evaluate the four assumptions used in selecting an appropriate inferential statistic.
Differentiate between nonparametric and parametric statistics.
Understand and calculate the chi-square statistic.
Understand and calculate two types of t-tests.
Understand and calculate a one-way analysis of variance.
Differentiate between a priori and a posteriori tests.
Understand and calculate a Tukey test.
Interpret a factorial analysis of variance.
Interpret an analysis of covariance.
Understand what is a multivariate statistic.
Understand how data are prepared and used in computer analysis.
Develop and evaluate a Results section using a five-step format.

—— TERMS ——————————————

alpha
analysis of covariance
analysis of variance
ANOVA summary table
a posteriori or post hoc comparisons
a priori or planned comparisons
BMD-P
ceiling effect
chi-square
error variance
F-max test
F-ratio
F-test
factorial analysis of variance
floor effect
homogeneity of variance
independence
inferential statistics
interaction
kurtosis
leptokurtic curve

main effect
Mann-Whitney U Test
mesokurtic curve
multivariate statistics
nonparametric statistics
normality
one-way analysis of variance
parametric statistics
platykurtic curve
power
practical significance
repeated measures analysis of variance
SAS
skewness
SPSS
sum squares
t-test for independent groups
t-test for related groups
Type I error
Type II error
Wilcoxon Signed-Rank Test

PART **4**

Analysis of the Discussion Section and Writing the Research Report

We have completed our consideration of the first three components of the research journal article: the Introduction, the Method, and the Results. The fourth major component is the Discussion section. This corresponds to the seventh and last step of the scientific method: Generate conclusions based upon the data related to hypotheses. In this fourth section we attempt to answer the question: What are the implications of the results for theory, research, or application? In other words, in the Discussion section we attempt to answer the broader question: "So what?" or "What is the practical significance of the statistical significance obtained in the Results section?"

In Chapter 11 we will discuss a strategy for understanding the results of the study and for drawing the major implications from the findings.

After presenting the four main components of the research article, in Chapter 12 we will describe an organizational format and strategy for writing the research article or report. Here we shall discuss ways of integrating all the sections of the journal article into a concise, organized entity.

Discussing the Results

What are the four main organizational components of the
  Discussion section, and how does each affect the writing or
  evaluating of the Discussion?

What ethical and legal considerations should researchers be
  aware of?

How is a research project differentiated from an evaluation
  project?

What questions should be considered in planning a program
  evaluation?

Research and Evaluation

Discussion section	Ethical considerations	Planning program evaluation	Developing an evaluation plan
Restatement of the purpose or hypothesis	APA and APGA standards	Why is the program being evaluated?	Specify purposes
Discussion of the theoretical, research, or educational implications	Measurement and evaluation and the use of assessment techniques	Who will receive the information and what will they do with it?	Describe program
Limitations of the research usually expressed in terms of threats to external validity	Research activities and publication	What kind of information do the decision-makers want?	Specify curriculum objectives
Statement of future research implications		Who should conduct the evaluation?	Identify program components
		Staff commitment	Assign relative importance to components of criteria for evaluation
		Time	Specify data collection requirements and criteria for evaluation
		Costs	Evaluation plan approved
			Implement evaluation plan

After we present a typical format for organizing a Discussion section and analyze two examples of a Discussion, we shall consider two additional important areas in educational research. One is a summary of the ethical considerations that researchers must implement in their research endeavors. The second is a brief discussion of the distinctions between research and evaluation. Evaluation was briefly defined in Chapter 1, and we shall elaborate on the evaluation project for those who should be aware of both types of process. First, then, let us consider the Discussion section of the research article.

Organization of the Discussion Section

In the Discussion section of the research article we attempt to present the major implications of the results for theory, research, or educational application. Ideally derived logically from the Results section, the Discussion section should answer the question: "So what?" That is, what is the practical significance of the results in terms of theory, research, or application? In terms of theoretical implications, how is existing theory modified or expanded based on the findings? In terms of research implications, how do the findings support or question the existing body of research? Finally, in terms of application, how do the results suggest instructional or individual modifications in what we do in psychology and in education?

Key Features

Well-written Discussion sections typically include at least these two key features:

1. Restatement of the purpose or hypothesis
2. Discussion of the implications of the major findings as related to the purpose or hypothesis based on theory, research, or application

These two steps are repeated as necessary in discussing the implications of the results. Not all of the results are usually discussed. A strategy used by researchers to determine which results to discuss is to list all the significant results in order of importance and then discuss only the top few (say, 2 to 6). Otherwise, the Discussion section becomes disjointed and fragmented rather than integrated or organized, with the purpose or hypothesis related to the most significant results obtained.

Many research articles also include a third and fourth step in the Discussion section:

3. Discussion of the limitations of the research study
4. Discussion of implications for future research

The decision to include these last two steps in a published journal article is usually the province of the editors and their journal's policy. Some editors will ask for this information to be omitted, others will ask for it to be included. Since you have already examined a few articles in your respective field, you should by now have a pretty good idea of each journal's policy.

The third step—discussing limitations—usually focuses on the major threats to internal and external validity that operated in the study. It is frequently included in the Discussion section rather than in the Method section so that, if there are limitations to the ability to generalize results, they may be discussed along with consideration of the main implications.

The fourth step—discussing implications—usually attempts to answer the question: "Where do I go from here?" Based on the obtained results and the derived implications, what steps in this line of research will I next pursue? In other words, what are the important follow-up questions which need to be answered?

These last two steps are usually a paragraph or two each in length, and they typically conclude the research article. The restatement of purpose and discussion of implications normally encompass the bulk of the Discussion section. We will expand further on these four points as we consider two examples of a Discussion section.

Examples of a Discussion Section

Many poorly constructed Discussion sections may be attributed to the failure to integrate the implications with any of the other components of the research article. An example is researchers who develop an entire study to test a set of hypotheses and then, when they write the Discussion section, consider only the implications of secondary results that obtained statistical significance while ignoring their original hypotheses, questions, or statements of purpose. Thus, the Discussion section does not logically flow from the prior research components. For instance, if we constructed a study and hypothesis to determine whether treatment A produces significant gains as compared to treatments B and C on measures X, Y, and Z, and the results produced no significant differences except on a minor independent variable, the entire focus of the Discussion section would consider the implications surrounding that significant finding. The lack of treatment effects is never referred to again in the article. Thus, the article will lack continuity and integration.

In order to have an integrated flow, even if statistical significance is lacking, the major hypotheses and research questions posed in the Introduction should be addressed, and the implications of this nonsignificance should be considered, even if only briefly. Then the logical transition can be to those major findings and their implications which did produce statistical significance.

A second example of a poorly constructed Discussion section involves the tendency of researchers to overgeneralize. In other words, some will generalize implications that are not directly supported by the

Among the Many Treasures Research Yields, a New Question Is Often the Most Valuable

results. The threats to external validity that we examined in Chapter 6 are useful to keep in mind when evaluating or writing a Discussion section, since they are all concerned with the problem of overgeneralizing beyond the results.

The educational literature is full of variations from the format we have given for the Discussion section. For instance, some studies combine the last two journal article components into one section called Results and Discussion. Others delineate subsections of the Discussion section with such headings as Interpretation, Limitations of Findings, and Conclusions. Regardless of the specific headings used in any section of the research article, the basic components we have mentioned throughout the book should be presented and considered. It may be more difficult to analyze a Discussion section by itself than to analyze the other components we have examined, since it would appear significantly out of context. Therefore, we shall consider examples of the Discussion section in which all of the article is included.

Consider the article by Ashby and Wittmaier (1978) on attitude changes in fourth-grade girls after exposure to stories about women in traditional and nontraditional occupations. We analyzed the Introduction section at the end of Chapter 4. Read the entire article with special attention to the Discussion section; see if you can identify the four key features listed at the beginning of this chapter.

Attitude Changes in Children After Exposure to Stories About Women in Traditional or Nontraditional Occupations

Marylee Stull Ashby
Alfred University

Bruce C. Wittmaier
Lancaster Guidance Clinic
Lancaster, Pennsylvania

Previous research has demonstrated that children's literature frequently presents girls and women only in limited, "traditional" roles, with the result that girls exposed to such literature may limit their own self-perceptions and aspirations. In an experiment with fourth graders, 29 girls were read two stories with women in traditional roles or two with women in nontraditional roles. Attitude changes were measured by a picture-choice test, two job checklists, and two adjective checklists. As predicted, girls who heard nontraditional stories rated traditionally male jobs and characteristics as appropriate for females more than girls who heard traditional stories. These results underline the importance of nonsexist books and textbooks in widening girls' aspirations and self-images.

Much attention has been given in recent years to the issue of sexism in children's books. Social learning theory predicts that children learn what constitutes sex-appropriate behavior from the sex role expectations and role models they observe around them. The books they read, both in and out of school, provide a major source of role models (Frasher & Walker, 1972). If these models show women in limited, stereotyped roles, girls may tend to limit their own aspirations.

Stull (Note 1) examined books that appeal to older children, including Newbery award winning books. She found that many, but not all, of the books presented girls and women only in limited, traditional roles. Newbery award winners were no better in this respect than books that had won no awards. Older books were more likely than recent books to present sexist images of females.

A study by Hillman (1974) compared children's books written in the 1930s and in the 1970s. She found that books written in the 1970s have more female characters than those written in the 1930s, but female characters are still greatly outnumbered by males.

Frasher and Walker (1972) examined widely used reading textbooks and found that males outnumber females by a large majority. Few of the females work outside the home, and those who do hold only traditionally female jobs. Fathers hold the position of family leadership. Fathers are shown mainly outdoors, while mothers are indoors. Girls are shown engaged in more quiet activities than boys.

A large number of studies point out the widespread sexism that exists in children's books and predict that this influences girls' self-images and aspirations. There is evidence that positive outcomes result from exposing children to nonstereotypical stories. Litcher and Johnson (1969), using multiethnic reading textbooks, succeeded in changing the attitudes of white school children toward blacks. McArthur and Eisen (1976) obtained more achievement behavior from nursery school girls who had heard a story about an achieving girl than those who heard about an achieving boy. This suggests that the content of reading books is important in influencing children's attitudes. By changing the content of the books children are exposed to, one may hope to change their attitudes toward themselves and others.

The current study was undertaken to determine the effects on girls of stories that portray women in nontraditional occupations. It was predicted that girls who were exposed to such women would perceive typically male jobs as more attractive than girls who were read stories about women in traditional occupations. It was also predicted that these girls would judge typically male adjectives to refer to both males and females more than girls read traditional stories.

Method

Subjects

Subjects were 137 fourth-grade students in two public schools. Six experimental groups were formed using all the students from the three fourth-grade classrooms at Alfred-Almond Central School, Almond, New York, a total of 66 students. Within each room students were assigned to traditional and nontraditional story groups. A total of 16 females and 16 males were assigned to the traditional groups and 18 females and 16 males to the nontraditional groups. The experimenter was interested mainly in the data from the girls, although the data from boys were also examined. Five girls and four boys were absent for one or both of the treatment sessions, and their data were not included in the results. This left 15 girls and 16 boys in the nontraditional group and 14 girls and 12 boys in the traditional group. Two girls and five boys were absent for one of the posttests; their data were included in the results for the other posttests.

The control group consisted of 71 students in three fourth-grade classrooms at Clinton Elementary School, Clinton, New York. Both schools are located in rural college towns. The student body in each is diverse, including middle- and lower-class students, faculty children, store owners' children, and farmers' children. Most students in both schools are white.

Materials

Four stories were used, two with women in traditional careers (telephone operator and nurse) and two with women in nontraditional careers (television director and veterinarian). The stories were based on the following children's books: *Linda Goes to a TV Studio,* by Nancy Dudley (1957); *I Know a Telephone Operator,* by J. A. Evans (1971); *What Can She Be? A Veterinarian,* by Gloria and Esther Goldreich (1972); and *The First Book of Nurses,* by Eleanor Kay (1968). The stories were edited or rewritten to fit the purposes of the experiment. For example, the sex of the director in *Linda Goes to a TV Studio* had to be changed. After rewriting, the stories were of the same length and approximately the same complexity.

The posttests used included a picture-choice test, two adjective checklists, and two job checklists. The picture-choice test was given only to the experimental groups, and the job and adjective checklists were given to both the experimental and control groups.

The picture-choice test consisted of eight pairs of photographs. Each pair had a photograph of a woman in a traditional role and a woman in a nontraditional role (e.g., a woman watering plants and a female telephone lineperson). The experimenter decided whether the job was traditional or nontraditional. As much as was possible, the size of the pictures and the size, attractiveness, and facial expressions of the woman were the same in each pair. Black-and-white pictures were paired with black-and-white pictures; and color, with color. Girls were asked which woman in each pair they would rather be, and boys were asked which woman they thought was happier in what she was doing.

Two adjective checklists were used, each with 20 words or phrases. Words were selected from the adjective checklist used by Berdie (1959) and simplified for fourth graders (e.g., "skeptical" became "doesn't trust people"). Students were asked whether each word or phrase described a male, a female, or both. A list of the adjectives used appears in Table 1.

Two job checklists were used, each with 25 jobs. Thirteen of the jobs appeared on both checklists, including the jobs of the women in the stories. The jobs were listed in a nonsexist manner (e.g., "mail carrier" instead of "mailman"), and certain common jobs were not used because they could not be both nonsexist and understandable to fourth graders (e.g., "stewardess" is sexist, and most fourth graders have never heard of a "flight attendant"). Students in the experimental groups were asked to rate each job from 1 to 5 according to how much they thought they would enjoy doing it. Control group students were asked whether each job was done by males, females, or both. A list of the jobs used appears in Table 2.

The adjectives and jobs were read one at a time to the students. It was thought that students would recognize more words by listening than they would if they were able to read the words themselves.

Table 1
Adjective Checklist

Adjective	Ratings[a]
Able	M
Bullying	M
Cheerful	B
Clever	B
Confident	B
Cool	M
Doesn't trust people	B
Does things without planning them	M
Feelings are easily hurt	F
Gentle	F
Graceful	F
Helpful	B
Is very careful	F
Kind	B
Likes art and music	F
Likes many things	B
Likes sports	M
Likes the outdoors	B
Likes to ask questions	B
Likes to be told what to do	B
Likes to do things on one's own	M
Nervous	F
Noisy	M
Plans ahead	B
Polite	F
Rough	M
Selfish	B
Shows one's feelings	F
Shy	F
Slow	B
Smart	B
Soft-hearted	F
Strong	M
Timid	F
Tough	M
Trusting	F
Wants to get a lot done	B
Warm	F

[a] Ratings by control group; M = male; F = female; B = both.

Procedures

Students in the experimental groups were told that the experimenter was interested in what kinds of stories fourth graders liked and that the stories were written by a friend of hers. Each group heard two stories, one in each of two sessions held outside the students' classrooms on consecutive days. Half of the groups heard the two traditional role stories, while half heard the two nontraditional role stories. After each story,

Table 2
Job Checklist

Job	Rating[a]
Army officer	M
Artist	B
Athlete	B
Carpenter	M
College Professor	M
Dancer	F
Dentist	M
Doctor	M
Factory worker	M
Fire fighter	M
Gas station attendant	M
Homemaker	F
Judge	M
Lawyer	M
Librarian	F
Mail carrier	M
Mechanic	M
Minister	M
Movie star	B
Musician	M
Newspaper reporter	M
Nurse	F
Parent	B
Pilot	M
Plumber	M
Police officer	M
Principal	M
Restaurant worker	B
Sales clerk	M
Scientist	M
Secretary	F
Senator	M
Teacher	B
Telephone operator	F
Television director	M
Veterinarian	M
Writer	B

[a] Ratings by control group; M = male; F = female; B = both.

students filled out a questionnaire asking what they liked and didn't like about each story, since ostensibly this was the experimenter's interest. The day after each group had heard the second story, the classroom teachers had the students fill out the first adjective and job checklists in class without the experimenter's presence. The experimenter then met with each student individually to administer the picture-choice test. The classroom teachers gave the second adjective and job checklists a week after the first.

The experimenter administered the job and adjective checklists to the control group. Students were told that

the experimenter had given the checklists to fourth graders in another school and wanted to see how it compared with this school.

Results

The results generally supported the prediction that girls in nontraditional story groups would select more nontraditional pictures, jobs, and adjectives than girls in traditional story groups. On the picture-choice tests, nontraditional girls picked significantly fewer traditional pictures than traditional girls (5.1 out of 8 compared with 6.2). Using a one-tailed test of significance, $t(27) = 1.741, p < .05$.

On the job checklists, there was a slight tendency for the traditional girls to rate the female jobs more positively, $t(8) = 2.06, p < .05$, one-tailed test. This effect was not evident on the second testing. There were no differences in the ratings of male jobs.

Words on the adjective checklist were classified as male, female, or both on the basis of the ratings made by the control group. A numerical score for each adjective was obtained by giving 2 points for each child who rated the word as the control group had, 1 point for every *both* rating, and -2 points for every rating opposite that of the control group. The scores for each adjective were then summed for each group.

On both checklists, the nontraditional females' ratings of the adjectives were less stereotyped: first list, $t(30) = 3.19, p < .01$; second list, $t(16) = 1.85, p < .05$, one-tailed tests.

On the picture-choice test, males who heard nontraditional stories picked slightly more traditional pictures than males who heard traditional stories, contrary to prediction. This difference was not significant, $t(26) = .28, ns$. There were no differences between the groups on the adjective checklists. The results of the job checklists were judged to be irrelevant for males, since they reflected the boys' attitudes toward the jobs and not toward females in these jobs.

Discussion

The results of this experiment suggest the importance of the type of role models girls see in the books they read. Girls in this study who heard stories with women in traditional roles showed a clear tendency to make more traditional, stereotypical responses than girls who heard stories involving nontraditional women. They preferred pictures of women in traditional roles and indicated that traditionally female jobs sounded more appealing than nontraditional jobs. Girls who heard stories about nontraditional women were more likely to pick nontraditional jobs.

The presence of a female experimenter may have contributed to these results. She served as a live role model who could have been interpreted as supporting or representing the women in the stories she was reading. Since she could be regarded as an authority figure, this would give more weight to the viewpoints presented in the stories. The observed effect might not have been so great if the children had read the stories themselves.

The setting of the experiment may also have had an effect. The children were allowed to leave their classrooms and their work during the school day to hear a story. This change in their usual routine may have made them particularly receptive to whatever material was presented.

The magnitude of the results is somewhat surprising, considering the limitations of the experiment. Students in the experimental groups received only two treatment sessions. They heard only two stories lasting about 15 minutes each. One might have expected that no effect would have been shown over such a short period of time. In contrast, Litcher and Johnson (1969) exposed students to multiethnic readers for a period of 4 months. As the experimenter read the stories and administered the picture-choice tests, she may have unknowingly influenced the results. However, a different person administered the adjective checklists in a different setting, and these results also support the hypothesis. Thus, the overall effect cannot be explained solely on the basis of experimenter bias or experimental demand characteristics.

The results of three of the five posttests were significant for females, and the results of the others were in the predicted direction in spite of the brief treatment conditions. This suggests that the effect of sexually stereotyped children's books on girls over a long period of time can be major. Surveys of current children's literature suggest that this is indeed the type of book that is generally available to girls. It can no longer be suggested that such books will have little impact on the girls who read them. Further research should examine the effect of more prolonged treatment conditions on the attitudes of girls to more closely approximate the actual effect of reading such books for years.

Further research needs to be done on the effect of sexually stereotyped books on males. It may be that nontraditional stories would widen males' perceptions of what constitutes appropriate behavior and characteristics for females. This idea should be tested.

The results of this study suggest that more effort must be made to eliminate the sexual bias in children's books and textbooks. One cannot expose girls to sexist books throughout childhood and then grant them a "free" choice of the role they want as an adult because such choices will not actually **be free. If girls have been told by books all their lives that the role of mother is the highest to which they can aspire, they are not** likely to consider **the role of doctor or carpenter as a real option. By widening the** range of options available **to girls and women** in children's books, one may **hope to widen** the range of options that girls will consider appropriate for themselves.

Reference Note

1. Stull, M. *"Isn't that just like a girl!" The sex typing of girls and women in children's literature.* Unpublished manuscript, Kirkland College, 1973.

References

Berdie, R. F. A femininity adjective check list. *Journal of Applied Psychology,* 1959, *43,* 327–333.

Dudley, N. *Linda goes to a TV studio.* New York: Coward-McCann, 1957.

Evans, J. A. *I know a telephone operator.* New York: Putnam, 1971.

Frasher, R., & Walker, A. Sex roles in early reading textbooks. *The Reading Teacher,* 1972, *25,* 741–749.

Goldreich, G., & Goldreich, E., *What can she be? A veterinarian.* New York: Lothrop, Lee & Shepard, 1972.

Hillman, J. S. An analysis of male and female roles in two periods of children's literature. *Journal of Educational Research,* 1974, *68*(2), 84–88.

Kay, E. *The first book of nurses.* New York: Franklin Watts, 1968.

Litcher, J. H., & Johnson, D. W. Changes in attitudes toward Negroes of white elementary school students after use of multiethnic readers. *Journal of Educational Psychology,* 1969, *60,* 148–152.

McArthur, L. Z., & Eisen, S. V. Achievements of male and female storybook characters as determinants of achievement behavior by boys and girls. *Journal of Personality and Social Psychology,* 1976, *33,* 467–473.

The first paragraph of the Discussion section summarizes the statistically significant findings obtained in the Results section. Instead of continuing in the following paragraphs to discuss the theoretical, research, or educational implications of the findings, the second, third, and fourth paragraphs each present a threat to the external validity of the study. The second paragraph discusses a threat due to a possible active experimenter effect. Similar findings may not be generalizable to studies which incorporate a male model or to those studies in which the children read the stories themselves. The third paragraph discusses a novelty effect threat due to having children leave their classrooms to participate in the study. The fourth paragraph discusses a further threat due to an experimenter effect or bias, that of unknowingly influencing the results. However, the researchers did not perceive that this threat was a viable confounding variable.

The fifth paragraph discusses an implication of the study, namely, the long-term effect on girls of sexually stereotyped children's books. This implication results in a suggestion for future research to examine the longer term effect of reading sex-stereotyped children's literature.

The sixth paragraph discusses a second implication for further research, namely, the effect of sexually stereotyped books on males. Males were included in the present study, but nonsignificance was not obtained on the dependent measures. Thus either the results or the implication for subsequent research needs elaboration. Finally, the last paragraph discusses the long-term implication of sexual bias in girls' and women's subsequent choices of occupational roles.

This Discussion section is an example of one that does not completely consider the theoretical, research, or practical implications of its findings. Only the last three paragraphs present implications, either for research or, in the case of the last paragraph, for practical implications.

How these results are integrated into the existing body of theory and/or research has not been covered. Thus the context we might have developed for understanding the current results is missing.

Consider the Discussion section from the article we reprinted in Chapter 1 by Morris, Surber, and Bijou (1978). You may want to reread the first three components of the article prior to reading the Discussion section.

Discussion

A comparison between a student self-paced instruction system and a flexible, instructor-paced point system revealed that students procrastinated when they self-paced, yet proceeded evenly through course material when given incentives to do so. As noted elsewhere, students do not *self*-pace; they pace according to the conditions that control the pacing behavior (Bijou et al., 1976). In most cases when we say a student self-paces, we are admitting that the conditions which produce pacing are unknown. These results are also in agreement with other research demonstrating that whether students self-pace or have their pacing regulated, they score similarly on criterion measures of course achievement (Atkins & Lockhart, 1976; Bitgood & Segrave, 1974; Burt, 1975; Lloyd et al., in press; Robin & Graham, 1974; Semb et al., 1974) and are highly and equally satisfied with the ways in which they were instructed (Bitgood & Segrave, 1974; Robin & Graham, 1974; Semb et al., 1974).

In addition to the similarity of course achievement and course satisfaction measures, the two groups showed no differences in (a) the number of units completed, (b) final grade distributions, or (c) course withdrawal rates. However, the self-paced group did have to repeat fewer quizzes, and this would seem to be an advantage. Why this difference occurred is not immediately apparent, but it could be that students took quizzes when they were prepared, rather than being forced to take them at the end of a week, prepared or not.

The data indicating that the self-pacing component had no differential effect on course withdrawal are particularly interesting. The PSI courses generally have higher withdrawal rates than lecture–discussion courses and the presumption is often that the self-pacing feature is the cause; however, there is only a small amount of empirical evidence for this latter claim (see Semb et al., 1974). Certainly the matter is not settled; the wide procedural variations from one PSI course to the next preclude a final answer. But the point can be made that self-pacing need not lead to greater student withdrawal. When it does, the other components of the PSI package should be scrutinized; indeed, they may be interacting with the self-pacing component, thereby inducing high withdrawal rates. This need not occur.

Although the results show striking similarities between the two groups on dependent measures relevant to educational achievement, many educators would still be troubled over student procrastination in the self-paced group. Course management logistics aside, cramming typically has been considered less desirable than regularly paced study; however, there are as yet no supportive data in the PSI literature for this conclusion (Burt, 1975). Therefore, the inclusion of a follow-up retention measure was a logical step for assessing possible differences. But no statistical retention differences were apparent. If anything, the data suggested that the benefit might go to the procrastinating self-paced group. Perhaps contingencies that allow self-pacing are important after all.

In addition to this retention trend, the difference between the two groups in quiz repeat rates was in favor of the self-paced group; they failed significantly fewer quizzes. But when all other achievement measures are the same, it is difficult to know how to interpret a high or low repeat rate. One conclusion is that more students in the instructor-paced group took quizzes before being adequately prepared. However, the supposedly aversive event of quiz failure did not seem to influence the course evaluation measures. On the other hand, it might be suggested that we did not measure the appropriate behaviors. Perhaps instructor-pacing and the quiz repeats are teaching students something else, something unrelated to achievement. Perhaps they are teaching pacing skills that will be more im-portant to future learning than the content of any single course.

Future PSI research should attempt to determine whether pacing skills, once acquired in a course, will then be applied in subsequent courses. However, a caveat needs to be entered. Analogous to the difficulties of generalization from clinical and educational programs, pacing skills should not be expected to appear magically in other learning settings. They must be planned for and programmed. Perhaps instructor-paced systems would be part of the program, perhaps not. But we should begin to find out. If instructor-paced systems are not part of a learning-to-self-pace program, then we must examine the possible benefits of self-paced systems for content retention despite the course management problems they generate.

The first four and one half paragraphs discuss the implications of the significant results in terms of either prior research or a conceptual explanation or reason for the findings. These latter reasons could become hypotheses for subsequent research. Finally, the last one and one half paragraphs consider implications for future research. A context for the results was arrived at based in prior research and current interpretations. The question "So what?" has been addressed in this Discussion section.

In many Discussion sections you will find a predominant focus on the limitations of the study and/or implications for future research, and little or no discussion of the theoretical, research, or practical implications. Another type of Discussion section, already mentioned, discusses results that are not related to or integrated with the prior research components. These Discussion sections may appear disjointed or irrelevant to the previous sections of the article. The task of understanding the implications and of separating knowledge from illusion or error becomes a difficult chore.

In Chapter 12, on writing the research article, we shall consider examples of evaluating the entire research process, and summarize suggestions for integrating the research components into a journal article. In the remainder of this chapter we discuss the question of ethics in research and make a further distinction between research and evaluation and give examples of two evaluation models.

Ethical Considerations

As experimenters and researchers in psychological and educational research we have a responsibility to protect the lives and the right to privacy of our subjects. Protecting the lives of subjects concerns their social and emotional well-being as well as their inherent dignity as human beings. The research process must ensure that we in no way expect subjects to engage in any procedure that would affect them negatively. Inanimate objects and phenomena, such as rock formations and snow avalanches, can be studied extensively without fear of irreparable damage, but research that involves human beings assumes the added risk and responsibility of seeing that they are protected. Harassment, excessive stress, and invasion of privacy violate any moral or ethical guidelines established by schools and universities, or in state and federal regulations. Physical and psychological trauma must be avoided, "research at any cost" has no place in our profession. Moral, ethical, and legal considerations arise when we attempt to manipulate an independent variable that should not be manipulated. For instance, taking children away from their parents and other adults to study language development during the first five years of life or inducing significant stress into a subject's life to determine how various neurotic defense mechanisms are used could produce irreparable damage.

Human subjects or vertebrate animals are not to be manipulated at the whim of a researcher. Prior consent to a procedure and permission to be tested are the right of every subject. Subjects should be informed of any risks involved, and all precautions must be taken by the investigator. Also the *debriefing* of every subject is necessary in psychological research. Debriefing is a meeting between the subject and the researcher after the study is completed in which the purpose of the research is explained. Not only are subjects asked to provide information about their experience during the study, but care is usually taken by the experimenter to ensure that no adverse effects to the subject have been produced during the research.

In the *Ethical Standards of Psychologists* (1981) published by the American Psychological Association, the following preamble introduces the code of ethics:

Psychologists respect the dignity and worth of the individual and strive for the preservation and protection of fundamental human rights. They are committed to increasing knowledge of human behavior and of people's understanding of themselves and others and to the utilization of such knowledge for the promotion of human welfare. While pursuing these objectives, they make every effort to protect the welfare of those who seek their services and of the research participants that may be the object of study. They use their skills only for purposes consistent with these values and do not knowingly permit their misuse by others. While demanding for themselves freedom of inquiry and communication, psychologists accept the responsibility this *freedom requires: competence, objectivity in the application of skills, and concern for the best interests of clients, colleagues, students, research participants, and society. In the pursuit of these ideals, psychologists subscribe to principles in the following areas: 1. Responsibility, 2. Competence, 3. Moral and Legal Standards, 4. Public Statements, 5. Confidentiality, 6. Welfare of the Consumer, 7. Professional Relationships, 8. Assessment Techniques, 9. Research With Human Participants, and 10. Care and Use of Animals.*

Acceptance of membership in the American Psycho-logical Association commits the member to adherence to these principles.

Psychologists cooperate with duly constituted committees of the American Psychological Association, in particular, the Committee on Scientific and Professional Ethics and Conduct, by responding to inquiries promptly and completely. Members also respond promptly and completely to inquiries from duly constituted state association ethics committees and professional standards review committees.

Two of the principles that relate to utilization of assessment techniques and pursuit of research activities are reprinted here.

Principle 8
ASSESSMENT TECHNIQUES

In the development, publication, and utilization of psychological assessment techniques, psychologists make every effort to promote the welfare and best interests of the client. They guard against the misuse of assessment results. They respect the client's right to know the results, the interpretations made, and the bases for their conclusions and recommendations. Psychologists make every effort to maintain the security of tests and other assessment techniques within limits of legal mandates. They strive to ensure the appropriate use of assessment techniques by others.

a. In using assessment techniques, psychologists respect the right of clients to have full explanations of the nature and purpose of the techniques in language the clients can understand, unless an explicit exception to this right has been agreed upon in advance. When the explanations are to be provided by others, psychologists establish procedures for ensuring the adequacy of these explanations.

b. Psychologists responsible for the development and standardization of psychological tests and other assessment techniques utilize established scientific procedures and observe the relevant APA standards.

c. In reporting assessment results, psychologists indicate any reservations that exist regarding validity or reliability because of the circumstances of the assessment or the inappropriateness of the norms for the person tested. Psychologists strive to ensure that the results of assessments and their interpretations are not misused by others.

d. Psychologists recognize that assessment results may become obsolete. They make every effort to avoid and prevent the misuse of obsolete measures.

e. Psychologists offering scoring and interpretation services are able to produce appropriate evidence for the validity of the programs and procedures used in arriving at interpretations. The public offering of an automated interpretation service is considered a professional-to-professional consultation. Psychologists make every effort to avoid misuse of assessment reports.

f. Psychologists do not encourage or promote the use of psychological assessment techniques by inappropriately trained or otherwise unqualified persons through teaching, sponsorship, or supervision.

Principle 9
RESEARCH WITH HUMAN PARTICIPANTS

The decision to undertake research rests upon a considered judgment by the individual psychologist about how best to contribute to psychological science and human welfare. Having made the decision to conduct research, the psychologist considers alternative directions in which research energies and resources might be invested. On the basis of this consideration, the psychologist carries out the investigation with respect and concern for the dignity and welfare of the people who participate and with cognizance of federal and state regulations and professional standards governing the conduct of research with human participants.

a. In planning a study, the investigator has the responsibility to make a careful evaluation of its ethical acceptability. To the extent that the weighing of scientific and human values suggests a compromise of any principle, the investigator incurs a correspondingly serious obligation to seek ethical advice and to observe stringent safeguards to protect the rights of human participants.

b. Considering whether a participant in a planned study will be a "subject at risk" or a "subject at minimal risk," according to recognized standards, is of primary ethical concern to the investigator.

c. The investigator always retains the responsibility for ensuring ethical practice in research. The investigator is also responsible for the ethical treatment of research participants by collaborators, assistants, students, and employees, all of whom, however, incur similar obligations.

d. Except in minimal-risk research, the investigator establishes a clear and fair agreement with research participants, prior to their participation, that clarifies the obligations and responsibilities of each. The investigator has the obligation to honor all promises and commitments included in that agreement. The investigator informs the participants of all aspects of the research that might reasonably be expected to influence willingness to participate and explains all other aspects of the research about which the participants inquire. Failure to make full disclosure prior to obtaining informed consent requires additional safeguards to protect the welfare and dignity of the research participants. Research with children or with participants who have impairments that would limit understanding and/or communication requires special safeguarding procedures.

e. Methodological requirements of a study may make the use of concealment or deception necessary. Before conducting such a study, the investigator has a special responsibility to (i) determine whether the use of such techniques is justified by the study's prospective scientific, educational, or applied value; (ii) determine whether alternative procedures are available that do not use concealment or deception; and (iii) ensure that the participants are provided with sufficient explanation as soon as possible.

f. The investigator respects the individual's freedom to decline to participate in or to withdraw from the research at any time. The obligation to protect this freedom requires careful thought and consideration when the investigator is in a position of authority or influence over the participant. Such positions of authority include, but are not limited to, situations in which research participation is required as part of employment or in which the participant is a student, client, or employee of the investigator.

g. The investigator protects the participant from physical and mental discomfort, harm, and danger that may arise from research procedures. If risks of such consequences exist, the investigator informs the participant of that fact. Research procedures likely to cause serious or lasting harm to a participant are not used unless the failure to use these procedures might expose the participant to risk of greater harm, or unless the research has great potential benefit and fully informed and voluntary consent is obtained from each participant. The participant should be informed of procedures for contacting the investigator within a reasonable time period following participation should stress, potential harm, or related questions or concerns arise.

h. After the data are collected, the investigator provides the participant with information about the nature of the study and attempts to remove any misconceptions that may have arisen. Where scientific or humane values justify delaying or withholding this information, the investigator incurs a special responsibility to monitor the research and to ensure that there are no damaging consequences for the participant.

i. Where research procedures result in undesirable consequences for the individual participant, the investigator has the responsibility to detect and remove or correct these consequences, including long-term effects.

j. Information obtained about a research participant during the course of an investigation is confidential unless otherwise agreed upon in advance. When the possibility exists that others may obtain access to such information, this possibility, together with the plans for protecting confidentiality, is explained to the participant as part of the procedure for obtaining informed consent.

A similar set of ethical standards was developed by the American Personnel and Guidance Association (APGA, 1974). The sections on measurement and evaluation and research and publication are reprinted here.

Section C: Measurement and Evaluation

The primary purpose of educational and psychological testing is to provide descriptive measures that are objective and interpretable in either comparative or absolute terms. The member must recognize the need to interpret the statements that follow as applying to the whole range of appraisal techniques including test and nontest data. Test results constitute only one of a variety of pertinent sources of information for personnel, guidance, and counseling decisions.

1. It is the member's responsibility to provide adequate orientation or information to the examinee(s) prior to and following the test administration so that the results of testing may be placed in proper perspective with other relevant factors. In so doing, the member must recognize the effects of socioeconomic, ethnic, and cultural factors on test scores. It is the member's professional responsibility to use additional unvalidated information cautiously in modifying interpretation of the test results.

2. In selecting tests for use in a given situation or with a particular counselee, the member must consider carefully the specific validity, reliability, and appropriateness of the test(s). "General" validity, reliability, and the like may be questioned legally as well as ethically when tests are used for vocational and educational selection, placement, or counseling.

3. When making any statements to the public about tests and testing, the member is expected to give accurate information and to avoid false claims or misconceptions. Special efforts are often required to avoid unwarranted connotations of such terms as IQ and grade equivalent scores.

4. Different tests demand different levels of competence for administration, scoring, and interpretation. Members have a responsibility to recognize the limits of their competence and to perform only those functions for which they are prepared.

5. Tests should be administered under the same conditions that were established in their standardization. When tests are not administered under standard conditions or when unusual behavior or irregularities occur during the testing session, those conditions should be noted and the results designated as invalid or of questionable validity. Unsupervised or inadequately supervised test-taking, such as the use of tests through the mails, is considered unethical. On the other hand, the use of instruments that are so designed or standardized to be self-administered and self-scored, such as interest inventories, is to be encouraged.

6. The meaningfulness of test results used in personnel, guidance, and counseling functions generally depends on the examinee's unfamiliarity with the specific items on the test. Any prior coaching or dissemination of the test materials can invalidate test results. Therefore, test security is one of the professional obligations of the member. Conditions that produce most favorable test results should be made known to the examinee.

7. The purpose of testing and the explicit use of the results should be made known to the examinee prior to testing. The counselor has a responsibility to ensure that instrument limitations are not exceeded and that periodic review and/or retesting are made to prevent counselee stereotyping.

8. The examinee's welfare and explicit prior understanding should be the criteria for determining the recipients of the test results. The member is obligated to see that adequate interpretation accompanies any release of individual or group test data. The interpretation of test data should be related to the examinee's particular concerns.

9. The member is expected to be cautious when interpreting the results of research instruments possessing insufficient technical data. The specific purposes

for the use of such instruments must be stated explicitly to examinees.

10. The member must proceed with extreme caution when attempting to evaluate and interpret the performance of minority group members or other persons who are not represented in the norm group on which the instrument was standardized.

11. The member is obligated to guard against the appropriation, reproduction, or modifications of published tests or parts thereof without the express permission and adequate recognition of the original author or publisher.

12. Regarding the preparation, publication, and distribution of tests, reference should be made to:

a. *Standards for Educational and Psychological Tests and Manuals,* revised edition, 1973, published by the American Psychological Association on behalf of itself, the American Educational Research Association, and the National Council on Measurement in Education.

b. "The Responsible Use of Tests: A Position Paper of AMEG, APGA, and NCME," published in *Measurement and Evaluation in Guidance* Vol. 5, No. 2, July 1972, pp. 385–388.

Section D: Research and Publication

1. Current American Psychological Association guidelines on research with human subjects shall be adhered to (*Ethical Principles in the Conduct of Research with Human Participants.* Washington, D.C.: American Psychological Association. Inc., 1973).

2. In planning any research activity dealing with human subjects, the member is expected to be aware of and responsive to all pertinent ethical principles and to ensure that the research problem, design, and execution are in full compliance with them.

3. Responsibility for ethical research practice lies with the principal researcher, while others involved in the research activities share ethical obligation and full responsibility for their own actions.

4. In research with human subjects, researchers are responsible for their subjects' welfare throughout the experiment, and they must take all reasonable precautions to avoid causing injurious psychological, physical, or social effects on their subjects.

5. It is expected that all research subjects be informed of the purpose of the study except when withholding information or providing misinformation to them is essential to the investigation. In such research, the member is responsible for corrective action as soon as possible following the research.

6. Participation in research is expected to be voluntary. Involuntary participation is appropriate only when it can be demonstrated that participation will have no harmful effects on subjects.

7. When reporting research results, explicit mention must be made of all variables and conditions known to the investigator that might affect the outcome of the investigation or the interpretation of the data.

8. The member is responsible for conducting and reporting investigations in a manner that minimizes the possibility that results will be misleading.

9. The member has an obligation to make available sufficient original research data to qualified others who may wish to replicate the study.

10. When supplying data, aiding in the research of another person, reporting research results, or in making original data available, due care must be taken to disguise the identity of the subjects in the absence of specific authorization from such subjects to do otherwise.

11. When conducting and reporting research, the member is expected to be familiar with and to give recognition to previous work on the topic, as well as to observe all copyright laws and follow the principle of giving full credit to all to whom credit is due.

12. The member has the obligation to give due credit through joint authorship, acknowledgement, footnote statements, or other appropriate means to those who have contributed significantly to the research, in accordance with such contributions.

13. The member is expected to communicate to other members the results of any research judged to be of professional or scientific value. Results reflect-ing unfavorably on institutions, programs, services, or vested interests should not be withheld for such reasons.

14. If members agree to cooperate with another individual in research and/or publication, they incur an obligation to cooperate as promised in terms of punctuality of performance and with full regard to the completeness and accuracy of the information provided.

As mentioned in Chapter 9, ethical and legal responsibilities of users of standardized tests are expected to be followed in any testing procedure, whether it be in a research or evaluation project or in the periodic assessment of student performance routinely conducted by school districts. These previous statements, as well as the APGA policy statement for users of standardized tests (see Appendix C), summarize these responsibilities. The protection, safety, and well-being of our subjects, human or animal, take precedence over any other research concern.

Research and Evaluation

In Chapter 1 we made a basic distinction between research and evaluation activities. Both use the scientific method, whose manifest components in connection with the research article we have examined in the previous chapters. The main difference is in their outcomes; research seeks conclusions to develop theory, principles, and generalizations which were derived from the analysis of the relationship between variables, that is, the goals of explanation, prediction, and control. The outcome of an evaluation study is to determine the advantages and disadvantages of a particular educational program, process, or product in terms of specific objectives and criteria for evaluation. Evaluation projects seek conclusions which lead to recommendations and decisions.

Planning a Program Evaluation

In planning an evaluation, several questions should be answered by those involved. The first is: *Why is the program, process, or product being evaluated?* Providing specific answers to this question will help clarify the purpose as well as the potential outcomes and instruments to be used. For instance, we might want to evaluate our district's staff development program to determine if training needs are being met. Po-

The Reseacher Is Responsible for the Safety, Well-being, and Integrity of the Subjects

tential outcomes and instruments, such as participant evaluations and related workshop records, might be generated as measures to consider.

Evaluations are conducted for a multitude of reasons. Sometimes the real purpose may be hidden. Results provided by evaluations are used to meet a variety of goals. Evaluation results may be used to provide information on whether a program or components of a program should be continued, terminated, or improved. Are key program objectives being correctly implemented? Evaluations may also be conducted as one aspect of staff development. Others may be conducted to meet evaluation requirements of outside agencies, such as state departments of education, accrediting agencies, and so forth. Thus, the first step for a group of individuals planning an evaluation is to specify clear and explicit purpose statements for planning the evaluation.

A second question that individuals involved in an evaluation should consider is: *Who will receive the information and what will they do with it?* Answering this question adequately includes identifying the key administrators or decision makers who will receive the data as well as determining their willingness to make decisions supported by the data you will collect. Such decisions may include changes which will affect student identification procedures, personnel, program structure, program objectives, inservice training, and the dissemination of information.

A third question that relates directly to the second should also be discussed: *What kind of information do the decision makers want?* Many comprehensive evaluation reports containing hundreds of pages are never read by anyone outside the evaluation team or used in the decision making process. Knowing the precise information needed will ensure that the evaluation effort plays a role in the decisions to be made. A succinct report that provides the desired information often has more use and value than an exhaustive treatise on evaluation.

The fourth and last question that should be considered is: *Who should conduct the evaluation?* Sometimes outside district evaluators are used, if finances are available, to provide a necessary objectivity to the evaluation process. Typically, though, someone inside the district serves as the evaluator. If an internal evaluation is conducted, should it be the supervisor, principal, teacher, or if your district is large enough, an internal evaluator on the staff?

After these four questions are answered, key criteria for planning should be examined, such as staff commitment, time, and cost requirements. We shall discuss these elements and develop an eight-step overview of the process of planning an evaluation to provide you with an overview of a typical planning process.

Staff commitment.   Ideally, a program evaluation should be coordinated by a small number of individuals within a school district who are interested in the program to be evaluated, working with one or two individuals who will receive the results. Committee members should be selected who can make the commitment of time and effort required by the planning process. If possible, release time or monetary payment should be provided to compensate each committee member. The committee should be a small working group of three to seven members. Too many members dilute its working effectiveness and make the scheduling of meetings cumbersome.

A project director from the committee should be selected to coordinate the total planning process with all the activities that this entails. The project director should be skilled in two major areas: leadership ability and research and evaluation experience. Specifically, the project director should have excellent interpersonal skills, credibility with both teachers and administrators, problem-solving and communication skills, and the ability to manage resources available to the planning committee. At the same time, the project director should have experience in research design, questionnaire development, data collection and analysis, and report writing, as well as previous planning experience. The project director should not only coordinate the planning process, but should also coordinate the implementation phase of the evaluation.

When a project fails, it can usually be attributed to a weakness on the part of the project director. If you want an evaluation project to succeed, do not select the project director randomly or based on who would like most to add it to their resume. Use the guidelines enumerated above. The selection of a project director is the most crucial component of a successful completion. Thus a planning committee should be able to answer these three questions affirmatively:

1. Are the individuals committed to serve as committee members?
2. Is a qualified project director committed to lead the planning process?
3. Is the program area, department, school, or school district committed to allocating the necessary staff, faculty, and administrator time?

Time. A specific time schedule is required to complete all the steps in the planning process. In addition, time should be allocated for any necessary administrative review of the final evaluation plan. The time schedule should include specific dates and the exact range of meeting times as well as a completion date for each component of the planning process. A good project director will be task-oriented in the meetings in order to keep extraneous discussions minimal and respect the other commitments of committee members. A meeting scheduled from 10:00 to 12:00 should start at 10:00 and run no later than 12:00. Frequently, a planning committee will set up three time schedules for each part of the planning process and implementation phase: optimistic, most likely, and pessimistic. The discrepancies among the three time estimates are a measure of the uncertainty of the process.

There are two main approaches used by planning committees when developing an evaluation plan. Some committees schedule meetings for two to four days, all day, either consecutively or spread out over one or two weeks. Other committees schedule a whole series of three-hour meetings once or twice a month for as long as six months. The shorter time block frequently costs less. Although it is difficult for committee members to find a block of time when everyone is free, it is usually a more efficient procedure since too much time between meetings results in wasted time reviewing and summarizing past tasks.

Two more approaches also are used by planning committees when scheduling the planning process. Some committees are appointed at the beginning of the academic year and complete the planning during that time. The remainder of the semester and spring term is spent by the project director and any technical consultant pilot testing the plan. The full-scale implementation of the evaluation project is then begun the following academic year in the fall. Other committees complete the evaluation plan during the spring semester or summer and then implement the evaluation plan at the beginning of the new academic year. Thus the following two questions should also be answered affirmatively:

1. Can a specific time schedule be developed?
2. Can it realistically complete the planning and implementation process?

Costs.   Any costs associated with the planning process should be analyzed before deciding to develop an evaluation plan. Typical costs encountered in the planning process include release time or monetary payment for staff, secretarial and clerical expenses, and costs for duplicating questionnaires, forms, committee minutes, and reports. Costs must be accurately estimated, because this is one criterion which, by itself, frequently determines whether a program evaluation will ever get off the ground. It is unlikely that a school district will be able to plan a program evaluation if these two questions cannot be answered positively:

1. Have costs in planning an evaluation been specified and analyzed?
2. Can the costs be provided by the department, school, or school district?

Developing an Evaluation Plan

The following seven steps comprise the planning process for evaluating a curriculum:

1. Specify the purposes or goals.
2. Describe the curriculum program.

3. Specify the curriculum objectives.
4. Identify and determine the relative importance of program components.
5. Specify the data collection requirements and criteria for evaluating the results.
6. Review, modify, and approve the evaluation plan.
7. Implement the evaluation plan.

In the first step the committee members should clarify their questions, concerns, and reasons for deciding to plan a program evaluation. Specific purposes for the evaluation plan are required in order to reach a common understanding. To paraphrase Nay, Scanlon, Schmidt, and Wholey (1976), if you don't know where you're going, it won't matter how you get there; and you also won't know when you get there. In Chapter 2 we discuss specifying a statement of purpose; it is useful for this process.

The second step is to describe or summarize the basic information related to the program to be evaluated. This information includes as much pertinent demographic data as possible to accurately describe the program, its components, and the target population it serves.

The third step is to specify the curriculum objectives for the program considered by the committee to be crucial to the purposes and goals in step one. This requires that specific and clear objectives be delineated. They are usually related to the general purposes or goals previously stated, but are presented at a more operational level. The objectives are analogous to a road map of untraveled territory. Without them you will usually lose your way.

The fourth step is to identify and prioritize the program components that relate to the objectives. These components should be the most relevant ones to your objectives and earlier purposes. There are five common program components, though others may be added as they are generated: (1) student outcomes, including basic skills, memorization, higher level cognitive reasoning processes, attitudes or values, and social or personality development; (2) instructional strategies, such as behavioral objectives, motivation, instructional methods, sequence or setting, student or teacher role, and evaluation of achievement; (3) curriculum content, including academic content areas, personal experiences of students, problem-solving or creative strategies and techniques, and societal influences; (4) content sequencing, such as observation, existing knowledge, developmental differences, and abstract reasoning techniques; and (5) program resources, including equipment, facilities, materials, schedule, staff, and student organization.

The fifth step relates to the five program components just listed. The relative importance of each is determined in relation to curriculum objectives and purposes. The program components selected as most important are then further examined. This step requires a specific operational statement for each selected program component as to how the data will be obtained and which criteria will be used for evaluating results obtained from the data analysis.

The sixth step assumes that an evaluation plan has been developed and written out, and is ready to be reviewed, revised, and approved. The review and revisions should focus on the consistency of the purposes, objectives, and data collection requirements related to the program objectives. Approval usually must come first from the committee and then from the administrative body that ordered the program evaluation.

The seventh step is the implementation of the evaluation plan. Here the project director or research consultant will have major responsibility for project control and eventual termination of the project. This implementation step involves the same seven steps as carried out in the research study. The entire seven-step process for planning an evaluation is represented by the flow chart in Figure 11.1.

Two Models of Evaluation

Many specific models of evaluation are used within the educational setting. Two frequently used models are *formative* and *summative evaluation*. Formative evaluation is a process that assists the developer of programs or products (meaning curricula or books) by applying research methodology. Formative evaluation goes on in close collaboration with the program or product development. Summative evaluation consists of evaluating the overall program after it is implemented. Summative evaluation is independent of the program or product developer.

Another frequently used model is *discrepancy evaluation.* This involves the analysis of differences between two or more variables or components of a program that logically or statistically should be in agreement. Areas for discrepancy evaluation include the discrepancies between program plans and actual operation, predicted and obtained program outcomes, student achievement and desired student outcomes, and goals or objectives of different system units.

Figures 11.2 and 11.3 are examples of questionnaires that have been used in school districts. The first is an instrument used for a summative evaluation of an elementary program for gifted/talented pupils. The second is an instrument used in a discrepancy evaluation of a staff development training workshop on problem-solving. Compare the two questionnaires and observe the differences in evaluation models as they are presented in these examples.

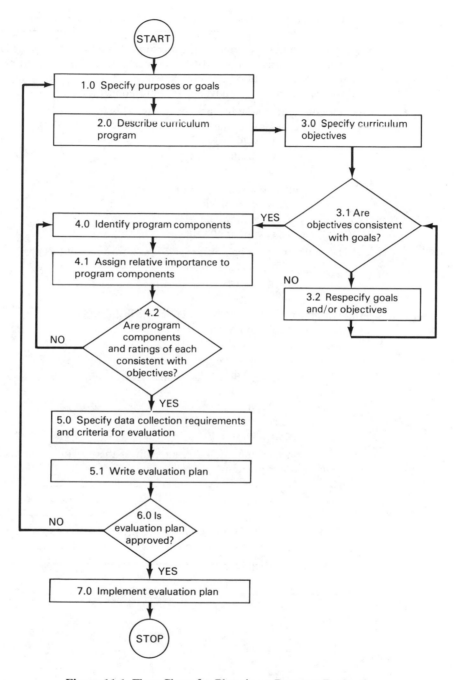

Figure 11.1 Flow Chart for Planning a Program Evaluation

Figure 11.2 Example of a Summative Evaluation Questionnaire

Directions: Please respond to the questions below based on your experience of having completed the summer Gifted and Talented program. The information you provide will assist us in planning future programs. Thank you in advance for your cooperation.

1. Please rate the program in terms of its value to you.
   ___ A. very valuable
   ___ B. valuable
   ___ C. of little value
   ___ D. of no value

2. Are you glad you were a part of this program?
   ___ A. very much so
   ___ B. somewhat
   ___ C. not at all

3. Do you think your parents are glad you were a part of this program?
   ___ A. very much so
   ___ B. somewhat
   ___ C. not at all

4. Do you think the work you were given in this program was
   ___ A. too hard
   ___ B. about right
   ___ C. too easy

5. If this program is offered again next year, would you want to join the group?
   ___ A. yes
   ___ B. maybe
   ___ C. no

6. Please comment on any other strength of the program which will help us in our planning:

   _____
   _____
   _____

7. Please comment on any area of the program that could be improved the next time it is offered:

   _____
   _____
   _____

Figure 11.3 Example of a Discrepancy Evaluation Questionnaire

Directions: Please respond to each question below using the scale at the right (Y = yes, S = somewhat, N = no). After responding to each item, please indicate how important you perceive this factor was to the success of the workshop by checking the appropriate scale at the left (E = essential, I = important, NI = not important).

E   I   NI   Y   S   N

1. Were the objectives of this workshop made clear?
___ ___ ___   ___ ___ ___

2. Were the objectives of this workshop attained?
___ ___ ___   ___ ___ ___

3. Did the techniques presented throughout the workshop help you increase your problem-solving ability?
___ ___ ___   ___ ___ ___

4. Were you given sufficient instruction in applying these problem-solving concepts to the classroom setting?
___ ___ ___   ___ ___ ___

5. Were you given sufficient time to practice these problem-solving techniques?
___ ___ ___   ___ ___ ___

6. Did you feel embarrassed or ill at ease as a result of the group activities?
___ ___ ___   ___ ___ ___

7. How will your teaching behavior change as a result of this workshop?

_____

_____

_____

8. How will your general behavior change as a result of this workshop?

_____

_____

_____

9. Please comment on any other aspect of the workshop that will facilitate our subsequent planning:

_____

_____

_____

There are many other evaluation models. All, however, incorporate the essential research process that we have discussed throughout the book. What usually varies among them is the jargon used to describe the idiosyncratic characteristics of each evaluation model.

SUMMARY

We have examined the four main components of a Discussion section: a restatement of the purpose or hypotheses; a discussion of the theoretical, research, or educational implications; limitations of the research, usually expressed in terms of the threats to external validity; and a statement of implications for future research. The last two steps may be omitted in some research articles depending upon the policy of the journal editors. Next, we examined two Discussion sections to compare the relative focus assigned to the theoretical, research, or educational implications. There followed the ethical considerations related to testing and research activities as set down by the APA and APGA. We then made further distinctions between research and evaluation, and delineated questions for planning, and a seven-step process for developing a program evaluation. Finally, we illustrated two evaluation models with examples of how each has been operationally defined through the use of a questionnaire.

OBJECTIVES

In Chapter 11 we have considered the components of the Discussion section as well as the ethical and legal aspects of testing and research. Questions to consider in planning a program evaluation and a summary for developing an educational plan were presented. Confirm your understanding of the material in Chapter 11 using the following objectives:

Evaluate the Discussion section in terms of its four main components.
Understand the important ethical and legal standards and guidelines.
Recognize whether a study is a research or an evaluation project.
Develop an evaluation project based on the questions and seven-step summary for planning an evaluation.
Recognize whether an evaluation project was formative or summative, or whether it employed a discrepancy evaluation model.

TERMS

discrepancy evaluation model   formative evaluation
evaluation   summative evaluation

Writing the Research Article

What are the key components of the research process, and how are they integrated into the journal article?

What is a typical outline for organizing a journal article?

What technical qualities of style and format should be considered when writing a journal article?

How are the substantive components of the research article integrated into the mechanics of writing?

Summary of the Research Process

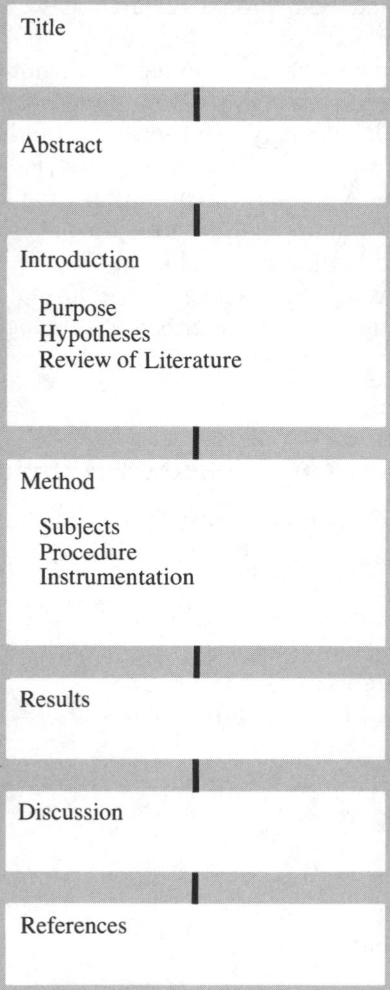

Title

Abstract

Introduction

    Purpose
    Hypotheses
    Review of Literature

Method

    Subjects
    Procedure
    Instrumentation

Results

Discussion

References

In the previous chapters we have discussed the various components of the research process and their relationship to the scientific method and to the typical journal article format encountered in educational research. We have included the technical information needed to understand and evaluate educational research as well as organizational and writing recommendations for conducting your own research. If the many suggestions we have presented throughout are incorporated and implemented in the research process, the probability of error operating in our results will be greatly reduced. We should be able to attribute our findings to real differences among the variables.

In this chapter we shall first summarize the key components of the research process and apply them to a journal article. Then we shall delineate the basic outline and technical considerations for writing a research article using the organizational format recommended in the publication manual of the American Psychological Association (APA, 1974).

Key Components of the Research Article

The major components comprising the key features of the research article are summarized in the following outline:

1. Introduction
   A. statement of purpose or problem
   B. hypotheses
   C. review of the literature
2. Method
   A. subjects
   B. procedure
   C. instrumentation
3. Results
   A. descriptive statistics
   B. inferential statistics
4. Discussion
   A. restatement of purpose or hypotheses
   B. theoretical, research, or educational implications
   C. limitations of study
   D. future research

As pointed out in Chapter 1, there are other components included in the research article, such as title, abstract, references, and reference notes. However, the key elements relating directly to the scientific

Writing the Research Article

method are included above. We shall discuss these other components when we consider the organizational format for writing the research article.

For each of the key components of the research process we have presented criteria and recommendations for integrating and writing the research article. We shall summarize these criteria for each component and then analyze a complete research article in terms of these criteria. We begin with the three components of the Introduction section.

Introduction

There are three main subsections to the Introduction section, as shown in the outline.

Statement of purpose or problem.   The four main criteria for writing a purpose statement are:

1. The purpose should be presented clearly and unambiguously in either declarative or question form.
2. The purpose should present the relationship between two or more variables and state the population to be examined.
3. The variables and population specified in the purpose should be consistent with the variables operationalized in the Instrumentation subsection and with the population defined in the Subjects subsection.
4. The purpose should be researchable or be amenable to empirical verification.

Hypotheses.   The four main criteria for writing any hypothesis are:

1. The hypothesis should be stated briefly and clearly.
2. The hypothesis should express the relationship between two variables.
3. The hypothesis should be testable.
4. The hypothesis should be supported by a rationale derived from theory, research, or personal experience.

If a hypothesis is included in the Introduction section, it is stated at a conceptual level (as either a theoretical, educational, or scientific hypothesis) in the form of a directional or nondirectional alternative hypothesis. It should be linked to a review of pertinent literature that serves as a rationale for the proposed hypothesis.

Review of the literature.   The review of the relevant literature should meet two main criteria or answer two main questions:

1. Why is this problem area the subject of this research investigation?
2. Why is this outcome predicted for the hypothesis?

Using predominantly primary sources, a general rationale to support the statement of purpose should be developed, as well as a specific rationale to support any proposed alternative hypotheses.

The three components above are integrated into the first major component of the research article—the Introduction section. The Introduction section flows from a general to a specific focus that typically includes these five features:

1. General rationale—review of the literature
2. More specific rationale—review of the literature
3. Purpose of research—statement of purpose
4. Specific rationale for the hypothesis—review of the literature
5. Hypothesis—statement of the hypothesis

Ideally, the general and specific rationale will provide a supportive context for two or more of the main variables in the study. Frequently, however, a rationale is provided for only one variable. This supportive context should flow smoothly into the purpose for conducting the research. Steps 4 and 5 are then implemented for each hypothesis. If a study proposes multiple hypotheses, steps 4 and 5 are repeated for each one.

Method

The Method section also contains three main subsections, as shown in the outline.

Subjects.   In writing the Subjects subsection of the research article, three questions should be answered:

1. Who participated in the study? Give the major demographic characteristics.
2. How many subjects participated? Give the number for each subgroup.
3. How were the subjects selected? Describe the assignment to groups.

The publication manual of the APA (1974, p. 17) recommends that not only the number of subjects assigned to each treatment or condition be stated, but also the type, number, and reason for those who dropped out of the study; any payments and promises made should also be stated, as well as the location of the study both by geographic region and institution. Furthermore, if a statistical technique for determining the sample size was used, that rationale should also be presented.

Procedure.   The Procedure subsection of the research article should contain a clear and specific presentation of the steps of the research process and an operational description of the independent variables to enable other researchers to replicate the study. The two main criteria are:

1. Describe and summarize clearly and concisely each step in the research process.
2. Operationally define each independent variable in the study.

In addition to a specific summary of the study, in the description of the independent variables, all key features needed for replication should be included. The summary and operational statement should include formation of groups, training of researchers, instructions to subjects, and any special procedures for minimizing the operation of any confounding variables.

Instrumentation.   The goal of the Instrumentation subsection is to convey completely and accurately the operational statements of the dependent variables in the study. In writing the Instrumentation subsection, the following questions should be answered:

1. What measure or test is used to assess each dependent variable?
2. What population is appropriate for the test?
3. What is the type of score (and its range of values) obtained from each measure?
4. What is the interrater reliability for the different measures?
5. As appropriate, what is the alternate form or test-retest reliability coefficient for the measure?
6. What validity evidence is there to support the use of each instrument for the corresponding conceptual level dependent variable?
7. If the researcher develops a measure, are there enough item examples and is the test construction phase adequately described? Finally, is sufficient information related to points 1 through 6 included?

The three components of the Method section all attempt to present the basic information of the research process. An integrated Method section will succinctly answer:

1. Who? — subjects
2. How? — procedure
3. What? — instrumentation

These operational statements of the population, the independent variables, and the dependent variables should flow logically from, and be integrated with, the conceptual-level presentation of the Introduction section.

Results

There are five main subsections in the Results section, which includes the descriptive and inferential statistics according to the outline:

1. An overview of the statistics to be used.
2. Results from the descriptive statistics.
3. Assumptions for the use of the inferential statistics.
4. Results of the main inferential statistics.
5. Results of the supporting inferential statistics, such as a priori or a posteriori tests.

If multiple analyses are conducted, then steps 3, 4, and 5 are usually repeated in sequence. Frequently, an overview of the statistics to be used is contained in the last paragraph of the Method section and serves as a transition to the Results section. Also, there is often a table or two to summarize the descriptive information. In addition, if a study is particularly complex, relationships may be graphically illustrated by means of frequency polygons, bar graphs, and the like. The goal of the Results section is to summarize the data and to convey the statistical treatment of these results.

Discussion

The fourth and last main component of the research article is the Discussion section. Its goal is to answer the question: "So what?" or "What are the theoretical, research, or educational implications of the findings?" The Discussion section attempts to impart meaning or utility to the results that were statistically significant in the Results section. Typically, the Discussion section is written to clearly summarize the following four types of information:

1. Restate the research question or hypotheses and indicate whether or not the results support the predictions.
2. Discuss the theoretical, research, or educational implications.
3. Discuss the major limitations of the study.
4. Suggest future research.

In order for an integrated flow to exist with the previous sections of the research article, the original hypotheses are examined in terms of whether or not they are supported by the results. Even if nonsignificance was obtained, the implications or reasons for the findings should be included. This provides the important link to the previous sections. The longest part of the Discussion section is the theoretical, research, or educational meaning of the significant findings. Points 3 and 4 are usually covered by one paragraph each. The major limitations are expressed in terms of threats to the external validity of the study. Suggestions for future research usually are also brief.

We now turn to consideration of the previous points in terms of a complete research article.

Integrating the Journal Article

Successfully analyzing an entire journal article is primarily a matter of applying the knowledge we've shared throughout this book. There are even different ways recommended for reading an article. Some researchers recommend reading the Abstract, Introduction, and Discussion sections first, and then reading the Method and Results sections only if the study is pertinent to their needs. Others recommend reading only the abstract first, then, if it seems pertinent, reading the rest of the article in order from Introduction through Method and Results to Discussion.

Read the following research article by Huber, Treffinger, Tracy, and Rand (1979). Some of the sections have been considered earlier in this book. Following the article you will find a set of comments evaluating the article based on what we have learned.

Self-Instructional Use of Programmed Creativity-Training Materials With Gifted and Regular Students

Jaclyn Huber, Donald Treffinger, and Dick Tracy
University of Kansas

Dave Rand
Wichita State University

The effects of the self-instructional use of programmed creativity materials for gifted and regular students were investigated. Programmed creativity-training materials were used on an individualized basis. The Purdue Creativity Training Program was made available for self-instruction for 12 weeks by half of the 648 fourth-, fifth-, and sixth-grade students; the other students comprised the control groups. Pre- and posttests of creative thinking were administered. Experimental students attained significantly greater gains on verbal fluency. Creative thinking abilities can be improved through self-instructional programmed materials for gifted and regular students.

Fostering creative thinking abilities in children has been a subject of educational concern for more than 20 years. The accumulation of knowledge has exceeded our ability to keep pace with new ideas. New emphases on information processing, abstraction of ideas, and generation of new knowledge are emerging. These processes certainly call for creative thinking; all problem solving may require at least some minimum level of creative thinking (Guilford, 1975).

Creative thinking abilities of children can be enhanced by many diverse means (Davis, 1973; Torrance, 1972a; Treffinger, 1977). Creativity training programs are one class of instructional materials designed to this end. Several programs have been established as effective in enhancing students' creative thinking abilities; none, however, has been tested on an individualized, self-paced basis, or for specific use with gifted students.

Individualization of instruction is generally viewed as a means of maximizing learning for each student. The needs, preferences, and capabilities of the individual have become a prime consideration in education (Weisgerber, 1971). Individualized, self-directed learning may hold particular promise for intellectually and creatively gifted students (Treffinger, 1975). Characteristics of gifted students typically include mention of the predisposition to be independent in thought and judgment (Gallagher, 1975; Martinson, Note 1).

The research vehicle used for this study, the Purdue Creativity Training Program (PCTP; Feldhusen, Treffinger, & Bahlke, 1970) is a set of programmed materials that has been the focus of several previous investigations. It consists of 28 audiotaped stories and presentations, each accompanied by printed exercises for the development of verbal and figural creative thinking abilities. Previous research with the PCTP has shown that it is effective in fostering creative thinking abilities, problem solving, and related attitudes (Feldhusen, Bahlke, &

Treffinger, 1969; Feldhusen, Treffinger, & Bahlke, 1970; Feldhusen, Treffinger, & Thomas, 1971; Robinson, 1969; Shively, Feldhusen, & Treffinger, 1972; Treffinger, Speedie, & Brunner, 1974).

The present study involved utilization of the PCTP on a self-instructional basis. Research with the PCTP and other programmed creativity instructional materials led to an expectation that the program would be effective on a self-instructional basis (Olton, Wardrop, Covington, Crutchfield, Goodwin, Klausmeier, & Ronda, 1967; Shackel & Lawrence, 1969; Shively et al., 1972; Treffinger, Speedie, & Brunner, 1974). In these studies the teacher's role was deliberately held to a minimum: Teachers gave instructions, played the tapes, and distributed the exercise sheets. The results indicated that several programs, including the PCTP, were successful in enhancing subjects' divergent thinking, with minimal teacher interaction.

Training gifted students' creative thinking abilities is also commonly emphasized in the literature on the education of the gifted and talented (Barbe & Renzulli, 1975; Gallagher, 1975). Thus programmed creativity training materials were used in an effort to enhance the creative thinking abilities of gifted students.

The specific research question was, Can the PCTP, if used in a self-paced mode, improve the creative thinking of regular and gifted children? In addition, the following questions were asked: Will the implementation of the PCTP be equally effective for Grades 4, 5, and 6? Will there be differential effects for grade level and class type for the treatment groups?

Method

Subjects

Six hundred forty-eight subjects from six school buildings in Grades 4, 5, and 6 were selected from an urban public school system. Three hundred nine subjects were enrolled in self-contained classes for in-

Table 1
Distribution of Subjects by Cell

| Grade | Experimental | | Control | |
	Gifted	Regular	Gifted	Regular
4	55	64	49	52
5	47	60	51	46
6	52	63	55	54

tellectually gifted students, and 339 were enrolled in regular classrooms in the same attendance centers. Eighteen classes, consisting of one gifted and one regular class at each grade level in each of three schools, were randomly designated as experimental groups. The remaining 18 classes received no experimental instructional program. The number of students for each cell is presented in Table 1.

The school population was representative of those in other cities of its size (200,000–300,000). The schools in the sample were comparable in socioeconomic status and distribution of sex and race of students and were substantially representative of the total school population in the city.

The gifted program provides an enriched learning environment for pupils of high academic potential. Specific criteria for eligibility for this program include the following: (a) academic excellence in the regular program, prior to selection; (b) IQ score of 125 on an individual test, and at least 2 years above grade level on standardized achievement tests; (c) good emotional, social, and personal development, as evaluated by the professional staff.

Research Design

A $2 \times 2 \times 3$ multivariate analysis of variance (MANOVA) was employed. The independent variables were instructional program or no program (PCTP vs. control), class type (gifted vs. regular), and grade (four, five, or six). The six dependent variables were the verbal and figural fluency, flexibility, and originality scores from the Torrance Tests of Creative Thinking (Torrance, 1974a). Pre- and posttest score differences (posttest minus pretest score) were computed, and the unit of analysis was the gains of individual students.

There were unequal numbers of subjects in each cell of this research design (Table 1). The computer program used for this research (BMD $\times$ 64), was modified by E. B. Cobb of the University of Kansas Department of Mathematics to handle MANOVA designs and unequal cell sizes; therefore, no effort was made to randomly equalize group sizes.

Instruments and Scoring

A battery of tests from the Torrance Tests of Creative Thinking (TTCT; Torrance, 1974a) were used as criterion measures. As operationally defined for this study, creative thinking abilities consisted of verbal and figural fluency, flexibility, and originality. Fluency was defined as the number of relevant responses to the test tasks. Flexibility was the number of different approaches or categories used in producing responses. Originality was measured by summing the response weights provided by the scoring manual; these weights reflect the statistical infrequency of responses. All scoring was conducted by trained scorers following the procedures described by Torrance (1974b).

Five subtests of the TTCT, three verbal and two figural, were employed. The verbal tests were Product Improvement, Just Suppose, and Unusual Uses; the figural subtests were Repeated Figures and Incomplete Figures. Alternate forms of these tests were administered as pre- and posttests. Scores for each of the verbal and figural tasks were analyzed separately, yielding six dependent variables. Rater reliabilities ranged from .85 to 1.0 for the six variables.

Reliability and Validity of the TTCT

Numerous studies were cited by Torrance (1974b) supporting the reliability of the Torrance Tests of Creative Thinking. Of particular interest was the report by Torrance (1972b) concerning the predictive validity of the TTCT for both short-range and long-range studies. The evidence presented was highly supportive of the ability of the TTCT to predict creative behavior on a wide range of criterion measures.

Although the TTCT are not comprehensive in the measurement of all facets of creative behavior, Torrance (1974b) contended that the tests sample a wide range of the abilities in such a universe. Treffinger, Renzulli, and Feldhusen (1971) proposed that measures of divergent thinking such as the TTCT may be viewed as necessary and useful, but not a sufficient component in the assessment of creative potential. Treffinger and Poggio (1972) suggested that divergent thinking tasks would be correlated with a more comprehensive measure of creative functioning but that the more comprehensive measure would also be related to other cognitive abilities.

Data Collection Procedures

Prior to placing the PCTP in the classrooms, two meetings were held with the teachers whose classes received the treatment. The nature and purpose of the research were outlined and discussed. Mimeographed instructions were distributed that included a description of the PCTP and suggestions for individualizing the program. The instructions asked the teachers to avoid examples of specific responses to the exercises, avoid evaluations of students' responses to exercises, provide opportunities for students to use the PCTP at their own discretion, and permit as much time as possible for a student to complete the exercises before listening to the next tape.

Five subtests from the TTCT, Form B, were administered to all students before the instructional period with the PCTP began in the experimental groups. Three verbal and two figural tasks were administered, with 8 minutes allowed for each task. The tests were administered by trained members of the research staff in the students' regular classrooms.

The students in the experimental classes used the PCTP over a 12-week period. There were a variety of program implementation strategies observed during this period. These included use of a specific, scheduled time period during the day; a free-time activity option; a free-choice activity for students upon completion of their regular class work; and a free-choice activity any time during the school day. Records of the amount of time spent with specific tapes were not uniformly kept across all experimental groups. The classes in the control group continued normal activities with no special instructional treatment during these same 12 weeks. At the end of the 12-week instructional period the corresponding five subtests from TTCT, Form A, were administered to all students.

Treatment of Data

The data were analyzed using a $2 \times 2 \times 3$ multivariate analysis of variance for unequal cells. The independent variables were class type (gifted or regular), treatment (PCTP or control), and grade (four, five, or six). The six dependent variables were verbal and figural fluency, flexibility, and originality. Analyses were conducted using simple gain scores (posttest minus pretest).

A multivariate analysis of variance was conducted; where significant values occurred for Wilks's (1932) lambda criterion (λ) univariate analyses (ANOVAs) were conducted for each dependent variable. The significance of Wilks's lambda was tested using the table in Timm (1975, p. 635). When significant Fs were obtained on the ANOVAs, appropriate Scheffé post hoc contrasts were conducted. The .05 level of significance was the criterion for all tests.

Results

Differences among groups prior to treatment were determined by 4×1 ANOVAs and post hoc Scheffé tests on TTCT pretest scores. For the ANOVAs the independent variables were four groups of subjects: (a) gifted experimentals, (b) gifted controls, (c) regular students in experimental groups, and (d) regular students in control groups. The dependent variable for each of the ANOVAs was a creative thinking component (verbal and figural fluency, flexibility, or originality) for each of the verbal and nonverbal subtest tasks. For example, on one ANOVA the dependent variable was the fluency score derived from the verbal task Product Improvement. Results from the analyses indicated a trend for gifted subjects to score higher on verbal subtests and for subjects in regular classes to score higher on nonverbal tasks, except for the sixth grade. The gifted sixth-grade subjects exhibited a trend to also be superior to regular students on figural tasks. A trend for the fifth- and sixth-grade gifted experimentals to be superior initially to gifted controls on verbal tasks was indicated.

At the end of the experimental period TTCT posttests were administered and difference scores computed. As shown in Table 2, the MANOVA on these difference scores revealed significant ($p < .05$) differences in the group centroids for the main

Table 2
Results of Multivariate Analysis of Variance in Order of Hypotheses Tested

Effect tested	U^a	$U_{.95}{}^b$	df
A × B × C	.9646*	.9654	6, 2,600
Class type (A)	.9577*	.9791	6, 1,600
Treatment (B)	.9560*	.9791	6, 1,600
Grade (C)	.9591*	.9654	6, 2,600
A × B	.9860	.9791	6, 1,600
B × C	.9584*	.9654	6, 2,600
A × C	.9823	.9654	6, 2,600

[a] Computed value of Wilks's lambda (result of multivariate analysis of variance). Significant values are smaller than critical values.
[b] Critical value of Wilks's lambda (see Timm, 1975).
* $p < .05$.

Table 3
Mean Torrance Tests of Creative Thinking Gain Scores

Variable	Gifted		Regular	
	Treatment	Control	Treatment	Control
		Grade 4		
1	5.55	3.27	1.89	−.31
2	−.49	−.49	.13	−.58
3	1.04	.55	3.81	−5.58
4	3.38	5.33	3.64	1.42
5	3.02	4.45	4.44	2.60
6	.58	−2.94	.56	−1.38
		Grade 5		
1	7.94	4.49	6.05	−5.26
2	.11	2.80	1.92	−1.78
3	3.23	1.61	3.83	−10.00
4	4.40	3.94	3.90	2.39
5	3.38	5.10	5.05	4.37
6	.94	.02	6.30	−1.63
		Grade 6		
1	4.88	.71	.40	−2.94
2	.50	−.65	−2.68	−3.39
3	−.62	−.16	−6.38	−3.78
4	5.60	6.07	4.56	6.59
5	3.71	4.07	4.06	4.72
6	−.62	3.82	2.95	1.19

Note. Variables: 1 = verbal fluency; 2 = verbal flexibility; 3 = verbal originality; 4 = figural fluency; 5 = figural flexibility; 6 = figural originality.

effects of class type, treatment, and grade. The Treatment × Grade and Treatment × Grade × Class Type interactions were also significant. There were no significant differences in the group centroids of either Class Type × Treatment or Class Type × Grade interactions. Table 3 gives the mean TTCT gain scores on each dependent variable. Table 4 gives the mean TTCT gain scores for experimentals and controls by class type on verbal fluency.

To determine the source of the differences that were significant on the MANOVA,

univariate ANOVAs were conducted for each dependent variable. Table 5 summarizes the significant results of the univariate ANOVAs on TTCT gain scores. For verbal fluency two main effects were significant: class type, $F(1, 636) = 11.41$, $p < .05$, and treatment, $F(1, 636) = 11.56$, $p < .05$. Since the hypotheses for this research concerned treatment effects, no other results are discussed. For verbal fluency the treatment group (PCTP) mean gain scores (4.23) were significantly greater than the mean gain scores (.04) of the no-treatment group. Although the Class Type × Treatment interaction for figural flexibility was significant in the univariate analysis, it was not further analyzed due to its nonsignificance on the MANOVA. The Grade × Treatment interaction on the MANOVA was significant; however, there were no significant differences on any of the ANOVAs.

Interpretation and Discussion

In general, the results of this research warrant the conclusion that the self-instructional use of the PCTP enhanced some divergent thinking abilities among students. The experimental groups had significantly greater gain scores for verbal fluency than did the control groups. This finding is consistent with previous research employing the PCTP with elementary school students (Feldhusen, Bahlke, & Treffinger, 1969;

Table 4
Mean Verbal Fluency Gain Scores by Group and Class Type Averaged Across Grades

Class type	Group	
	Experimental	Control
Regular	2.72	−2.74
Gifted	6.05	2.76
M	4.23	.04

Feldhusen, Treffinger, & Thomas, 1971; Speedie, Treffinger, & Feldhusen, 1971; Shively et al. 1972; Treffinger, Speedie, & Brunner, 1974). The PCTP seems to be an effective instructional program for fostering the divergent thinking variable of verbal fluency when used with classroom groups or in a self-instructional approach.

Prior research has suggested that gifted students make greater achievement gains with programmed materials than through traditional instruction (Hanson & Komoski, 1965; Shackel & Lawrence, 1969; Stolurow, 1962). The results of the present study, however, do not indicate any significant interaction between class type and treatment.

The absence of a significant interaction between treatment and class type may have been influenced by several factors. Given the initially high divergent thinking scores of students in the gifted classes, for example, there may have been less opportunity for gains (cf. Olton et al., 1967; Wardrop, Olton, Goodwin, Covington, Klausmeier, Crutchfield, & Ronda, 1969). The PCTP activities and format may not have been as attractive or interesting to gifted students as to students in regular classes (cf. Feldhusen, Elias, & Treffinger, 1969). The self-contained classes for gifted students were fast-paced, with many diverse activities competing for the student's time and energy.

Although the results of the MANOVA yielded a significant Treatment × Grade interaction, subsequent analyses failed to indicate the source of that interaction. The program was equally effective for Grades 4, 5, and 6.

A significant interaction for Class Type × Treatment × Grade was found by MANOVA. However, univariate analyses on each dependent variable failed to clarify the source of the interaction. This is not unusual in MANOVA, since the correlated variables can reach significance if considered

Table 5
Summary of Significant Effects in Univariate Analysis of Variance on Each Dependent Variable

Dependent variables	Significant independent variables
Verbal fluency	Class type**
	Treatment**
Verbal flexibility	Grade*
Verbal originality	ns
Figural fluency	Grade*
Figural flexibility	Class Type × Treatment*
Figural originality	ns

* $p < .05$.   ** $p < .001$.

in combination but may not be significant singly (Winer, 1962).

Implementing any educational program or curriculum on an individualized basis is fraught with problems. Many experienced teachers were not trained to individualize instruction for their students. It may be very difficult for such teachers to move away from teacher-controlled expository teaching. Other teachers do not believe that children can direct their own learning activities effectively. This attitude can influence the success of efforts in that direction by colleagues, researchers, or students. In the classroom the PCTP constituted only a very small part of the total school program and classroom environment. It may not have involved ample time for students to learn to develop the skills needed for self-directed learning, even among gifted students. Learning styles, personality variables, and previous experiences can influence the willingness of children to undertake learning on their own. Systematic assistance may therefore be needed to assist students and teachers to implement self-directed learning models successfully and efficiently (Mosston, 1972; Treffinger, 1975, 1978).

Absence of gains on the figural variables may have been related to the specific choices of tapes and exercises made by the students. Some of the tapes and exercises provided more opportunities for the exercise of figural abilities than others. It is also possible that the figural abilities require greater instructional efforts, student practice, or teacher interaction.

Limitations of Research

The analyses of pretest scores for all subjects revealed a trend toward superiority of the gifted subject on verbal tasks for the fourth-grade students and for verbal and figural tasks for fifth- and sixth-grade students. To the degree that the TTCT have ceilings, this initial superiority could have contributed to two effects: (a) the lack of superior gain scores for the gifted students as was hypothesized; and (b) the lack of significant gain scores on nonverbal tasks, possibly due to the numbers of circles, pairs of lines, and incomplete figures presented to the subjects. Since the verbal tasks are more open-ended, a ceiling effect is more difficult to discern, although there is a limit to the number of pages where children may write their ideas and the amount of time given to each subtest. Future research with gifted children might take these considerations into account and elucidate this problem.

Conclusions

The results of this study provide limited, but significant, support for the effectiveness of programmed creativity instructional materials when implemented on a student-directed basis. The program was successful in influencing verbal fluency for gifted and regular students in Grades 4, 5, and 6.

Future research may be directed profitably to several questions: What are the effects of group instruction with the PCTP on gifted students' creative thinking abilities? What are the effects of using other creativity instructional programs on a self-instructional basis? How can students learn to manage and direct their own learning, creative thinking, and problem-solving? What are the influences of various student characteristics and teacher influences upon the success of individualized, learner-directed, creativity instructional programs?

Reference Note

1. Martinson, R. A. *The identification of the gifted and talented.* Office of the Ventura County Superintendent of Schools, Ventura, California, 1974.

References

Barbe, W. B., & Renzulli, J. S. (Eds.). *Psychology and education of the gifted* (2nd ed.). New York: Irvington, 1975.

Davis, G. A. *Psychology of problem solving.* New York: Basic Books, 1973.

Feldhusen, J. F. Programming and the talented pupil. *Clearinghouse,* 1963, *38,* 151–154.

Feldhusen, J. F., Bahlke, S. J., & Treffinger, D. J. Teaching creative thinking. *Elementary School Journal,* 1969, *70,* 48–53.

Feldhusen, J. F., Elias, R. M., & Treffinger, D. J. The right kind of programmed instruction for the gifted and talented. *NSPI Journal,* 1969, *8,* 6–11.

Feldhusen, J. F., Treffinger, D. J., & Bahlke, S. J. Developing creative thinking: The Purdue Creativity Program. *Journal of Creative Behavior,* 1970, *4,* 85–90.

Feldhusen, J. F., Treffinger, D. J., & Thomas, S. J. *Global and componential evaluation of creativity training materials* (Creative Education Foundation Monograph). Buffalo, N.Y.: Creative Education Foundation, State University College, 1971.

Gallagher, J. J. Characteristics of gifted children: A research summary. In W. B. Barbe & J. S. Renzulli (Eds.), *Psychology and education of the gifted* (2nd ed.). New York: Irvington, 1975.

Guilford, J. P. Three faces of intellect. In W. B. Barbe & J. S. Renzulli (Eds.), *Psychology and education of the gifted* (2nd ed.). New York: Irvington, 1975.

Hanson, L. F., & Komoski, P. K. School use of programmed instruction. In R. Glaser (Ed.), *Teaching machines and programmed instruction. II: Data and directions.* Washington, D.C.: Department of Audio-Visual Instruction, National Education Association, 1965.

Mosston, M. *Teaching: From command to discovery.* Belmont, Calif.: Wadsworth, 1972.

Olton, R. M., Wardrop, J. L., Covington, M. V., Crutchfield, R. S., Goodwin, W. L., Klausmeier, H. J., & Ronda, T. *The development of productive thinking skills in fifth-grade children.* Madison: Wisconsin Research and Development Center for Cognitive Learning, University of Wisconsin, November 1967.

Robinson, W. L. T. *Taped creativity series vs. conventional teaching and learning.* Unpublished master's thesis, Atlanta University, 1969.

Shackel, D. S. J., & Lawrence, F. J. Improving creativity through programmed instruction. *New Zealand Journal of Educational Studies,* 1969, *4,* 41–56.

Shively, J. E., Feldhusen, J. F., & Treffinger, D. J. Developing creativity and related attitudes. *Journal of Experimental Education,* 1972, *41,* 63–69.

Speedie, S. M., Treffinger, D. J., & Feldhusen, J. F. Evaluation of components of the Purdue Creative Thinking Program: A longitudinal study. *Psychological Reports,* 1971, *29,* 395–398.

Stolurow, L. M. Implications of current research and future trends in programmed instruction. *Journal of Educational Research,* 1962, *55,* 517–519.

Timm, N. H. *Multivariate analysis with applications in education and psychology.* Belmont, Calif.: Wadsworth, 1975.

Torrance, E. P. Can we teach children to think creatively? *Journal of Creative Behavior,* 1972, *6,* 114–143. (a)

Torrance, E. P. Predictive validity of the Torrance Tests of Creative Thinking. *Journal of Creative Behavior,* 1972, *6,* 236–262. (b)

Torrance, E. P. *Torrance Tests of Creative Thinking.* Princeton, N.J.: Personnel Press, 1974. (a)

Torrance, E. P. *Torrance Tests of Creative Thinking: Norms-technical manual.* Princeton, N.J.: Personnel Press, 1974. (b)

Treffinger, D. J. Teaching for self-directed learning: A priority for the gifted and talented. *Gifted Child Quarterly,* 1975, *29,* 46–59.

Treffinger, D. J. Methods, techniques, and educational programs for stimulating creativity (1975 revision). In S. J. Parnes, R. B. Noller, & A. M. Biondi (Eds.), *Guide to creative action.* New York: Scribner, 1977.

Treffinger, D. J. Guidelines for encouraging independence and self-direction among gifted students. *Journal of Creative Behavior,* 1978, *12,* 14–20.

Treffinger, D. J., & Poggio, J. P. Needed research on the measurement of creatvity. *Journal of Creative Behavior,* 1972, *6,* 253–267.

Treffinger, D. J., Renzulli, J. S., & Feldhusen, J. F. Problems in the assessment of creative thinking. *Journal of Creative Behavior,* 1971, *5,* 104–112.

Treffinger, D. J., Speedie, S. M., & Brunner, W. D. Improving children's creative problem solving ability: The Purdue creativity project. *Journal of Creative Behavior,* 1974, *8,* 20–30.

Wardrop, J. L., Olton, R. M., Goodwin, W. L., Covington, M. V., Klausmeier, H. J., Crutchfield, R. S., & Ronda, T. The development of productive thinking skills in fifth grade children. *Journal of Experimental Education,* 1969, *37,* 67–77.

Weisgerber, R. A. *Perspectives in individualized learning.* Itasca, Ill.: Peacock, 1971.

Wilks, S. S. Certain generalizations in the analysis of variance. *Biometrika,* 1932, *24,* 471–494.

Winer, B. J. *Statistical principles in experimental design.* New York: McGraw-Hill, 1962.

Comments on the Introduction Section

We shall comment on each paragraph of the Introduction section.

1. *First paragraph.* Gives a general rationale for "fostering creative thinking" and "new emphases."

2. *Second paragraph.* Gives a slightly more specific rationale on materials for "creativity training programs." The last sentence provides a specific initial rationale for the study, namely, "none . . . has been tested on an individualized, self-paced basis, or for specific use with gifted students."

3. *Third paragraph.* Gives a specific rationale for using individualized instruction with gifted students.

4. *Fourth paragraph.* Specifies a rationale for using a particular individualized program, namely, the Purdue Creativity Training Program (PCTP). Is the description of the specific treatment appropriate here or should it appear under a Procedure subsection that describes the main independent variables in the study?

5. *Fifth paragraph.* Gives a more specific rationale for using the Purdue Creativity Training Program on a self-instructional basis. Again, should this appear in the Procedure subsection? If the main thrust of the research is to evaluate the effectiveness of a particular instrument (the PCTP) rather than the conceptual variable (programmed instruction materials), then an extensive rationale in the Introduction is not unusual for a particular instrument. However, if the conceptual level variable is the main focus—that is, more broadly, instructional programs—then the PCTP is only one operational statement of that conceptual variable and should be discussed more appropriately in the Procedure subsection.

6. *Sixth paragraph.* Presents a more specific rationale for using programmed creativity training materials to facilitate the creative thinking of gifted students, along with an initial indication that the dependent measure may be a creativity measure.

7. *Seventh paragraph.* Presents one main and two secondary hypotheses in a research question format. The first asks, is the PCTP effective regardless of the type of student, "gifted or regular?" Thus a significant main effect due to PCTP is being proposed. The second hypothesis relates to whether there will be an interaction between grade and type of student. No rationale was presented for these two predictions. Based on the general rationale in paragraphs four and five, a rationale was presented for the main hypothesis related to PCTP effectiveness.

In the Introduction, there is no explicit statement of the purpose or problem. From the information presented we can infer the following variables: (1) program at two levels: PCTP and no-PCTP; (2) class type at two levels: gifted and regular; (3) grade at three levels; four, five, and six. There is no explicit statement of the dependent variable either. However, a rationale for a creativity measure is found in the Method section, where six dependent variables are presented: verbal fluency, flexibility, and originality scores; and figural fluency, flexibility, and originality scores. More specifically, gain scores (posttest minus pretest scores) for each of the six measures are calculated.

Now, based on the additional information in the Method section, we can give a complete purpose statement:

> The main purpose of this study is to determine
> the effectiveness of self-paced programmed
> creativity instruction compared to no instruc-

> tion in increasing creativity in elementary school children. Gain scores on six creativity measures are calculated for both verbal and figural creativity: fluency, flexibility, and originality. In addition, the type of student at two levels (gifted and regular) and grade at three levels (four, five, and six) are also examined.

Returning to the statement of hypotheses in paragraph seven of the Introduction, we have no specific statement as to whether a prediction relates to all six dependent measures or to the verbal or to the figural scores. Thus, if we infer an effect for all of the six measures, we can restate the first hypothesis as follows:

> PCTP will result in significantly increased gain scores on the six creativity measures compared to no-PCTP.

Since there is no rationale or specific comparison given for the other two research questions, they can either be omitted or presented as nondirectional alternative hypotheses.

Considering the review of the literature as it relates to the purpose and hypothesis, we find that the first five paragraphs relate to a rationale for the main independent variable: instructional program at two levels: PCTP and no-PCTP. In paragraph six there is a brief initial rationale for examining creativity as the dependent measure. Also, in the last sentences of paragraphs two and three, there is a brief rationale for examining gifted students.

Comments on the Method Section

Subjects. In the Subjects section, paragraph one gives the total number of subjects, but not how they were selected from the schools. Sentences three and four indicate that 18 classes were randomly assigned or designated as the experimental classes; the remaining 18 became the control. Thus, it is not clear whether the 309 or the 339 subjects in the two groups represent a random selection from the 36 classes or whether the classrooms were selected randomly and these numbers represent the total number of subjects in each class. In other words, it is not clear whether simple random or cluster random sampling was employed.

In paragraph two, we find important environmental and personological variables described: city size, socioeconomic status, sex, and race. Perhaps statistical comparisons between the groups on the pretest measured by these variables would have provided technical support rather than just descriptive support that these groups a priori were equivalent. In other words, multiple *t*-tests, for example, could have been performed on each of the environmental and personological variables with the pretest scores to determine whether pretest performance by sex, race, socioeconomic status, or city size were comparable.

In paragraph three, we find a description of criteria that distinguishes the gifted from the regular student. The phrase "academic excellence" could be operationally defined in terms of G.P.A. perhaps; "individual test" for the IQ measure could also be defined. Finally, "good" development could be more specifically delineated. Table 1 usefully presents the number of subjects in each cell; however, the subjects could easily be included in Table 3.

Research design.   In the first paragraph we find the research design, a 2 × 2 × 3 MANOVA, as well as the independent and dependent variables. In paragraph two there is a statistical modification of an existing computer program. However, MANOVA analyses are available; these modifications should be extensively documented and available for examination by interested researchers.

Instruments and scoring.   Paragraph one contains an operational statement of the dependent measure. Type and extent of training might also have been included; the Torrance Test of Creative Thinking (TTCT) requires considerable expertise in scoring subjects' responses validly and reliably.

Paragraph two delineates specific subtests. It might well have stated which alternate forms were used, and when. Appropriate alternate form reliability coefficients could be presented in this section or the next. Rater reliabilities are given and are high. It might well have stated how many raters were used and the median rating. Also, it could have given a description of the norms and the appropriateness of the TTCT for this population.

Reliability and validity of the TTCT.   In paragraph one, the first sentence concerns the reliability of the TTCT, and the remaining two sentences concern its criterion-related predictive validity. More specific information might have been provided, such as the type of reliability; alternate form reliability would be most appropriate here, since different forms were used. In addition, the range or median of the pertinent reliability coefficients could be presented. Do differences exist in the reliability or validity of the TTCT when measured by the six scoring procedures? That is to say, are some subtests more reliable or valid than others? Specific pertinent criterion measures should be reported as well as the range and median of the validity coefficients. As mentioned in the last section, is the reliability and validity of the TTCT derived from a comparable standardization sample? That is to say, is the norm group appropriate?

In paragraph two, there is evidence of the content validity of the TTCT. Citing its author and others, the basic conclusion reached is that the abilities measured by the TTCT comprise a necessary subset of the total set of creative abilities, but are not complete. In other words, divergent thinking ability measured by the TTCT is only one of many characteristics of the creative individual.

Data collection procedures.   In paragraph one we find the specific training and instructions given to the teachers who would be using the PCTP in the classroom.

In paragraph two is given the pretest administration procedure for the TTCT, Form B. In paragraph three is a description of the use of the PCTP. The last sentence states that the posttest was also administered. An important confounding variable which is not given is the total amount of time each child used the PCTP or comparable measures, such as the number of tapes completed or the exercises scored. In other words, the amount of time in the treatment may affect the subjects' scores on the TTCT. Also, what is the rationale for a twelve-week training period? Is twelve weeks too short a time to significantly affect one's level of creativity? In the Procedure subsection it might be useful to consider these possible confounding variables and any others that might operate. Discussion would focus on how the procedures employed in this study minimized threats to internal or external validity.

Treatment of data.   The first paragraph summarizes the statistical design and the independent and dependent variables. The second paragraph gives an overview of the statistics in the Results section. It serves as a transition to the Results section.

Comments on the Results Section

The first paragraph of the Results section confusingly attempts to equate the groups prior to the treatment. In the fifth sentence an attempt is made to give the results of the descriptive and/or inferential statistics on the pretest scores. It is not clear what the intention of the first paragraph is. If it is an attempt to empirically determine whether the groups are equivalent on the pretest scores according to the main independent variables, then descriptive statistics as the mean and standard deviation should be included for the pretest and posttest scores.

In the second paragraph we find the significant results of the multivariate analysis of variance (MANOVA), and the reader is directed to tables 2, 3, and 4. This paragraph presents the results of the inferential statistics calculated, and paragraph three gives the results of the supporting inferential statistics, in this case one-way ANOVAs. With multivariate statistics, the post hoc or a posteriori tests that may be calculated are univariate ANOVAs rather than a Tukey HSD or Scheffé test. The third and fourth sentences of paragraph three reveal that significance was obtained, for class type and for treatment, but, since each main effect had two levels, inspection of gain score means was adequate—that is, ANOVAs did not need to be calculated for those main effects with only two levels. The last two sentences discuss results that were not further analyzed, in the first instance because of the overall nonsignificance of the MANOVA. Thus the significant difference obtained from the ANOVA was attributed to chance or error. In the second instance, an overall grade X treatment interaction was significant on the MANOVA, but no significant differences were obtained on the ANOVAs. This analysis uses a conservative approach inasmuch as the authors did not wish to conclude that differences existed (based on the MANOVA) when significant differences were not obtained subsequently (based on the ANOVA). A rationale for this relationship is given in the fifth paragraph of the Discussion section.

Comments on the Discussion Section

Interpretation and discussion.   The first paragraph expresses the general conclusion that self-instruction enhances some divergent thinking skills, specifically verbal fluency. The second and third paragraphs discuss the nonsignificance of the class type and treatment interaction, and give some possible reasons from the research literature for the nonsignificance. The fourth and fifth paragraphs discuss the overall MANOVA significance and the subsequent nonsignificance of the univariate analyses. A statistical rationale is provided. The sixth paragraph presents educational implications for implementing an individualized program. Possible confounding variables are also given: teacher attitudes, time, learning styles, personality variables, and previous experience. Systematic assistance is a vehicle proposed to minimize the influence of these confounding variables. The seventh paragraph presents a rationale for the absence of gains on the figural variables.

Limitations of research.   This paragraph points out a limitation because of a ceiling effect of the TTCT for gifted children. Supporting research from the literature for this statement would be useful.

Conclusions. The first paragraph summarizes the main findings, and the second paragraph generates questions for future research. Thus, in this study the third and fourth steps of the Discussion section are included under separate headings. In the remaining section we shall give an organizational format for communicating the research process.

Writing the Research Article

The format and style of professional writing in educational research typically involves two main aspects: the substantive information in the article and its logical arrangement, and the technical format or the way the information is written; that is, the mechanics of the writing (Angell, 1973). Up to this point in the book, we have discussed the basic information and its logical arrangement for each section of the research article. We shall now focus on the mechanics of style.

The mechanics of writing includes the format and placement of headings, tables, figures, quotations, footnotes, and references, as well as punctuation, capitalization, and spelling. Most departments and schools within universities have their accepted style for papers, theses, and dissertations; many have developed a style manual for students to follow. If your research is for a graduate school, you will want to use their style manual. If you are writing for journal publication, find out the required style for that journal. Style manuals used in educational writing include the APA manual (1974), Turabian (1973), Campbell and Ballou (1977), and Dugdale (1972). You are urged to choose one style and use it consistently as specified. The technical recommendations in each manual are given in order to standardize the presentation and format of articles throughout the journal publications.

Using APA style, an example of a recommended organization for a journal article is given here:

Journal Article Organization

Title (12-15 words)

Author's name and institutional affiliation

Abstract (100-175 words)

Introduction (presented without a heading and without side headings)

Method (first-level heading, a side heading as needed, and an indented paragraph heading as needed)

Results (first-level heading, a side heading as needed, and an indented paragraph heading as needed)

Discussion (first-level heading, a side heading as needed, and an indented paragraph heading as needed)

References (first-level heading; only references cited in the article are included)

Appendix (first-level heading; only infrequently needed)

A summary checklist for each section of the research article is helpful for clearly and concisely communicating the research process.

Title
— 1. Length is 12–15 words
— 2. Main variables are stated
— 3. Relationship of variables is presented
— 4. Population is stated
— 5. Redundancy is avoided (such as "a study of")

Title Page
— 1. Title
— 2. Author's name(s)
— 3. Institutional affiliation
— 4. Running head (2- to 5-word shortened title placed on each page of manuscript)

Abstract
— 1. Write it after completing the entire article
— 2. State purpose or problem
— 3. Include method and population
— 4. Give main results
— 5. State main conclusions
— 6. Make it succinct, accurate, and self-contained
— 7. Keep it to 100–175 words

Introduction
— 1. No heading
— 2. General to specific review of literature
— 3. Complete purpose or problem statement
— 4. Specific rationale for hypothesis
— 5. Complete hypothesis

Method
— 1. Present first-level heading for *Method* section
— 2. Present side headings for *Subjects, Procedure,* and *Instrumentation*
— 3. Present indented paragraph headings for each subheading under the three subsections above

Subjects

__ 1. Present sample demographic information
__ 2. Give number of subjects
__ 3. Detail selection of subjects
__ 4. Present other unique conditions as appropriate, such as payments, ethical considerations, and so on

Procedure

__ 1. State specific, succinct summary of steps in the research process
__ 2. Give operational definition of each independent variable
__ 3. Present other unique conditions as appropriate, such as control variables

Instrumentation

__ 1. State operational definition of each dependent variable
__ 2. Provide technical information as appropriate: norms, reliability, validity

Results

__ 1. Present first-level heading for *Results* section
__ 2. Present side headings as appropriate
__ 3. Present overview statement of statistics
__ 4. Give descriptive statistics
__ 5. State assumptions for inferential statistics
__ 6. Detail main inferential statistics
__ 7. Present supporting inferential statistics
__ 8. Use tables and figures as appropriate

Discussion

__ 1. Present first-level heading for *Discussion* section
__ 2. Present side headings as appropriate
__ 3. Present support (or nonsupport) statement of hypothesis
__ 4. Discuss theoretical, research, and educational implications
__ 5. Present brief limitations of study
__ 6. Present brief suggestions for future research
__ 7. Avoid overgeneralizations
__ 8. Integrate *Discussion* with previous components

References

__ 1. Present first-level heading for *References* section
__ 2. Include only cited references
__ 3. Provide complete documentation for each reference

Additional technical considerations

__ 1. Abbreviations
__ 2. Metrication
__ 3. Table titles and format

— 4. Figure captions and format
— 5. Quotations
— 6. Reference citations in text
— 7. Reference notes
— 8. Footnotes
— 9. Punctuation
—10. Spelling
—11. Capitalization
—12. Italic and boldface type

Additional writing style considerations

— 1. Use words correctly
— 2. Avoid ambiguity
— 3. Present logical arrangement of ideas
— 4. Use smooth or straightforward phrasing
— 5. Give complete information

In the field of educational research, the journal article is one format that has evolved to enable professionals in the field to communicate

Completed Research Is as a Work of Art

with each other in a standard, sensible, and succinct style. It has evolved as a conventional and acceptable format with known components and particular substantive expectations. Other forms of communication obviously are employed, but the research journal article continues to be the main vehicle for interaction throughout a field of research. Thus, throughout this book the author has tried to detail the role of the scientific method and the educational research process in the complementary processes of developing or evaluating a research-based journal article.

SUMMARY

We have summarized the key substantive features that should be included in each section and subsection of the research article. We have examined these features in a complete journal article. Finally, we have given suggestions for the mechanics of writing the research article and included a summary checklist for integrating the substantive information of the research process with the mechanics and technical information.

OBJECTIVES

We have come a long way in our consideration of educational research and the scientific method as presented within a journal article. We know the substantive components of each section of the research process as well as the basic mechanics of writing for communicating with others. Confirm your understanding of the material in Chapter 12 using the following objectives:

Evaluate each component of the research process in terms of its completeness and the specificity of information.
Determine the technical considerations required by each journal.
Determine the usefulness or utility of that research for your professional concerns.

TERMS

Style manuals: Dugdale
APA manual   Turabian
Campbell and Ballou

Appendix A

Review of Selected Standardized Tests

Intelligence Tests

The major individually administered intelligence tests we will describe are:

Wechsler Preschool and Primary Scale of Intelligence (WPPSI)
Wechsler Intelligence Scale for Children–Revised (WISC–R)
Wechsler Adult Intelligence Scale–Revised (WAIS–R)
Stanford-Binet Intelligence Scale

The major group administered intelligence tests we will examine are:

Cognitive Abilities Test (CAT)
Otis-Lennon Mental Ability Test (OLMAT)
Test of Cognitive Skills (TCS)

Other measures will be discussed in the context of examining these tests.

Individually Administered Intelligence Tests

Wechsler Preschool and Primary Scale of Intelligence (WPPSI). This test was published by The Psychological Corporation in 1967 and is designed to be individually administered to children between the ages of 4 and 6½ years. Six main subtests comprise the Verbal Scale: information, vocabulary, arithmetic, similarities, comprehension, and sentences. Five main subtests comprise the Performance Scale: animal house, picture completion, mazes, geometric design, and block design. Total testing time ranges from fifty to seventy-five minutes; one or two testing sessions typically are used. Verbal, Performance, and Full Scale IQs are obtained from the subtests. IQ score is derived from a mean of 100 and a standard deviation of 15; subtest scores are converted from a raw score to a standard or scaled score with a mean of 10 and a standard deviation of 3. Twelve hundred children—100 boys and 100 girls in six half-year age groups from 4 to 6½—comprised the standardization sample. According to the proportions derived from the 1960 census, the group was stratified by age, sex, geographical region, urban-rural, proportion of whites and nonwhites, and occupational levels of fathers.

Wechsler Intelligence Scale for Children-Revised (WISC-R). The WISC-R, published in 1974 by The Psychological Corporation, is designed to be individually administered to children between the ages of 6 and 16 in fifty to seventy-five minutes. Six main subtests comparable to both the WPPSI and the WAIS comprise the Verbal Scale: information, similarities, arithmetic, vocabulary, comprehension, and digit span. Five main subtests, of which three are comparable to the WPPSI and all are comparable to the WAIS, comprise the Performance Scale: picture completion, picture arrangement, block design, object assembly, and coding (or mazes). As in both the WPPSI and the WAIS, Verbal, Performance, and Full Scale IQs are obtained from the subject's performance on the subtests. Each IQ score is standardized on a mean of 100 and a standard deviation of 15; subtest scores are converted in the norm tables from raw scores to scaled or standard scores with a mean of 10 and a standard deviation of 3. Twenty-two hundred children—100 boys and 100 girls at each of eleven age levels—comprised the standardization sample. Based on the distributions obtained from the 1970 census, the group was stratified by three main variables in addition to age and sex: geographical region, urban-rural, and proportion of whites and nonwhites.

Wechsler Adult Intelligence Scale-Revised (WAIS-R). The WAIS-R was published in 1981 by The Psychological Corporation and is the first revision of the original WAIS published in 1955. It is designed to be individually administered, and testing time for adults ranges from sixty to ninety minutes. Norms are available from 16 years to 74 years, 11 months. Six subtests comprise the Verbal Scale: information, digit span, vocabulary, arithmetic, comprehension, and similarities. Five subtests comprise the Performance Scale: picture completion, picture arrangement, block design, object assembly, and digit symbol. Verbal, Performance, and Full Scale IQs are obtained and are standardized on a mean of 100 and a standard deviation of 15; subtest scaled scores are standardized on a mean of 10 and a standard deviation of 3. The WAIS-R standardization sample was composed of 1,880 adults separated into nine age groups. The sample also was stratified by sex, proportion of whites and nonwhites, geographical region, occupation, and education.

Stanford-Binet Intelligence Scale.   The current revision of the Stanford-Binet was published in 1973 by Houghton Mifflin. This revision, entitled Form L-M, incorporates the best subtests from previous separate versions published in 1937, which were combined in a 1960 version. The test content of the 1973 version essentially remained the same as that of the 1960 version, with only two minor changes. A major change did take place, however: the test was restandardized. Form L-M may be administered to individuals from age 2 through the adult years; testing time ranges from thirty minutes for younger subjects to ninety minutes for older subjects. However, the test is not recommended for adults of normal or superior intelligence (Anastasi, 1976, p. 236). There is an insufficient difficulty level or ceiling to the test, i.e., items are too easy for most superior adults or adolescents. In addition, the test has more appeal and interest for children. The Stanford-Binet consists of tests grouped into age levels from age II to superior adult. From age II to age V, the test proceeds by half-year intervals, e.g., II, II-6, III, III-6, and so on. From age V to age XIV, yearly age-level tests are presented. The four remaining levels include the Average Adult level and Superior Adult levels I, II, and III. There are six tests for each age level except the Average Adult, which has eight tests. The test obtains a mental age and an IQ, which is standardized on a mean of 100 and a standard deviation of 16. Most of the tests are of a verbal nature. For example, the six tasks at the VIII year level are vocabulary, memory for stories, verbal absurdities, similarities and differences, comprehension, and naming the days of the week. Other age levels do have nonverbal tasks, such as copying a square at year V or copying a diamond at year VII; but verbal tasks are predominant. The 1973 restandardization sample was comprised of approximately 2,100 subjects, with 100 at each half-year age group from 2 to 5½ and 100 at each one-year age group from 6 to 18.

All three of the Wechsler tests as well as the Stanford-Binet require special training for test examiners in administering, scoring, and interpretation. An obvious disadvantage of an individually administered test is that it is time consuming and thus costly. A main advantage is the greater depth and breadth of information obtainable from one subject. In those situations where individual measures are not feasible, group intelligence tests are employed.

Group Administered Intelligence Tests

Cognitive Abilities Test (CAT).   This test, published in 1978 by Houghton Mifflin, is a revision of the older Lorge-Thorndike Intelligence Test published in 1954. The CAT is a group test designed to assess the mental ability of subjects from kindergarten through twelfth grade.

It includes two primary levels for K–1 and grades 2–3 and a multilevel edition for grades 3–12. The multilevel edition contains eight levels: each level overlaps items with other levels, and each has ten subtests arranged into three batteries. The verbal battery has four subtests: vocabulary, sentence completion, verbal classification, and verbal analogies. The quantitative battery has three subtests: quantitative relations, number series, and equation building. The nonverbal battery has three subtests also: figure classification, figure analogies, and figure synthesis. The primary levels contain four subtests that include oral vocabulary, multimental concepts, qualitative concepts, and relational concepts. Administration time is thirty-five minutes for each battery of the multilevel edition and twelve to sixteen minutes for each of the separate subtests of the primary level. The scores on each battery are expressed as a standard score with a mean of 100 and a standard deviation of 16. The manual does not advise combining the three battery scores into a single combined or total score. Percentile ranks, stanines, and grade equivalents also are available. The standardization sample consisted of approximately 19,000 subjects representing each grade of the school population of the country, and stratified variables included size of school district, geographical region, family income, education, and racial/ethnic population. The CAT was standardized on the same normative sample as were the Iowa Tests of Basic Skills (ITBS) and the Tests of Achievement and Proficiency (TAP).

Otis-Lennon Mental Ability Test.   The Otis-Lennon test was published in 1967 by The Psychological Corporation and was revised in 1979. It is the latest sequel to the Otis tests developed during the 1920s, the Otis Self-Administering Tests of Mental Ability, and the Otis Quick-Scoring Mental Ability tests developed in the 1930s and revised in the 1950s. Five levels comprise the current Otis-Lennon Mental Ability Test, used to measure the range of mental ability commonly found in grades 1–12. The Primary I level is recommended for use with most pupils in the first half of grade 1; less mature first graders should be tested in the second half-year. Norms are provided for both uses. The Primary I level has four main types of test items: classification or relations, following of directions, quantitative reasoning, and comprehension of verbal concepts; one total score is obtained. The test is orally administrated. The Elementary I level is recommended for use with students from the last half of grade 1 through the end of grade 3. Also orally administered, the test uses a total time of approximately fifty-five to sixty minutes in two testing sessions. Its items are similar to those in the previous level, with additional items to assess the ability to reason by analogy. One total score summarizes the performance on the eighty items. The final three levels,

Elementary II (grades 4–6). Intermediate (grades 7–9). and Advanced (grades 10–12). contain eighty verbal and figural items. e.g.. verbal and figural analogies. comprehension of verbal concepts. and quantitative reasoning to assess abstract reasoning ability. Time required for testing is approximately sixty to eighty-five minutes. An IQ standardized on a mean of 100 and a standard deviation of 16 was derived from each level with the 1967 edition of the test: however. the principal score in the 1979 edition is called the School Ability Index (SAI). Age and grade percentile ranks and stanines also are obtained through age 17 years and 11 months. or grade 12. The standardization sample included more than 200.000 subjects in 100 school systems from all fifty states.

Test of Cognitive Skills (TCS).   The TCS was published in 1981 by the California Test Bureau/McGraw-Hill and is a major revision of. and successor to. the Short Form Test of Academic Aptitude (SFTAA). published in 1970. The SFTAA was derived from the early 1963 California Test of Mental Maturity (CTMM). The TCS is based upon the Item Response Theory (IRT) developed by Lord. The TCS has four subtests: sequences (the ability to understand a rule of principle implicit in a sequence or pattern of numbers. letters. or figures): analogies (the ability to see concrete or abstract relationships and to classify relationships): memory (the ability to recall previously presented materials): and verbal reasoning (the ability to discern relationship and reason logically). Five levels are available: level 1 for grades 2–3: level 2 for grades 3–5: level 3 for grades 5–7: level 4 for grades 7–9: and level 5 for grades 9–12. Approximate time for administration is fifty-three minutes. Four subtest scores and a composite Cognitive Skills Index (CSI) score are derived. The CSI is standardized on a mean of 100 and a standard deviation of 16. Additional scores for percentile rank and stanine by age and grade. and a scaled score that ranges from 0 to 999. are available. The test was normed concurrently with the Comprehensive Tests of Basic Skills (CTBS) Form U. The standardization sample was comprised of 82.400 subjects in grades 2 through 12 from public. Catholic. and private schools stratified by four geographic regions in the second week of October 1980. Size of district was also considered in stratifying the public and Catholic populations.

Additional Intelligence and Aptitude Tests

A variety of individual and group intelligence tests are used in educational and psychological research. and many are used for particular functions. One is the Peabody Picture Vocabulary Test (PPVT). published by the American Guidance Service: it provides a relatively quick measure (fifteen minutes or less) of vocabulary and is especially useful with subjects unable to verbalize well, e.g., the cerebral palsied or the deaf. The Haptic Intelligence Scale for the Adult Blind (HIS–AB), published by Psychology Research, was developed as a nonverbal performance test for blind subjects aged 18 or over. The Bayley Scales of Infant Development, published by The Psychological Corporation, assesses the current developmental level of children between the ages of 2 months and 2½ years on three scales: Mental Scale, Motor Scale, and the Infant Behavior Record. The McCarthy Scales of Children's Abilities, also published by The Psychological Corporation, assesses children between the ages of 2½ and 8½ years on eighteen tests grouped into six scales that overlap: Verbal, Perceptual-Performance, Quantitative, General Cognitive, Memory, and Motor. Other tests such as the Goodenough-Harris Drawing Test and the Culture Fair Intelligence Test, published respectively by Harcourt Brace Jovanovich and the Institute of Personality and Ability Testing, have been used in cross-cultural testing and testing of different ethnic groups. They attempt to minimize the verbal dependency that tests have incorporated in them as well as to minimize cultural differences that might operate.

College qualification and aptitude tests also are used frequently in educational research. Two main ones are the American College Testing Program (ACT); and the College Board Scholastic Aptitude Test (SAT), published by the Educational Testing Service (ETS). The ACT test battery obtains five scores: English usage, mathematics usage, social studies reading, natural sciences reading, and a total combined score. For college bound seniors the mean is approximately 19 with a standard deviation of 5; testing time is approximately 160 minutes. From the SAT, verbal and mathematical scores are obtained, each with a mean of 500 and a standard deviation of 100; testing time is approximately 150 minutes.

Two of the most frequently used graduate aptitude tests are the Graduate Record Examination (GRE) and the Miller Analogies Tests (MAT), published respectively by ETS and The Psychological Corporation. The GRE yields three scores: verbal, quantitative, and analytical abilities. Each is standardized on a mean of 500 and a standard deviation of 100; range of scores is 200–800. Testing time is three hours. The MAT contains one hundred verbal analogy items in increasing difficulty with an allotted testing time of fifty minutes; five forms are available. Numerous norm groups have been derived; for example, the mean and the standard deviation for education students across six areas of specialty who applied to graduate programs between 1974 and 1978 are 48.6 and 16.8 respectively. The total number in the norm group was 4,005.

Achievement Tests

Achievement tests purport to measure the accomplishments of a student after a period of learning in order to determine the level of achievement that was attained. We will examine several of the general achievement tests that are used to assess a student's learning over a broad field of knowledge and that are typically used by school districts as part of their district testing plans to assess student growth. The main ones we will examine include:

Comprehensive Tests of Basic Skills (CTBS)
Iowa Tests of Basic Skills (ITBS)
Tests of Achievement and Proficiency (TAP)
Metropolitan Achievement Tests
SRA Achievement Series
Stanford Achievement Tests (SAT)
Stanford Test of Academic Skills (TASK)

Other measures will be discussed in the context of examining these tests.

Comprehensive Tests of Basic Skills (CTBS). The CTBS Form U was last published in 1981 by the California Test Bureau/McGraw-Hill. It is a revision of and replacement for the earlier California Achievement Tests. It assesses five areas of basic skills: mathematics, language, reading, spelling, and reference skills. Form U is available at nine levels: K–K.9, K.5–1.8, 1.0–2.9, 1.6–2.9, 2.5–3.9, 3.6–4.9, 4.5–6.9, 6.5–8.9, and 8.6–12.9. Two other versions, Form S and a Spanish edition, are available. Usually administered over four sessions, the test requires a total time ranging from 68 minutes for the lower level to 198 minutes for the higher level. Depending on the level, up to fifteen scores are obtained; standard scores are expressed with a mean of 600 and a standard deviation of 100. Percentile ranks, stanines, and grade equivalents also are available. The standardization sample for the final version was the same as that for the Test of Cognitive Skills (TCS) presented above.

Iowa Tests of Basic Skills (ITBS). The ITBS, published in 1978 by Houghton Mifflin, is the latest edition of the Iowa basic skills assessment begun in 1935. Two main batteries of the standard edition are available: a Primary Battery, which has four levels for grades K.1–1.5, K.8–1.9, 1.7–2.6, and 2.7–3.5; and a Multilevel Battery, which has six levels for grades 3, 4, 5, 6, 7, and 8–9. A basic edition also is available, with fewer subtests if testing time is limited: four hours and four minutes for the standard multilevel edition as compared to two hours and nineteen minutes for the basic edition. The eleven subtests of the Multilevel Battery are vocabulary and reading; a language section that includes subtests on spelling, capitalization, punctuation, and usage; a work-study section that includes subtests on visual materials and reference materials; and a mathematics section that includes subtests on concepts, problem solving, and computation. Two additional subtests in the content areas on science and social studies also are available in a separate booklet. Age equivalents, grade equivalents, percentile ranks, stanines, and normal curve equivalents are available. In addition, standard scores with a mean of 80 and a standard deviation of 20 are provided. Criterion-referenced interpretation of skills also is provided. The ITBS was standardized with the Cognitive Abilities Test and the Tests of Achievement and Proficiency. A total of approximately 19,000 students representing each grade was used for the standardization sample, and variables stratified were geographical region, size of school district, family income and education, and racial/ethnic population.

Tests of Achievement and Proficiency (TAP).   The appropriate upward extension achievement test to be used with the ITBS for grades 9 through 12 is the TAP. Also published in 1978 by Houghton Mifflin, it is the latest revision of the earlier Tests of Academic Progress. Four levels at each of grades 9–12 comprise the current test. Six main subtests, each forty minutes in length, have been developed: reading comprehension, mathematics, written expression, sources of information, social studies, and science. Percentile ranks, grade equivalent scores, stanines, and two nonscale scores—a minimum competency score and an applied proficiency skills score—are available.

Metropolitan Achievement Tests.   The Metropolitan Achievement Tests, last published in 1978 by Harcourt Brace Jovanovich, should not be confused with the Metropolitan Readiness Tests. Six levels of the test battery are available: primer, K.7–1.4; primary I, 1.5–2.4; primary II, 2.5–3.4; elementary, 3.5–4.9; intermediate, 5.0–6.9; and advanced, 7.0–9.5. Variations of six different subtests are used at different levels. For instance, at the primer level three skills are tested: word analysis or listening for sounds, reading, and mathematical concepts or numbers. At the primary II level seven subtests are used: word knowledge, word analysis, reading, spelling, mathematical computation, mathematical concepts, and mathematical problem solving. At the advanced level nine subtests are used; word analysis is omitted, and language, science, and social studies are added to those tests at the primary II level. Early levels such as the primer are administered orally; total testing time ranges from two to five hours in six to eight sessions. Stanines, grade equivalents, and percentile ranks are reported; standard scores are available, but their use is not encouraged. The mean and the standard deviation based on the latest test manual are not provided because, based on the examples presented, the scaled score value ranges from 0 to 999 and the mean and standard deviation will vary for each subtest. The standardization sample was comprised of over 550,000 students, and stratified variables included size of school district, public/nonpublic affiliation, geographical region, socioeconomic status, and ethnic background.

Science Research Associates (SRA) Achievement Series. The SRA Achievement Series, published in 1971 by Science Research Associates, is the latest revision of the series published in 1954, 1961, and 1964; it is designed to measure the educational development in basic curriculum areas of students in grades 1–9. The test publishers recommend that the appropriate upward extension for grades 9–12, the Iowa Tests of Educational Development, be used concurrently. A multilevel battery of the series, composed of three separate but overlapping tests, is designed for use in grades 4–9: the blue level for grades 4–6; the green level for grades 6–8; and the red level for grades 8–9. A primary level for grades 1–2, and an intermediate level for grades 2–4, also are available. Total testing time is five hours and fifteen minutes, with two sessions over two days recommended. The Short Test of Educational Ability (STEA), which requires thirty additional minutes, also can be included. Subtests of the multilevel achievement series include: reading, vocabulary, mathematics concepts, mathematics computation, language arts, spelling, social studies, use of sources, and science. Obtained scores include percentile ranks, grade equivalents, and stanines. An SRA Growth Scale Value (GSV) also expresses test results in similar units for the subject areas covered by the Iowa Tests of Educational Development; the GSV ranges from 0 to 850 for grades 1–12. The mean and the standard deviation are not standardized across subtests. In addition to the GSV, percentile ranks, stanines, and grade equivalents are available. Norms were obtained from 118,000 students in grades 1–9, and geographical region and type of school were included in the stratification. Norms are provided for large city schools, Title I schools, rural and small town schools, nonpublic schools, and high socioeconomic schools.

Stanford Achievement Tests (SAT). The SAT originally appeared in 1923 and was last published in 1973 by Harcourt Brace Jovanovich. Subsequent restandardization was conducted in the spring of 1982; however, results were not available at the time of this writing. The SAT has six levels: primary level I for grades 1.5–2.4; primary level II for grades 2.5–3.4; primary level III for grades 3.5–4.4; intermediate level I for grades 4.5–5.4; intermediate level II for grades 5.5–6.9; and advanced for grades, 7.0–9.5. Each level yields from twelve to sixteen scores; two forms, A and B, also are available at each level. For example, the primary level III has fifteen scores derived from the following subtests and combined subtests: reading (comprehension, work-study skills, total); mathematics (concepts, computation, application, total); spelling, language, social science, science, auditory (vocabulary, listening comprehension, total); total. Partial batteries are available without science, social science, and listening comprehension, and the mathematics and reading subtests also are available separately. Total time required ranges, depending on level, from 250 to 405 minutes administered over several (five to seven) sessions. Four types of scores are provided: percentile rank, stanine, grade equivalents, and scaled scores. The scaled scores are not standardized across the different subtests; however, they are comparable to the different levels and to the appropriate upward and downward extensions of the SAT. Criterion-referenced interpretations also are possible. The standardization sample was comprised of 275,000 students in 109 school systems in forty-three states. The main variables considered in the norm group were community size, geographic region, family income, class size, public/nonpublic schools, and ethnic group. The Stanford Early School Achievement Test (SESAT), a recommended downward extension of the SAT, has two levels, K.1–1.1 and 1.1–1.8. The recommended upward extension of the SAT is the Stanford Test of Academic Skills (TASK).

Stanford Test of Academic Skills (TASK).   The TASK, published by Harcourt Brace Jovanovich from 1972 to 1975, has three levels: level I for grades 8–10; and level II for grades 11–12; and grade 13 for junior/community colleges. Two forms, A and B, are available for all levels except for grade 13, which has only form A. Three main scores are obtained: reading, English, and mathematics. The reading test has two subtests, comprehension and vocabulary. The English test has four parts: reference skills; punctuation, grammar, and capitalization; spelling; and English expression. The mathematics test is a combination of processes and operations that surveys basic mathematics skills. The standardization sample was comprised of over 17,000 students in nineteen schools and later administered to students in thirty-two schools in twenty-nine states. Norms are provided by grade level for grades 8–12; a second norm group comprised of community college freshmen also is available. Three types of scores are possible: percentile rank, stanine, and scaled scores. The scaled scores are comparable with the SESAT and the SAT; however, no mean or standard deviation is provided nor are comparisons across subtests possible. It also provides criterion-referenced interpretations.

Other Achievement Tests

Many other achievement tests have been used in educational and psychological research. For instance, the Sequential Tests of Educational Progress (STEP) and its corresponding ability test, the Cooperative School and College Ability Tests (SCAT), published in 1966 by the Educational Testing Service (ETS), have been extensively researched. Several individually administered achievement tests that require shorter testing time also have been developed. For example, the Peabody Individual Achievement Test (PIAT), published by American Guidance Service, is used widely. In addition, the Wide Range Achievement Test–Revised Edition, published by Guidance Associates of Delaware, can be administered individually or to groups, and it can provide percentiles, grade equivalents, or standard scores for three subtests: reading, spelling, and arithmetic, from pre-school to college. The Woodcock-Johnson Psycho-Educational Battery, published by Teaching Resources Corporation in 1977, is also now being used widely. It consists of three main parts: cognitive ability, scholastic achievement, and interest. It is designed primarily for the school-age population, but norms are provided from age 3 through age 80+. The test is comprised of twenty-seven subtests. The cognitive ability part, for example, has twelve subtests. Numerous comparison scores are provided, including percentile ranks, standard scores with a mean of 100 and a standard deviation of 15, and normal curve equivalents (NCE). Testing time is approximately two hours for the complete battery.

Numerous educational tests also have been developed for specific diagnostic or achievement assessment purposes for such content areas as reading, foreign languages, mathematics, and artistic and musical aptitude. In addition, many tests have been developed to assess cognitive dysfunction and learning disabilities. As you explore the tests used in your particular educational field, you will become familiar with many of these tests as well.

Projective, Personality, and Interest Measures

Personality tests, broadly speaking, encompass both projective and interest measures. Generally, personality tests are measures used to assess attitudinal, emotional, motivational, or social characteristics as compared to tests that measure general intellectual abilities or achievement. Except for the projective tests, personality tests are paper-and-pencil, self-report inventories or questionnaires used for either individual or group administration. Several of the most widely used tests will be briefly described. The main projective tests to be described are:

Rorschach
Thematic Apperception Test (TAT)

The main personality measures to be described are:

Minnesota Multiphasic Personality Inventory (MMPI)
California Psychological Inventory (CPI)
Sixteen Personality Factor Questionnaire (16PF)

Finally, the main interest, attitude, or value scales we will consider are:

Strong-Campbell Interest Inventory (SCII)
Differential Aptitude Tests (DAT)

Additional tests will be presented in the context of examining these measures.

Projective Measures

Rorschach.   The Rorschach ink blots technique developed by Hermann Rorschach was first described in 1921. This technique is composed of ten symmetrical bilateral ink blots, five in black and grey and five containing pastel shades or touches of bright red. The subject is shown each card and asked to tell what he sees or what the ink blot could represent. The clinician also systematically asks the subject to relate or associate the responses to the parts or aspects of each ink blot. The scoring and interpreting of the response have received much criticism for their apparent lack of standardization. Typically, however, four scoring categories are employed: location, determinants, content, and popularity. The location category refers to the part of the ink blot with which the subject associates each response. The determinants category refers to responses associated with form, color, shading, or movement. The content category typically includes responses associated with human figures and their parts, animal figures and details, inanimate objects, and others such as sexual objects and symbolic representations. A popularity category score, which represents the relative frequency or common occurrence of different responses among the general population, also is obtained.

Because of the difficulty in scoring and interpreting the Rorschach, additional techniques have been developed. One, Piotrowski's Automated Rorschach (PAR) published by Hays Associates, is a computerized scoring and interpretative system. A second is the Holtzman Inkblot Technique (HIT), published by The Psychological Corporation.

It is comprised of two parallel forms of forty-five cards each, and only one response per card is obtained. Administration and scoring of the HIT are standardized and appear to improve on the earlier Rorschach; however, both continue to be widely used. For each of twenty-two response variables scored on the HIT, percentile scores for age 5 to adult, as well as for several specific groups such as schizophrenics and juvenile delinquents, are available.

Thematic Apperception Test (TAT).   The TAT, published by Harvard University Press, was originally developed by Henry A. Murray and his associates in 1938. It is comprised of twenty cards, nineteen of which contain hazy, vague, or ambiguous pictures in black and white and one of which is a blank card. Developed for use with children from age 4 to adult, the test requires the subject to make up a story for each picture, telling what led up to the event shown and describing what is currently happening, what the people are feeling and thinking, and what the outcome will be. On the blank card the subject is asked to construct a picture, describe it, and then tell a story about it. Approximately two 1-hour sessions using ten cards each are required. The TAT stories are interpreted as the responses reflect Murray's theory of needs and environmental press. Murray's theory includes needs for achievement, affiliation, aggression, dominance, and so forth. Environmental press concerns those forces which facilitate or interfere with meeting or satisfying needs, such as being comforted or being criticized.

Subsequent adaptations and variations of the TAT have been developed. For example, the Children's Apperception Test (CAT) was designed for children between the ages of 3 and 10, and the Senior Apperception Technique for use with the elderly contains cards with problems of concern to the aged. Both are published by CPS Incorporated. Additional variations include the H-T-P (House-Tree-Person) Projective Technique published by Western Psychological Services and the Make a Picture Story (MAPS) published by The Psychological Corporation. Another variation of the projective technique is to have numerous incomplete sentences filled or completed by the subjects and their responses inferred to reflect their internal processing: for instance, "I am happiest when _____." The Rotter Incomplete Sentences Blank published by The Psychological Corporation is an example of this type of projective sentence-completion test.

Personality Measures

Minnesota Multiphasic Personality Inventory (MMPI).   The MMPI, published by The Psychological Corporation, is one of the most widely used and researched paper-and-pencil, self-report personality inventories. The test comprises 550 statements to which one responds "true" or "mostly true" as applied to oneself, or "false" or "not usually true" as applied to oneself. Designed for subjects from age 16 to adult, the inventory also has norms that have been developed for younger adolescent subjects. Thirteen scores are obtained from the MMPI, including ten clinical scales and three validating scales. The ten clinical scales are: hypochondriasis, depression, hysteria, psychopathic deviate, masculinity-femininity, paranoia, psychasthenia, schizophrenia, hypomania, and social introversion. The three validating scales obtain a lie score, a validity score, and a correction score. Each of the thirteen scores is standardized with a mean of 50 and a standard deviation of 10. Any score that is two standard deviations or more above the mean, 70 or above, is considered a cutoff for the identification of psychological disorder.

California Psychological Inventory (CPI). The CPI, published by Consulting Psychologists Press, was developed specifically for use with non-psychiatrically disturbed subjects from age 13 through 70. It attempts to measure characteristics of personality important for social living and social interaction. The test booklet contains 480 items that the subject answers true or false; approximately half of the items were taken from the MMPI. Testing time is usually about one hour. The CPI includes eighteen scales, three of which were designed to assess attitudes toward test taking: sense of well-being, good impression, and communality. The remaining fifteen scales include: dominance, capacity for status, sociability, social presence, self-acceptance, responsibility, socialization, self-control, tolerance, achievement via conformity, achievement via independence, intellectual efficiency, psychological-mindedness, flexibility, and femininity. Each scale provides a standard score with a mean of 50 and a standard deviation of 10. The normative sample contained approximately 6,200 males and 7,150 females stratified by age, socioeconomic level, and geographical area. Norms for several educational and occupational groups also are provided. In order to minimize interpretation bias both the MMPI and the CPI require extensive training in interpreting the profile of obtained scores.

Sixteen Personality Factor Questionnaire (16PF). The 16PF, developed from the theory and research of Cattell and his associates, is a multidimensional personality inventory published by the Institute for Personality and Ability Testing in 1967. Five forms are available dependent upon the subject's reading level, and the inventory is usually administered in an essentially untimed procedure in forty to sixty minutes. Developed for use with subjects 16 years of age and over, sixteen scales comprise the measures, including fifteen personality scales and one general intelligence scale. The sixteen scales expressed on a bipolar dimension are: reserved vs. outgoing; less intelligent vs. more intelligent; affected by feelings vs. emotionally stable; humble vs. assertive; sober vs. happy-go-lucky; expedient vs. conscientious; shy vs. venturesome; tough-minded vs. tender-minded; trusting vs. suspicious; practical vs. imaginative; forthright vs. shrewd; self-assured vs. apprehensive; conservative vs. experimenting; group dependent vs. self-sufficient; undisciplined self-conflict vs. controlled; and relaxed vs. tense. Six combined or second-order scores also are obtained: introversion vs. extroversion; low anxiety vs. high anxiety; tender-minded emotionality vs. tough poise; naturalness vs. discreetness; subduedness vs. independence; and cool realism vs. prodigal subjectivity. Norms are available for junior and senior high school students, university and college undergraduates, and the general adult population. Stanines and percentile ranks for each scale are reported; means and standard deviations for the obtained raw scores also are calculated. Comparable questionnaires have been developed as a downward extension of the 16PF: the Early School Personality Questionnaire for ages 6 to 8; the Children's Personality Questionnaire for ages 8 to 12; and the Junior and Senior High School Personality Questionnaire for ages 12 to 18.

Other Personality Measures

Numerous personality measures also have been developed to assess more specific personality constructs. In the area of self-concept, the Piers-Harris Children's Self-Concept Scale (CSCS), published by Counselor Recordings and Tests, has been widely used. Appropriate for children with an approximate third-grade reading level, the scale provides norms up to twelfth grade. Oral administration of the eighty items answered as yes or no is possible for younger ages; administration time is approximately twenty minutes. Six scales are used: behavior, intellectual school status, physical appearance, anxiety, popularity, and happiness/satisfaction. The Tennessee Self-Concept Scale (TSCS) was developed for subjects aged 12 to 68 with at least a sixth-grade reading level. Also published by Counselor Recordings and Tests, the scale provides ninety items to be answered yes or no. Percentiles and scores with a mean of 50 and a standard deviation of 10 are obtained. The Personal Orientation Inventory (POI), published by the Educational and Industrial Testing Service, is a measure to assess one's level of self-actualization as described in Maslow's theory of motivation. Administered individually or in groups of subjects from the age of 13 and up, the inventory provides 150 dual choice items, positive and negative, and the subject selects the one that reflects his perception about his life. Usually taking approximately thirty minutes, the inventory yields two basic orientation scale scores and ten subscale scores. The two basic scales are an other- vs. inner-directed support scale and a time-competent vs. time-incompetent scale. The ten subscales are: self-actualizing value, existentiality, feeling reactivity, spontaneity, self-regard, self-acceptance, nature of man, synergy, acceptance of aggression, and capacity for intimate contact. Percentiles and standard scores based on a mean of 50 and a standard deviation of 10 are obtained for numerous norm groups from male psychopathic felons to male and female high school and college students.

Numerous measures used to assess creativity also are available. Two widely used tests are the Remote Associates Test (RAT), published by Houghton Mifflin, and the Torrance Tests of Creative Thinking, published by Personnel Press. The psychological construct of anxiety is another concept frequently examined in the research literature. Two frequently used tests are the Taylor Manifest Anxiety Scale (Taylor 1953) and the State-Trait Anxiety Inventory (STAI), published by Consulting Psychologists Press.

Interest Measures.

Strong-Campbell Interest Inventory (SCII). The SCII, published by Stanford University Press in 1974, is a revision of the widely used and researched Strong Vocational Interest Blank (SVIB) first published in 1927. The SCII is designed to determine one's interest in or attitude toward a particular concept. The subject's perception then is compared to the interests expressed by numerous norm groups collected over extensive testing. The inventory includes 325 items, and it is administered in thirty to sixty minutes depending on the reading speed of each subject. Written at the sixth-grade level, the inventory asks subjects aged 13 or over to respond to each question with like, indifferent, or dislike. The test is divided into seven sections: occupations, school subjects, activities, amusements, types of people, preferences between two activities, and characteristics. Scores are provided on a variety of dimensions, each standardized with a mean of 50 and a standard deviation of 10. Individuals trained in interpreting the SCII are necessary to maximize the degree of useful information obtained. A profile of scores usually contains information related to subjects on their general occupational theme, academic orientation, introversion-extroversion, interest on twenty-three basic scales from sales and merchandising to religious activities, and interest as related to the expressed interest of individuals in 124 occupations.

Differential Aptitude Tests (DAT). The DAT, last published in 1973 by The Psychological Corporation, is one of the most widely used multiple-aptitude batteries. Designed for educational and vocational counseling of students in grades 8–12, nine main scores are obtained from eight scales: verbal reasoning, numerical ability, abstract reasoning, clerical speed and accuracy, mechanical reasoning, space relations, spelling, and language usage. The ninth is a combined verbal reasoning plus numerical ability score. Administration time is four hours in two to six sessions for the two forms. Percentile ranks and stanines are obtained for local or national norms. The standardization sample used seventy-six school districts in thirty-three states; a total of 5,000–7,350 students representing each grade level were tested. Norms for Catholic and vocational schools also are available. A DAT Career Planning Program and report also are available, which integrate the aptitude tests on the DAT with the subject's interests and perceptions obtained from the Career Planning Questionnaire.

Additional aptitude batteries are used for numerous purposes. For instance, the General Aptitude Test Battery (GATB) still is used by state employment service offices. The Minnesota Vocational Interest Inventory (MVII) published by The Psychological Corporation assesses interest in various skilled and semi-skilled occupations. It provides scores on scales similar to the basic interest skills of the SCII.

Summary

We have described many of the most frequently used intelligence, achievement, personality, and interest tests used in psychological and educational research. However, the test reviews were not meant to be exhaustive, nor do we conclude that all tests are of equal quality. As you become more experienced in your particular educational setting, you will be reviewing firsthand many of these tests in more depth. You will need to consider the reliability, validity, and norms of each test for your specific testing or research purpose. Many of the tests described are well developed in terms of technical quality; however, they still may not be appropriate for your particular purpose.

Appendix B

List of Test Publishers

American College Testing Program
(ACT)
P.O. Box 168
Iowa City, Iowa 52240

American Guidance Service, Inc.
720 Washington Avenue SE
Minneapolis, Minnesota 55414

The Bobbs-Merrill Co., Inc.
Box 558
4300 West 62nd Street
Indianapolis, Indiana 46206

Bureau of Educational Research and Service
University of Iowa
Iowa City, Iowa 52240

College Entrance Examination Board
(CEEB)
888 Seventh Avenue
New York, New York 10019
Order Department: Box 2815
Princeton, New Jersey 08541

Consulting Psychologists Press, Inc.
577 College Avenue
Palo Alto, California 94306

CTB/McGraw-Hill
Del Monte Research Park
Monterey, California 93940

Educational and Industrial Testing Service
P.O. Box 7234
San Diego, California 92107

Educational Testing Service
(ETS)
Rosedale Road
Princeton, New Jersey 08540

Harcourt Brace Jovanovich, Inc.
757 Third Avenue
New York, New York 10017

Houghton Mifflin Company
One Beacon Street
Boston, Massachusetts 02107

Institute for Personality and Ability Testing
1602 Coronado Drive
Champaign, Illinois 61820

Personnel Press
191 Spring Street
Lexington, Massachusetts 02173

The Psychological Corporation
757 Third Avenue
New York, New York 10017

Psychological Test Specialists
Box 1441
Missoula, Montana 59801

Psychometric Affiliates
1743 Monterey
Chicago, Illinois 60643

Science Research Associates, Inc.
155 North Wacker Drive
Chicago, Illinois 60606

Sheridan Psychological Services, Inc.
P.O. Box 6101
Orange, California 92667

C. H. Stoelting Co.
424 North Homan Avenue
Chicago, Illinois 60624

Teachers College Press
Teachers College, Columbia University
1234 Amsterdam Avenue
New York, New York 10027

Western Psychological Services
12031 Wilshire Boulevard
Los Angeles, California 90025

Appendix C

APGA POLICY STATEMENT

Responsibilities of Users of Standardized Tests

INTRODUCTION

During the past several years, individual APGA members have been under increasing pressure from their various constituencies to define, provide and employ safeguards against the misuse of standardized tests. APGA as an organization has also been challenged by individuals and agencies to provide leadership in the face of growing concern about the effects of testing on clients of all ages and all subpopulations, and in all settings.

At the 1976 APGA convention, the board of directors requested action on the development of a statement on the responsible use of standardized tests. A committee representing all APGA divisions and regions spent two years studying the issues and developing the following statement.

Target audience: The statement is intended to present the position and address the needs of the professional members of APGA divisions and regions. Although this position may provide guidance for test developers, teachers, administrators, parents, press or the general public, it is not designed to represent these audiences. The statement is built on the assumption that test data of themselves are neutral and that guidelines are needed to promote constructive use of tests.

Organization and focus: The statement is organized into eight sections: Introduction, Decision Rules, Test Selection, Qualifications of Test Users, Test Administration, Scoring of Tests, Test Interpretation and Communication. Each section is directed toward the various uses and decisions that must be made by the test user (e.g., whether to test, which test(s) to use, what data to obtain, how to interpret, etc.). The committee developed a classification system for the uses of standardized tests and treated only those issues that fit into the use classification scheme.

The next step was to define issues related to the classification system. Issues were sought from individuals, professional statements, literature and the popular press. Issues were examined in terms of their relevance to APGA members and to their importance in terms of the possible consequences to the person(s) tested.

Only the principles underlying each issue are specified. These principles are appropriate as standards for all APGA divisions and regions. Divisions and regions are encouraged to develop their own statements, expanding on each prrinciple with specific procedures and examples and appropriate to their members. The principles are grouped around similar issues and are indexed for easy reference.

Composition of Committee: Each division president and the representative of each region was asked to appoint to the committee a member who was: (1) knowledgable in the use of standardized tests; (2) aware of the national concerns about the use of tests; (3) willing to involve the division/region membership in identification of the concerns, needs and propositions of the division/region as these relate to the responsible use of tests; (4) able to participate actively and to respond promptly to requests for review of draft documents; (5) capable of securing cooperation of division/region officers in developing procedures for division/region implementation of the statement; (6) willing to accept specific assignments such as providing current organizational statements.

In addition to the division/region appointment, the committee included two members-at-large and a chairperson, all appointed by the APGA president, and three test experts to serve as a core committee to assist the chairperson in analyzing and synthesizing input from committee members and in preparing draft statements for committee review.

To furnish perspective for the work of this committee, a review of relevant literature was conducted and each member of the committee received copies of nu-

Source: From APGA Policy Statement, Responsibilities of users of standardized tests, *Guidepost,* October 5, 1978, 5–8. Reprinted by permission.

merous position papers, reports, articles and mono-graps that added to understanding the issues and the consequences of alternative principles.

Among these papers were the interim report of the 1975-76 APGA Committee on Standardized Testing; the 1972 APGA/AMEG Statement on the Responsible Use of Tests; position papers of individual divisions and of other professional organizations such as the American Psychological Association, the American Education Research Association and the National Council on Measurement in Education; journal articles; and conference presentations.

The committee's statement is intended to be sensitive to current and emerging problems and concerns that are generic to all APGA divisions/regions and to address these problems and concerns with principles that are specific enough to serve as a template to develop division/region statements addressed to the specific disciplines/settings of individual divisions/regions.

DECISION RULES

In human service agencies, decisions about client needs may be made on the basis of direct observation or historical information alone. Further refinement of direct observation and historical data can often be obtained by employing standardized tests.

Deciding whether to test creates the possibility of **three classes of errors** relative to the agency functions **of description**, diagnosis, prescription, selection, place-**ment, prediction**, growth evaluation, etc.

First, a decision not to test can result in misjudgments that stem solely from inadequate data.

Second, tests may be used well, producing data that could improve accuracy in decisions affecting the client but that are not utilized.

Third, tests may be misused through inappropriate selection, improper administration, inaccurate scoring, incompetent interpretation or indiscriminate, inadequate, or inaccurate communication.

To reduce the chance for errors, the responsible practitioner will always determine in advance **why** a given test should be used. This provides protection and benefits for both the client and the agency. Having a clearly developed rationale increases the probable benefits of testing by indicating how a particular set of information, when used by an individual or set of individuals, will contribute to a sounder decision without prejudice to either the client or the agency.

The guidelines that follow are intended to provide decision rules to help agencies and practitioners avoid charge of irresponsible practice.

Defining purposes for testing:
1. Decide whether you will be testing to evaluate individuals, groups or both.
2. Identify your interests in the particular target population in terms of the agency's purposes and capabilities.
3. Determine limits to diagnosis, prediction or selection created by age, racial, sexual, ethnic or cultural characteristics of those to be tested.
4. Develop specific objectives and limits for the use of test data in relation to each of the component service areas of placement/selection, prediction (expectancies), description/diagnosis and growth studies (assessing change over time).

A. Placement: If the purpose is selection or placement (selection is a simple in-out sort of placement), the test selector and interpreter must know about the programs or institutions in which the client may be placed and be able to judge the consequences of such placement or exclusion for the client.

B. Prediction/expectancies: If the purpose is prediction, the persons deciding to test and/or interpret the results must understand the pitfalls of labeling, stereotyping and prejudging people. Ways to avoid these potentially invidious outcomes should be known.

C. Description/diagnosis: If the purpose is diagnosis or description, the selector or interpreter should understand enough about the general domain being measured to be able to identify those aspects adequately measured and those not.

D. Growth/change assessment: If the purpose is to examine growth, the person designing the study and interpreting the results needs to know the many problems associated with such measurement:
1) the unreliability of change measures;
2) the pitfalls in using norms as reference points;
3) the associated problems of articulation and comparability;
4) the limitations of scoring scales, such as grade equivalents, that may not have the comparable meaning which they appear to have at different scale levels.

Determining information needs:
1. Assess the consequences for the clients of both testing or not testing.
2. Determine what decisions can be made with existing information to avoid unnecessary data-gathering efforts.
3. Limit data gathering to those functions or aptitude, achievement, interests/attitudes/values and perceptual-motor skills that are directly relevant in making decisions about delivery of services to a particular individual or group.
4. Identify whether the test being considered can provide acceptable levels of precision (reliability) for the decision being made.
5. Identify whether the data obtained can be cross-validated against other available data as a part of the decision-making process.
6. Determine the amount and form of data to be shared on the basis of maximum relevance to the agency's purposes and capabilities.

Identifying users of test information:
1. Data should be prepared so that they can be comprehended by the persons using the data for decision-making.
2. Limit access to users specifically authorized by the law or by the client.
3. Identify obsolescence schedules so that stored

personal test data may be systematically reclassified and relocated to historical files or destroyed.

4. Process personal data used for research or program evaluation so as to assure individual anonymity.

QUALIFICATIONS OF TEST USERS

All professional personnel and guidance workers should have formal training in psychological and educational measurement and testing. Nevertheless, it is unreasonable to expect that this training necessarily makes one an expert or even that an expert always has all the knowledge and skill appropriate to any particular situation. Thus, questions of user qualifications should always arise when testing is being considered.

Those who participate in any aspect of testing should be qualified to do so. Lack of proper qualifications leads to misuse, errors and sometimes damage to clients. Each professional is responsible for making judgment on this matter in each situation and cannot leave that responsibility either to clients or to those in authority.

In many instances information or skills that may be lacking can be acquired quite readily by those with a background of professional training and experience. In all instances it is incumbent upon the individual to obtain that training or arrange for proper supervision and assistance when engaged in, or planning to engage in, testing.

The requisite qualifications for test users depend on four factors: (1) the particular role of the user: (2) the setting in which the use takes place; (3) the nature of the test; and (4) the purpose of the testing.

These factors interact with each other but may nevertheless be considered separately for the purposes of these standards.

Roles of test users, selectors, administrators, scorers and interpreters:

A test user may play all of these roles or any subset of them when working with other professional personnel. In some situations each role may be the responsibility of a different person. The knowledge and skills that pertain to these roles are listed under the sections so headed. The general principle is that the test users should engage in only those testing activities for which their training and experience qualify them.

Settings and conditions of test use:

Counselors and personnel workers should assess the quality and relevance of their knowledge and skills to the situation before deciding to test or to participate in a testing program.

Characteristics of tests:

Tests differ in many ways, and users need to understand the peculiarities of the instruments they are using.

Purposes of testing:

The purpose of the testing dictates how the test is used and thus may influence requisite qualifications of users beyond those entailed by their testing roles. Technically proper use for ill-understood purposes may constitute misuse.

TEST SELECTION

Tests should be selected for a specific measurement purpose, use and interpretation. The selection of tests should be guided by information obtained from a careful analysis of the following major considerations:

— What are the characteristics of the population to be tested?

— What knowledge, skills, abilities or attitudes are to be assessed?

— What are the purposes for testing?

— How will the test scores be used and interpreted?

When complete answers to these questions have been obtained, selection or development of tests should be directed toward obtaining measures that are congruent with the stated needs for assessment in terms of the purposes, content, use, interpretation and particular characteristics of the individuals who are to be tested.

Selection of tests must also be guided by the criteria of technical quality recommended by the measurement profession and published by APA/AERA/NCME in "Standards for Educational and Psychological Tests" (1974). Full recognition and analysis of these considerations should become the focus of a process to select appropriate tests. The responsible test selector will:

Select appropriate tests:

1. Select tests that have been demonstrated, to the satisfaction of professional specialists, as appropriate for the characteristics of the population to be tested.

2. Select tests that are within the level of skills of administration and interpretation possessed by the practitioner.

3. Determine whether a common test or different tests are required for the accurate measurement of groups with different characteristics.

4. Recognize that different tests for cultural, ethnic and racial groups constitute inefficient means for making corrections for differences in prior life experiences, except where different languages are involved.

5. Determine whether persons or groups that use different languages should be tested in either or both languages and in some instance by prior testing for bilingualism.

Relate evidence or validity to particular usage:

1. Apply tests or selection only when they show predictive validity for the specific tasks or competencies needed in an educational or employment assignment to maintain legal prescriptions for non-discriminatory practices in selection, employment or placement.

3. Determine validity of a test (whether the test measures what it claims to measure) through evidence of the contructs used in developing the measures, the correlation of the test performance with another appraisal of the characteristics being measured, or the predictions of specified behavior from the test performance.

3. Determine that the content of the test has high congruence with the users' definition of the knowledge and skills that are the desired criteria of human performance to be appraised.

4. Confirm that the criteria of human performance to be appraised are contained in the tasks and results of the testing procedure.

Employ user participation in test selection:

Actively involve the persons who will be using the tests (administering, scoring, summarizing, interpreting, making decisions) in the selection of tests that are congruent with the locally determined purposes, conditions and uses of the measurement.

Select tests to satisfy local use:

1. Give specific attention to how the test is designed to handle the variation of motivation among persons taking the test, the variation or bias in response to the test content and the effects of the presence or absence of guessing in the responses to the test questions.

2. Determine whether tests standardized for nationwide use show evidence that such tests yield comparable results for individuals or groups with cultural differences.

3. Identify and analyze the effects of working speed and language facility in relation to the criteria of human performance that are expected to result from the test.

Consider technical characteristics of tests:

1. Select only published or locally developed tests that have documented evidence of the reliability or consistency of the measure.

2. Select tests that have documented evidence of the effectiveness of the measure for the purpose to be served: placement/selection, prediction (expectancy), description/diagnosis, or growth studies (change over time). A test is rarely equally effective for the four common test uses.

3. Consider the procedures used in standardization and norming for relevance to the local population and the desired use and interpretation.

4. Use separate norms for men and women only when empirical evidence indicates this is necessary to minimize bias.

5. Determine the degree of reliability (or validity) demanded of a test on the basis of the nature of the decisions to be based on test scores.

6. A test for final diagnosis or selection requires a higher degree of reliability than an initial screening test.

7. Explicitly list and use the ease and accuracy of the procedures for scoring, summarizing and communicating test performance as criteria for selecting a test.

8. Recognize that the technical characteristics and norms of standardized tests may vary when used with different populations. The selection process should include trial administrations to verify that the test is functioning with the technical characteristics and desired results for the local population and local uses.

Practical constraints of cost, conditions and time for testing must be considered but not used as the primary criteria for test selection.

TEST ADMINISTRATION

Test administration includes all procedures that are used to ensure that the test is presented consistently in the manner specified by the test developers and used in the standardization and that the individuals being tested have orientation and conditions that maximize opportunity for optimum performance.

Standardized tests should provide manuals giving specific directions for administering, scoring and interpreting tests. Tests developed for a specific local purpose, use or population should be administered in a prescribed and consistent manner to obtain optimum performance from the individuals being tested. Effective administration of tests requires that the administrator have knowledge and training with the instruments and the processes of presentation.

Orientation:

1. Inform testing candidates, relevant institutions or agencies and the community about the testing procedure. The orientation should describe the purposes and contents sampled by the test, how it is administered and how the scores will be reported and used.

2. Provide annual training for test administrators by qualified professional specialists if your agency or institution uses tests or sponsors testing programs.

3. Routinely review the test materials and administration conditions well in advance of the time for testing so that full preparation will ensure standardized administration and recognition of any irregularities that may occur.

4. Ensure that the orientation is sufficient to make the test relevant for the individual or group being tested before beginning test administration.

5. Ensure that all persons being tested have the specified practice with sample problems or test taking skills prior to their performance on the test.

6. Demonstrate the techniques and requirements for marking machine-scorable answer sheets. Check all individuals taking a test for competency in the techniques of recording their answers prior to the specific period of testing.

Qualifications of test administrators:

1. Administer standardized tests only if you are qualified by training and experience as competent to administer particular tests.

2. Know the exact population and procedures used in standardizing the test and determine that the test is appropriate for the local population that is to be tested.

3. Acquire extensive training required to administer, score or interpret tests requiring test-specific training.

Giving directions:

1. Administer standardized tests with the verbatim instructions, exact sequence and timing and the identical materials that were used in the test standardization.

2. Present all tests (whether standardized, published or locally constructed) in an identical manner to ensure that the test is a fair and comparable demonstration of the performance of each individual taking the test.

Recognize that taking a test may be a new and frightening experience or stimulate anxiety or frustration for some individuals. Communicate to the examinees that they should attempt each task with positive application of their skills and knowledge and the anticipation that they will do their best.

Testing conditions:

1. Devote concentrated attention to observing the condition and reactions of the individuals being tested. Observe those being tested and identify environmental, health or emotional conditions that should be recorded and considered as invalidating elements for the test performance.

2. Possess and demonstrate clear verbal articulation, calmness and positive anticipation, empathy for and social identification with the examiness, and, impartial treatment for all being tested.

3. Determine whether the testing environment (seating, work surfaces, lighting, heating, freedom from distractions, etc.) is conducive to the best possible performance of the test-takers.

4. Administer tests in physical facilities and psychological climates that allow each individual being tested to achieve optimum performance.

5. Record any deviation from standardized test administration procedure (such as used to accommodate handicapping conditions) and make it a permanent attachment to the test score or record.

6. Develop and complete for each test a systematic and objective procedure for observing and recording the behavior of those being tested (and recording conventional or deviant conditions of testing). Attach this record to the test scores of the persons tested.

7. Provide a written record of any circumstances that may have increased or reduced the opportunity of an individual being tested to demonstrate his or her best performance.

Accept responsibility for seeing that invalid or questionable test scores are not recorded, or not recorded without written qualification of the conditions that may have affected optimum test performance.

9. Arrange assistance from trained personnel in providing uniform conditions and in observing the conduct of the examinees when large groups of individuals must be tested.

Professional collaboration:

Recognize that in institutional settings, and wherever skill and knowledge can be pooled and responsibility shared, it is the qualifications of the team as a whole that count rather than those of individuals. However, coordination and consistency must be maintained.

TEST SCORING

The measurement of human performance depends on accurate and consistent application of defined procedures for crediting the responses made by persons being tested. The procedures for scoring and recording test performance must be continuously audited for consistency and accuracy.

1. Routinely rescore a sample of the test answer sheets to verify the accuracy of the initial scoring.

2. Employ systematic procedures to verify the accuracy and consistency of machine scoring of answer sheets.

3. Obtain a separate and independent verification that appropriate scoring rules and normative conversions are used for each person tested.

4. Verify as accurate the computation of raw scores

and the conversion of raw scores to normative or descriptive scales prior to release of such information to the tested person or to users of the test results.

5. Routinely check machine or manual reports of test results for accuracy. The person performing this task must be qualified to recognize inappropriate or impossible scores.

6. Develop and use systematic and objective procedures for observing and recording the conditions and behaviors of persons being tested and make this a part of the scores or test results that are reported.

7. Clearly label the scores that are reported and the date that a particular test was administered.

TEST INTERPRETATION

Test interpretation encompasses all the ways we assign value to the scores.

A test can be described as a systematic set or series of standard observations of performances that all fall in some particular domain. Typically each observation yields a rating of the performance (such as right or wrong and pass or fail), then these ratings are counted and this count becomes the basis of the scores. Such scores are usually much more stable than the result of any single performance. This score reliability creates the possibility of validity greater than can be obtained from unsystematic or nonaggregated observations.

The proper interpretation of test scores starts with understanding these fundamental characteristics of tests. Given this, the interpretation of scores from a test entails knowledge about (1) administration and scoring procedures; (2) scores, norms, and related technical features; (3) reliability; and (4) validity.

Adequate test interpretation requires knowledge and skill in each of these areas. Some of this information can be mastered only by studying the manual and other materials of the test; no one should undertake the interpretation of scores on any test without such study.

Administration and Scoring:

Standard procedures for administering and scoring the test limit the possible meanings of scores. Departures from standard conditions and procedures modify and often invalidate the criteria for score interpretation.

1. The principles in the section on administration and scoring need to be understood by those engaged in interpretation.

2. Ascertain the circumstances peculiar to the particular administration and scoring of the test.

A. Examine all reports from administrators, proctors and scorers concerning irregularities or conditions, such as excessive anxiety, which may have affected performance.

B. Weigh the possible effects on test scores of examiner-examinee differences in ethnic and cultural background, attitudes and values in light of research on these matters. Recognize that such effects are probably larger in individual testing situations.

c. Look for administrators' reports of examinee behavior that indicate the responses were made on some basis other than that intended — as when a student being tested for knowledge of addition-number-facts adds by making tallies and then counting them.

3. Consider differences among clients in their reaction to instructions about guessing and scoring.

4. Recognize or judge the effect of scorer biases and judgment when subjective elements enter into scoring.

Scores, norms and related technical features:

The result of scoring a test is usually a number (or a set of numbers) called a raw score. Raw scores taken by themselves are not usually interpretable. Some additional steps must be taken.

The procedures either translate the numbers directly into descriptions of their meaning (e.g., pass or fail) or into other numbers called derived scores (e.g., standard scores) whose meaning stems from the test norms.

To interpret test scores, these procedures and the resulting descriptions or derived scores need to be thoroughly understood. Anything less than full understanding is likely to produce at least some, and probably many, serious errors in interpretation. The following are imperatives for interpreting tests:

1. Examine the test manuals, handbooks, users' guides and technical reports to determine what descriptions or derived scores are produced and what unique characteristics each may have.

2. Recognize that direct score interpretations such as mastery and nonmastery in criterion-referenced tests depend on arbitrary rules or standards.

A. Report number or percent of items right in addition to the indicated interpretation whenever it will help others understand the quality of the examinee's test performance.

B. Recognize that the difficulty of a fixed standard, such as 80 percent right, will vary widely from objective objective. Such scores are not comparable in the normative sense.

C. Recognize that when each score is classified as pass fail, mastery-nonmastery or the like, that each element is being given equal weight.

3. Use the derived scores that fit the needs of the current use of the test.

A. Use percentile ranks for direct comparison of individuals to the norm or reference group.

B. Use standard scores or equal unit scaled scores whenever means and variances are calculated or other arithmetic operations are being used.

4. Recognize that only those derived scores that are based on the same norm group can be compared.

5. Consider the effect of any differences between the tests in what they measure when one test or form is equated with another, as well as the errors stemming from the equating itself.

Give greater credence to growth or change shown by the same test (including level and form) than to equated measures except where practice effects or feedback have destroyed the validity of a second use.

6. Evaluate the appropriateness of the norm groups available as bases for interpreting the scores of clients.

A. Use the norms for the group to which the client belongs.

B. Consider using local norms and derived scores based on these local norms whenever possible.

7. Acquire knowledge of specific psychological or educational concepts and theories before interpreting the scores of tests based on such knowledge.

Reliability:

Reliability is a prerequisite to validity. Generally, the greater the number of items the greater the reliability of the test. The degree to which a score or a set of scores may vary because of measurement error is a central factor in interpretation.

1. Use the standard error of measurement to obtain a rough estimate of the probable variation in scores due to unreliability.

2. Use the reliability coefficient to estimate the proportion of score variance that is not due to error.

3. Consider the sources of variance attributable to error in the particular reliability indexes reported in relationship to the uses being made of the scores.

4. Assess reported reliabilities in light of the many extraneous factors that may have artificially raised or lowered these estimates, such as test speededness, sample homogeneity or heterogeneity, restrictions in range and the like.

5. Distinguish indexes of rater reliability (i.e., of objectivity) from test reliability.

Validity:

Proper test interpretation requires knowledge of the validity evidence available for the test as used. Its validity for other uses is not relevant. The purpose of testing dictates how a test is used. Technically proper use for ill-understood purposes may constitute misuse. The nature of the validity evidence required for a test is a function of its use.

Prediction — developing expectancies: The relationship of the test scores to an independently developed criterion measure is the basis for predictive validity.

1. Consider both the reliability and the relevance of the criterion measures used.

2. Use cross validation data to judge the validity of predictions.

3. Question the meaning of an apparently valid predictor that lacks both construct and content validity. Assess the role of underlying and concomitant variables.

4. Consider the validity of a given measure in the context of all the predictors used or available. Does the measure make an independent contribution to the prediction over and above that provided by other measures?

5. Consider the pitfalls of labeling, stereotyping and prejudging people. The self-fulfilling prophecies that may result are often undesirable.

Placement/selection: Predictive validity is the usual basis for valid placement. Consider the evidence of validity for each alternative (i.e., each placement) when inferring the meaning of scores.

1. Obtain adequate information about the programs or institutions in which the client may be placed in order to judge the consequences of such placement.

2. Estimate the probability of favorable outcomes for each possible placement (e.g., both selection and rejection) before judging the import of the scores.

3. Consider the possibility that outcomes favorable from an institutional point of view may differ from those that are favorable from the examinees' point of view.

4. Examine the possibility that the clients' group membership (race, sex, etc.) may alter the reported validity relationships.

5. Use all the available evidence about the individual to infer the validity of the score for that individual. Each single piece of information about an individual, (e.g, test score, teacher report, or counselor opinion) improves the probability that proper judgments and decisions can be made.

A. Test scores should be considered in context; they do not have absolute meaning.

B. Single test scores should not be the sole basis for placement or selection.

Description/diagnosis: Distinguish between those descriptions and diagnoses using psychological constructs that can be validated only indirectly and those for which content specifications suffice.

1. Identify clearly the domain specified by those asserting content validity. Assess the adequacy of the content sampling procedures used in writing and selecting items.

2. Identify the dimensions of the construct being measured when multiple scores from a battery or inventory are used for description.

A. Examine the content validity and/or the construct validity of each score separately.

B. Consider the relative importance of the various subtests, parts, objectives or elements yielding separate scores and judge the weight they each should be given in interpretation.

C. Recognize that when scores are summed or averaged their weight is a function of their variances.

D. Recognize that when each score is classified as pass-fail, mastery-nonmastery or the like, each element is being given equal weight.

3. Examine the completeness of the description provided, recognizing that no set of test scores completely describes a human being.

Growth — Studies of change: Valid assessment of growth or change requires both a test having descriptive validity and a procedure for establishing that the scores obtained differ from those that might arise when no change has occurred.

1. Report as possibilities all the interpretations the study or evaluation design permits. Point out those interpretations that are precluded by the design used.

A. When standard procedures such as the RMC models (see Tallmadge, GK. and Horst, D.P., A procedural guide for validating achievement gains in educational projects: Mountain View, Calif: RMC Research Corp., Dec. 1975) for measuring growth in achievement are employed, use the descriptions of strengths and weaknesses provided.

B. Look for naturally occurring control groups not part of design whenever possible.

2. Consider the strengths and weaknesses of the particular tests used with respect to this use.

Consider the possibility of floor or ceiling effects, the content changes level to level, the adequacy of articulation in multilevel tests, the comparability of alternate forms, the adequacy of the score-equating across forms, and the comparability of timing of the testing to that of the norming.

3. Recognize the unreliability of individual score differences as measures of change.

4. Recognize the limitations of scoring scales such as grade equivalents that may not have the comparable meaning they appear to have at different levels of the scale.

5. Recognize the need for equal interval scales when trying to assess the amount of change.

COMMUNICATING TEST RESULTS

Communication consists of reporting data in such a way that it is comprehensible and informative. The responsible practitioner reports test data with a concern for the user's need for information and the purposes of evaluating the significance of the information.

There must also be a concern for the right of the individual tested to be informed regarding how the results will be used for his or her benefit (informed consent), who will have access to the results (right to privacy), and what safeguards exist to prevent misuse.

Where standardized test data are being used to enhance decisions about an **individual,** the practitioner's responsibilities are as follows:

Know the manual:

1. Become thoroughly familiar with the publisher's manual before attempting to "explain" any results.

2. Develop skills needed to communicate results of tests, using concepts that are frequently misunderstood before communicating results to clients, the public, or other recipients of the information.

Know the limits:

1. Inform the person receiving the test information that "scores" are approximations, not absolutes, and indicate the SEM or the margin of error in some other way, such as by reporting score intervals rather than points.

2. Candidly discuss with the person receiving the test information any qualifications necessary to understand potential sources of bias for a given set of test results relative to their use with a specific individual;

3. Emphasize that test data represent just one source of information and should rarely, if ever, be used alone for decision making.

Informed consent:

1. Inform the person receiving the test information of any circumstances that could have affected the validity or reliability of the results.

2. Inform the examinee of what action will be taken by the agency and who will be using the results.

3. Obtain the consent of the examinee before using test results for any purpose other than that advanced prior to testing.

Right to privacy:

Inform the examinee of steps to be taken to correct any erroneous information that may be on file as a result of testing.

Where standardized test data are being used to describe **groups** for the purpose of evaluation, the practitioner's responsibilities are as follows:

Background information:

1. Include background information to improve the accuracy of understanding about any numerical data.

2. Identify the purposes for which the reported data would be appropriate.

Politics:

Be aware that public release of test information provides data for all kinds of purposes and that some of these may be adverse to the interests of those tested.

Averages and norms:

1. Clarify in particular that "average" on a standardized test is a range, not a point, and typically includes the middle 50 percent of the group being considered.

2. Qualify all group data in terms of the appropriateness of the norms for that group.

Agency policies:

1. Work for agency test-reporting policies designed to strengthen and protect the benefits of the groups being measured.

2. Work within the agency to establish procedures for periodic review of internal test use.

Appendix D

Statistical Tables

Table D.1 Random Numbers

03 47 43 73 86	36 96 47 36 61	46 98 63 71 62	33 26 16 80 45	60 11 14 10 95
97 74 24 67 62	42 81 14 57 20	42 53 32 37 32	27 07 36 07 51	24 51 79 89 73
16 76 62 27 66	56 50 26 71 07	32 90 79 78 53	13 55 38 58 59	88 97 54 14 10
12 56 85 99 26	96 96 68 27 31	05 03 72 93 15	57 12 10 14 21	88 26 49 81 76
55 59 56 35 64	38 54 82 46 22	31 62 43 09 90	06 18 44 32 53	23 83 01 30 30
16 22 77 94 39	49 54 43 54 82	17 37 93 23 78	87 35 20 96 43	84 26 34 91 64
84 42 17 53 31	57 24 55 06 88	77 04 74 47 67	21 76 33 50 25	83 92 12 06 76
63 01 63 78 59	16 95 55 67 19	98 10 50 71 75	12 86 73 58 07	44 39 52 38 79
33 21 12 34 29	78 64 56 07 82	52 42 07 44 38	15 51 00 13 42	99 66 02 79 54
57 60 86 32 44	09 47 27 96 54	49 17 46 09 62	90 52 84 77 27	08 02 73 43 28
18 18 07 92 46	44 17 16 58 09	79 83 86 19 62	06 76 50 03 10	55 23 64 05 05
26 62 38 97 75	84 16 07 44 99	83 11 46 32 24	20 14 85 88 45	10 93 72 88 71
23 42 40 64 74	82 97 77 77 81	07 45 32 14 08	32 98 94 07 72	93 85 79 10 75
32 36 28 19 95	50 92 26 11 97	00 56 76 31 38	80 22 02 53 53	86 60 42 04 53
37 85 94 35 12	83 39 50 08 30	42 34 07 96 88	54 42 06 87 98	35 85 29 48 39
70 29 17 12 13	40 33 20 38 26	13 89 51 03 74	17 76 37 13 04	07 74 21 19 30
56 62 18 37 35	96 83 50 87 75	97 12 25 93 47	70 33 24 03 54	97 77 46 44 80
99 49 57 22 77	88 42 95 45 72	16 64 36 16 00	04 43 18 66 79	94 77 24 21 90
16 08 15 04 72	33 27 14 34 09	45 59 34 68 49	12 72 07 34 45	99 27 72 95 14
31 16 93 32 43	50 27 89 87 19	20 15 37 00 49	52 85 66 60 44	38 68 88 11 80
68 34 30 13 70	55 74 30 77 40	44 22 78 84 26	04 33 46 09 52	68 07 97 06 57
74 57 25 65 76	59 29 97 68 60	71 91 38 67 54	13 58 18 24 76	15 54 55 95 52
27 42 37 86 53	48 55 90 65 72	96 57 69 36 10	96 46 92 42 45	97 60 49 04 91
00 39 68 29 61	66 37 32 20 30	77 84 57 03 29	10 45 65 04 26	11 04 96 67 24
29 94 98 94 24	68 49 69 10 82	53 75 91 93 30	34 25 20 57 27	40 48 73 51 92
16 90 82 66 59	83 62 64 11 12	67 19 00 71 74	60 47 21 29 68	02 02 37 03 31
11 27 94 75 06	06 09 19 74 66	02 94 37 34 02	76 70 90 30 86	38 45 94 30 38
35 24 10 16 20	33 32 51 26 38	79 78 45 04 91	16 92 53 56 16	02 75 50 95 98
38 23 16 86 38	42 38 97 01 50	87 75 66 81 41	40 01 74 91 62	48 51 84 08 32
31 96 25 91 47	96 44 33 49 13	34 86 82 53 91	00 52 43 48 85	27 55 26 89 62
56 67 40 67 14	64 05 71 95 86	11 05 65 09 68	76 83 20 37 90	57 16 00 11 66
14 90 84 45 11	75 73 88 05 90	52 27 41 14 86	22 98 12 22 08	07 52 74 95 80
68 05 51 18 00	33 96 02 75 19	07 60 62 93 55	59 33 82 43 90	49 37 38 44 59
20 46 78 73 90	97 51 40 14 02	04 02 33 31 08	39 54 16 49 36	47 95 93 13 30
64 19 58 97 79	15 06 15 93 20	01 90 10 75 06	40 78 78 89 62	02 67 74 17 33
05 26 93 70 60	22 35 85 15 13	92 03 51 59 77	59 56 78 06 83	52 91 05 70 74
07 97 10 88 23	09 98 42 99 64	61 71 62 99 15	06 51 29 16 93	58 05 77 09 51
68 71 86 85 85	54 87 66 47 54	73 32 08 11 12	44 95 92 63 16	29 56 24 29 48
26 99 61 65 53	58 37 78 80 70	42 10 50 67 42	32 17 55 85 74	94 44 67 16 94
14 65 52 68 75	87 59 36 22 41	26 78 63 06 55	13 08 27 01 50	15 29 39 39 43
17 53 77 58 71	71 41 61 50 72	12 41 94 96 26	44 95 27 36 99	02 96 74 30 83
90 26 59 21 19	23 52 23 33 12	96 93 02 18 39	07 02 18 36 07	25 99 32 70 23
41 23 52 55 99	31 04 49 69 96	10 47 48 45 88	13 41 43 89 20	97 17 14 49 17
60 20 50 81 69	31 99 73 68 68	35 81 33 03 76	24 30 12 48 60	18 99 10 72 34
91 25 38 05 90	94 58 28 41 36	45 37 59 03 09	90 35 57 29 12	82 62 54 65 60
34 50 57 74 37	98 80 33 00 91	09 77 93 19 82	74 94 80 04 04	45 07 31 66 49
85 22 04 39 43	73 81 53 94 79	33 62 46 86 28	08 31 54 46 31	53 94 13 38 47
09 79 13 77 48	73 82 97 22 21	05 03 27 24 83	72 89 44 05 60	35 80 39 94 88
88 75 80 18 14	22 95 75 42 49	39 32 82 22 49	02 48 07 70 37	16 04 61 67 87
90 96 23 70 00	39 00 03 06 90	55 85 78 38 36	94 37 30 69 32	90 89 00 76 33

Source: Table D.1 is taken from Table XXXII, page 134–135, of Fisher & Yates: *Statistical Tables for Biological, Agricultural and Medical Research* published by Longman Group Ltd., London (previously published by Oliver and Boyd Ltd., Edinburgh) and by permission of the authors and publishers.

Table D.2 Areas of a Standard Normal Distribution

An entry in the table is the proportion under the entire curve which is between z = 0 and a positive value of z. Areas for negative values of z are obtained by symmetry. For percentage move the decimal point two places to the right. To obtain the percentile rank, add the percentage below to 50 percent for a positive z or subtract the percentage below from 50 percent for a negative z. For both, round to the nearest whole number to obtain Pr.

z	.00	.01	.02	.03	.04	.05	.06	.07	.08	.09
0.0	.0000	.0040	.0080	.0120	.0160	.0199	.0239	.0279	.0319	.0359
0.1	.0398	.0438	.0478	.0517	.0557	.0596	.0636	.0675	.0714	.0753
0.2	.0793	.0832	.0871	.0910	.0948	.0987	.1026	.1064	.1103	.1141
0.3	.1179	.1217	.1255	.1293	.1331	.1368	.1406	.1443	.1480	.1517
0.4	.1554	.1591	.1628	.1664	.1700	.1736	.1772	.1808	.1844	.1879
0.5	.1915	.1950	.1985	.2019	.2054	.2088	.2123	.2157	.2190	.2224
0.6	.2257	.2291	.2324	.2357	.2389	.2422	.2454	.2486	.2517	.2549
0.7	.2580	.2611	.2642	.2673	.2703	.2734	.2764	.2794	.2823	.2852
0.8	.2881	.2910	.2939	.2967	.2995	.3023	.3051	.3078	.3106	.3133
0.9	.3159	.3186	.3212	.3238	.3264	.3289	.3315	.3340	.3365	.3389
1.0	.3413	.3438	.3461	.3485	.3508	.3531	.3554	.3577	.3599	.3621
1.1	.3643	.3665	.3686	.3708	.3729	.3749	.3770	.3790	.3810	.3830
1.2	.3849	.3869	.3888	.3907	.3925	.3944	.3962	.3980	.3997	.4015
1.3	.4032	.4049	.4066	.4082	.4099	.4115	.4131	.4147	.4162	.4177
1.4	.4192	.4207	.4222	.4236	.4251	.4265	.4279	.4292	.4306	.4319
1.5	.4332	.4345	.4357	.4370	.4382	.4394	.4406	.4418	.4429	.4441
1.6	.4452	.4463	.4474	.4484	.4495	.4505	.4515	.4525	.4535	.4545
1.7	.4554	.4564	.4573	.4582	.4591	.4599	.4608	.4616	.4625	.4633
1.8	.4641	.4649	.4656	.4664	.4671	.4678	.4686	.4693	.4699	.4706
1.9	.4713	.4719	.4726	.4732	.4738	.4744	.4750	.4756	.4761	.4767
2.0	.4772	.4778	.4783	.4788	.4793	.4798	.4803	.4808	.4812	.4817
2.1	.4821	.4826	.4830	.4834	.4838	.4842	.4846	.4850	.4854	.4857
2.2	.4861	.4864	.4868	.4871	.4875	.4878	.4881	.4884	.4887	.4890
2.3	.4893	.4896	.4898	.4901	.4904	.4906	.4909	.4911	.4913	.4916
2.4	.4918	.4920	.4922	.4925	.4927	.4929	.4931	.4932	.4934	.4936
2.5	.4938	.4940	.4941	.4943	.4945	.4946	.4948	.4949	.4951	.4952
2.6	.4953	.4955	.4956	.4957	.4959	.4960	.4961	.4962	.4963	.4964
2.7	.4965	.4966	.4967	.4968	.4969	.4970	.4971	.4972	.4973	.4974
2.8	.4974	.4975	.4976	.4977	.4977	.4978	.4979	.4979	.4980	.4981
2.9	.4981	.4982	.4982	.4983	.4984	.4984	.4985	.4985	.4986	.4986
3.0	.4987	.4987	.4987	.4988	.4988	.4989	.4989	.4989	.4990	.4990

Source: From *Elementary Statistics,* Fourth Edition, by Paul G. Hoel, copyright © 1976, John Wiley & Sons, Inc. Reprinted by permission of John Wiley & Sons, Inc.

Table D.3 Percentile Ranks to Normal Curve Equivalents

Pr Percentile rank	NCE	Pr	NCE	Pr	NCE	Pr	NCE
99	99	73	63	47	48	21	33
98	93	72	62	46	48	20	32
97	90	71	62	45	47	19	32
96	87	70	61	44	47	18	31
95	85	69	60	43	46	17	30
94	83	68	60	42	46	16	29
93	81	67	59	41	45	15	28
92	80	66	59	40	45	14	28
91	78	65	58	39	44	13	26
90	77	64	58	38	44	12	25
89	76	63	57	37	43	11	24
88	75	62	56	36	42	10	23
87	74	61	56	35	42	9	22
86	73	60	55	34	41	8	20
85	72	59	55	33	41	7	19
84	71	58	54	32	40	6	17
83	70	57	54	31	40	5	15
82	69	56	53	30	39	4	13
81	68	55	53	29	38	3	10
80	68	54	52	28	38	2	7
79	67	53	52	27	37	1	1
78	66	52	51	26	36		
77	66	51	51	25	36		
76	65	50	50	24	35		
75	64	49	49	23	34		
74	64	48	49	22	34		

Table D.4 F Distribution: 5% (roman type) and 1% (boldface type) Levels for the Distribution of F

Between group df

Within group df	1	2	3	4	5	6	7	8	9	10	11	12	14	16	20	24	30	40	50	75	100	200	500	∞
1	161 **4052**	200 **4999**	216 **5403**	225 **5625**	230 **5764**	234 **5859**	237 **5928**	239 **5981**	241 **6022**	242 **6056**	243 **6082**	244 **6106**	245 **6142**	246 **6169**	248 **6208**	249 **6234**	250 **6258**	251 **6286**	252 **6302**	253 **6323**	253 **6334**	254 **6352**	254 **6361**	254 **6366**
2	18.51 **98.49**	19.00 **99.01**	19.16 **99.17**	19.25 **99.25**	19.30 **99.30**	19.33 **99.33**	19.36 **99.34**	19.37 **99.36**	19.38 **99.38**	19.39 **99.40**	19.40 **99.41**	19.41 **99.42**	19.42 **99.43**	19.43 **99.44**	19.44 **99.45**	19.45 **99.46**	19.46 **99.47**	19.47 **99.48**	19.47 **99.48**	19.48 **99.49**	19.49 **99.49**	19.49 **99.49**	19.50 **99.50**	19.50 **99.50**
3	10.13 **34.12**	9.55 **30.81**	9.28 **29.46**	9.12 **28.71**	9.01 **28.24**	8.94 **27.91**	8.88 **27.67**	8.84 **27.49**	8.81 **27.34**	8.78 **27.23**	8.76 **27.13**	8.74 **27.05**	8.71 **26.92**	8.69 **26.83**	8.66 **26.69**	8.64 **26.60**	8.62 **26.50**	8.60 **26.41**	8.58 **26.30**	8.57 **26.27**	8.56 **26.23**	8.54 **26.18**	8.54 **26.14**	8.53 **26.12**
4	7.71 **21.20**	6.94 **18.00**	6.59 **16.69**	6.39 **15.98**	6.26 **15.52**	6.16 **15.21**	6.09 **14.98**	6.04 **14.80**	6.00 **14.66**	5.96 **14.54**	5.93 **14.45**	5.91 **14.37**	5.87 **14.24**	5.84 **14.15**	5.80 **14.02**	5.77 **13.93**	5.74 **13.83**	5.71 **13.74**	5.70 **13.69**	5.68 **13.61**	5.66 **13.57**	5.65 **13.52**	5.64 **13.48**	5.63 **13.46**
5	6.61 **16.26**	5.79 **13.27**	5.41 **12.06**	5.19 **11.39**	5.05 **10.97**	4.95 **10.67**	4.88 **10.45**	4.82 **10.27**	4.78 **10.15**	4.74 **10.05**	4.70 **9.96**	4.68 **9.89**	4.64 **9.77**	4.60 **9.68**	4.56 **9.55**	4.53 **9.47**	4.50 **9.38**	4.46 **9.29**	4.44 **9.24**	4.42 **9.17**	4.40 **9.13**	4.38 **9.07**	4.37 **9.04**	4.36 **9.02**
6	5.99 **13.74**	5.14 **10.92**	4.76 **9.78**	4.53 **9.15**	4.39 **8.75**	4.28 **8.47**	4.21 **8.26**	4.15 **8.10**	4.10 **7.98**	4.06 **7.87**	4.03 **7.79**	4.00 **7.72**	3.96 **7.60**	3.92 **7.52**	3.87 **7.39**	3.84 **7.31**	3.81 **7.23**	3.77 **7.14**	3.75 **7.09**	3.72 **7.02**	3.71 **6.99**	3.69 **6.94**	3.68 **6.90**	3.67 **6.88**
7	5.59 **12.25**	4.74 **9.55**	4.35 **8.45**	4.12 **7.85**	3.97 **7.46**	3.87 **7.19**	3.79 **7.00**	3.73 **6.84**	3.68 **6.71**	3.63 **6.62**	3.60 **6.54**	3.57 **6.47**	3.52 **6.35**	3.49 **6.27**	3.44 **6.15**	3.41 **6.07**	3.38 **5.98**	3.34 **5.90**	3.32 **5.85**	3.29 **5.78**	3.28 **5.75**	3.25 **5.70**	3.24 **5.67**	3.23 **5.65**
8	5.32 **11.26**	4.46 **8.65**	4.07 **7.59**	3.84 **7.01**	3.69 **6.63**	3.58 **6.37**	3.50 **6.19**	3.44 **6.03**	3.39 **5.91**	3.34 **5.82**	3.31 **5.74**	3.28 **5.67**	3.23 **5.56**	3.20 **5.48**	3.15 **5.36**	3.12 **5.28**	3.08 **5.20**	3.05 **5.11**	3.03 **5.06**	3.00 **5.00**	2.98 **4.96**	2.96 **4.91**	2.94 **4.88**	2.93 **4.86**
9	5.12 **10.56**	4.26 **8.02**	3.86 **6.99**	3.63 **6.42**	3.48 **6.06**	3.37 **5.80**	3.29 **5.62**	3.23 **5.47**	3.18 **5.35**	3.13 **5.26**	3.10 **5.18**	3.07 **5.11**	3.02 **5.00**	2.98 **4.92**	2.93 **4.80**	2.90 **4.73**	2.86 **4.64**	2.82 **4.56**	2.80 **4.51**	2.77 **4.45**	2.76 **4.41**	2.73 **4.36**	2.72 **4.33**	2.71 **4.31**

Source: From *Elementary Statistics*, Fourth Edition, by Paul G. Hoel, copyright © 1976, John Wiley & Sons, Inc. Reprinted by permission of John Wiley & Sons, Inc.

Table D.4 (continued)

Between group df

Each cell shows the upper value (top) over the lower value (bottom).

Within group df	∞	500	200	100	75	50	40	30	24	20	16	14	12	11	10	9	8	7	6	5	4	3	2	1
10	2.54 / 3.91	2.55 / 3.93	2.56 / 3.96	2.59 / 4.01	2.61 / 4.05	2.64 / 4.12	2.67 / 4.17	2.70 / 4.25	2.74 / 4.33	2.77 / 4.41	2.82 / 4.52	2.86 / 4.60	2.91 / 4.71	2.94 / 4.78	2.97 / 4.85	3.02 / 4.95	3.07 / 5.06	3.14 / 5.21	3.22 / 5.39	3.33 / 5.64	3.48 / 5.99	3.71 / 6.55	4.10 / 7.56	4.96 / 10.04
11	2.40 / 3.60	2.41 / 3.62	2.42 / 3.66	2.45 / 3.70	2.47 / 3.74	2.50 / 3.80	2.53 / 3.86	2.57 / 3.94	2.61 / 4.02	2.65 / 4.10	2.70 / 4.21	2.74 / 4.29	2.79 / 4.40	2.82 / 4.46	2.86 / 4.54	2.90 / 4.63	2.95 / 4.74	3.01 / 4.88	3.09 / 5.07	3.20 / 5.32	3.36 / 5.67	3.59 / 6.22	3.98 / 7.20	4.84 / 9.65
12	2.30 / 3.36	2.31 / 3.38	2.32 / 3.41	2.35 / 3.46	2.36 / 3.49	2.40 / 3.56	2.42 / 3.61	2.46 / 3.70	2.50 / 3.78	2.54 / 3.86	2.60 / 3.98	2.64 / 4.05	2.69 / 4.16	2.72 / 4.22	2.76 / 4.30	2.80 / 4.39	2.85 / 4.50	2.92 / 4.65	3.00 / 4.82	3.11 / 5.06	3.26 / 5.41	3.49 / 5.95	3.88 / 6.93	4.75 / 9.33
13	2.21 / 3.16	2.22 / 3.18	2.24 / 3.21	2.26 / 3.27	2.28 / 3.30	2.32 / 3.37	2.34 / 3.42	2.38 / 3.51	2.42 / 3.59	2.46 / 3.67	2.51 / 3.78	2.55 / 3.85	2.60 / 3.96	2.63 / 4.02	2.67 / 4.10	2.72 / 4.19	2.77 / 4.30	2.84 / 4.44	2.92 / 4.62	3.02 / 4.86	3.18 / 5.20	3.41 / 5.74	3.80 / 6.70	4.67 / 9.07
14	2.13 / 3.00	2.14 / 3.02	2.16 / 3.06	2.19 / 3.11	2.21 / 3.14	2.24 / 3.21	2.27 / 3.26	2.31 / 3.34	2.35 / 3.43	2.39 / 3.51	2.44 / 3.62	2.48 / 3.70	2.53 / 3.80	2.56 / 3.86	2.60 / 3.94	2.65 / 4.03	2.70 / 4.14	2.77 / 4.28	2.85 / 4.46	2.96 / 4.69	3.11 / 5.03	3.34 / 5.56	3.74 / 6.51	4.60 / 8.86
15	2.07 / 2.87	2.08 / 2.89	2.10 / 2.92	2.12 / 2.97	2.15 / 3.00	2.18 / 3.07	2.21 / 3.12	2.25 / 3.20	2.29 / 3.29	2.33 / 3.36	2.39 / 3.48	2.43 / 3.56	2.48 / 3.67	2.51 / 3.73	2.55 / 3.80	2.59 / 3.89	2.64 / 4.00	2.70 / 4.14	2.79 / 4.32	2.90 / 4.56	3.06 / 4.89	3.29 / 5.42	3.68 / 6.36	4.54 / 8.68
16	2.01 / 2.75	2.02 / 2.77	2.04 / 2.80	2.07 / 2.86	2.09 / 2.89	2.13 / 2.96	2.16 / 3.01	2.20 / 3.10	2.24 / 3.18	2.28 / 3.25	2.33 / 3.37	2.37 / 3.45	2.42 / 3.55	2.45 / 3.61	2.49 / 3.69	2.54 / 3.78	2.59 / 3.89	2.66 / 4.03	2.74 / 4.20	2.85 / 4.44	3.01 / 4.77	3.24 / 5.29	3.63 / 6.23	4.49 / 8.53
17	1.96 / 2.65	1.97 / 2.67	1.99 / 2.70	2.02 / 2.76	2.04 / 2.79	2.08 / 2.86	2.11 / 2.92	2.15 / 3.00	2.19 / 3.08	2.23 / 3.16	2.29 / 3.27	2.33 / 3.35	2.38 / 3.45	2.41 / 3.52	2.45 / 3.59	2.50 / 3.68	2.55 / 3.79	2.62 / 3.93	2.70 / 4.10	2.81 / 4.34	2.96 / 4.67	3.20 / 5.18	3.59 / 6.11	4.45 / 8.40
18	1.92 / 2.57	1.93 / 2.59	1.95 / 2.62	1.98 / 2.68	2.00 / 2.71	2.04 / 2.78	2.07 / 2.83	2.11 / 2.91	2.15 / 3.00	2.19 / 3.07	2.25 / 3.19	2.29 / 3.27	2.34 / 3.37	2.37 / 3.44	2.41 / 3.51	2.46 / 3.60	2.51 / 3.71	2.58 / 3.85	2.66 / 4.01	2.77 / 4.25	2.93 / 4.58	3.16 / 5.09	3.55 / 6.01	4.41 / 8.28
19	1.88 / 2.49	1.90 / 2.51	1.91 / 2.54	1.94 / 2.60	1.96 / 2.63	2.00 / 2.70	2.02 / 2.76	2.07 / 2.84	2.11 / 2.92	2.15 / 3.00	2.21 / 3.12	2.26 / 3.19	2.31 / 3.30	2.34 / 3.36	2.38 / 3.43	2.43 / 3.52	2.48 / 3.63	2.55 / 3.77	2.63 / 3.94	2.74 / 4.17	2.90 / 4.50	3.13 / 5.01	3.52 / 5.93	4.38 / 8.18
20	1.84 / 2.42	1.85 / 2.44	1.87 / 2.47	1.90 / 2.53	1.92 / 2.56	1.96 / 2.63	1.99 / 2.69	2.04 / 2.77	2.08 / 2.86	2.12 / 2.94	2.18 / 3.05	2.23 / 3.13	2.28 / 3.23	2.31 / 3.30	2.35 / 3.37	2.40 / 3.45	2.45 / 3.56	2.52 / 3.71	2.60 / 3.87	2.71 / 4.10	2.87 / 4.43	3.10 / 4.94	3.49 / 5.85	4.35 / 8.10
21	1.81 / 2.36	1.82 / 2.38	1.84 / 2.42	1.87 / 2.47	1.89 / 2.51	1.93 / 2.58	1.96 / 2.64	2.00 / 2.72	2.05 / 2.80	2.09 / 2.88	2.15 / 2.99	2.20 / 3.07	2.25 / 3.17	2.28 / 3.24	2.32 / 3.31	2.37 / 3.40	2.42 / 3.51	2.49 / 3.65	2.57 / 3.81	2.68 / 4.04	2.84 / 4.37	3.07 / 4.87	3.47 / 5.78	4.32 / 8.02
22	1.78 / 2.31	1.80 / 2.33	1.81 / 2.37	1.84 / 2.42	1.87 / 2.46	1.91 / 2.53	1.93 / 2.58	1.98 / 2.67	2.03 / 2.75	2.07 / 2.83	2.13 / 2.94	2.18 / 3.02	2.23 / 3.12	2.26 / 3.18	2.30 / 3.26	2.35 / 3.35	2.38 / 3.45	2.45 / 3.59	2.55 / 3.76	2.66 / 3.99	2.82 / 4.31	3.05 / 4.82	3.44 / 5.72	4.30 / 7.94
23	1.76 / 2.26	1.77 / 2.28	1.79 / 2.32	1.82 / 2.37	1.84 / 2.41	1.88 / 2.48	1.91 / 2.54	1.96 / 2.62	2.00 / 2.70	2.04 / 2.78	2.10 / 2.89	2.14 / 2.97	2.20 / 3.07	2.24 / 3.14	2.28 / 3.21	2.32 / 3.30	2.38 / 3.41	2.43 / 3.54	2.53 / 3.71	2.64 / 3.94	2.80 / 4.26	3.03 / 4.76	3.42 / 5.66	4.28 / 7.88
24	1.73 / 2.21	1.74 / 2.23	1.76 / 2.27	1.80 / 2.33	1.82 / 2.36	1.86 / 2.44	1.89 / 2.49	1.94 / 2.58	1.98 / 2.66	2.02 / 2.74	2.09 / 2.85	2.13 / 2.93	2.18 / 3.03	2.22 / 3.09	2.26 / 3.17	2.30 / 3.25	2.36 / 3.36	2.43 / 3.50	2.51 / 3.67	2.62 / 3.90	2.78 / 4.22	3.01 / 4.72	3.40 / 5.61	4.26 / 7.82

Table D.4 (continued)

Each cell lists the 0.05 critical value (top) and the **0.01 critical value (bottom, bold)**.

Within group df	Between group df																							
	1	**2**	**3**	**4**	**5**	**6**	**7**	**8**	**9**	**10**	**11**	**12**	**14**	**16**	**20**	**24**	**30**	**40**	**50**	**75**	**100**	**200**	**500**	**∞**
25	4.24 **7.77**	3.38 **5.57**	2.99 **4.68**	2.76 **4.18**	2.60 **3.86**	2.49 **3.63**	2.41 **3.46**	2.34 **3.32**	2.28 **3.21**	2.24 **3.13**	2.20 **3.05**	2.16 **2.99**	2.11 **2.89**	2.06 **2.81**	2.00 **2.70**	1.96 **2.62**	1.92 **2.54**	1.87 **2.45**	1.84 **2.40**	1.80 **2.32**	1.77 **2.29**	1.74 **2.23**	1.72 **2.19**	1.71 **2.17**
26	4.22 **7.72**	3.37 **5.53**	2.98 **4.64**	2.74 **4.14**	2.59 **3.82**	2.47 **3.59**	2.39 **3.42**	2.32 **3.29**	2.27 **3.17**	2.22 **3.09**	2.18 **3.02**	2.15 **2.96**	2.10 **2.86**	2.05 **2.77**	1.99 **2.66**	1.95 **2.58**	1.90 **2.50**	1.85 **2.41**	1.82 **2.36**	1.78 **2.28**	1.76 **2.25**	1.72 **2.19**	1.70 **2.15**	1.69 **2.13**
27	4.21 **7.68**	3.35 **5.49**	2.96 **4.60**	2.73 **4.11**	2.57 **3.79**	2.46 **3.56**	2.37 **3.39**	2.30 **3.26**	2.25 **3.14**	2.20 **3.06**	2.16 **2.98**	2.13 **2.93**	2.08 **2.83**	2.03 **2.74**	1.97 **2.63**	1.93 **2.55**	1.88 **2.47**	1.84 **2.38**	1.80 **2.33**	1.76 **2.25**	1.74 **2.21**	1.71 **2.16**	1.68 **2.12**	1.67 **2.10**
28	4.20 **7.64**	3.34 **5.45**	2.95 **4.57**	2.71 **4.07**	2.56 **3.76**	2.44 **3.53**	2.36 **3.36**	2.29 **3.23**	2.24 **3.11**	2.19 **3.03**	2.15 **2.95**	2.12 **2.90**	2.06 **2.80**	2.02 **2.71**	1.96 **2.60**	1.91 **2.52**	1.87 **2.44**	1.81 **2.35**	1.78 **2.30**	1.75 **2.22**	1.72 **2.18**	1.69 **2.13**	1.67 **2.09**	1.65 **2.06**
29	4.18 **7.60**	3.33 **5.52**	2.93 **4.54**	2.70 **4.04**	2.54 **3.73**	2.43 **3.50**	2.35 **3.33**	2.28 **3.20**	2.22 **3.08**	2.18 **3.00**	2.14 **2.92**	2.10 **2.87**	2.05 **2.77**	2.00 **2.68**	1.94 **2.57**	1.90 **2.49**	1.85 **2.41**	1.80 **2.32**	1.77 **2.27**	1.73 **2.19**	1.71 **2.15**	1.68 **2.10**	1.65 **2.06**	1.64 **2.03**
30	4.17 **7.56**	3.32 **5.39**	2.92 **4.51**	2.69 **4.02**	2.53 **3.70**	2.42 **3.47**	2.34 **3.30**	2.27 **3.17**	2.21 **3.06**	2.16 **2.98**	2.12 **2.90**	2.09 **2.84**	2.04 **2.74**	1.99 **2.66**	1.93 **2.55**	1.89 **2.47**	1.84 **2.38**	1.79 **2.29**	1.76 **2.24**	1.72 **2.16**	1.69 **2.13**	1.66 **2.07**	1.64 **2.03**	1.62 **2.01**
32	4.15 **7.50**	3.30 **5.34**	2.90 **4.46**	2.67 **3.97**	2.51 **3.66**	2.40 **3.42**	2.32 **3.25**	2.25 **3.12**	2.19 **3.01**	2.14 **2.94**	2.10 **2.86**	2.07 **2.80**	2.02 **2.70**	1.97 **2.62**	1.91 **2.51**	1.86 **2.42**	1.82 **2.34**	1.76 **2.25**	1.74 **2.20**	1.69 **2.12**	1.67 **2.08**	1.64 **2.02**	1.61 **1.98**	1.59 **1.96**
34	4.13 **7.44**	3.28 **5.29**	2.88 **4.42**	2.65 **3.93**	2.49 **3.61**	2.38 **3.38**	2.30 **3.21**	2.23 **3.08**	2.17 **2.97**	2.12 **2.89**	2.08 **2.82**	2.05 **2.76**	2.00 **2.66**	1.95 **2.58**	1.89 **2.47**	1.84 **2.38**	1.80 **2.30**	1.74 **2.21**	1.71 **2.15**	1.67 **2.08**	1.64 **2.04**	1.61 **1.98**	1.59 **1.94**	1.57 **1.91**
36	4.11 **7.39**	3.26 **5.25**	2.86 **4.38**	2.63 **3.89**	2.48 **3.58**	2.36 **3.35**	2.28 **3.18**	2.21 **3.04**	2.15 **2.94**	2.10 **2.86**	2.06 **2.78**	2.03 **2.72**	1.98 **2.62**	1.93 **2.54**	1.87 **2.43**	1.82 **2.35**	1.78 **2.26**	1.72 **2.17**	1.69 **2.12**	1.65 **2.04**	1.62 **2.00**	1.59 **1.94**	1.56 **1.90**	1.55 **1.87**
38	4.10 **7.35**	3.25 **5.21**	2.85 **4.34**	2.62 **3.86**	2.46 **3.54**	2.35 **3.32**	2.26 **3.15**	2.19 **3.02**	2.14 **2.91**	2.09 **2.82**	2.05 **2.75**	2.02 **2.69**	1.96 **2.59**	1.92 **2.51**	1.85 **2.40**	1.80 **2.32**	1.76 **2.22**	1.71 **2.14**	1.67 **2.08**	1.63 **2.00**	1.60 **1.97**	1.57 **1.90**	1.54 **1.86**	1.53 **1.84**
40	4.08 **7.31**	3.23 **5.18**	2.84 **4.31**	2.61 **3.83**	2.45 **3.51**	2.34 **3.29**	2.25 **3.12**	2.18 **2.99**	2.12 **2.88**	2.07 **2.80**	2.04 **2.73**	2.00 **2.66**	1.95 **2.56**	1.90 **2.49**	1.84 **2.37**	1.79 **2.29**	1.74 **2.20**	1.69 **2.11**	1.66 **2.05**	1.61 **1.97**	1.59 **1.94**	1.55 **1.88**	1.53 **1.84**	1.51 **1.81**
42	4.07 **7.27**	3.22 **5.15**	2.83 **4.29**	2.59 **3.80**	2.44 **3.49**	2.32 **3.26**	2.24 **3.10**	2.17 **2.96**	2.11 **2.86**	2.06 **2.77**	2.02 **2.70**	1.99 **2.64**	1.94 **2.54**	1.89 **2.46**	1.82 **2.35**	1.78 **2.26**	1.73 **2.17**	1.68 **2.08**	1.64 **2.02**	1.60 **1.94**	1.57 **1.91**	1.54 **1.85**	1.51 **1.80**	1.49 **1.78**
44	4.06 **7.24**	3.21 **5.12**	2.82 **4.26**	2.58 **3.78**	2.43 **3.46**	2.31 **3.24**	2.23 **3.07**	2.16 **2.94**	2.10 **2.84**	2.05 **2.75**	2.01 **2.68**	1.98 **2.62**	1.92 **2.52**	1.88 **2.44**	1.81 **2.32**	1.76 **2.24**	1.72 **2.15**	1.66 **2.06**	1.63 **2.00**	1.58 **1.92**	1.56 **1.88**	1.52 **1.82**	1.50 **1.78**	1.48 **1.75**
46	4.05 **7.21**	3.20 **5.10**	2.81 **4.24**	2.57 **3.76**	2.42 **3.44**	2.30 **3.22**	2.22 **3.05**	2.14 **2.92**	2.09 **2.82**	2.04 **2.73**	2.00 **2.66**	1.97 **2.60**	1.91 **2.50**	1.87 **2.42**	1.80 **2.30**	1.75 **2.22**	1.71 **2.13**	1.65 **2.04**	1.62 **1.98**	1.57 **1.90**	1.54 **1.86**	1.51 **1.80**	1.48 **1.76**	1.46 **1.72**

Table D.4 (continued)

Between group df

Within group df	1	2	3	4	5	6	7	8	9	10	11	12	14	16	20	24	30	40	50	75	100	200	500	∞
48	4.04 / 7.19	3.19 / 5.08	2.80 / 4.22	2.56 / 3.74	2.41 / 3.42	2.30 / 3.20	2.21 / 3.04	2.14 / 2.90	2.08 / 2.80	2.03 / 2.71	1.99 / 2.64	1.96 / 2.58	1.90 / 2.48	1.86 / 2.40	1.79 / 2.28	1.74 / 2.20	1.70 / 2.11	1.64 / 2.02	1.61 / 1.96	1.56 / 1.88	1.53 / 1.84	1.50 / 1.78	1.47 / 1.73	1.45 / 1.70
50	4.03 / 7.17	3.18 / 5.06	2.79 / 4.20	2.56 / 3.72	2.40 / 3.41	2.29 / 3.18	2.20 / 3.02	2.13 / 2.88	2.07 / 2.78	2.02 / 2.70	1.98 / 2.62	1.95 / 2.56	1.90 / 2.46	1.85 / 2.39	1.78 / 2.26	1.74 / 2.18	1.69 / 2.10	1.63 / 2.00	1.60 / 1.94	1.55 / 1.86	1.52 / 1.82	1.48 / 1.76	1.46 / 1.71	1.44 / 1.68
55	4.02 / 7.12	3.17 / 5.01	2.78 / 4.16	2.54 / 3.68	2.38 / 3.37	2.27 / 3.15	2.18 / 2.98	2.11 / 2.85	2.05 / 2.75	2.00 / 2.66	1.97 / 2.59	1.93 / 2.53	1.88 / 2.43	1.83 / 2.35	1.76 / 2.23	1.72 / 2.15	1.67 / 2.06	1.61 / 1.96	1.58 / 1.90	1.52 / 1.82	1.50 / 1.78	1.46 / 1.71	1.43 / 1.66	1.41 / 1.64
60	4.00 / 7.08	3.15 / 4.98	2.76 / 4.13	2.52 / 3.65	2.37 / 3.34	2.25 / 3.12	2.17 / 2.95	2.10 / 2.82	2.04 / 2.72	1.99 / 2.63	1.95 / 2.56	1.92 / 2.50	1.85 / 2.40	1.81 / 2.32	1.75 / 2.20	1.70 / 2.12	1.65 / 2.03	1.59 / 1.93	1.56 / 1.87	1.50 / 1.79	1.48 / 1.74	1.44 / 1.68	1.41 / 1.63	1.39 / 1.60
65	3.99 / 7.04	3.14 / 4.95	2.75 / 4.10	2.51 / 3.62	2.36 / 3.31	2.24 / 3.09	2.15 / 2.93	2.08 / 2.79	2.02 / 2.70	1.98 / 2.61	1.94 / 2.54	1.90 / 2.47	1.85 / 2.37	1.80 / 2.30	1.73 / 2.18	1.68 / 2.09	1.63 / 2.00	1.57 / 1.90	1.54 / 1.84	1.49 / 1.76	1.46 / 1.71	1.42 / 1.64	1.39 / 1.60	1.37 / 1.56
70	3.98 / 7.01	3.13 / 4.92	2.74 / 4.08	2.50 / 3.60	2.35 / 3.29	2.23 / 3.07	2.14 / 2.91	2.07 / 2.77	2.01 / 2.67	1.97 / 2.59	1.93 / 2.51	1.89 / 2.45	1.84 / 2.35	1.79 / 2.28	1.72 / 2.15	1.67 / 2.07	1.62 / 1.98	1.56 / 1.88	1.53 / 1.82	1.47 / 1.74	1.45 / 1.69	1.40 / 1.63	1.37 / 1.56	1.35 / 1.53
80	3.96 / 6.96	3.11 / 4.88	2.72 / 4.04	2.48 / 3.56	2.33 / 3.25	2.21 / 3.04	2.12 / 2.87	2.05 / 2.74	1.99 / 2.64	1.95 / 2.55	1.91 / 2.48	1.88 / 2.41	1.82 / 2.32	1.77 / 2.24	1.70 / 2.11	1.65 / 2.03	1.60 / 1.94	1.54 / 1.84	1.51 / 1.78	1.45 / 1.70	1.42 / 1.65	1.38 / 1.57	1.35 / 1.52	1.32 / 1.49
100	3.94 / 6.90	3.09 / 4.82	2.70 / 3.98	2.46 / 3.51	2.30 / 3.20	2.19 / 2.99	2.10 / 2.82	2.03 / 2.69	1.97 / 2.59	1.92 / 2.51	1.88 / 2.43	1.85 / 2.36	1.79 / 2.26	1.75 / 2.19	1.68 / 2.06	1.63 / 1.98	1.57 / 1.89	1.51 / 1.79	1.48 / 1.73	1.42 / 1.64	1.39 / 1.59	1.34 / 1.51	1.30 / 1.46	1.28 / 1.43
125	3.92 / 6.84	3.07 / 4.78	2.68 / 3.94	2.44 / 3.47	2.29 / 3.17	2.17 / 2.95	2.08 / 2.79	2.01 / 2.65	1.95 / 2.56	1.90 / 2.47	1.86 / 2.40	1.83 / 2.33	1.77 / 2.23	1.72 / 2.15	1.65 / 2.03	1.60 / 1.94	1.55 / 1.85	1.49 / 1.75	1.45 / 1.68	1.39 / 1.59	1.36 / 1.54	1.31 / 1.46	1.27 / 1.40	1.25 / 1.37
150	3.91 / 6.81	3.06 / 4.75	2.67 / 3.91	2.43 / 3.44	2.27 / 3.13	2.16 / 2.92	2.07 / 2.76	2.00 / 2.62	1.94 / 2.53	1.89 / 2.44	1.85 / 2.37	1.82 / 2.30	1.76 / 2.20	1.71 / 2.12	1.64 / 2.00	1.59 / 1.91	1.54 / 1.83	1.47 / 1.72	1.44 / 1.66	1.37 / 1.56	1.34 / 1.51	1.29 / 1.43	1.25 / 1.37	1.22 / 1.33
200	3.89 / 6.76	3.04 / 4.71	2.65 / 3.88	2.41 / 3.41	2.26 / 3.11	2.14 / 2.90	2.05 / 2.73	1.98 / 2.60	1.92 / 2.50	1.87 / 2.41	1.83 / 2.34	1.80 / 2.28	1.74 / 2.17	1.69 / 2.09	1.62 / 1.97	1.57 / 1.88	1.52 / 1.79	1.45 / 1.69	1.42 / 1.62	1.35 / 1.53	1.32 / 1.48	1.26 / 1.39	1.22 / 1.33	1.19 / 1.28
400	3.86 / 6.70	3.02 / 4.66	2.62 / 3.83	2.39 / 3.36	2.23 / 3.06	2.12 / 2.85	2.03 / 2.69	1.96 / 2.55	1.90 / 2.46	1.85 / 2.37	1.81 / 2.29	1.78 / 2.23	1.72 / 2.12	1.67 / 2.04	1.60 / 1.92	1.54 / 1.84	1.49 / 1.74	1.42 / 1.64	1.38 / 1.57	1.32 / 1.47	1.28 / 1.42	1.22 / 1.32	1.16 / 1.24	1.13 / 1.19
1000	3.85 / 6.66	3.00 / 4.62	2.61 / 3.80	2.38 / 3.34	2.22 / 3.04	2.10 / 2.82	2.02 / 2.66	1.95 / 2.53	1.89 / 2.43	1.84 / 2.34	1.80 / 2.26	1.76 / 2.20	1.70 / 2.09	1.65 / 2.01	1.58 / 1.89	1.53 / 1.81	1.47 / 1.71	1.41 / 1.61	1.36 / 1.54	1.30 / 1.44	1.26 / 1.38	1.19 / 1.28	1.13 / 1.19	1.08 / 1.11
∞	3.84 / 6.64	2.99 / 4.60	2.60 / 3.78	2.37 / 3.32	2.21 / 3.02	2.09 / 2.80	2.01 / 2.64	1.94 / 2.51	1.88 / 2.41	1.83 / 2.32	1.79 / 2.24	1.75 / 2.18	1.69 / 2.07	1.64 / 1.99	1.57 / 1.87	1.52 / 1.79	1.46 / 1.69	1.40 / 1.59	1.35 / 1.52	1.28 / 1.41	1.24 / 1.36	1.17 / 1.25	1.11 / 1.15	1.00 / 1.00

Table D.5 Upper Percentage Points of the F_{max} Statistic

$$F_{max} = (\sigma^2_{largest})/(\sigma^2_{smallest})$$

df for σ^2	α	k = number of variances								
		2	3	4	5	6	7	8	9	10
4	.05	9.60	15.5	20.6	25.2	29.5	33.6	37.5	41.4	44.6
	.01	23.2	37.	49.	59.	69.	79.	89.	97.	106.
5	.05	7.15	10.8	13.7	16.3	18.7	20.8	22.9	24.7	26.5
	.01	14.9	22.	28.	33.	38.	42.	46.	50.	54.
6	.05	5.82	8.38	10.4	12.1	13.7	15.0	16.3	17.5	18.6
	.01	11.1	15.5	19.1	22.	25.	27.	30.	32.	34.
7	.05	4.99	6.94	8.44	9.70	10.8	11.8	12.7	13.5	14.3
	.01	8.89	12.1	14.5	16.5	18.4	20.	22.	23.	24.
8	.05	4.43	6.00	7.18	8.12	9.03	9.78	10.5	11.1	11.7
	.01	7.50	9.9	11.7	13.2	14.5	15.8	16.9	17.9	18.9
9	.05	4.03	5.34	6.31	7.11	7.80	8.41	8.95	9.45	9.91
	.01	6.54	8.5	9.9	11.1	12.1	13.1	13.9	14.7	15.3
10	.05	3.72	4.85	5.67	6.34	6.92	7.42	7.87	8.28	8.66
	.01	5.85	7.4	8.6	9.6	10.4	11.1	11.8	12.4	12.9
12	.05	3.28	4.16	4.79	5.30	5.72	6.09	6.42	6.72	7.00
	.01	4.91	6.1	6.9	7.6	8.2	8.7	9.1	9.5	9.9
15	.05	2.86	3.54	4.01	4.37	4.68	4.95	5.19	5.40	5.59
	.01	4.07	4.9	5.5	6.0	6.4	6.7	7.1	7.3	7.5
20	.05	2.46	2.95	3.29	3.54	3.76	3.94	4.10	4.24	4.37
	.01	3.32	3.8	4.3	4.6	4.9	5.1	5.3	5.5	5.6
30	.05	2.07	2.40	2.61	2.78	2.91	3.02	3.12	3.21	3.29
	.01	2.63	3.0	3.3	3.4	3.6	3.7	3.8	3.9	4.0
∞	.05	1.00	1.00	1.00	1.00	1.00	1.00	1.00	1.00	1.00
	.01	1.00	1.00	1.00	1.00	1.00	1.00	1.00	1.00	1.00

Table D.6 Critical Values of Chi Square

df	.99	.98	.95	.90	.80	.70	.50	.30	.20	.10	.05	.02	.01	.001
1	.0002	.0006	.0039	.016	.064	.15	.46	1.07	1.64	2.71	3.84	5.41	6.64	10.83
2	.02	.04	.10	.21	.45	.71	1.39	2.41	3.22	4.60	5.99	7.82	9.21	13.82
3	.12	.18	.35	.58	1.00	1.42	2.37	3.66	4.64	6.25	7.82	9.84	11.34	16.27
4	.30	.43	.71	1.06	1.65	2.20	3.36	4.88	5.99	7.78	9.49	11.67	13.28	18.47
5	.55	.75	1.14	1.61	2.34	3.00	4.35	6.06	7.29	9.24	11.07	13.39	15.09	20.52
6	.87	1.13	1.64	2.20	3.07	3.83	5.35	7.23	8.56	10.64	12.59	15.03	16.81	22.46
7	1.24	1.56	2.17	2.83	3.82	4.67	6.35	8.38	9.80	12.02	14.07	16.62	18.48	24.32
8	1.65	2.03	2.73	3.49	4.59	5.53	7.34	9.52	11.03	13.36	15.51	18.17	20.09	26.12
9	2.09	2.53	3.32	4.17	5.38	6.39	8.34	10.66	12.24	14.68	16.92	19.68	21.67	27.88
10	2.56	3.06	3.94	4.86	6.18	7.27	9.34	11.78	13.44	15.99	18.31	21.16	23.21	29.59
11	3.05	3.61	4.58	5.58	6.99	8.15	10.34	12.90	14.63	17.28	19.68	22.62	24.72	31.26
12	3.57	4.18	5.23	6.30	7.81	9.03	11.34	14.01	15.81	18.55	21.03	24.05	26.22	32.91
13	4.11	4.76	5.89	7.04	8.63	9.93	12.34	15.12	16.98	19.81	22.36	25.47	27.69	34.53
14	4.66	5.37	6.57	7.79	9.47	10.82	13.34	16.22	18.15	21.06	23.68	26.87	29.14	36.12
15	5.23	5.98	7.26	8.55	10.31	11.72	14.34	17.32	19.31	22.31	25.00	28.26	30.58	37.70
16	5.81	6.61	7.96	9.31	11.15	12.62	15.34	18.42	20.46	23.54	26.30	29.63	32.00	39.25
17	6.41	7.26	8.67	10.08	12.00	13.53	16.34	19.51	21.62	24.77	27.59	31.00	33.41	40.79
18	7.02	7.91	9.39	10.86	12.86	14.44	17.34	20.60	22.76	25.99	28.87	32.35	34.80	42.31
19	7.63	8.57	10.12	11.65	13.72	15.35	18.34	21.69	23.90	27.20	30.14	33.69	36.19	43.82
20	8.26	9.24	10.85	12.44	14.58	16.27	19.34	22.78	25.04	28.41	31.41	35.02	37.57	45.32
21	8.90	9.92	11.59	13.24	15.44	17.18	20.34	23.86	26.17	29.62	32.67	36.34	38.93	46.80
22	9.54	10.60	12.34	14.04	16.31	18.10	21.34	24.94	27.30	30.81	33.92	37.66	40.29	48.27
23	10.20	11.29	13.09	14.85	17.19	19.02	22.34	26.02	28.43	32.01	35.17	38.97	41.64	49.73
24	10.86	11.99	13.85	15.66	18.06	19.94	23.34	27.10	29.55	33.20	36.42	40.27	42.98	51.18
25	11.52	12.70	14.61	16.47	18.94	20.87	24.34	28.17	30.68	34.38	37.65	41.57	44.31	52.62
26	12.20	13.41	15.38	17.29	19.82	21.79	25.34	29.25	31.80	35.56	38.88	42.86	45.64	54.05
27	12.88	14.12	16.15	18.11	20.70	22.72	26.34	30.32	32.91	36.74	40.11	44.14	46.96	55.48
28	13.56	14.85	16.93	18.94	21.59	23.65	27.34	31.39	34.03	37.92	41.34	45.42	48.28	56.89
29	14.26	15.57	17.71	19.77	22.48	24.58	28.34	32.46	35.14	39.09	42.56	46.69	49.59	58.30
30	14.95	16.31	18.49	20.60	23.36	25.51	29.34	33.53	36.25	40.26	43.77	47.96	50.89	59.70

Source: Table D.6 is taken from Table IV, page 47, of Fisher & Yates: *Statistical Tables for Biological, Agricultural and Medical Research* published by Longman Group Ltd., London (previously published by Oliver and Boyd Ltd., Edinburgh) and by permission of the authors and publishers.

Table D.7 Critical Values of t

	Level of significance for a one-tail test				
	.05	.025	.01	.005	.0005
	Level of significance for a two-tail test				
df	.10	.05	.02	.01	.001
1	6·314	12·706	31·821	63·657	636·619
2	2·920	4·303	6·965	9·925	31·598
3	2·353	3·182	4·541	5·841	12·924
4	2·132	2·776	3·747	4·604	8·610
5	2·015	2·571	3·365	4·032	6·869
6	1·943	2·447	3·143	3·707	5·959
7	1·895	2·365	2·998	3·499	5·408
8	1·860	2·306	2·896	3·355	5·041
9	1·833	2·262	2·821	3·250	4·781
10	1·812	2·228	2·764	3·169	4·587
11	1·796	2·201	2·718	3·106	4·437
12	1·782	2·179	2·681	3·055	4·318
13	1·771	2·160	2·650	3·012	4·221
14	1·761	2·145	2·624	2·977	4·140
15	1·753	2·131	2·602	2·947	4·073
16	1·746	2·120	2·583	2·921	4·015
17	1·740	2·110	2·567	2·898	3·965
18	1·734	2·101	2·552	2·878	3·922
19	1·729	2·093	2·539	2·861	3·883
20	1·725	2·086	2·528	2·845	3·850
21	1·721	2·080	2·518	2·831	3·819
22	1·717	2·074	2·508	2·819	3·792
23	1·714	2·069	2·500	2·807	3·767
24	1·711	2·064	2·492	2·797	3·745
25	1·708	2·060	2·485	2·787	3·725
26	1·706	2·056	2·479	2·779	3·707
27	1·703	2·052	2·473	2·771	3·690
28	1·701	2·048	2·467	2·763	3·674
29	1·699	2·045	2·462	2·756	3·659
30	1·697	2·042	2·457	2·750	3·646
40	1·684	2·021	2·423	2·704	·3·551
60	1·671	2·000	2·390	2·660	3·460
120	1·658	1·980	2·358	2·617	3·373
∞	1·645	1·960	2·326	2·576	3·291

Source: Table D.7 is taken from Table III, page 46, of Fisher & Yates: *Statistical Tables for Biological, Agricultural and Medical Research* published by Longman Group Ltd., London (previously published by Oliver and Boyd Ltd., Edinburgh) and by permission of the authors and publishers.

Table D.8 Percentage Points of the Studentized Range

Error df	α	r = number of means or number of steps between ordered means									
		2	3	4	5	6	7	8	9	10	11
5	.05	3.64	4.60	5.22	5.67	6.03	6.33	6.58	6.80	6.99	7.17
	.01	5.70	6.98	7.80	8.42	8.91	9.32	9.67	9.97	10.24	10.48
6	.05	3.46	4.34	4.90	5.30	5.63	5.90	6.12	6.32	6.49	6.65
	.01	5.24	6.33	7.03	7.56	7.97	8.32	8.61	8.87	9.10	9.30
7	.05	3.34	4.16	4.68	5.06	5.36	5.61	5.82	6.00	6.16	6.30
	.01	4.95	5.92	6.54	7.01	7.37	7.68	7.94	8.17	8.37	8.55
8	.05	3.26	4.04	4.53	4.89	5.17	5.40	5.60	5.77	5.92	6.05
	.01	4.75	5.64	6.20	6.62	6.96	7.24	7.47	7.68	7.86	8.03
9	.05	3.20	3.95	4.41	4.76	5.02	5.24	5.43	5.59	5.74	5.87
	.01	4.60	5.43	5.96	6.35	6.66	6.91	7.13	7.33	7.49	7.65
10	.05	3.15	3.88	4.33	4.65	4.91	5.12	5.30	5.46	5.60	5.72
	.01	4.48	5.27	5.77	6.14	6.43	6.67	6.87	7.05	7.21	7.36
11	.05	3.11	3.82	4.26	4.57	4.82	5.03	5.20	5.35	5.49	5.61
	.01	4.39	5.15	5.62	5.97	6.25	6.48	6.67	6.84	6.99	7.13
12	.05	3.08	3.77	4.20	4.51	4.75	4.95	5.12	5.27	5.39	5.51
	.01	4.32	5.05	5.50	5.84	6.10	6.32	6.51	6.67	6.81	6.94
13	.05	3.06	3.73	4.15	4.45	4.69	4.88	5.05	5.19	5.32	5.43
	.01	4.26	4.96	5.40	5.73	5.98	6.19	6.37	6.53	6.67	6.79
14	.05	3.03	3.70	4.11	4.41	4.64	4.83	4.99	5.13	5.25	5.36
	.01	4.21	4.89	5.32	5.63	5.88	6.08	6.26	6.41	6.54	6.66
15	.05	3.01	3.67	4.08	4.37	4.59	4.78	4.94	5.08	5.20	5.31
	.01	4.17	4.84	5.25	5.56	5.80	5.99	6.16	6.31	6.44	6.55
16	.05	3.00	3.65	4.05	4.33	4.56	4.74	4.90	5.03	5.15	5.26
	.01	4.13	4.79	5.19	5.49	5.72	5.92	6.08	6.22	6.35	6.46
17	.05	2.98	3.63	4.02	4.30	4.52	4.70	4.86	4.99	5.11	5.21
	.01	4.10	4.74	5.14	5.43	5.66	5.85	6.01	6.15	6.27	6.38
18	.05	2.97	3.61	4.00	4.28	4.49	4.67	4.82	4.96	5.07	5.17
	.01	4.07	4.70	5.09	5.38	5.60	5.79	5.94	6.08	6.20	6.31
19	.05	2.96	3.59	3.98	4.25	4.47	4.65	4.79	4.92	5.04	5.14
	.01	4.05	4.67	5.05	5.33	5.55	5.73	5.89	6.02	6.14	6.25
20	.05	2.95	3.58	3.96	4.23	4.45	4.62	4.77	4.90	5.01	5.11
	.01	4.02	4.64	5.02	5.29	5.51	5.69	5.84	5.97	6.09	6.19
24	.05	2.92	3.53	3.90	4.17	4.37	4.54	4.68	4.81	4.92	5.01
	.01	3.96	4.55	4.91	5.17	5.37	5.54	5.69	5.81	5.92	6.02
30	.05	2.89	3.49	3.85	4.10	4.30	4.46	4.60	4.72	4.82	4.92
	.01	3.89	4.45	4.80	5.05	5.24	5.40	5.54	5.65	5.76	5.85
40	.05	2.86	3.44	3.79	4.04	4.23	4.39	4.52	4.63	4.73	4.82
	.01	3.82	4.37	4.70	4.93	5.11	5.26	5.39	5.50	5.60	5.69
60	.05	2.83	3.40	3.74	3.98	4.16	4.31	4.44	4.55	4.65	4.73
	.01	3.76	4.28	4.59	4.82	4.99	5.13	5.25	5.36	5.45	5.53
120	.05	2.80	3.36	3.68	3.92	4.10	4.24	4.36	4.47	4.56	4.64
	.01	3.70	4.20	4.50	4.71	4.87	5.01	5.12	5.21	5.30	5.37
∞	.05	2.77	3.31	3.63	3.86	4.03	4.17	4.29	4.39	4.47	4.55
	.01	3.64	4.12	4.40	4.60	4.76	4.88	4.99	5.08	5.16	5.23

Source: Adapted from Table 29 in *Biometrika Tables for Statisticians,* Vol. 1, Third Edition, edited by E. S. Pearson and H. O. Hartley, New York: Cambridge, 1966. Reprinted by permission of the Biometrika Trustees.

Table D.9 Critical Values of the Spearman rho Rank-Order Correlation Coefficient

*n	Significance level for one-tailed test		Significance level for two-tailed test	
	.05	.01	.05	.01
5	.900	.999	.999	.999
6	.829	.943	.886	.999
7	.714	.893	.786	.929
8	.643	.833	.738	.881
9	.600	.783	.683	.833
10	.564	.746	.648	.794
12	.506	.712	.591	.777
14	.456	.645	.544	.715
16	.425	.601	.506	.665
18	.399	.564	.475	.625
20	.377	.534	.450	.591
22	.359	.508	.428	.562
24	.343	.485	.409	.537
26	.329	.448	.392	.515
28	.317	.448	.377	.496
30	.306	.432	.364	.478

*n=number of pairs of scores (or subjects)

Table D.10 Critical Values for the Pearson Correlation Coefficient

	Level of significance for a one-tail test				
	.05	.025	.01	.005	.0005
	Level of significance for a two-tail test				
df	.10	.05	.02	.01	.001
1	.9877	.9969	.9995	.9999	1.0000
2	.9000	.9500	.9800	.9900	.9990
3	.8054	.8783	.9343	.9587	.9912
4	.7293	.8114	.8822	.9172	.9741
5	.6694	.7545	.8329	.8745	.9507
6	.6215	.7067	.7887	.8343	.9249
7	.5822	.6664	.7498	.7977	.8982
8	.5494	.6319	.7155	.7646	.8721
9	.5214	.6021	.6851	.7348	.8471
10	.4973	.5760	.6581	.7079	.8233
11	.4762	.5529	.6339	.6835	.8010
12	.4575	.5324	.6120	.6614	.7800
13	.4409	.5139	.5923	.6411	.7603
14	.4259	.4973	.5742	.6226	.7420
15	.4124	.4821	.5577	.6055	.7246
16	.4000	.4683	.5425	.5897	.7084
17	.3887	.4555	.5285	.5751	.6932
18	.3783	.4438	.5155	.5614	.6787
19	.3687	.4329	.5034	.5487	.6652
20	.3598	.4227	.4921	.5368	.6524
25	.3233	.3809	.4451	.4869	.5974
30	.2960	.3494	.4093	.4487	.5541
35	.2746	.3246	.3810	.4182	.5189
40	.2573	.3044	.3578	.3932	.4896
45	.2428	.2875	.3384	.3721	.4648
50	.2306	.2732	.3218	.3541	.4433
60	.2108	.2500	.2948	.3248	.4078
70	.1954	.2319	.2737	.3017	.3799
80	.1829	.2172	.2565	.2830	.3568
90	.1726	.2050	.2422	.2673	.3375
100	.1638	.1946	.2301	.2540	.3211

Source: Table D.10 is taken from Table VII, page 63, of Fisher & Yates: *Statistical Tables for Biological, Agricultural and Medical Research* published by Longman Group Ltd., London (previously published by Oliver and Boyd Ltd., Edinburgh) and by permission of the authors and publishers.

References

Aiello, N. C., and Wolfle, L. M. A meta-analysis of individualized instruction in science. *Resources in Education,* December 1980, ED 190 404.

Alexander, L., Frankiewicz, R., and Williams, R. Facilitation of learning and retention of oral instruction using advance and post organizers. *Journal of Educational Psychology,* 1979, *71,* 701–707.

American personnel and guidance association ethical standards. Washington, D.C.: APGA, 1974.

Anastasi, A. *Psychological testing* (4th ed.). New York: The Macmillan Company, 1976.

Angell, J. Technical aspects of writing form and style. In R. H. Jones (Ed.), *Methods and techniques of educational research.* Danville, Ill.: The Interstate, 1973.

APGA policy statement on responsibilities of users of standardized tests. *Guideposts,* October 1978, 5–8.

Ashby, M. S., and Wittmaier, B. C. Attitude changes in children after exposure to stories about women in traditional or nontraditional occupations. *Journal of Educational Psychology,* 1978, *70* (6), 945–949.

Barr, A. J., Goodnight, S., and Helwig, G. *A user's guide to SAS 76.* Raleigh, N.C.: SAS Institute, Inc., 1976.

Berliner, C. C., and Cahen, L. S. Trait-treatment interaction and learning. In. F. N. Kerlinger (Ed.), *Review of research and education.* Itasca, Ill.: F. E. Peacock, 1973.

Borg. W., and Gall, M. *Educational research: An introduction* (3rd ed.). New York: Longman, 1979.

Bracht, G., and Glass, G. The external validity of experiments. *American Educational Research Journal,* 1968, *5,* 437–474.

Buros, O. K. (Ed.). *Tests in print II.* Highland Park, N.J.: Gryphon Press, 1974.

Campbell, D. T., and Stanley, J. C. Experimental and quasi-experimental designs for research on teaching. In N. L. Gage (Ed.), *Handbook of research on teaching.* Chicago: Rand McNally, 1963.

Campbell, W. G., and Ballou, S. V. *Form and style: Theses, reports, term papers.* Boston: Houghton Mifflin, 1977.

Chun, K., Cobb, S., and French, J. R. P. *Measures for psychological assessment.* Ann Arbor, Mich.: Institute for Social Research, 1975.

Cohen, J. *Statistical power analysis for the behavioral sciences.* New York: Academic Press, 1977.

Cohen, L. S., and Fieby, N. M. The class size/achievement issue: New evidence and a research plan. *Phi Delta Kappan,* 1979, *60* (7), 492–495, 538.

Comrey, A. L., Backer, T. E., and Glaser, E. M. *A sourcebook for mental health measures.* Los Angeles: Human Interaction Resource Institute, 1973.

Cook, T. D., and Leviton, L. C. Reviewing the literature; a comparision of traditional methods with meta-analysis. *Journal of Personality,* 1980, *48,* 449–471.

Cooley, W. W., and Lohnes, P. R. *Multivariate data analysis.* New York: Wiley, 1971.

Cooper, H. M., and Arkin, R. M. On quantitative reviewing. *Journal of Personality,* 1981, *49* (2), 225–229.

D'Agostino, R. B. Simple compact portable test of normality: Geary's test revisited. *Psychological Bulletin,* 1970, *74* (2), 138–140.

Dixon, W. J., and Brown, M. B. (Eds.). *BMDP: biomedical computer programs, P-series.* Berkeley: University of California Press, 1979.

Dugdale, K. *A manual of form for theses and term reports* (4th ed.). Bloomington: Indiana University Press, 1972.

Ethical standards of psychologists. Washington, D.C.: American Psychological Association, 1977.

Foulds, M. L., and Hannigan, P. S. Effects of Gestalt marathon workshops on measured self-actualization: A replication and follow-up. *Journal of Counseling Psychology.* January 1976, *23,* 60–65.

Gage, N. L. (Ed.). *Handbook of research on teaching.* Chicago: Rand McNally, 1963.

Glass, G. V. Primary, secondary, and meta-analysis of research. *The Educational Researcher,* 1976, *10,* 3–8.

Glass, G. V. On criticism of our class size/achievement issue: New evidence and a research plan. *Phi Delta Kappan,* 1980, *62* (4), 242–244.

Glass, G. V., Peckham, P. P., and Sanders, J. R. Consequences of failure to meet assumptions underlying the fixed effects analyses of variance and covariance. *Review of Educational Research,* 1972, *42* (3), 237–288.

Glass, G. V., and Smith, M. L. Meta-analysis of research on class-size and achievement. *Educational Evaluation and Policy Analysis,* 1979, *1* (1), 2–16.

Glass, G. V., and Smith, M. L. Meta-analysis of research on the relationship of class-size and achievement. *Resources in Education,* August 1979, ED 169 129.

Glass, G. V., and Stanley, J. C. *Statistical methods in education and psychology.* Englewood Cliffs, N.J.: Prentice-Hall, 1970.

Gronlund, N. E. *Sociometry in the classroom.* New York: Harper, 1959.

Gronlund, N. E. *Measurement and evaluation in teaching* (4th ed.). New York: The Macmillan Company, 1981.

Hays, W. L. *Statistics for the social sciences* (2nd ed.). New York: Holt, Rinehart and Winston, 1973.

Hearold, S. L. Meta-analysis of the effects of television on social behavior. *Resources in Education,* January 1980, ED 175 432.

Herrnstein, R. J. IQ. *Atlantic Monthly,* September 1971, 228, 43–64.

Hersen, M., and Barlow, D. H. *Single case experimental designs.* New York: Pergamon, 1976.

Hess, F. Class size revisited; Glass and Smith in perspective. *Resources in Education,* November 1979, ED 172 402.

Hillman, J. S. An analysis of male and female roles in two periods of children's literature. *Journal of Educational Research,* 1974, *68* (2), 84–88.

Hoel, P. *Elementary statistics* (4th ed.). New York: Wiley, 1976.

Hopkins, C. D. *Educational research: A structure for inquiry.* Columbus, Ohio: Charles E. Merrill, 1976.

Hopkins, C. D. *Understanding educational research.* Columbus, Ohio: Charles E. Merrill, 1980.

Hopkins, K. D., and Glass, G. V. *Basic statistics for the behavioral sciences.* Englewood Cliffs, N.J.: Prentice-Hall, 1978.

Huber, J., Treffinger, D., Tracy, D., and Rand, D. Self-instructional use of programmed creativity-training materials with gifted and regular students. *Journal of Educational Psychology,* 1979, *71,* 303–309.

Johnson, O. G. *Tests and measurements in child development: Handbook II* (2 Vols.). San Francisco: Jossey-Bass, 1976.

Johnson, O. G., and Bommarito, J. W. *Tests and measurements in child development: A handbook.* San Francisco: Jossey-Bass, 1971.

Kerlinger, F. N. *Foundations of behavioral research* (2nd ed.). New York: Holt, Rinehart and Winston, 1973.

Kirk, R. *Experimental design: Procedures for the behavioral sciences.* Belmont, Calif.: Brooks/Cole, 1968.

Krol, R. A. A meta-analysis of the effects of desegregation on academic achievement. *Resources in Education,* May 1981, ED 196 988.

Krozybski, A. *Science and sanity: An introduction to non-Aristotelian systems and general semantics* (4th ed.). Lakeville, Conn.: The International Non-Aristotelian Library Publishing Company, 1958.

Lachowicz, J. M. The relative effects of praise, praise-plus-description and praise-plus-instructions with pre-school children. *Dissertation Abstracts International,* January 1972, *32,* 12–13.

Lahey, B., and Drabman, R. S. Facilitation of the acquisition and retention of sight-word vocabulary through token reinforcement. *Journal of Applied Behavior Analysis. 7,* Summer 1974, 307–312.

Lee, A. The child in pedagogy and culture: Concepts of American preadolescence as revealed in teaching theories and as related to the culture, 1900–1914. *Educational Horizons,* 1968, *46* (3), 134–140.

Leviton, L. C., and Cook, T. D. What differentiates meta-analysis from other forms of review. *Journal of Personality,* 1981, *49* (2), 231–235.

McReynolds, W. T., and Coleman, J. Token economy: Patient and staff changes. *Behavior Research and Therapy, 10,* February 1972, 29–34.

Moore, G. W. Transitive inferences within seriation problems assessed by explanations, judgments, and strategies. *Child Development,* 1979, *50,* 1164–1172.

Morris, E. K., Surber, C. F., and Bijou, S. Self-pacing versus instructor-pacing: Achievement, evaluations, and retention. *Journal of Educational Psychology,* 1978, *70* (2), 224–234.

Morrison, D.. F. *Multivariate statistical methods.* New York: McGraw-Hill, 1967.

Nay, J. N., Scanlon, J. W., Schmidt, R. E., and Wholey, J. If you don't care where you get to, then it doesn't matter which way you go. In C. C. Abt (Ed.), *The evaluation of social programs.* Beverly Hills, Calif.: Sage, 1976, 97–120.

Nie, N. H., Hull, C. H., Jenkins, J. G., Steinbrenner, K., and Bent, D. H. *Statistical package for the social sciences* (2nd ed.). New York: McGraw-Hill, 1975.

Nunnally, J. C. *Introduction to statistics for psychology and education.* New York: McGraw-Hill, 1975.

Osgood, C. E., Suci, G. J., and Tannenbaum, O. H. *The measurement of meaning.* Urbana, Ill.: University of Illinois Press, 1957.

Publication Manual of the American Psychological Association, Second Edition. Washington, D.C.: American Psychological Association, 1974.

Redfield, D. L., and Rousseau, E. W. A meta-analysis of experimental research on teacher questioning behavior. *Review of Educational Research,* 181, *51* (2), 237–245.

Ribes, E., Galesso-Coaracy, S., and Durán, L. The effects of punishment on the acquisition and maintenance of reading behavior in retarded children. *Revista Interamericana de Psicologia.* 1973, *7,* 33–42.

Robinson, J. P., and Shaver, P. R. *Measures of social psychological attitudes.* Ann Arbor, Mich.: Institute for Social Research, 1973.

Rosenthal, R. *Experimenter effects in behavioral research.* New York: Appleton-Century-Crofts, 1966.

Seagoe, M. V. *Terman and the gifted.* Los Altos, Calif.: W. Kaufman, 1975.

Siegel, S. *Nonparametric statistics.* New York: McGraw-Hill, 1975.

Simpson, S. N. Comment on "meta-analysis of research on class size and achievement." *Educational Evaluation and Policy Analysis,* 1980, *2* (3), 81–83.

Smith, M. L., and Glass, G. V. Meta-analysis of psychotherapy outcome studies. *American Psychologist,* 1977, *32* (9), 752–760.

Smith, M. L., and Glass, G. V. Relationship of class-size to classroom processes, teacher satisfaction and pupil affect: a meta-analysis. *Resources in Education,* December 1980, ED 190 698.

Snedecor, G. W., and Cochran, W. G. *Statistical methods* (6th ed.). Ames, Iowa: University of Iowa Press, 1967.

Standards for educational and psychological tests. Washington, D.C.: American Psychological Association, 1974.

Taylor, J. A. A personality scale of manifest anxiety. *Journal of Abnormal and Social Psychology,* 1953, *48,* 285–290.

Terman, L. M. *Genetic studies of genius.* Stanford, Calif.: Stanford University Press, 1925.

Thesaurus of ERIC descriptors. Phoenix, Ariz.: Oryx Press, 1980.

Thesaurus of psychological index terms (2nd ed.). Washington, D.C.: American Psychological Association, 1977.

Thorndike, R. L., and Hagen, E. P. *Measurement and evaluation in psychology and education* (4th ed.). New York: Wiley, 1977.

Travis, R. P., and Travis, P. Y. Self-actualization in marital enrichment. *Journal of Marriage and Family Counseling,* January 1976, 73–79.

Trayers, R. M. W. (Ed.). *Second handbook of research on teaching.* Chicago: Rand McNally, 1973.

Tuckman, B. W. *Measuring educational outcomes: Fundamentals of testing.* New York: Harcourt Brace Jovanovich, 1975.

Turabian, K. U. *A manual for writers of term papers, theses, and dissertations* (4th ed.). Chicago: University of Chicago Press, 1973.

Walberg, H. J., Schiller, D., and Haertel, G. D. The quiet revolution in educational research. *Phi Delta Kappan,* November 1979, 179–183.

Webb, E., Campbell, D. T., Schwartz, R. D., and Sechrest, L. *Unobtrusive measures: Nonreactive research in the social sciences.* Chicago: Rand-McNally, 1966.

Winer, B. J. *Statistical principles in experimental design.* (2nd ed.). New York: McGraw-Hill, 1971.

Zimmerman, B. J., and Kinsler, K. Effects of exposure to a punished model and verbal prohibitions on children's toy play. *Journal of Educational Psychology,* 1979, *71,* 388–395.

Index